THE
COMPLETE
SOUTH AFRICAN
STITCH
ENCYCLOPEDIA

THE
COMPLETE
SOUTH AFRICAN
STITCH
ENCYCLOPEDIA

JAN EATON

δelος

Delos Publishers
40 Heerengracht
CAPE TOWN

Published in 1986 by Hamlyn Publishing
a division of The Hamlyn Publishing Group Limited
Bridge House, London Road,
Twickenham, Middlesex, England

Copyright © 1986 Quarto Publishing

All rights reserved. No part of this publication may be reproduced, stored in a retrieval system, or transmitted in any form or by any means, electronic, mechanical, photocopying, recording or otherwise, without the permission of Hamlyn Publishing and the copyright holder.

First South African edition 1989

ISBN 1-86826-002-X

This book was designed and produced by Quarto Publishing Ltd

Senior editor Jane Laing

Art editor Alex Arthur

Editorial Caroline Mordaunt, Alison Berry, Jac Buchan, Maggie McCormack

Designer Fraser Newman

Photographer Rose Jones

Indexer Hilary Bird

Art director Nigel Osborne

Editorial director Jim Miles

Typeset by Ampersand Communications Ltd, London
Paste-up by Patrizio Semproni
Manufactured in Hong Kong by Regent Publishing Services Ltd
Printed by Leefung-Asco Printers Ltd, Hong Kong

The author would like to take this opportunity to thank Gavin Fry and Ronald Wilson for their kind help and assistance.

Contents

Introduction	6
Basic stitches	8
Fabric stitches	16
Line stitches	16
Border stitches	44
Filling stitches	68
Detached filling stitches	88
Isolated stitches	92
Motif stitches	100
Edging stitches	108
Hem stitches	112
Insertion stitches	113
Other fabric stitches	116
Canvas stitches	120
Straight and slanted stitches	120
Crossed stitches	132
Composite stitches	152
Other canvas stitches	168
Glossary	172
Index	174

Introduction

From Algerian eye stitch to Gobelin stitch and from tête de boeuf filling stitch to zigzag stitch, every stitch in *The Complete South African Stitch Encyclopedia* is described in detail. A comprehensive reference book and a self-instruction manual combined, all the stitches are accompanied by clear, full-colour photographs, with step-by-step progressions for the more complicated stitches.

For every stitch, the method of working is clearly explained and advice is offered on the most suitable type of threads to use. Alternative names are provided and the interesting and involved history of some of the more unusual or older stitches is also given.

To make the book straightforward to use, the stitches are divided according to kind, so that if you know the type of stitch you require but do not have a specific stitch in mind, you need only turn to the relevant section from which you can easily choose the most appropriate stitch.

The introductory section contains easy-to-work stitches, such as chain stitch and cross stitch. If you are new to embroidery, practise these stitches first, as they form the basis for many of the complex, composite stitches found later in the book.

The next ten sections contain free embroidery stitches grouped according to their usage — for example, line stitches, filling stitches, isolated stitches, motif stitches, edging stitches and insertion stitches. Many of the line and isolated stitches can also be used as fillings and details of this can be found in the text, where appropriate.

Canvas stiches can be found in the final four sections of the book and are grouped according to their construction — for example, straight stitches and crossed stitches.

To further help you decide on the stitch you wish to use, the stitches are arranged in order of difficulty within each section and each one is accompanied by a degree-of-difficulty symbol to indicate the amount if skill needed to work the stitch successfully.

When looking for a stitch with a particular name, consult the index at the back of the book. This has been organized so that all the stitches that make up a family group can be found under the initial letter of the main stitch. For example, threaded herringbone stitch is also listed under 'H' as herringbone stitch – threaded. The technical terms mentioned in the text are fully explained in the glossary, which begins on page 172.

INTRODUCTION 7

Degree of difficulty ratings
Within each section, the stitches are arranged into three groups, according to the degree of difficulty involved in working them. The number of star symbols accompanying each entry indicates the group into which the stitch falls: a stitch with one star is easy to work, one with two requires a little more skill and a stitch with three stars is difficult to effect. These at-a-glance symbol ratings should further help you to decide which stitch to use.

☆   Easy

☆☆   Medium

☆☆☆   Difficult

Matching text and photographs
Each double page of photographs illustrates the stitches described on the preceding double page of text and for greatest benefit, text and photographs should be used in conjunction. Once you have decided on the stitch you wish to use, read through the method of working the stitch and follow the steps on the photograph of the corresponding stitched example. Every stitch is numbered so that you can quickly match the description of a stitch to its photograph.

94/1 Portuguese knotted stem stitch   ☆☆☆

LINE STITCHES 21

20 FABRIC STITCHES

32 Whipped chain stitch ☆
Whipped chain stitch is a simple line stitch used on plain- and even-weave fabrics and gives a neat, slightly raised, line. The whipping thread can be of a contrasting colour, weight or texture.
A foundation row of chain stitch (see page 12) is worked first, and then whipped at regular intervals

the threading will tighten them. A second thread, of a contrasting weight, colour or texture, is then laced through the back stitch foundation. The needle should enter the fabric only at the beginning and end of each row. Use a blunt-ended tapestry needle for the lacing to avoid splitting the foundation stitches. The lacing thread should be tightened

36 Rosette of thorns stitch ☆
Rosette of thorns stitch is an ornamental line stitch used on plain- and even-weave fabrics. It makes a pattern of crown shapes linked together to form a line and is a variation of buttonhole stitch (see page 13). It looks equally effective worked in straight rows or round

39 Twisted chain stitch and detached twisted chain stitch
Twisted chain stitch is a useful line stitch as it follows curves well and has a neat, slightly textured look. It is always worked downwards, and is used on plain- and even-weave fabrics. A simple variation of chain

as an edging stitch on a hemmed piece of fabric, the top row of stitching should follow the turned over edge of the hem; the second row is worked on the very edge of the hem.

worked first, and then a second thread is whipped over the line without picking up any ground fabric. Use a blunt-ended tapestry needle for the whipping to avoid splitting the stitches on the foundation row. The effect of whipped

---

22 FABRIC STITCHES

32 Whipped chain stitch
35/1 Plaited fly stitch
36 Rosette of thorns stitch
33 Pekinese stitch
35/2 Plaited fly stitch
37 Single feather stitch
34 Open Cretan stitch
35/3 Plaited fly stitch
38 Knotted cable stitch

LINE STITCHES 23

39 Twisted chain stitch and detached twisted chain stitch
42/1 Pearl stitch
43 Whipped stem stitch
40 Double buttonhole stitch
42/2 Pearl stitch
44 Ship's ladder stitch
41 Half chevron stitch
42/3 Pearl stitch
45 Thorn stitch

BASIC STITCHES

1 Couching ☆
also known as **convent stitch** *and* **kloster stitch**
and **puffy couching**
also known as **bunched couching**

Couching takes its name from the French word 'coucher', meaning to lay down. The technique involves laying a thread or group of threads on the surface of a plain- or even-weave fabric, and then tying them down by means of a second, often finer, thread. Couching was extensively used on Medieval embroideries to keep scarce and expensive threads, especially those made from precious metals, on the surface of the work to avoid any waste. It was also used to attach threads to the fabric when they were too thick, rigid or textured to be stitched directly into the fabric without damaging either fabric or thread. Couching can be used to work linear designs, to cover the edge of an appliquéd shape, or to fill an area solidly. This technique is used for laid-work *(see page 84)*: the surface threads are laid side by side on the fabric, and then anchored by a second thread, which is couched down in a pattern. In other types of couching, the thread is laid across the fabric, and then tied down with the same thread before the next line of thread is laid; Bokhara couching *(see page 77)* and Roumanian couching *(see page 81)* are good examples.

Ordinary couching is the simplest form of this technique, and it should always be worked with the fabric stretched in an embroidery hoop or frame. It is worked from right to left, usually along a guide-line marked on the fabric, unless it is being worked as a filling. The thick thread (or group of threads) is brought to the surface of the fabric, laid loosely along the line to be couched and, if you are right-handed, held in place and guided by the left hand. The couching thread is brought through, and small, straight stitches are taken over the thick thread and back through the fabric. The line of thick thread should lie evenly on the surface after it has been couched. When the line is completed, all the threads are taken to the back of the work and secured. When working curves, arrange the couching stitches closer together so that the curved line lies flat. An extra stitch or two may need to be worked when negotiating an angle to make sure that the corner of the couched thread lies flat. When this stitch is used solidly, row on row, for filling a shape, the couching stitches can be arranged so they form parallel rows across the laid threads. They can also be placed alternately on each row, or arranged to make a small geometric pattern.

Puffy couching is worked in a similar way but over a group of threads rather than a single one. The threads are laid on the surface and the couching stitches are made small enough to compress them into bunches. The couching thread should be pulled tightly after each stitch, and the laid threads should be kept fairly loose on the surface of the fabric, so that they puff out between each stitch.

2 Herringbone stitch ☆
also known as **Mossoul stitch, Persian stitch, Russian stitch, Russian cross stitch, plaited stitch, catch stitch** *and* **witch stitch**

Herringbone stitch is a line stitch which is used on plain- and even-weave fabrics. It makes a pretty, crossed zigzag line and the stitches must be perfectly regular. It is worked from left to right and is very easy and quick to work. Guide-lines may need to be marked on the fabric if the threads cannot be counted to keep the row straight. When the stitch is used as a filling, the rows can be placed so that the tips of the stitches on the second and subsequent rows touch those on the row immediately preceding them. This will give a light trellis effect. For a heavier look, arrange the rows underneath each other so that the zigzags interlock. Herringbone stitch is also used as the foundation row for a number of more complicated stitches. Any type of thread can be used for this stitch, the choice depending on the size of stitch required and the weight of the ground fabric.

3 Chevron stitch ☆

Chevron stitch is a line and filling stitch used on plain- and even-weave fabrics. It is also used as a smocking stitch to make both the diamond and surface honeycomb patterns. Chevron stitch is worked from left to right between two parallel lines, in a similar way to herringbone stitch *(see above)*, and makes a pretty, zigzag line. This stitch does not follow curves well unless they are very gradual. It is composed of diagonal stitches set at an angle with a shorter horizontal stitch worked where these stitches meet. To keep the width of the stitches even, guide-lines need to be marked on the fabric, unless the threads can be counted.

When used as a filling stitch, the rows are placed closely together to give a lattice effect, which benefits from being worked neatly and regularly. An isolated stitch such as daisy stitch *(see page 92)* or dot stitch *(see page 92)* can be worked in the centre of the diamond-shaped spaces to make the filling more decorative. Chevron stitch can be threaded with a contrasting colour in the same way as threaded herringbone stitch *(see page 45)*.

4 Holbein stitch ☆

also known as **double running stitch, line stitch, stroke stitch, square stitch, two-sided line stitch, two-sided stroke stitch, Roumanian stitch** *and* **Chiara stitch**

Holbein stitch is a simple line stitch used on even-weave fabrics. It is a very old stitch and is an important component of two distinct types of counted thread embroidery: Assisi work and black-work. Assisi work evolved in the town of that name in central Italy, probably during the fourteenth century, and is characterized by an unworked design and an embroidered background. The designs, often heraldic, were outlined by a row of Holbein stitch worked in black thread, with the background areas solidly filled in with long-armed cross stitch *(see page 141)*, and later with cross stitch *(see page 14)*. The backgrounds were of one colour only, traditionally red or blue, and these colours were also occasionally used for the Holbein stitch.

Black-work, also known as Spanish black-work or Spanish work, was worked in a black thread on a white or natural fabric, using Holbein stitch extensively as an outline. The designs were very formal, with strongly outlined shapes and regular geometric fillings, and were sometimes enlivened by the use of metal thread or spangles. The designs were probably of Moorish origin and black-work spread from Spain to England and the rest of Europe some time during the fifteenth century when it was used as a decoration for clothing, particularly on shirts, collars and ruffs, and household linens. The use of black-work as a costume decoration can be seen in many sixteenth-century English portraits, particularly those by Hans Holbein (1497-1543) after whom this stitch was named.

Holbein stitch is extremely easy to work and is a useful stitch, both for outlines and for intricate linear details. A row of evenly spaced running stitch *(see page 12)* is worked first and the spaces are filled in on the return journey. It is exactly the same on both sides of the fabric, and can also be stepped to give a zigzag line.

5 Split stitch ☆
also known as **Kensington outline stitch**

Split stitch is a line stitch used on plain- and even-weave fabrics. It is used for outlines, as it follows intricate designs well, and it is also worked solidly as a shaded filling, especially for figurative embroideries, because of its brush-stroke quality. The type of thread suitable for use with split stitch is confined to a soft, untwisted thread which can be split by the needle. The method of working this stitch is similar to stem stitch *(see below)* but in this case the thread is split by the needle as it emerges from the fabric. The result is rather like chain stitch *(see page 12)* in appearance.

Split stitch was used during the Middle Ages for embroidering figures, particularly hands and faces. Examples of 'opus anglicanum' still exist which show the extensive use of this stitch.

6 Coral stitch ☆
also known as **coral knot, beaded stitch, German knot stitch, knotted stitch, scroll stitch** *and* **snail trail**

Coral stitch is a knotted line stitch used on plain- and even-weave fabrics. It is one of the oldest embroidery stitches, and many examples of it can be found on seventeenth- and eighteenth-century English crewel embroidery work. It is worked from right to left.

Hold the thread loosely on the surface of the fabric with your left thumb (if you are right-handed) and pull the needle through the fabric and over the thread to form a knot. The stitch can be varied by altering the angle of the needle as it takes up the fabric, and by changing the spacing of the knots along the row. Any type of embroidery thread can be used; the effect made depends on the weight and composition of the thread. Coral stitch is used for outlines, as it follows curves well, and for linear details. It can also be worked solidly to cover an area with a pretty, knotted filling. The knots can be arranged so that they form lines across the filling, or they can be set alternately on every row.

7 Stem stitch ☆
also known as **crewel stitch, stalk stitch** *and* **South Kensington stitch**

Stem stitch is a line stitch used on plain- and even-weave fabrics. One of the most frequently used outline stitches, it is quite easy to work and follows curves and intricate linear details well. It can also be used for filling and shading areas *(see stem stitch filling, page 69)*.

The stitch is simply worked, with a forwards and backwards motion along the line; the stitches should be evenly worked and equally sized. The working thread must always be kept at the right of the needle; if it is at the left, the effect is slightly different, and the stitch is then known as outline stitch *(see page 12)*. A slightly wider stem stitch line can be made by inserting the needle into the fabric at a slight angle to the line instead of directly along it. Any type of embroidery thread can be used, providing that it is compatible with the size of the stitch and the weight of the ground fabric.

BASIC STITCHES

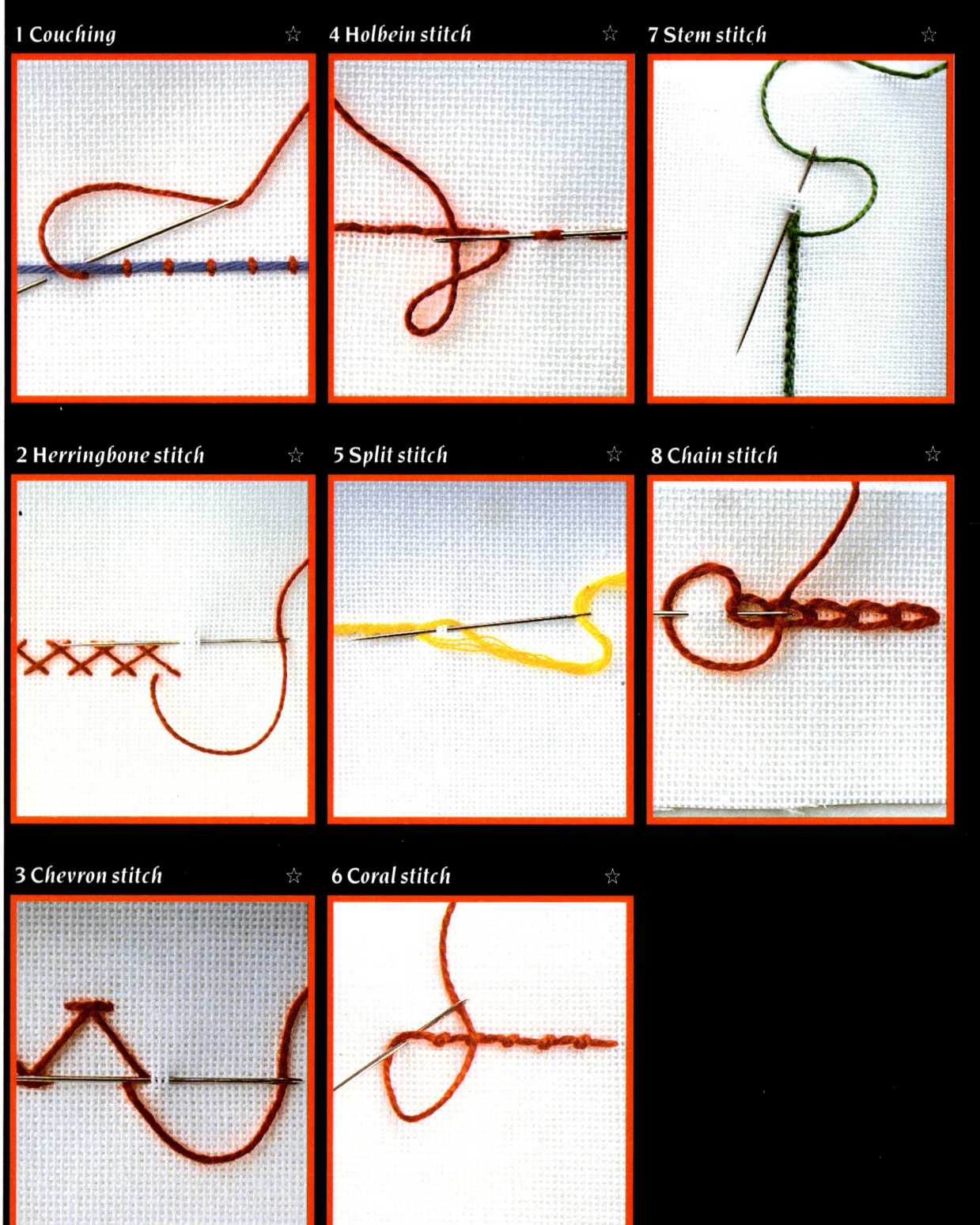

BASIC STITCHES **11**

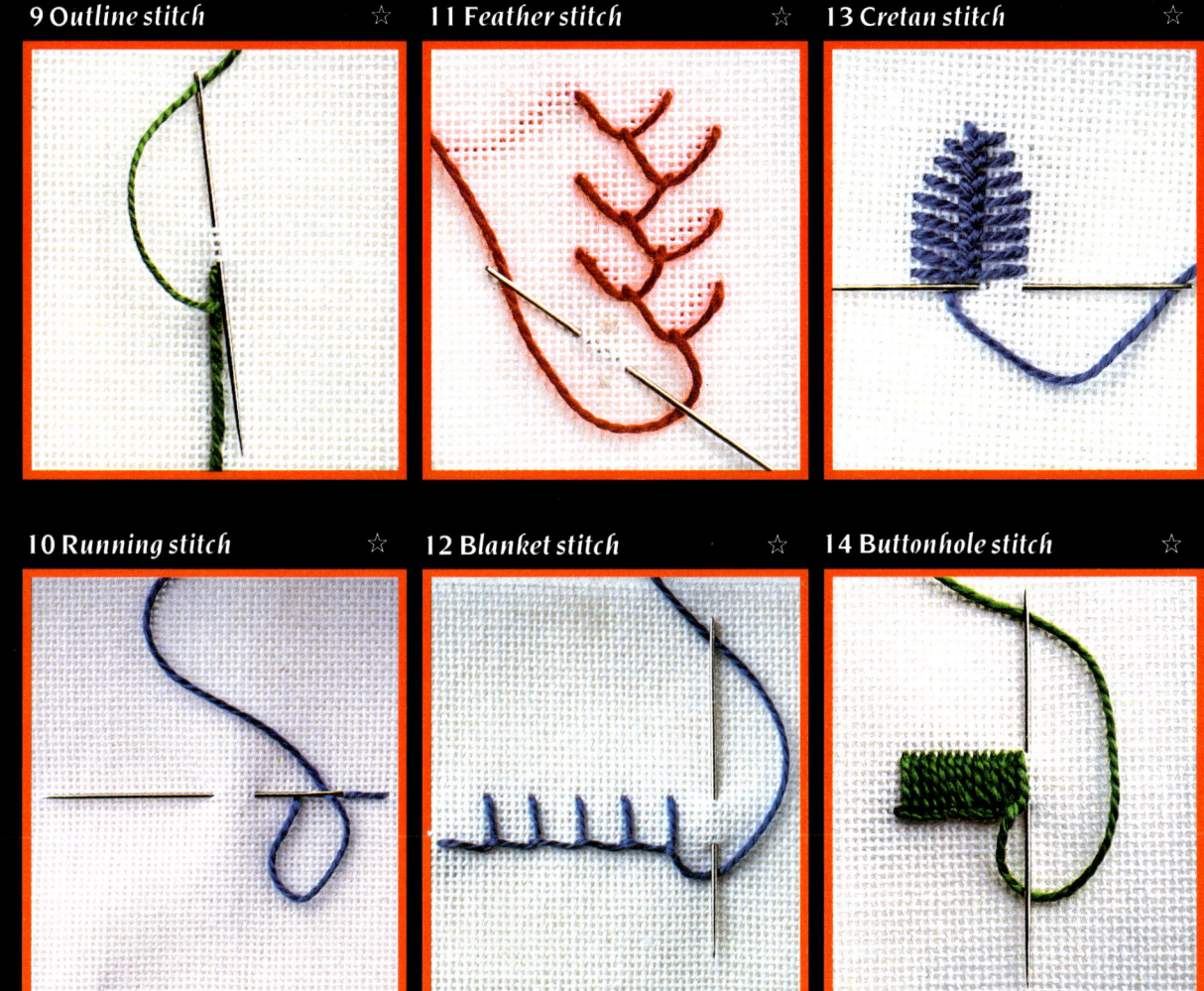

BASIC STITCHES

8 Chain stitch ☆
also known as **tambour stitch** *and* **point de chainette**

Chain stitch is one of the oldest embroidery stitches. Its use is widespread, and examples of the stitch can be found on many antique and contemporary textiles throughout the world. Chain stitch probably originated in Persia and India, where it is usually worked by hand with a fine hook known as an 'ari', which speeds up the work considerably. From the front of the embroidery, it is virtually impossible to distinguish chain stitch worked with a hook from that worked with a needle, although it is possible to tell from the back of the work: a continuous embroidery thread without any joins indicates that the chain stitch has been worked with a hook. Chain stitch is also worked in Western countries with a similar tool, known as a 'tambour' hook. The Eastern and Western methods differ slightly: in India, the rows of chain stitch are worked on the right side of the fabric, which is hand held; using the tambour method, the stitch is worked from the reverse of the fabric, which is always mounted in a frame with the wrong side uppermost. Chain stitch was also one of the two stitches produced by the early sewing machines.

Chain stitch, worked either by needle or hook, forms a line stitch on plain- and even-weave fabrics. It can also be worked solidly to produce a dense filling, which lends itself well to shading. It is a simple stitch to work, but care should be taken to keep the stitches even and of the same size. Chain stitch makes a good outline stitch and is very useful for defining curves and intricate shapes when worked quite small. Any thread is suitable, but the size of the stitch will depend on the weight of the embroidery thread used. When used as a filling, chain stitch can either be worked in close rows to fill the shape, or the rows can be worked from the centre outwards in a spiral, using one or more colours or textures.

Chain stitch can be worked with a needle on single canvas in the same way as on fabric. It is often used for backgrounds and gives a dense, almost knitted texture. Care should be taken when matching the weight of the thread to the gauge of the canvas to ensure that the canvas threads are completely covered. Chain stitch on fabric or canvas can have a row of back stitch *(see page 14)* worked down the centre, either in the same colour, or with a contrasting thread. This line of back stitch is useful for covering the background threads when chain stitch is worked on canvas.

9 Outline stitch ☆

Outline stitch is a line stitch used on plain- and even-weave fabrics. An extremely versatile stitch, it is used for outlining shapes in single or multiple rows and, as it follows intricate curves well, for complicated linear details. It makes a neat, twisted line and can be worked in any type of embroidery thread, depending on the required weight of the line. It is worked in almost the same way as stem stitch *(see page 9)*, but the working thread always lies to the left of the needle, rather than to the right. A line of outline stitches twists in a reverse direction to a line of stem stitches.

10 Running stitch ☆

Running stitch is a line stitch used on plain- and even-weave fabrics. It is the simplest and most basic of all stitches and is made by passing the needle and thread in and out of the fabric at regular intervals. This stitch has many uses: as an outline stitch, for working linear details, as it follows intricate shapes well; as a foundation row, for more complex stitches, such as Croatian stitch *(see page 73)*; as a strengthening stitch in cut-work; and for hand quilting. The stitches should all be of equal length and any type of embroidery thread can be used, providing that it is compatible with the weight of the ground fabric.

11 Feather stitch ☆
also known as **single coral stitch** *and* **briar stitch**

Feather stitch is a decorative line and smocking stitch used on plain- and even-weave fabrics. This stitch has been extensively used on traditional English smocks, both as a smocking stitch and as surface embroidery; it is also used as a decorative joining stitch on crazy patchwork. It makes a pretty, feathery line, which is equally effective when worked in straight lines or following curves. Worked downwards, it is a quick stitch, easy to perfect. The thread is brought through at the top of the line to be covered and a slanting loop stitch is made alternately to the left and to the right of the line. Any type of embroidery thread can be used with feather stitch but the effect required and the weight of the ground fabric must be taken into account.

12 Blanket stitch ☆
also known as **open buttonhole stitch**

Blanket stitch is a looped line stitch worked on plain- and even-weave fabrics in exactly the same way as buttonhole stitch *(see below)*. The only difference between the two stitches is the spacing between the uprights: in blanket stitch, a space is left between each upright. Blanket stitch is frequently used as an edging stitch to cover a turned-over raw edge and makes a good appliqué stitch. The name probably originates from the use of the stitch, sometimes worked by hand but more often by machine, as a method of finishing the edges of blankets. As a line stitch on the surface of the fabric, blanket stitch can be made more decorative by altering the lengths of the uprights; a simple variation is to make the stitches alternately long and short, either singly or in groups of two or three. The lengths can also be varied to form pyramid shapes or the loops at the bottom of the stitch can be whipped with a contrasting colour *(see whipped back stitch, page 16)*. Blanket stitch also forms the foundation for composite stitches, such as barb stitch *(see page 16)*.

13 Cretan stitch ☆
also known as **Persian stitch, long-armed feather stitch** *and* **quill stitch** *(when it is worked in a straight vertical line)*

Cretan stitch is a line stitch or filling for narrow shapes, used on plain- and even-weave fabrics. The name is derived from the island of Crete, where the stitch has been used for centuries to decorate clothing. It is also found on Persian embroideries, and the stitch is called Persian stitch in France.

When used as a filling, the stitch is worked from alternate sides of the shape to completely cover it. A plait forms down the centre of the shape to make a very decorative filling. This stitch can be worked with the stitches close together, or they can be spaced apart to let the ground fabric show through. Whether it is used as a filling or as a line stitch, different effects can be achieved by varying the amount of fabric picked up and by altering the slant of the needle. When used as a line stitch, it is usually worked with an open finish, and it makes a pretty, spiked line, which follows curves well. Any type of embroidery thread can be used with Cretan stitch, but when it is being used to fill a shape solidly, a stranded silk or cotton will give better cover.

14 Buttonhole stitch ☆
also known as **button stitch** *and* **close stitch**

Buttonhole stitch is a simple, looped line stitch used on plain- and even-weave fabrics and has a variety of applications both practical and decorative. It is frequently used for finishing raw edges and for buttonholes, although a knotted variation, tailor's buttonhole stitch *(see page 33)*, is more hard-wearing and therefore more suitable for this purpose. Variations of this stitch are used for many types of decorative embroidery, including cut-work, couching and filling. Work buttonhole stitch from left to right, pulling the needle through the fabric and over the working thread; this action forms a row of vertical straight stitches joined together by a looped edge at the bottom. The stitch is equally successful worked in straight lines or following curves, and the size of the vertical stitches can be graduated to give a wavy line or a sawtooth edge at the top of the row. The stitches are placed closely together so that no ground fabric shows between them; if they are widely spaced, the stitch is known as blanket stitch *(see above)*.

BASIC STITCHES

15 Cross stitch
*also known as **sampler stitch, Berlin stitch** and **point de marque***

Cross stitch is probably the oldest and best known of all decorative embroidery stitches. It has many variations and has been known world-wide for centuries. Cross stitch is still used on traditional embroideries in many areas, including the Greek Islands, Scandinavia, Central and Eastern Europe and India. It is extremely quick and easy to work and is used mainly on even-weave fabrics, and on canvas where the threads can be counted to keep the crosses even. The stitch can also be used on plain-weave fabrics, but guide-lines will need to be marked on the fabric unless a commercially produced transfer is being used. Among its many uses, cross stitch is excellent for outlines, solid fillings, formalized motifs, borders and lettering. Cross stitch on canvas makes an excellent and hard-wearing stitch, suitable for upholstery.

Although the actual construction of crossed diagonal stitches remains the same, there are different methods of working ordinary cross stitch, depending on the choice of ground fabric or canvas. One rule applies to all methods: the top diagonal stitches must always fall in the same direction, unless a deliberate light and shade effect is required, in which case their direction can be varied to catch the light.

1 Cross stitch worked individually
Work a complete cross stitch before proceeding to the next stitch to form neat, slightly raised crosses. Cross stitch on canvas should always be worked in this way, and double canvas should be used for the best result. Care should be taken when matching the weight of the thread to the gauge of the canvas to ensure that the canvas is completely covered.

2 Cross stitch worked in rows
This method works well on plain- and even-weave fabrics. First, work a line of diagonals in one direction. Then, cover them with the top diagonals on the second journey in the opposite direction.

3 Alternate cross stitch This method is only suitable for even-weave fabrics. It will ensure an even tension and finish, particularly important when covering a large area. The bottom diagonal rows are worked alternately on two journeys, and then the top diagonals are worked over them in two more journeys.

16 Darning
*also known as **tacking stitch***

Darning stitch is a simple line and filling stitch and is used on plain- and even-weave fabrics. It is a variation of running stitch *(see page 12)* but, instead of the stitches and spaces being of equal length, the surface stitches are made longer and only a tiny amount of fabric is picked up by the needle. Many different patterns can be made by varying the arrangement of rows of stitches; one of the simplest, a brick pattern, is shown. Any type of embroidery thread can be used; choose the thread according to the weight of the ground fabric and the size of the stitch required.

In many parts of the world, notably the Greek Islands and Eastern Europe, darning stitch is used to create complex, geometric patterns by using multiple rows of the stitch.

17 Back stitch
*also known as **stitching** and **point de sable***

Back stitch is one of the most adaptable stitches in this book. It can be used as a delicate line stitch on plain- and even-weave fabrics; as a firm foundation row for composite stitches, such as Pekinese stitch *(see page 20)* and herringbone ladder filling stitch *(see page 73);* and occasionally on canvas in conjunction with another stitch, where a well-defined outline or centre line is needed. When used alone it should be worked in small, even stitches to look rather like machine stitching. This stitch follows intricate curves well if the stitches are kept tiny to let the curve flow. The front of the work is similar in appearance to Holbein stitch *(see page 9)* but, where Holbein stitch is quite flat, back stitch is slightly raised.

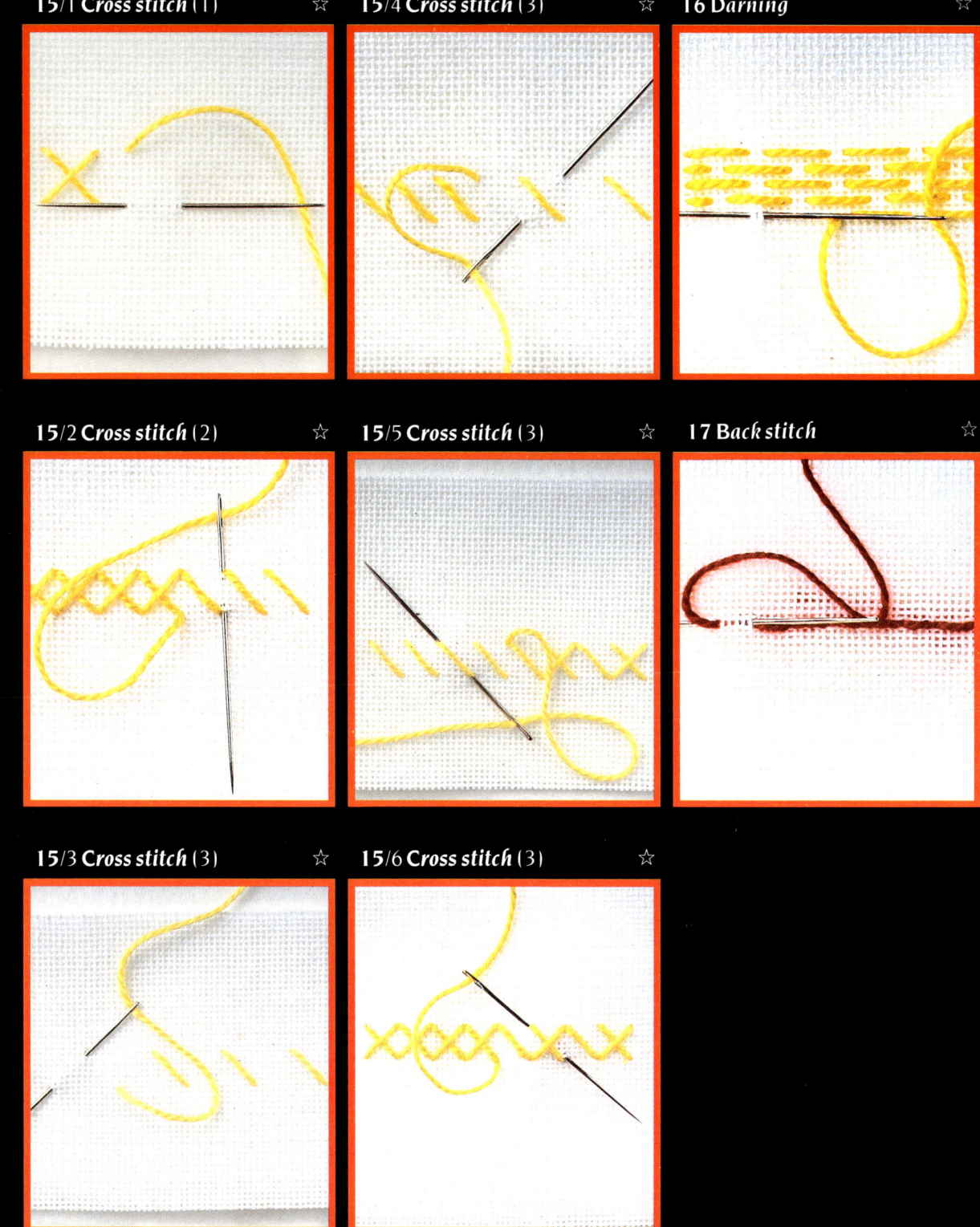

FABRIC STITCHES
Line stitches

18 Threaded back stitch
Threaded back stitch is quick to work and gives a decorative outline to a shape on plain- and even-weave fabrics; the line is heavier and wider than a plain back stitch line. A foundation row of ordinary back stitch is worked, although the stitches should be slightly longer than usual. Using a blunt-ended tapestry needle, a second thread is then passed alternately up and down behind these stitches, without entering the fabric. A third thread is then used to fill in the spaces left on the first journey to create a richer, heavier line. Threaded back stitch can be worked in one, two or three colours and will give an embossed effect if a much thicker yarn is used for the threading than the foundation row. If the back stitches are made fairly large, textured threads can be used for the threading to give an interesting effect on delicate fabric.

19 Whipped back stitch
Whipped back stitch is used as a line stitch on plain- and even-weave fabrics. It gives a heavier line than ordinary back stitch, and has a narrower, more raised appearance than threaded back stitch *(see page 16)*. First, work a foundation row of back stitches slightly longer than usual, and then whip a second thread over the line, without picking up any ground fabric; use a blunt-ended tapestry needle for the whipping to avoid splitting the foundation thread. The effect of whipped back stitch varies depending on the choice of whipping thread: if a heavy, shiny thread in the same colour as the foundation stitching is used, the line will look like a fine cord. Such a thread is employed when a raised line is required on a fabric that is too delicate for a thick thread to be embroidered through the weave: a very fine thread can be used for the foundation row and then whipped with the thick one.

20 Barb stitch
Barb stitch is an ornamental line stitch used on plain-weave fabrics. A foundation of two rows of blanket stitch *(see page 13)* worked close together is first laid down with the loops facing each other. These loops are then whipped together with a second thread without picking up the ground fabric. A blunt-ended tapestry needle should be used for the second thread, which can be of a contrasting colour, texture or thickness to the first thread, or a metallic yarn can be used for a richer effect. Barb stitch can be worked in a single line, or rows of the stitch can be repeated to make a wide border. The second row can be placed edge to edge with the first one, or the stitches of each row can interlock.

21 Basque stitch
also known as **twisted daisy border stitch**
Basque stitch, as its name suggests, has its origins in the Basque provinces of northern Spain. Often used in conjunction with the Basque knot *(see page 36)*, this stitch has been found on old embroideries of that area of Spain, and also in Portugal and southern France. Traditionally, the stitch was worked with red thread on green fabric, or white thread on a blue-green background. Basque stitch is a looped line stitch with a twist, which is always worked on plain-weave fabrics. It lends itself particularly well to curved lines and scroll shapes, and is most effective embroidered in white or another light-coloured thread on a dark fabric. At first sight, this stitch looks quite complicated, but it will prove quick and easy to work after some practice.

22 Berwick stitch
Berwick stitch is a line stitch worked on plain-weave fabrics. It forms a knotted base line with straight stitches protruding like spines from the top. Two rows of stitches can be worked with the knotted edges close together and the spines making a fishbone shape at each side. Each knot should be tightened slightly before proceeding to the next stitch. It is a quick and easy stitch to work, and is useful for outlining circular shapes, looking equally effective with the knotted edge on the inside or outside of the curve. Work French knots *(see page 96)* or Chinese knots *(see page 96)* at the top of the spines for a more ornate line, or vary the lengths of the spines to make a zigzag edge.

23 Closed feather stitch
Closed feather stitch is a wide line stitch used on plain- and even-weave fabrics and is a variation of feather stitch *(see page 12)*. It makes a decorative lacy line, which is worked downwards between two parallel lines, and it makes a pretty border when worked in multiple rows. To keep the rows even, guide-lines may need to be marked on the fabric if the threads cannot be counted. Closed feather stitch can be used as a couching stitch to anchor groups of threads and narrow ribbon or flat cord. This stitch does not follow curves well, unless they are extremely gradual, and it is usually worked in a straight line. It is worked in the same way as feather stitch but the needle is inserted vertically, rather than at an angle, and the loops are worked rather more closely together.

24 Whipped fly stitch
also known as **whipped attached fly stitch**
Whipped fly stitch is a line and filling stitch used on plain- and even-weave fabrics. It produces an attractive branched line with a ridged centre, which can be used on the straight or as an outline stitch. A variation of ordinary fly stitch *(see page 93)*, it is usually worked in two colours. A row of vertical fly stitch is worked with the tying-down stitches almost but not quite touching the centre of the 'V' shapes. A second thread is then used to whip the tying-down stitches, without picking up the ground fabric *(see whipped back stitch, page 16)*. Use a blunt-ended tapestry needle for the whipping thread to avoid splitting the stitches on the fly stitch row. The whipping thread can be of a contrasting weight, colour or texture and a metallic thread can look very attractive, providing that it is supple enough to follow the line well. Rows of whipped fly stitch can be worked solidly to fill a shape, giving a lacy, ridged effect.

LINE STITCHES

25 Open chain stitch ☆
also known as **ladder stitch, square chain stitch, Roman chain stitch, small writing** *(when the stitches are narrow) and* **big writing** *(when the stitches are wide)*
Open chain stitch is a line stitch worked downwards on plain- and even-weave fabrics. A variation of chain stitch *(see page 12)*, it is quick and easy to work. Carefully follow the sequence shown and anchor the last chain in each row by a tiny straight stitch through each of the bottom corners. Open chain stitch can be worked to give either an open or closed effect by simply adjusting the spacing between the stitches. It can be worked between parallel lines to make a heavy outline, and can couch down cords, narrow ribbons or other threads. This stitch is also suitable for filling narrow shapes of graduated widths, or it can be worked solidly row upon row to fill a larger area. It is essential that the line should be of an even width and guide-lines may need to be marked on the fabric when the stitch is worked in a straight line if the fabric threads cannot be counted.

When this stitch is spaced so that the ground fabric shows through, the space in the centre of each chain stitch can be decorated with an isolated stitch, such as a Chinese knot *(see page 96)*. Running stitch *(see page 12)* or chain stitch can be worked down the centre of each row in a contrasting colour or a different weight of embroidery thread. Open chain stitch worked closely together to make a solid line with no ground fabric showing through is characteristic of both Indian and East European embroidery, particularly that of Hungary and Yugoslavia.

26 Knotted Cretan stitch ☆
Knotted Cretan stitch is a decorative line stitch and filling used on plain- and even-weave fabrics. It is a simple variation of open Cretan stitch *(see page 20)* and is similar in appearance to zigzag coral stitch *(see page 25)*. It makes a pretty, zigzag line, with a knotted effect, and is suitable for use with any type of embroidery thread, the choice depending on the weight of line required. It is worked in the same way as open Cretan stitch but a knot is made after each slanting stitch is completed. Each knot should be tightened firmly, before proceeding to the next stitch.

Knotted Cretan stitch makes a good outline, especially when it is worked on a small scale, and it follows gradual curves well. It can also be used as a light filling over a shape, with the zigzags arranged to make an attractive lattice pattern.

27 Pagoda chevron stitch ☆
Pagoda chevron stitch is a line and filling stitch used on plain- and even-weave fabrics. It is a pretty and simply worked variation of chevron stitch *(see page 8)*, and is worked from left to right between two parallel lines. Any type of thread can be used with this stitch, the choice depending on the effect required. It is worked in a similar way to chevron stitch but in this case the diagonal stitches pass over the straight horizontal stitches, rather than underneath. Follow the sequence of stitches shown. To keep the stitches even, guide-lines may need to be marked on the fabric if the threads cannot be counted.

Pagoda chevron stitch can also be worked in closely placed rows to make a lattice filling.

28 Reversed fly stitch ☆
Reversed fly stitch is a line or filling stitch used on plain- and even-weave fabrics. It is a variation of ordinary fly stitch *(see page 93)* and, as the name suggests, consists of a row of vertical fly stitch with superimposed upside-down fly stitches. The tail stitches are normally kept quite short but can be made much longer to give a completely different effect. The stitch is usually worked in one journey, but two contrasting colours or weights of thread can be used if two journeys are made. It makes a pretty filling stitch worked either solidly in vertical rows over the shape, or each pair of fly stitches can be scattered to make a powdering.

29 Whipped running stitch ☆
also known as **cordonnet stitch**
Whipped running stitch is a line stitch used on plain- and even-weave fabrics. It makes a heavier line than ordinary running stitch *(see page 12)*, but has a narrower, more raised appearance than interlaced running stitch *(see page 25)*. This stitch is used for outlines and linear details, as it will follow intricate curves well.

First work a foundation of small, evenly spaced running stitches over the line to be covered. Then whip a second thread over this foundation, without picking up any ground fabric *(see whipped back stitch, page 16)*. A much heavier thread can be used for the whipping, and it can also be of a contrasting colour and texture. Alternatively a metallic thread can be used for the whipping, providing that it is quite supple.

30 Closed fly stitch ☆
Closed fly stitch is a line or filling stitch used on plain- and even-weave fabrics. A variation of ordinary fly stitch *(see page 93)*, it makes a heavy line and is worked downwards. It can be used as a filling for long, narrow shapes by graduating the widths of the stitches, or it can be worked solidly, row on row, for filling a larger shape. It is worked in exactly the same way as fly stitch when that stitch is worked in a vertical row, but the tying-down stitch is tiny and the V-shaped loops are packed very closely together. When this stitch is worked in a straight line, if the threads cannot be counted, guide-lines may need to be marked on the fabric to keep the row even.

31 Crossed buttonhole stitch ☆
Crossed buttonhole stitch is another simple but attractive variation of buttonhole stitch *(see page 13)*, and is used on plain- and even-weave fabrics. It can be used as an edging or line stitch, or as a filling, and consists of pairs of buttonhole stitches worked at an angle so that they cross each other. When the spaces between the stitches are narrowed and the stitch is worked row upon row as a filling, a pretty, trellis-like grid effect is achieved.

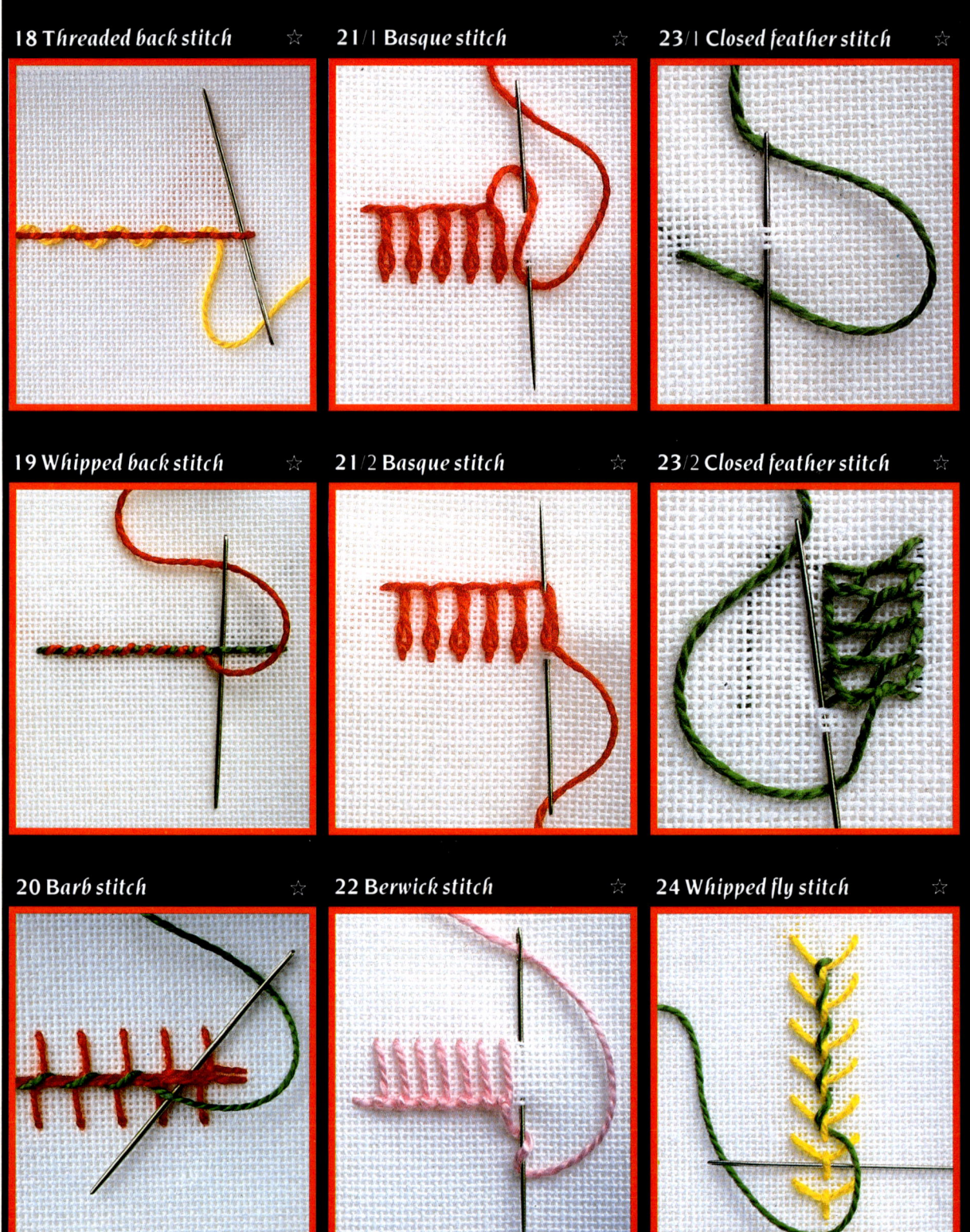

LINE STITCHES 19

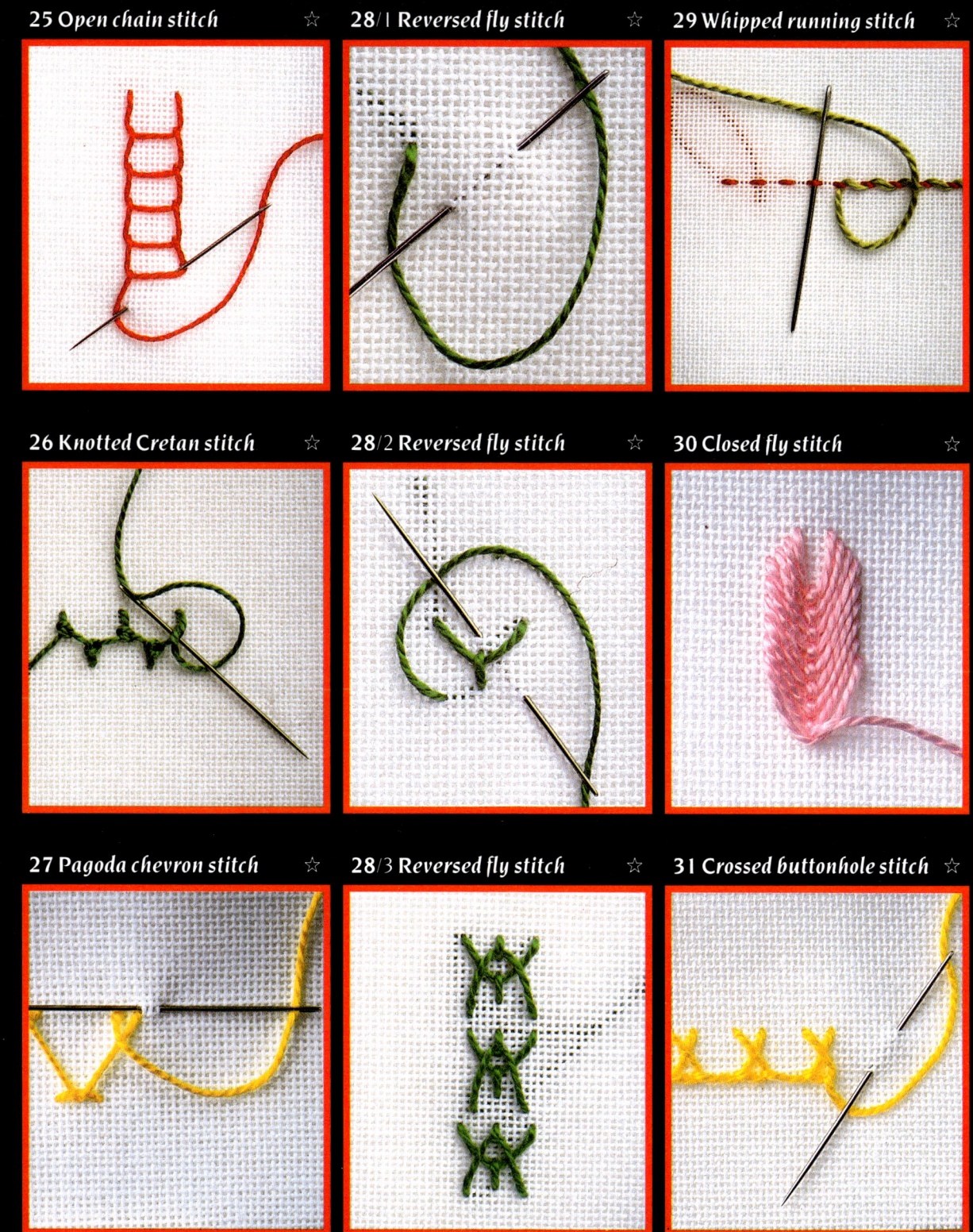

25 Open chain stitch
28/1 Reversed fly stitch
29 Whipped running stitch
26 Knotted Cretan stitch
28/2 Reversed fly stitch
30 Closed fly stitch
27 Pagoda chevron stitch
28/3 Reversed fly stitch
31 Crossed buttonhole stitch

FABRIC STITCHES

32 Whipped chain stitch

Whipped chain stitch is a simple line stitch used on plain- and even-weave fabrics and gives a neat, slightly raised, line. The whipping thread can be of a contrasting colour, weight or texture.

A foundation row of chain stitch *(see page 12)* is worked first, and then whipped at regular intervals with a second thread (do not pick up any ground fabric). The whipping stitches fall across the junctions of the chain stitches. Use a blunt-ended tapestry needle for the whipping to avoid splitting the stitches on the foundation row. Other variations of this stitch can also be worked:

1 The chain stitch row can be whipped back in the opposite direction to give a heavy, raised line.
2 The whipping stitches can be worked over the top and bottom of the chain loops, rather than over the whole stitch, to give a lighter effect.
3 An interesting solid filling can be made by working spaced parallel rows of chain stitch with the links directly underneath each other. These rows are then whipped loosely together through the opposite links, the whipping stitches spanning the spaces between the rows. This filling technique can also be worked with cable stitch *(see page 33)*, and looks very decorative when the whipping thread is shiny or metallic.

33 Pekinese stitch
also known as **Chinese stitch, blind stitch** *and* **forbidden stitch**

Pekinese stitch is a composite line stitch used on plain- and even-weave fabrics. One of the principal stitches used on old Chinese embroideries, it was worked on a tiny scale, and was reputed to affect the eyesight of the worker, hence its alternative name, blind stitch. It was worked in silk and used to fill shapes solidly with carefully blended shades. Pekinese stitch makes an attractive braided line which follows any linear design well, and can be used as a filling stitch in the Chinese manner.

The stitch is worked on a foundation of back stitch *(see page 14)*; the stitches should be left fairly loose, as the threading will tighten them. A second thread, of a contrasting weight, colour or texture, is then laced through the back stitch foundation. The needle should enter the fabric only at the beginning and end of each row. Use a blunt-ended tapestry needle for the lacing to avoid splitting the foundation stitches. The lacing thread should be tightened slightly after each loop has been formed to make a neat, textured line.

34 Open Cretan stitch

Open Cretan stitch is a line stitch and filling used on plain- and even-weave fabrics. A variation of ordinary Cretan stitch *(see page 13)*, the needle is inserted vertically into the fabric, rather than at a slant, and the stitches are spaced apart. It makes a light, zigzag line and follows gradual curves well. Any type of embroidery thread can be used; the choice depends on the size of the stitch and the weight of the fabric.

When used as a filling, the rows are arranged to make a lattice pattern, which can be decorated by the addition of isolated stitches worked in the spaces, and in a contrasting thread: French knots *(see page 96)*, Chinese knots *(see page 96)*, or daisy stitches *(see page 92)* all look effective. Isolated stitches can also be worked as a decoration when open Cretan stitch is worked in a single straight line to build up quite complex borders.

35 Plaited fly stitch

Plaited fly stitch is a line or filling stitch used on plain- and even-weave fabrics. It is an easily worked variation of ordinary fly stitch *(see page 93)* and makes an attractive plaited line or light filling. The stitch consists of a row of fly stitches with long tails, worked horizontally, from left to right. Each new stitch overlaps the previous stitch. A wide, double line can be made by working two rows of the stitch, with the 'V' shapes touching, creating spines along each side. By graduating the length of the tying-down stitches, a wavy edge can be made. Plaited fly stitch can be worked solidly, row on row, to fill a shape. The tying-down stitches can be made smaller.

36 Rosette of thorns stitch

Rosette of thorns stitch is an ornamental line stitch used on plain- and even-weave fabrics. It makes a pattern of crown shapes linked together to form a line and is a variation of buttonhole stitch *(see page 13)*. It looks equally effective worked in straight rows or round gradual curves, with the branching stitches fanning out along the outside of the curve. Any type of embroidery thread can be used, but a fine, rounded thread such as coton a broder shows off the delicacy of the stitch. The line is worked from left to right, and consists of groups of five buttonhole stitches worked with the bases close together and the upright stitches fanning out. A long buttonhole stitch links the groups of stitches. The crown shapes can be decorated by the addition of an isolated knot stitch, such as a Chinese knot *(see page 96)*, or a Danish knot *(see page 97)*, at the tip of each upright stitch.

37 Single feather stitch
also known as **slanted buttonhole stitch**

Single feather stitch is a line and smocking stitch used on plain- and even-weave fabrics. A variation of feather stitch *(see page 12)*, it makes a much plainer line, which is equally effective worked straight or following a curve. It is worked downwards and the looped stitches are made only at the right of the line. It has a similar appearance to blanket stitch *(see page 13)*, but the arms of the stitch are set at an angle.

38 Knotted cable stitch
also known as **knotted cable chain stitch**

Knotted cable stitch is a composite line stitch used on plain- and even-weave fabrics; it is made up of chain stitch *(see page 12)* and coral stitch *(see page 9)*. More ornate than ordinary cable stitch, it makes a broader line with a knotted appearance. Although this stitch looks more complicated to work than cable stitch, it is in fact easier, as the knots hold the chains in place during stitching. A round, twisted thread suits this stitch well.

39 Twisted chain stitch and detached twisted chain stitch ☆

Twisted chain stitch is a useful line stitch as it follows curves well and has a neat, slightly textured look. It is always worked downwards, and is used on plain- and even-weave fabrics. A simple variation of chain stitch *(see page 12)*, a twist is made at the top of each chain. It may help to hold the chain loop down on the fabric with the left thumb while pulling the working thread through the fabric (if you are right-handed). Twisted chain stitch gives a more satisfactory line than ordinary chain stitch and is ideal for outlining shapes and for linear details. Any type of embroidery thread can be used: a rounded thread, such as pearl cotton, will make the line slightly more raised than a flatter thread, such as stranded silk or cotton. The stitch is most effective when the stitches are fairly small and close together.

Twisted chain stitch can also be worked as an isolated stitch in the same way as daisy stitch *(see page 92)* when it is known as detached twisted chain stitch. Each loop is anchored to the fabric by a tiny straight stitch worked at the bottom. It can be used either as an accent stitch or in multiples as a pretty, textured powdering over a wide area of fabric.

40 Double buttonhole stitch ☆

Double buttonhole stitch is an attractive edging or outline stitch used on plain- and even-weave fabrics. It is quick and easy to work and consists of two parallel rows of blanket stitch *(see page 13)* worked facing each other. The second parallel row is placed so that the vertical stitches fit into the spaces of the first row. The spacing and size of the stitches can be varied, depending on the weight of thread used and the effect required. This stitch is equally effective worked in straight lines or following curves. When the two rows are worked close together with long verticals, a second thicker and contrasting thread or narrow ribbon can be slotted through the centre to make a more decorative line. When worked as an edging stitch on a hemmed piece of fabric, the top row of stitching should follow the turned over edge of the hem; the second row is worked on the very edge of the hem.

41 Half chevron stitch ☆

Half chevron stitch is a line stitch used on plain- and even-weave fabrics. It is a variation of chevron stitch *(see page 8)* and is worked from left to right. Half chevron stitch can be used with any type of embroidery thread and makes a useful border or outline stitch. The lower edge of the stitch is exactly the same as chevron stitch. This stitch follows curves well, and makes a good circular outline; the chevron edge can be worked on either the outside or inside of the circle. It can also be worked row on row to make a light, lacy filling stitch.

42 Pearl stitch ☆

Pearl stitch is a line stitch used on plain- and even-weave fabrics. It makes a raised, beaded line, which is suitable for outlines and intricate linear details, and looks most effective when worked with a heavy thread, such as pearl or soft cotton. It can also be worked with a more open finish, but the resulting line can look rather ragged. The line is worked from right to left of the area and, after the tiny horizontal stitch is made, the needle is inserted through the loop and then downwards through the fabric. The working thread should be tightened firmly before the needle is pulled through to begin the next stitch.

43 Whipped stem stitch ☆

Whipped stem stitch is a raised line stitch used on plain- and even-weave fabrics. It makes a heavier line than ordinary stem stitch *(see page 9)* and it is more raised than its sister stitches, whipped running stitch *(see page 17)* and whipped back stitch *(see page 16)*.

Whipped stem stitch is used where a bold line is needed as it follows curves and linear details well. It can be made more decorative by using a contrasting colour for the whipping. A foundation row of stem stitch is worked first, and then a second thread is whipped over the line without picking up any ground fabric. Use a blunt-ended tapestry needle for the whipping to avoid splitting the stitches on the foundation row. The effect of whipped stem stitch varies, depending on the choice of whipping thread: by using a heavy, lustrous thread in the same colour as the foundation row, the line will look like a fine cord; whereas a stranded thread in a contrasting colour will give a flatter effect.

44 Ship's ladder stitch ☆

Ship's ladder stitch is a line stitch used on plain- and even-weave fabrics. It makes a delicate, angular line, which is best used on the straight as it does not follow a curve well. It is very simple to work and is always worked from the bottom to the top. The stitch consists of a central line of vertical straight stitches divided by diagonal straight stitches set across the line. Any type of embroidery thread can be used, the choice depending on the weight of the ground fabric and the required width of the line. The central line of vertical stitches can be whipped, using the same or a contrasting weight of thread to give a heavier effect *(see whipped back stitch, page 16)*.

45 Thorn stitch ☆

Thorn stitch is a line stitch used on plain- and even-weave fabrics. It makes a pretty, branched line, and is often used to depict stems and ferns on a naturalistic embroidery. Actually a form of couching *(see page 8)*, a long, laid thread forms the centre of the line. Diagonal straight stitches are then worked in pairs, crossing over the central thread and anchoring it to the fabric. The diagonal stitches create the 'thorns' at each side of the line, and the lengths of these stitches can be varied as required. To prevent the fabric from puckering, thorn stitch is best worked on fabric that is stretched in an embroidery hoop or frame. The laid thread can be of a contrasting weight and colour to that used for the diagonal stitches.

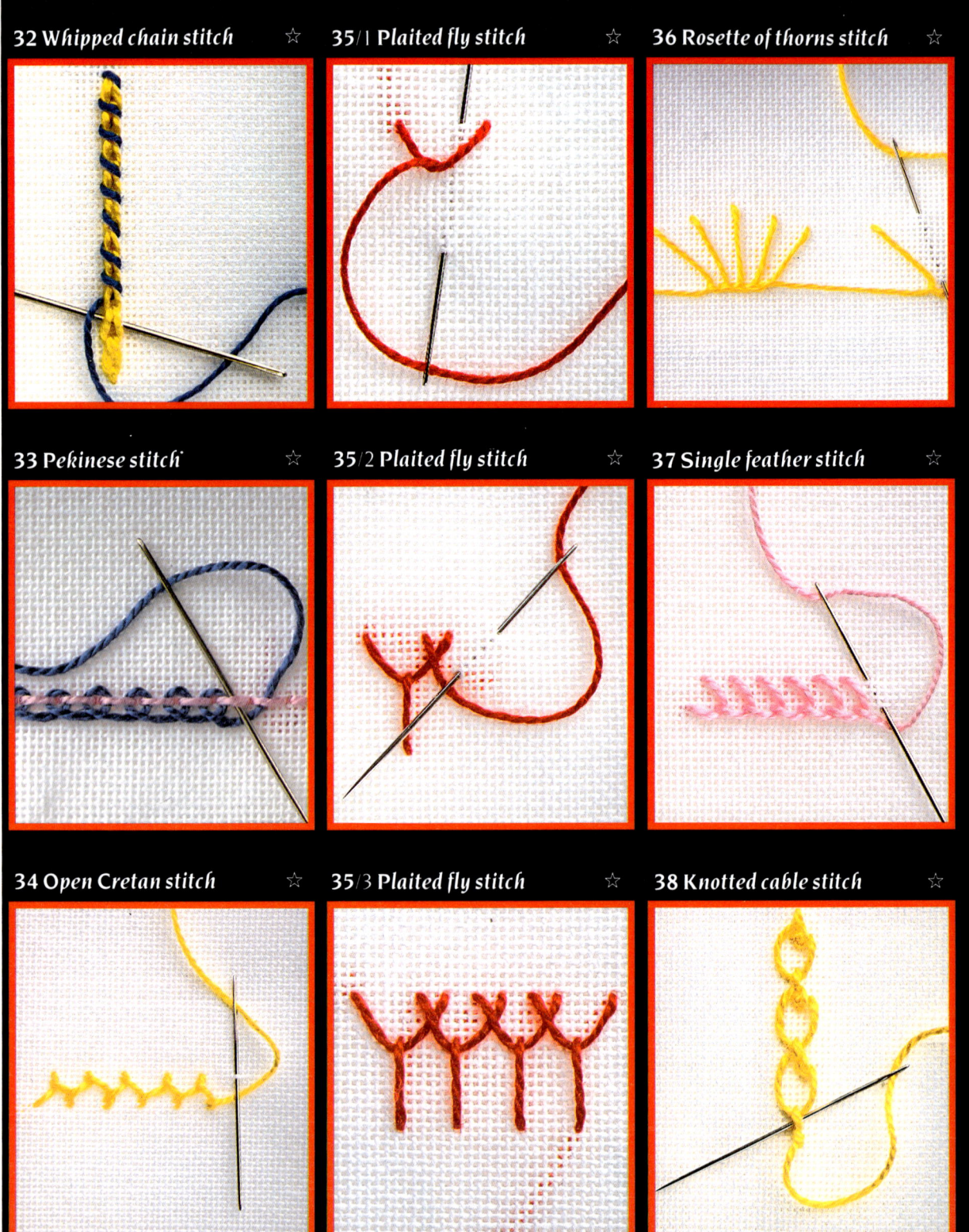

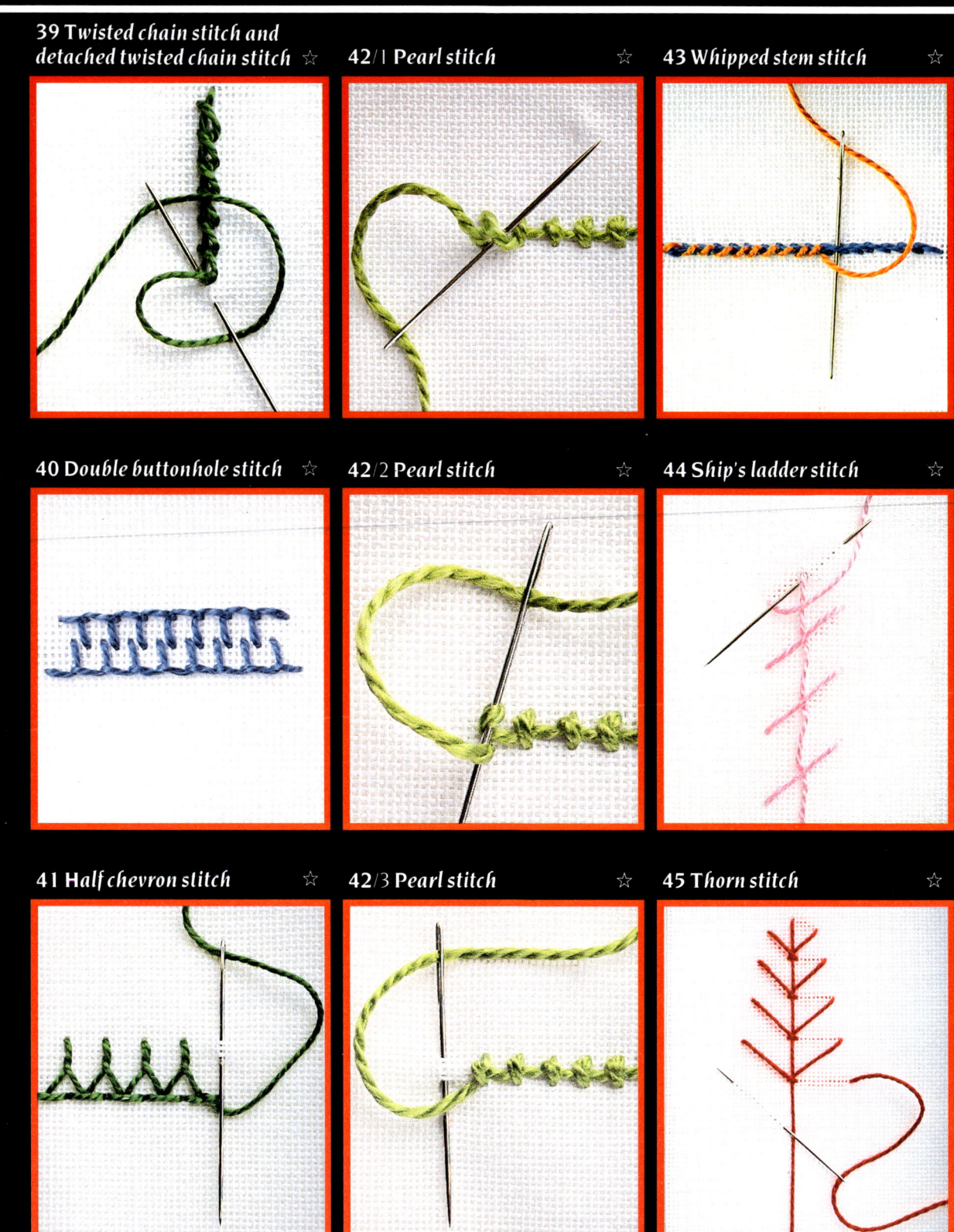

FABRIC STITCHES

46 Pueblo stitch ☆
Pueblo stitch is a line stitch used on plain- and even-weave fabrics. It is a variation of back stitch *(see page 14)* and must be worked with a two-ply, lightly twisted wool thread to achieve the correct appearance. Two strands of crewel wool can be used instead, perhaps in two contrasting colours, in which case the twists are made as each stitch is worked. The stitch makes an unusual twisted line and was probably invented by the Pueblo Indians of North America who have used it to produce some very fine examples of embroidery.

Pueblo stitch consists of large back stitches, and the effect of the line depends on the loosely twisted thread which is split as each section is made. It can be used for outlines and also looks extremely effective when worked solidly to make a filling.

47 Satin stitch ☆
also known as damask stitch

Satin stitch is a line and filling stitch used on plain- and even-weave fabrics. It is one of the oldest embroidery stitches and, like cross stitch *(see page 14)*, examples of satin stitch can be found worked on traditional embroideries in practically every country, but notably in China and Japan. Satin stitch consists of straight stitches worked side by side and, although it appears to be an easy stitch to work, some practice is required to work satin stitch evenly. It should be worked on fabric stretched in an embroidery hoop or frame to prevent the material from puckering, and the stitches should lie evenly and closely together to completely cover the ground fabric.

When used as a line stitch, it is worked between two lines with the stitches either slanting or at right angles to the lines to give a perfectly smooth surface. When worked as a filling, the stitches are taken right across the shape and can be worked vertically or diagonally, with changes of direction giving the effect of light and shade. This effect is enhanced by the use of a lustrous thread, such as stranded cotton or silk, but any other embroidery thread can be used, the choice depending on the effect required and the weight of the ground fabric. Since long satin stitches can become loose and untidy, only small shapes should be attempted, or, if a large shape is required, it should be split into smaller, more workable shapes first. For a very large shape, use long and short stitch *(see page 72)* or encroaching satin stitch *(see page 68)*. Areas of satin stitch can be made slightly raised by first working a padding of rows of stem stitch *(see page 9)*, chain stitch *(see page 12)*, or running stitch *(see page 12)* over the shape. Satin stitch can also be used on single canvas for outlines and small shapes, with the stitches running vertically, horizontally or diagonally.

48 Double fly stitch ☆
Double fly stitch is a line stitch used on plain- and even-weave fabrics. It is a simply worked variation of ordinary fly stitch *(see page 93)* and it makes a pretty line, which can be worked in two colours. The stitch consists of a row of spaced fly stitches worked vertically, with each fly stitch over-stitched by a second fly stitch. The tail of the second fly fills the space underneath the first, and so on. The line can be worked in one or two journeys, depending on how many colours are being used. If one colour only is being used, work the stitch as a continuous line. For two colours, work the underneath stitches on one journey, and the top stitches on the second journey.

49 Scroll stitch ☆
also known as single knotted line stitch; see also coral stitch

Scroll stitch is a line stitch used on plain- and even-weave fabrics. It makes a simple knotted line which flows round curves and follows intricate details well, and is often used to depict areas of water. Any type of embroidery thread can be used with scroll stitch, providing that it is compatible with the weight of the ground fabric. A stranded thread gives a much flatter effect than a rounded thread, such as pearl or soft cotton. It is very quick and easy to work and runs from left to right along the line. It consists of a series of simple knots which are linked together. The knots should not be pulled tightly and they can be worked closely together or spaced quite widely apart, depending on the effect required.

50 Closed buttonhole stitch ☆
Closed buttonhole stitch is a very simple variation of buttonhole stitch *(see page 13)*. It makes an attractive alternative edging for hems instead of blanket stitch *(see page 13)*, or it can be worked row upon row to make a border or filling. It is worked from left to right in the same way as buttonhole stitch, but the spacing between the stitches is more open. Each pair of verticals is worked into the same place in the fabric so that they form a triangular shape; a variation of this is to work three verticals in the same space. When working this stitch as a border or filling, different effects can be achieved by placing the rows with the loops facing one another, or with the vertical stitches touching each other, or interlocking.

51 Rope stitch ☆
Rope stitch is a line stitch used on plain- and even-weave fabrics. It makes a solidly stitched line, which is raised along the lower edge. This stitch is extremely effective for working curves and spirals, especially when a lustrous thread, such as stranded cotton or silk, is used. It is relatively easy to work, but the stitches should lie close together and evenly to give the correct effect. The stitch is worked from right to left by working slanting stitches which

LINE STITCHES

should slant sharply backwards. A small knot is formed by pulling the needle through over the working thread; these knots should not show on the surface but merely act as a padding to raise the lower edge of each stitch.

52 Broad chain stitch ☆
also known as **reverse chain stitch**
Broad chain stitch is a line stitch used on plain- and even-weave fabrics. It makes a bold, broad line, suitable for where a heavily defined outline is needed. A firm thread should be chosen so that the individual stitches keep their shape well. Begin the row by working a short straight stitch; this will anchor the top chain. Bring the needle out of the fabric further along the line and then work the top chain through the straight stitch; work the second and subsequent chains as shown. When the needle passes under the chain loops, no ground fabric should be picked up; the chain stitches should be left quite loose on the surface of the fabric to make the line flat and broad.

53 Spine chain stitch ☆
Spine chain stitch is a decorative variation of chain stitch *(see page 12)*. A line stitch, it is used on plain- and even-weave fabrics. It is most attractive when worked on a small scale and can be used for outlining, as it follows all types of curves well. Any kind of embroidery thread can be used for this stitch, depending on the weight of the ground fabric and the effect required. It is worked in exactly the same manner as chain stitch but with the addition of a diagonal straight stitch at the base of each chain. These diagonal stitches or 'spines' can be worked alternately to the right and left of the chains, or they can be grouped in multiples at either side. The spines can conform to one length or vary along the row. They can be embellished by the addition of an isolated stitch, such as a French knot *(see page 96)* or a daisy stitch *(see page 92)*, at the tip.

A variation of this stitch can be made by whipping the central chain stitch row in a contrasting colour or different texture of thread, or by working an isolated knot stitch in the centre of each chain.

54 Heavy chain stitch ☆
also known as **heavy braid chain stitch**
Heavy chain stitch is a solid line stitch used on plain- and even-weave fabrics. It makes a heavy, cord-like line which is useful where a well-defined outline is needed. It is similar in construction to broad chain stitch *(see page 25)* and is also worked downwards. The row starts with a vertical straight stitch worked in exactly the same way as broad chain stitch; the second and subsequent chains are then worked as shown. The difference between this stitch and broad chain stitch is that the needle is passed back under the previous two chain loops, rather than just the previous one, to form the next stitch. When the needle passes under the chain loops, no ground fabric should be picked up. This stitch can be worked row on row to fill an area, but the effect can be rather solid and uninteresting, and choice of thread is important. Any type of embroidery thread can be used when heavy chain stitch is worked in a single row, although a round, twisted thread will make the line stand out best from the background. A stranded cotton or silk will create a flatter, wider line.

55 Interlaced running stitch ☆
Interlaced running stitch is a line stitch used on plain- and even-weave fabrics. It makes an attractive threaded line, which follows curves and intricate shapes well and is used for outlines and decorative details. This stitch is an easily worked variation of ordinary running stitch *(see page 12)*, which is threaded in two journeys. A heavy thread is normally used for the interlacing and a rounded thread, such as pearl or soft cotton, gives a slightly raised line. The stitch can be monochrome, or contrasting colours can be used for the interlacing. Use a blunt-ended tapestry needle to avoid splitting the running stitches. Interlaced running stitch can also be worked solidly to fill a shape, either in vertical or horizontal rows, or arranged in a spiral, working outwards from the centre of the shape.

56 Paris stitch ☆
Paris stitch is a line stitch used only on even-weave fabrics. It makes a neat line with branched stitches along the upper edge, and should be worked in straight rows. It is a variation of back stitch *(see page 14)*, which is used to make a horizontal line. After each back stitch is worked, a vertical stitch is made. This vertical stitch can be worked diagonally to give a different effect. When used on a loosely woven fabric, each stitch can be pulled slightly to create a pattern of holes along the row. Paris stitch can also be worked row upon row to fill a shape.

57 Zigzag coral stitch ☆
Zigzag coral stitch is a wide, decorative line stitch used on plain- and even-weave fabrics. It forms a knotted zigzag line, which follows gradual curves well, and it makes an attractive outline when the stitches are kept small and even. It is a variation of coral stitch *(see page 9)* and is usually worked downwards between two parallel lines. Guidelines may need to be marked on the fabric to keep the lines of stitching straight and even. Each left-hand stitch is worked in exactly the same way as a coral stitch, but the right-hand stitches are worked slightly differently. Any type of thread can be used with zigzag coral stitch, but a medium weight, slightly twisted thread will give the most pleasing result.

FABRIC STITCHES

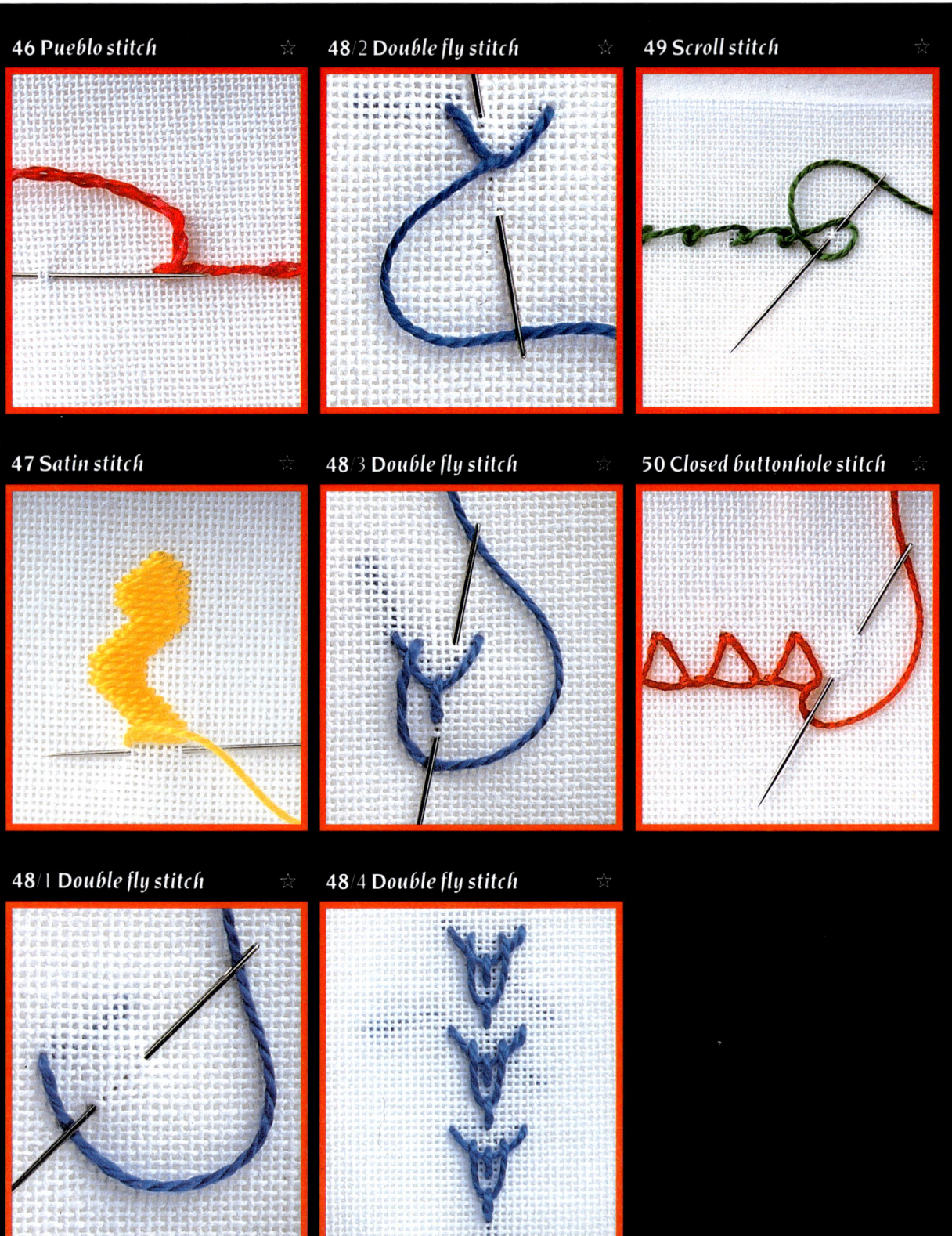

46 Pueblo stitch
48/2 Double fly stitch
49 Scroll stitch
47 Satin stitch
48/3 Double fly stitch
50 Closed buttonhole stitch
48/1 Double fly stitch
48/4 Double fly stitch

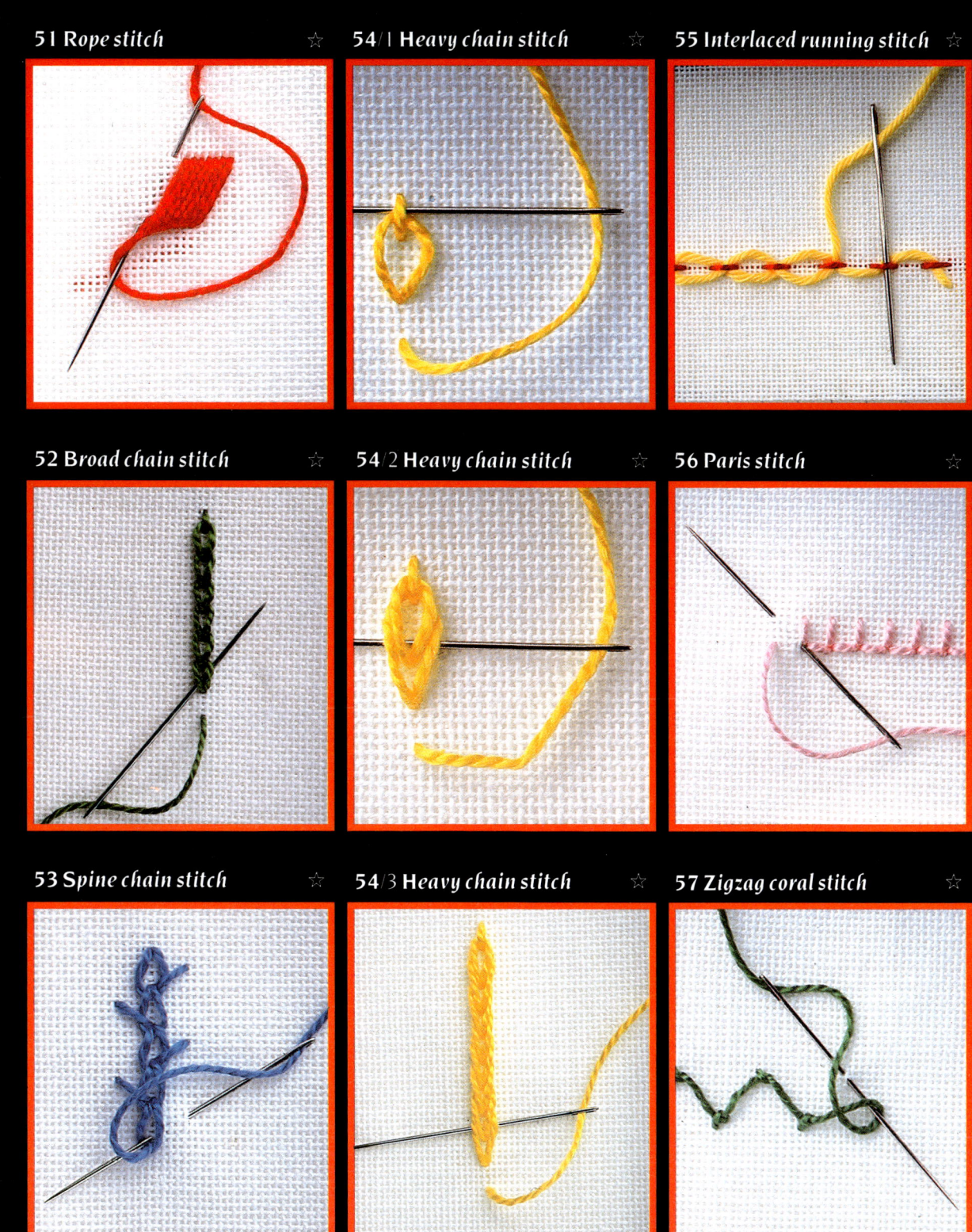

FABRIC STITCHES

58 Double feather stitch ☆
also known as **double coral stitch**
Double feather stitch is a wide line stitch used on plain- and even-weave fabrics. It is a great favourite as it makes a branched, feathery line, which is more decorative than that made by feather stitch *(see page 12)*. A variation of feather stitch, it is worked in a zigzag pattern. It is used for borders, or multiple rows can be worked to fill a shape. It is worked downwards in a similar way to feather stitch, but two or more stitches are made alternately to the right and the left of the line. It can also be worked irregularly, with the numbers of stitches at each side varying, depending on the shape of line required.

59 Petal stitch ☆
also known as **pendant chain stitch**
Petal stitch is a composite line stitch used on plain- and even-weave fabrics. It makes an attractive line with daisy stitches *(see page 92)* arranged so that they hang down to form pendants. This stitch is especially suited to working circular and spiral lines, but it can also be used on the straight, either singly or in multiple rows, to make a textured filling. It is worked from right to left and consists of a row of stem stitch *(see page 9)* with daisy stitches worked below each stem stitch, as shown. Any type of embroidery thread can be used, although the weight of the ground fabric must be taken into consideration, but this stitch looks very effective worked in stranded cotton or silk.

60 Bonnet stitch ☆
Bonnet stitch came by its name after an example of the stitch, which does not seem to have been previously known, was found embroidered on a bonnet in a 1923 issue of *Embroidery Magazine*. It is a looped line stitch with a twist, suitable for use on plain-weave fabrics. Worked from right to left, this stitch is a twisted variation of blanket stitch *(see page 13)*. Bonnet stitch can also be worked in rows that touch, to produce a light, lacy filling. The stitch can be varied by altering the lengths of the twisted uprights and the spaces between them. Most types of thread are suitable for use with this stitch, depending on the effect required and the weight of the fabric to be used. A fine pearl cotton, for example, will give a delicate, spidery look, while a thick wool will create a more solid texture.

61 Fern stitch ☆
Fern stitch is a line stitch used on plain- and even-weave fabric. It is extremely simple to work and any type of embroidery thread can be used, but the weight of the background fabric must be taken into account. Fern stitch makes a pretty, branched line and is often used for decorating leaf and flower shapes and for working fern-like sprays in a floral embroidery. It consists of groups of three straight stitches of equal length, worked at angles to each other and sharing the same base hole; the groups are arranged to form a line. Evenly sized and spaced stitches are essential, so care should be taken when working this stitch.

62 Overcast stitch and detached overcast stitch ☆☆
Overcast stitch is a raised line stitch used on plain- and even-weave fabrics. It is used for outlines, as it follows an intricate pattern well, and it is particularly useful for working letters and monograms, and for figurative designs. This stitch should always be worked with the fabric stretched in an embroidery hoop or frame, as the ground fabric can become puckered and distorted. A padding row of running stitch *(see page 12)* or Holbein stitch *(see page 9)* is worked along the desired line first. This line is then closely covered by small straight stitches, worked at right angles to the padding. The stitches must be worked tightly together and pick up a very small amount of ground fabric each time. A flat thread, such as stranded cotton or silk, gives better coverage to the overcasting, while a round thread, such as pearl cotton, should be used for the padding row.

Detached overcast stitch is worked in a similar way but with two differences. The padding consists of two loosely worked rows of stem stitch *(see page 9)*: the two rows pick up the fabric alternately. The overcast stitch over the padding is worked in the same way as above, but the ground fabric is not picked up. The stitches must be worked evenly and very close together to make a well-formed line. This stitch is especially useful for working branched lines and for lines that cross one another.

63 Basket stitch no. 1 ☆☆
This and basket stitch no. 2 *(see page 80)* bear the same name but are, in fact, entirely different. Basket stitch no. 1 is a line stitch used on plain-weave fabrics, which gives a braided effect, useful for both edgings and fillings. It can be worked to give an open or closed finish, and looks best when the outside edges are kept parallel: guide-lines drawn on the fabric are helpful here. Basket stitch no. 1 is worked with a forwards and backwards motion, and is similar in construction to long-armed cross stitch *(see page 141)*. These plaited or braided stitches are very effective when worked with a fairly shiny thread, such as stranded cotton, to enhance the light and shade effect made by the different slants of the stitched threads.

64 Zigzag cable stitch ☆☆
also known as **double cable stitch**
Zigzag cable stitch is a simple but effective variation of ordinary cable stitch *(see page 33)*. It is a line stitch and filling used on plain- and even-weave fabrics. The stitches are formed in exactly the same manner as cable stitch, but each one is worked at right angles to the previous one to make a zigzag line. When used as a line stitch, zigzag cable stitch is usually worked in straight lines, as it does not follow curves well. It makes an attractive light filling when several spaced parallel rows are worked together: the apex of each pair of stitches should be placed between those on the row below. This stitch works well with any type of embroidery thread.

65 Feathered chain stitch ☆
also known as chained feather stitch

Feathered chain stitch is a pretty, wide line stitch used on plain- and even-weave fabrics. It makes a delicate zigzag line, and is suitable for use with any type of embroidery thread, although a fine thread will enhance the delicacy of the stitch. It is essential that the stitches are of an even size and equally spaced along the line: if an even-weave fabric is used, the threads can be counted to keep the stitches evenly spaced; if a plain-weave fabric is used, guide-lines will need to be marked on the fabric, or the zigzag line will be lost. The stitch is always worked downwards and consists of chain stitches *(see page 12)* worked alternately to the left and right at a slant. These stitches are then connected by straight diagonal stitches. Short rows of feathered chain stitch can be scattered at random over an area to make a light powdering, or rows can be worked solidly to give an interesting texture to a shape.

66 Breton stitch ☆☆

Breton stitch is a relatively little-known stitch characteristic of the embroidery of Brittany, and is reminiscent of the shape of the carved spindles found on the furniture of that area. It is a line stitch used on plain- and even-weave fabrics and is traditionally worked with a dark blue thread on a white fabric, or with white thread on blue linen. Breton stitch is based on closed herringbone stitch *(see page 60)* but differs from that stitch in the way that the crossing stitches are twisted round each other. It is worked with the stitches quite close together between parallel lines; the width between these lines depends on the weight of the embroidery thread. When rows of Breton stitch are worked together to make a filling, an attractive grill-work pattern is created over the fabric, which allows the colour of the background to show through. This stitch should be worked on tightly stretched fabric in an embroidery hoop or frame, using a thread with a definite twist for best results. It is equally effective as a line or filling stitch, or to outline curved shapes.

67 Satin stitch couching ☆☆
also known as trailing stitch

Satin stitch couching makes a solid, raised line and is used on plain- and even-weave fabrics. A variation of ordinary couching *(see page 8)*, the laid threads are used as a padding and are completely covered by couching stitches. It is used exclusively as a line stitch; it follows both tight and gradual curves well, and can be used for very intricate linear patterns. To give a varying diameter of line, vary the weight of the laid threads. Any type of embroidery thread is suitable for the couching stitches, although a stranded cotton or silk will give the most effective cover. Bring the laid threads to the surface and guide them with your left hand (if you are right-handed) along the line to be stitched. Then bring through the couching thread, and work small, close satin stitches *(see page 24)* over the laid thread. The satin stitches can be worked either at right angles to the laid thread, or they can be slanted, depending on the effect required.

68 German buttonhole stitch ☆☆

German buttonhole stitch is a lacy, looped line stitch, which gives a knotted effect; it is used on plain- and even-weave fabrics. This stitch makes a very decorative line which looks complicated to work but is, in fact, quite easy. A rounded, twisted thread, such as pearl cotton will make the line stand out from the fabric, while stranded cotton or silk will give a flatter appearance. It is usually worked downwards on the fabric, unlike most other variations of buttonhole stitch, which are worked from left to right. A pair of buttonhole stitches *(see page 13)* are worked with a slant. The working thread is then looped under both stitches in an upward direction, without entering the fabric. To complete the stitch, the thread must be pulled in a downward direction. Like most decorative line stitches, German buttonhole stitch can be used as an outline or worked solidly to make a border or filling. It looks very unusual when worked in a spiral shape.

69 Laced Antwerp edging stitch and fringed Antwerp edging stitch ☆☆

Laced Antwerp edging stitch is a line stitch used on plain-weave fabric, not an edging stitch. It consists of two rows of Antwerp edging stitch running parallel to each other on the surface of the fabric, with the loops facing one another. A second thread is then laced through the loops with a blunt-ended tapestry needle, without picking up the ground fabric.

Fringed Antwerp edging stitch is another decorative border stitch but it can also be used as a fancy fringe edging. Work one row of Antwerp edging stitch, then, to form the fringe, attach lengths of thread to each loop using a lark's head knot *(see Glossary)*. This fringing technique can also be used with Armenian edging stitch *(see page 108)* and braid edging stitch *(see page 109)*.

70 Rosette chain stitch ☆☆
also known as bead edging stitch

Rosette chain stitch is a decorative line stitch used on plain- and even-weave fabrics. It makes a pretty, braided line, and is a useful finishing device, worked close to the turned under edge of a piece of fabric. A variation of twisted chain stitch *(see page 21)*, it is always worked from right to left and is fairly simple to stitch. The loop must be held loosely in place on the fabric with the left thumb (if you are right-handed) while the twisted chain stitch is completed. Next, the needle is passed under the right-hand top thread of the stitch, without picking up the ground fabric; the next twisted chain stitch can then be worked.

A heavy thread, such as pearl cotton, is the most suitable for this stitch, as stranded threads give a flat effect. Rosette chain stitch is a useful outline stitch, equally effective when worked in a straight line or when following a curve. It is also used to make floral motifs by working it in a small circle, with the chain stitches pointing outwards.

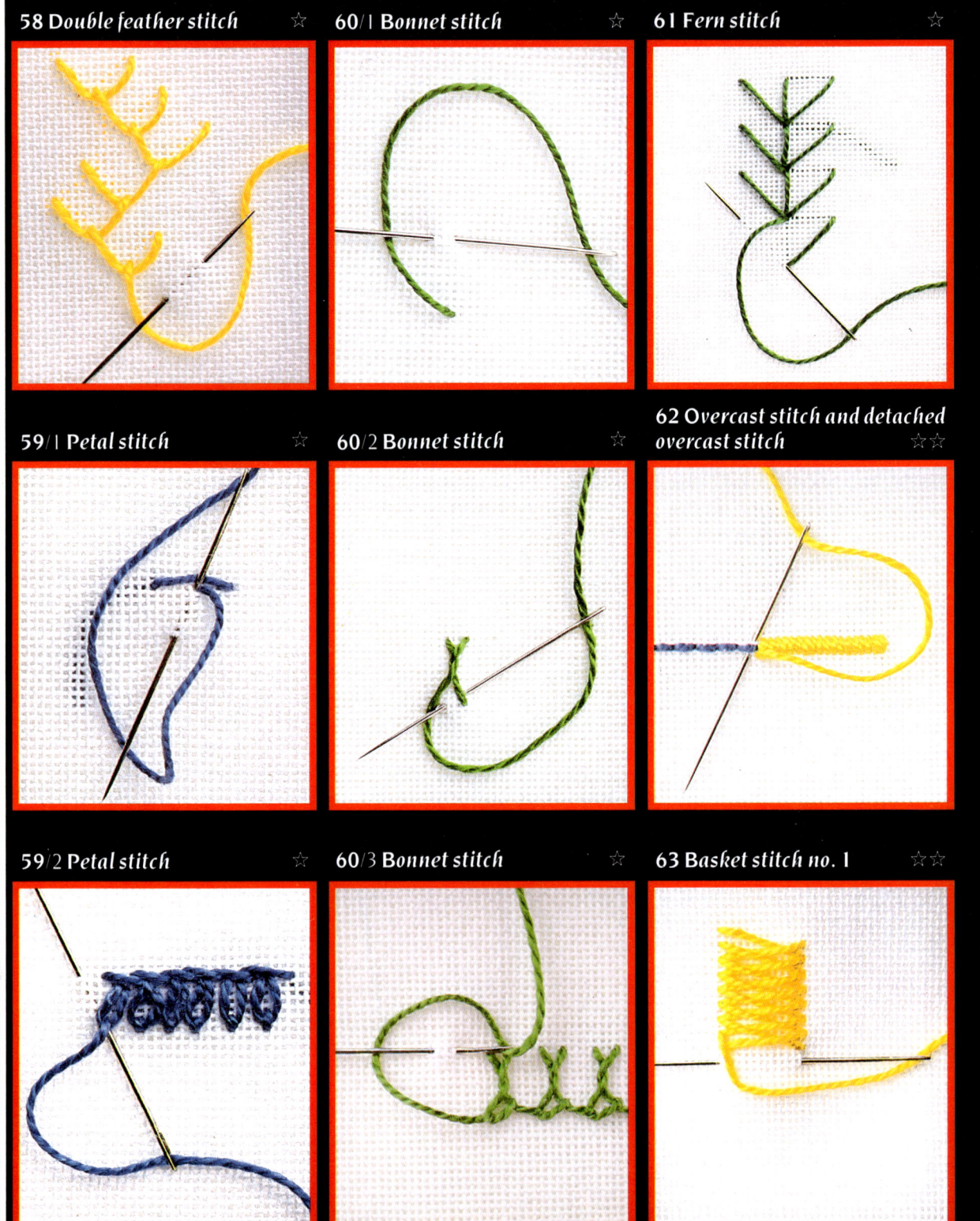

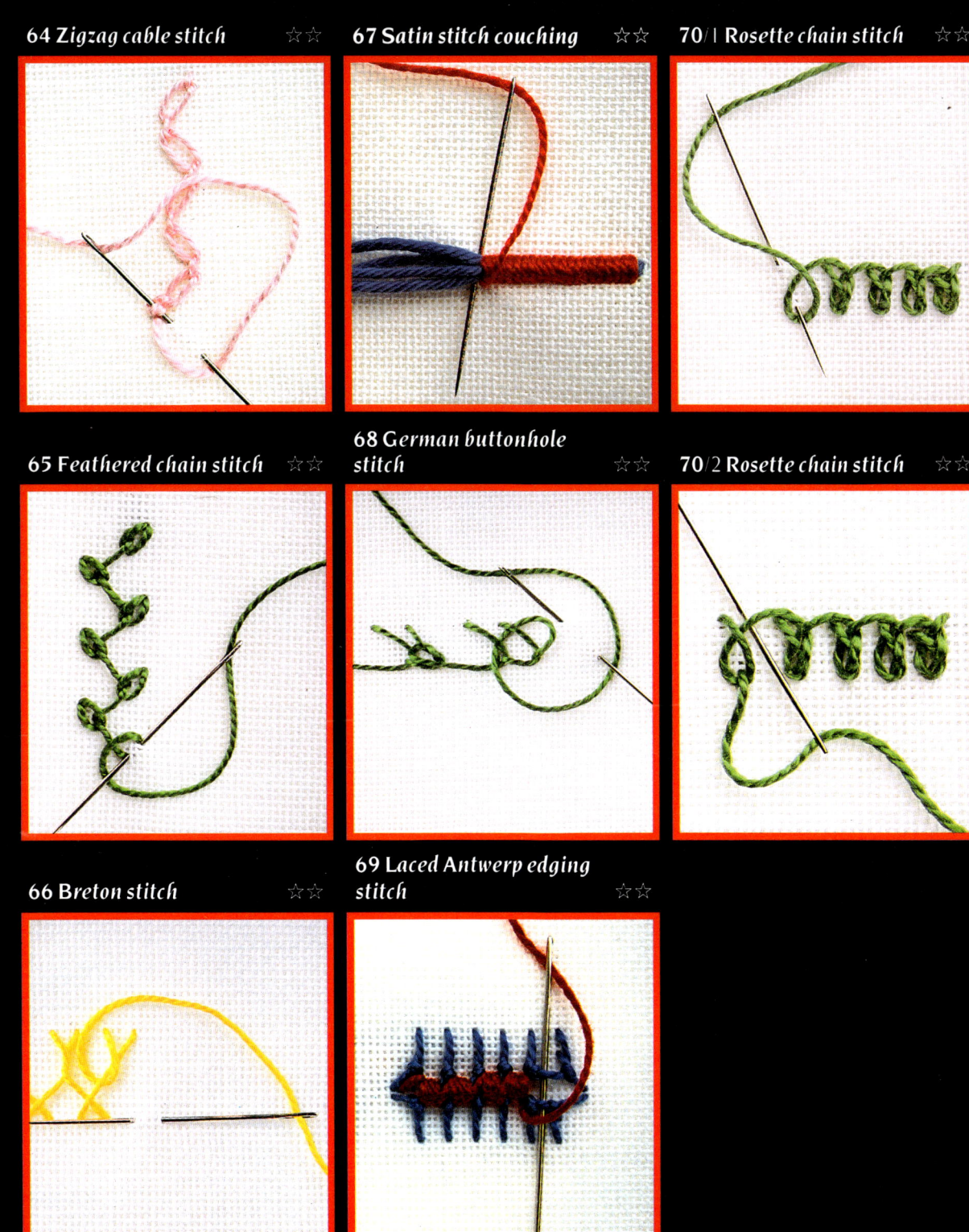

71 Whipped satin stitch ☆☆
Whipped satin stitch is a variation of ordinary satin stitch *(see page 24)* used on plain- and even-weave fabrics. It gives a raised, corded finish to lines and narrow shapes worked in satin stitch, by whipping the same or a contrasting thread across the surface. The satin stitches should be slanted, and the whipping stitches should be set at right angles to them and spaced slightly apart. The whipping stitches enter the ground fabric close to the outside of the shape or line, and should be perfectly regular.

72 Mirrored buttonhole stitch ☆☆
also known as **up and down buttonhole stitch**

Mirrored buttonhole stitch is a variation of buttonhole stitch *(see page 13)* and is used as a line stitch on plain- and even-weave fabrics. It forms pairs of vertical stitches crossed by a small bar, each pair linked by a loop. It is fairly simple to work; the pairs of stitches should be made in two separate movements. After the first stitch has been worked, hold down the loop with the left thumb to prevent it slipping while completing the second stitch. Mirrored buttonhole stitch makes a bold outline, which is particularly attractive when worked round curves and circles. It can be worked solidly for filling shapes, with the rows placed next to each other or overlapping.

73 Knotted pearl stitch ☆☆
Knotted pearl stitch is a line stitch used on plain- and even-weave fabrics. A variation of pearl stitch *(see page 21)*, it makes a more open line with a knotted surface. It is also suitable for outlines and linear details, but is not as effective as ordinary pearl stitch for following very intricate designs. A round thread, such as pearl cotton, accentuates the knotted appearance of the stitch more than a flat, stranded cotton thread. It is worked from right to left, and the working thread should be tightened after each knot before proceeding to the next stitch. The lower stitches can be made longer to create a less densely knotted effect, or the lengths can be varied to give an undulating line.

74 Wheat ear stitch ☆☆
Wheat ear stitch is a decorative line stitch used on plain- and even-weave fabrics. It makes a branched line with a heavy central strip and looks rather like an ear of corn, especially when used in short lengths. This stitch follows a gentle curve but is normally used on the straight. Wheat ear stitch was often used as a surface decoration on traditional English smocks. The stitch is worked downwards and consists of two diagonal stitches set at right angles and then joined by a broad chain stitch *(see page 25)*, as shown. The length of the diagonal stitches can be varied to give an attractive, irregular line, and any type of embroidery thread can be used.

75 Looped edging stitch no. 2 ☆☆
Looped edging stitch no. 2 is a line stitch used on plain- and even-weave fabrics and not an edging stitch as its name implies. It makes a looped line, with regular downward straight stitches, and follows a curve well, provided that the looped line is worked on the inside of the curve, with the straight stitches fanning out from it. This stitch can also be worked solidly, row on row, to make an attractive filling. It is simple to work, and each row is worked from right to left along parallel lines. Guide-lines may need to be marked on the fabric if the stitch is being worked in straight lines and the fabric threads cannot be counted. A short, horizontal stitch is made at the beginning of each row to act as a foundation for the first loop. A series of straight stitches and loops are then made along the row.

76 Tailor's buttonhole stitch ☆☆

Tailor's buttonhole stitch is similar to ordinary buttonhole stitch *(see page 13)* but it has a stronger edge, which is more hard-wearing and particularly suitable for heavyweight fabrics. It is used both to finish raw edges and as a line stitch on plain- and even-weave fabrics. It is worked from left to right in the same way as buttonhole stitch, but with an extra loop of thread, which is wound round the needle before it is pulled through the stitch. This extra loop makes a firm knotted edge to the stitch. Tailor's buttonhole stitch should be worked with the stitches very close together, so that no fabric shows between them. This will ensure that the knots lie neatly next to each other along the edge. The lengths of the uprights can be graduated to give a zigzag or undulating top edge to the stitch for a more decorative line.

77 Cable stitch ☆☆
also known as **cable chain stitch**

Cable stitch is a variation of chain stitch *(see page 12)* used as a line or filling stitch on plain- and even-weave fabrics. It is worked in a similar way to ordinary chain stitch but in this case the thread is twisted round the needle after each chain loop, and before it enters the fabric. This makes an intervening link between the chains. The stitch follows curved lines well and makes a good filling stitch when worked solidly. A contrasting stitch, such as coral stitch *(see page 9)* or stem stitch *(see page 9)* can be worked on alternate rows to make an unusual filling. Another method of filling a shape with cable stitch is to work evenly spaced parallel rows of it over the whole area to be filled. Then lace adjoining rows together through the chains with a contrasting thread and a blunt-ended tapestry needle.

78 Loop stitch ☆
also known as **centipede stitch** *and* **knotted loop stitch**; *see also* **daisy stitch**

Loop stitch is a line stitch used on plain- and even-weave fabrics, and it has a raised, plaited centre. It is normally used on the straight, but it will follow a curve, providing that it is gradual. Loop stitch can also be used to fill narrow shapes by varying the length of the outside stitches and outlining the shape with back stitch *(see page 14)* or stem stitch *(see page 9)* for greater definition. It is worked horizontally from right to left along parallel lines, and guide-lines may need to be drawn on the fabric to keep the stitches even, if the fabric threads cannot be counted. Straight stitches are worked between the two lines, and loop under each preceding stitch to make the plaited centre. Any type of thread can be used, but a round, twisted thread, such as pearl cotton, enhances the raised plait.

79 Double-sided cross stitch ☆☆
also known as **marking stitch** *and* **brave bred stitch**

Double-sided cross stitch is used on plain- and even-weave fabrics. As its name suggests, it makes an identical stitch on both sides of the fabric; it is a reversible variation of ordinary cross stitch *(see page 14)*. It is an ideal stitch for fine, semi-transparent fabrics, such as organdie or fine silk Habotai, and for work which is viewed from both sides. Each row is worked in four journeys: at the end of the first journey and the beginning of the fourth, work extra half-diagonals. If it is necessary to work over a cross stitch to get to a point of continuation (to keep the stitch identical on both sides) it should be done as neatly as possible. Care should be taken to secure the beginning and end of each length of embroidery thread under an existing stitch.

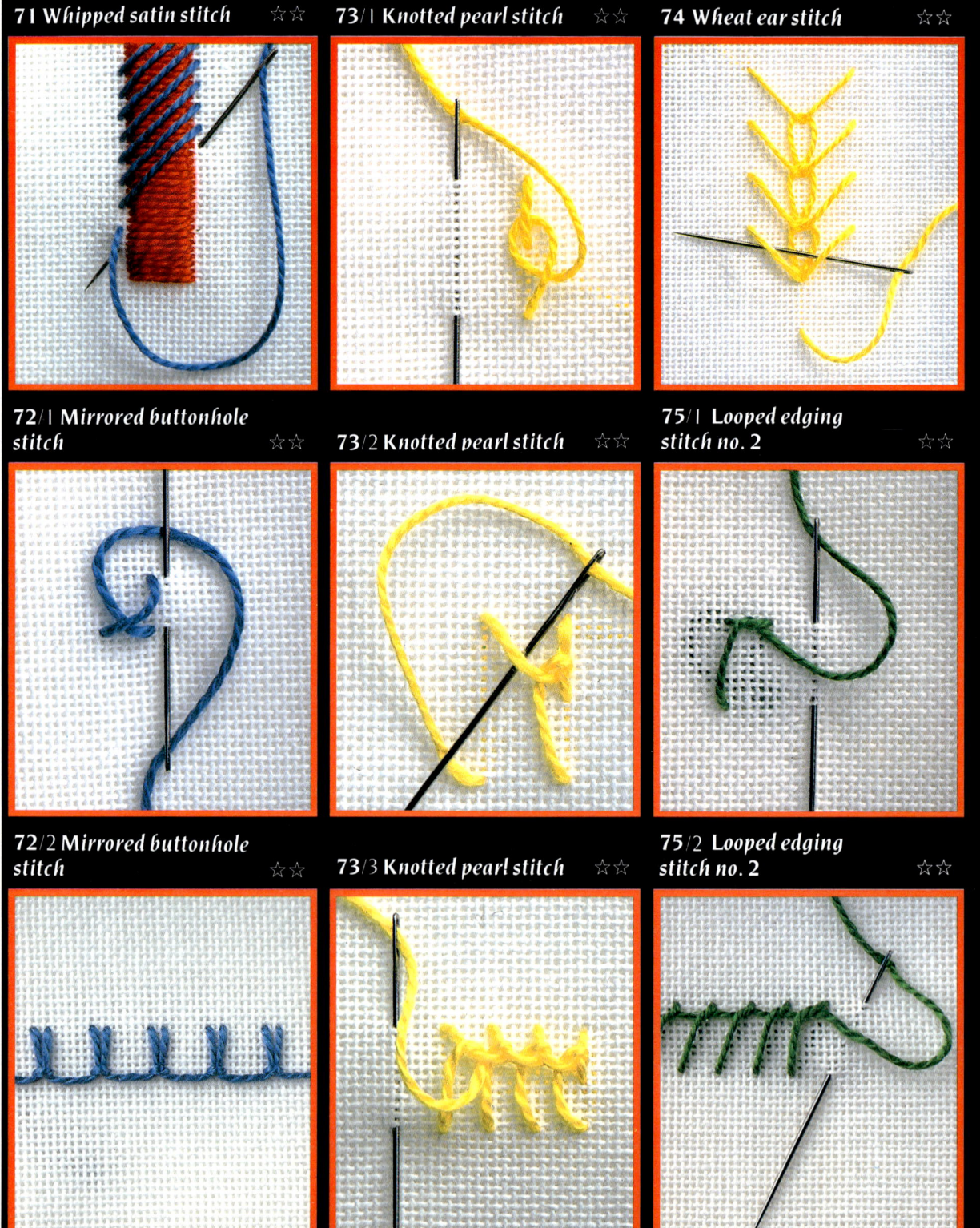

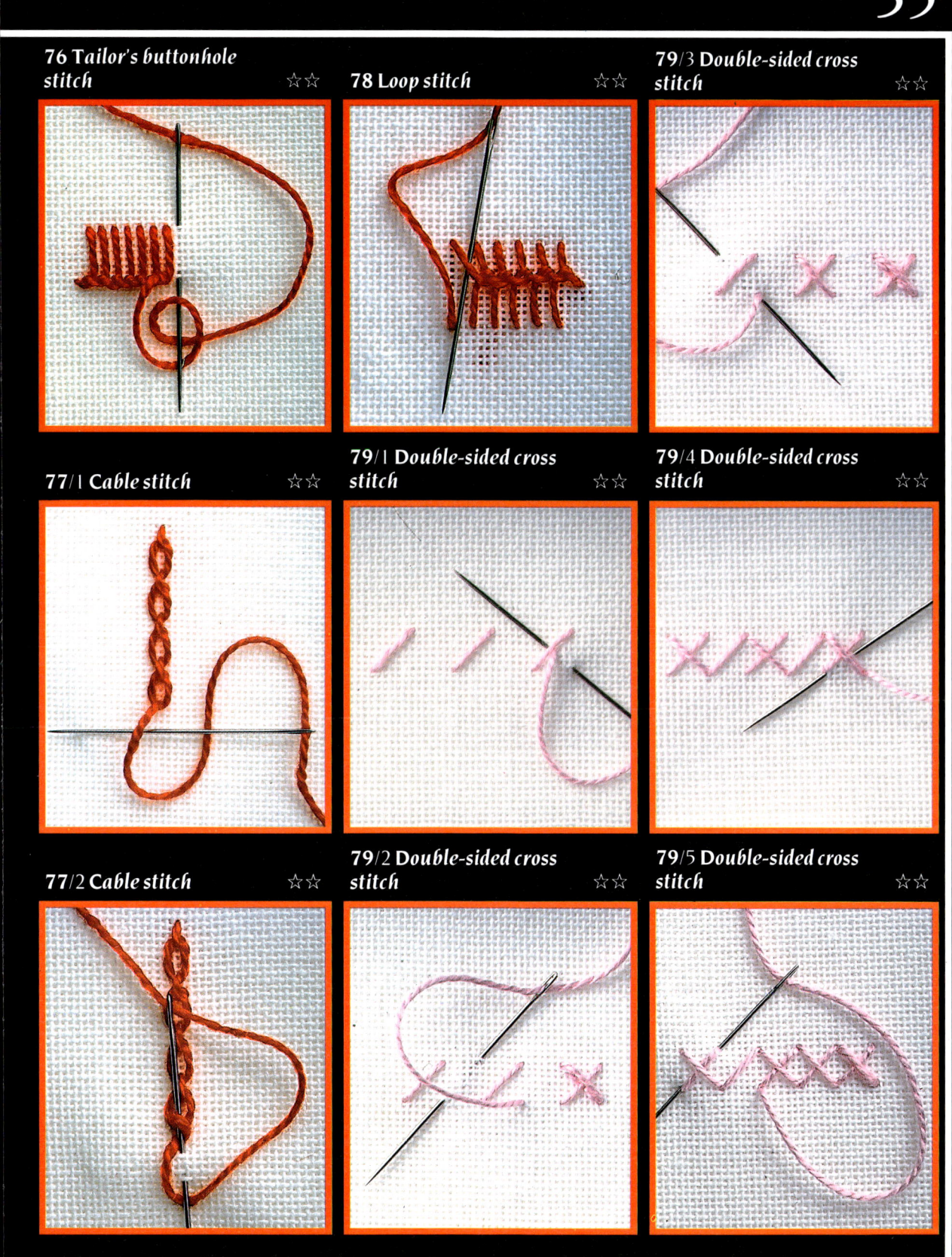

LINE STITCHES 35

76 Tailor's buttonhole stitch ☆☆

78 Loop stitch ☆☆

79/3 Double-sided cross stitch ☆☆

77/1 Cable stitch ☆☆

79/1 Double-sided cross stitch ☆☆

79/4 Double-sided cross stitch ☆☆

77/2 Cable stitch ☆☆

79/2 Double-sided cross stitch ☆☆

79/5 Double-sided cross stitch ☆☆

FABRIC STITCHES

80 Braid stitch ☆☆
also known as Gordian knot stitch
Braid stitch is a line stitch used on plain- and even-weave fabrics. It makes a textured border with a braided, slightly raised look, which can be worked easily round curves. It should be worked between close parallel lines, using a firm, twisted thread, such as pearl cotton or coton à broder; stranded cotton is too flat to work well with this stitch. The stitches should be kept small, otherwise the loops slip and become loose, and the braided effect is lost. When working braid stitch on an even-weave linen along the grain of the fabric, one or two of the fabric threads can be drawn out behind the stitches to give the stitch a lacy look. This stitch is not suitable for use on articles which will be laundered unless the stitches are less than 5mm (¼ in) high, as the loops are inclined to pull out of shape if they are any longer.

81 Basque knot ☆☆
also known as knotted loop stitch
Basque knots can be used singly, scattered at random over an area of plain-weave fabric to provide a textured finish, or they can be joined together to form a line stitch which gives a well-defined knotted line. By packing the row of lines closely together and using a heavy thread, this stitch can be used as a solid filling. Basque knot is similar to double knot stitch *(see page 36)*, but differs from it because it is always worked from right to left rather than left to right, and also because the base stitch is slightly larger. This knot was often used on old embroideries to ornament rows of Basque stitch *(see page 16)*.

82 Sorbello stitch ☆☆
Sorbello stitch is a looped stitch used on plain- and even-weave fabrics. The stitch originates in the Italian village of Sorbello where it is used extensively, often in a heavy white cotton thread on an unbleached linen background. The Italians use it not only for working straight and curved lines, but also as an individual stitch to fill complex geometric designs in the same way as cross stitch *(see page 14)*.

The stitch should be worked quite loosely and each stitch covers a small square area. First, a horizontal straight stitch is made at the top of the square; the thread is then brought through at the bottom left-hand corner, looped under and over the horizontal stitch and taken through the fabric at the bottom right-hand corner. The stitches are worked close together from left to right to make a line, or they can be used individually, in the Italian manner. A round thread, such as soft cotton, or the heaviest available weight of pearl cotton, shows off the textured quality of this stitch well, but it also looks effective when worked in a finer thread.

83 Double knot stitch ☆☆
also known as tied coral stitch, old English knot stitch, Smyrna stitch and Palestrina stitch
Double knot stitch is a line stitch used on plain- and even-weave fabrics. Characteristic of Italian embroidery, this stitch makes an attractive knotted line with a beaded effect. It is used for outlines, linear details, curves and, by working it solidly, as a textured filling. It can also be worked as an isolated stitch and be used as a powdering. Work the stitch from left to right: make a straight stitch and loop the thread under and over it to form a knot at the end. The knots can be arranged more closely together and the straight stitch made very small to give a heavy line. Use a round, twisted thread, such as pearl cotton, for this stitch to show the knots to their best advantage.

84 Zigzag chain stitch ☆☆
*also known as **Vandyke chain stitch***
Zigzag chain stitch is a line stitch and filling used on plain- and even-weave fabrics, and is suitable for use with any type of embroidery thread. It is a very old variation of chain stitch *(see page 12)* and small-scale examples of it have been found on ancient Chinese embroideries. As its name suggests, it makes a decorative zigzag line – an unusual outline for a shape. It is worked in the same way as ordinary chain stitch but each chain loop is set at right angles to the previous one to create the zigzag line. To ensure that the chains lie flat on the surface of the fabric, the needle should pierce the end of the previous loop as it enters the fabric. This stitch also makes an effective filling when worked solidly over an area and lends itself to being striped or shaded gradually in bands.

85 Marking cross stitch ☆☆
Marking cross stitch is a variation of ordinary cross stitch *(see page 14)*, and is used on plain- and even-weave fabrics. It is reversible and forms an ordinary cross stitch on one side of the fabric, and a neat square of four straight stitches on the reverse. As its name suggests, it is particularly useful for working lettering and monograms on clothing and household linen, or for any item where both sides are viewed. It is also extremely decorative when worked on a semi-transparent fabric, such as organdie or voile, since the squares on the back of the fabric show through, creating a shadow effect. Each cross is covered twice to form the square of stitches on the reverse. It is sometimes necessary to make further re-crosses, especially when working lettering, in order to complete the squares on the back, and this should be done very neatly. Care should be taken to secure the beginning and end of each length of embroidery thread under an existing stitch.

86 Chequered chain stitch ☆☆
*also known as **magic chain** and **magic stitch***
Chequered chain stitch is a variation of ordinary chain stitch *(see page 12)*. It is a decorative line or filling stitch used on plain- and even-weave fabrics, worked with two contrasting threads. Both threads are threaded through the same needle, and a row of chain stitch is worked using the threads alternately. When making a stitch with one of the threads, the thread not in use is kept above the point of the needle before both threads are pulled through. (If a loop of the wrong colour thread remains on the surface, a slight pull on the thread will cause it to disappear.) The position of the threads is then reversed, and the next stitch worked. The threads need not be altered after each stitch – two or more stitches can be worked in one colour, before reversing the position of the threads.

87 Knotted chain stitch ☆☆
*also known as **link stitch***
Knotted chain stitch is a fancy line stitch used on plain- and even-weave fabrics. It makes a raised, knotted line and follows intricate curves well. To show this stitch to its best advantage, work it in a rounded, fairly heavy thread, such as soft cotton or pearl cotton, in the heaviest weight available. Adjust the loop of each stitch to the required size, hold it in place on the fabric with the left thumb and at the same time pull the working thread through the loop to complete the knot. Although this stitch is easy to work by following the sequence shown, it takes practice to work the loops completely evenly.

38 FABRIC STITCHES

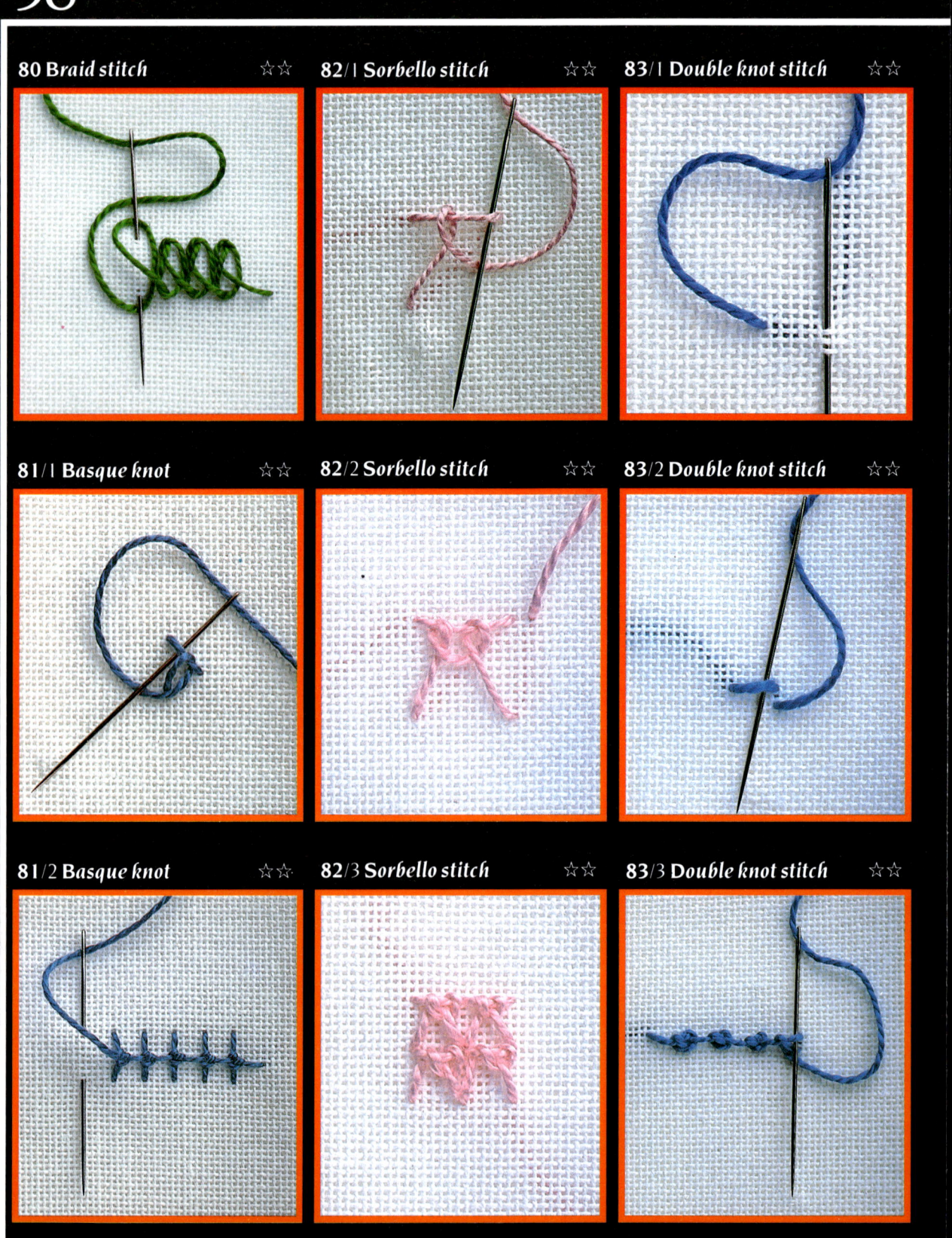

80 Braid stitch ☆☆

81/1 Basque knot ☆☆

81/2 Basque knot ☆☆

82/1 Sorbello stitch ☆☆

82/2 Sorbello stitch ☆☆

82/3 Sorbello stitch ☆☆

83/1 Double knot stitch ☆☆

83/2 Double knot stitch ☆☆

83/3 Double knot stitch ☆☆

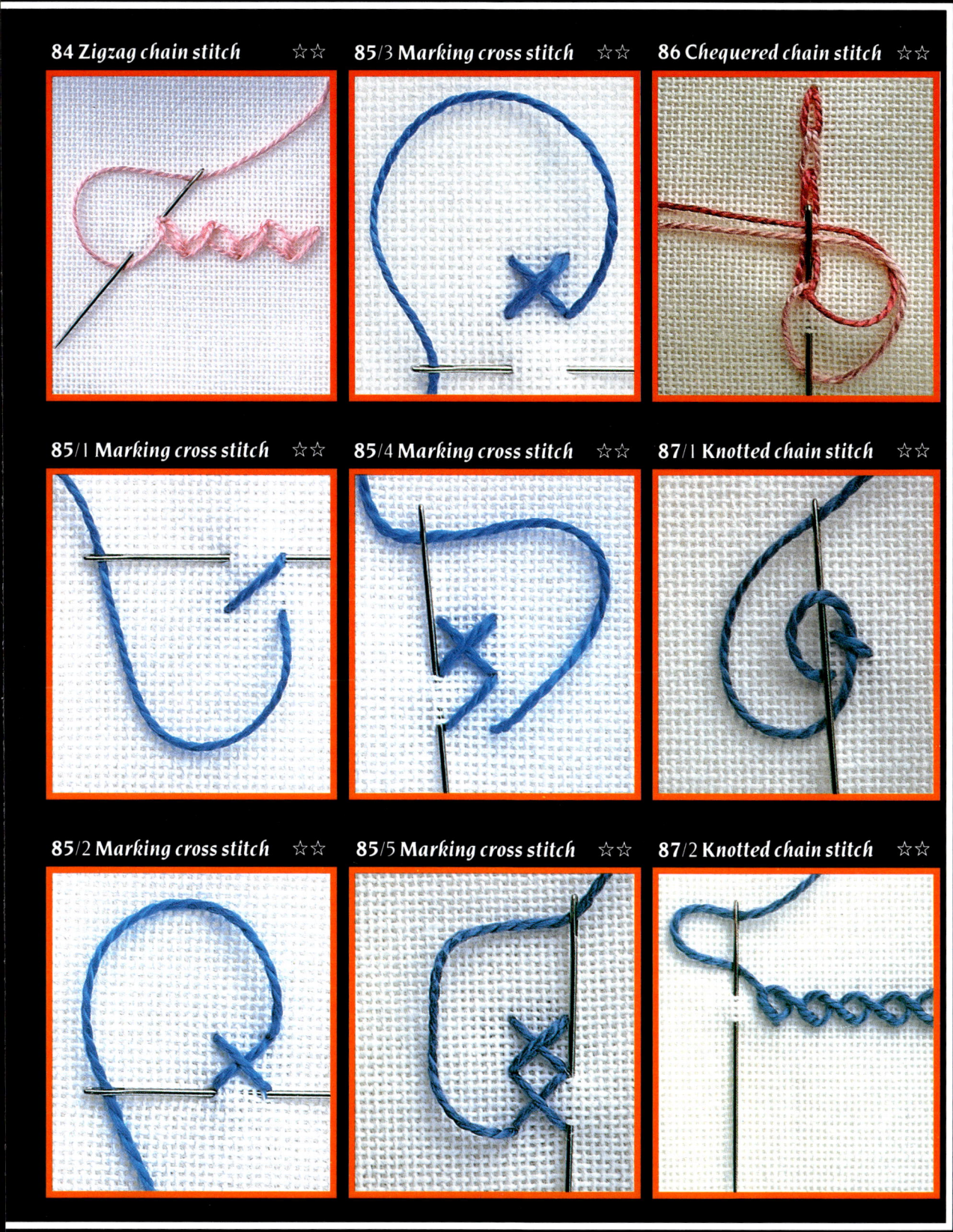

LINE STITCHES 39

84 Zigzag chain stitch ☆☆

85/3 Marking cross stitch ☆☆

86 Chequered chain stitch ☆☆

85/1 Marking cross stitch ☆☆

85/4 Marking cross stitch ☆☆

87/1 Knotted chain stitch ☆☆

85/2 Marking cross stitch ☆☆

85/5 Marking cross stitch ☆☆

87/2 Knotted chain stitch ☆☆

FABRIC STITCHES

88 Crested chain stitch ☆☆
also known as **Spanish coral stitch**
Crested chain stitch is a composite line stitch used on plain- and even-weave fabrics. It gives a decorative, braided line when worked closely together, and has a light, lacy appearance if the stitches are spread out. It is particularly effective when used to outline a gradual curve with the coral stitch edge on the outside of the curve. This stitch combines chain stitch *(see page 12)* and coral stitch *(see page 9)*, and it is much easier to work crested chain stitch successfully if both of these stitches are already familiar. It is worked downwards and spans two parallel lines, which may first need to be marked on the fabric to keep the stitches evenly spaced. First work a small chain stitch at the top right-hand side of the fabric, then work the coral and chain stitches alternately. A round, twisted thread, such as pearl cotton, illustrates the beauty of this stitch better than a flat, stranded thread.

89 Knotted diamond stitch ☆☆☆
Knotted diamond stitch is a complex line stitch used on plain- and even-weave fabrics. It makes a bold, strongly textured line, which can be worked as a border or an outline. Any type of thread can be used for this stitch, but a firm, rounded thread, such as the heaviest available weight of pearl cotton, makes the knots more pronounced than a flat, stranded thread. It is worked from left to right and consists of complicated knots linked together in a line. Each knot is worked on a foundation of a diagonal straight stitch slanting from bottom left to top right. The thread is brought through the fabric at the bottom right-hand corner and a series of loops is worked to make the knot over the foundation, without picking up the ground fabric. The thread should be tightened at each stage. When the knot is completed, the next foundation stitch is made, and so on to the end of the row.

90 Knotted buttonhole stitch ☆☆☆
Knotted buttonhole stitch is a very useful and decorative variation of ordinary buttonhole stitch *(see page 13)*. A line stitch used on plain- and even-weave fabrics, each vertical stitch has a knot at the tip. Knotted buttonhole stitch is effective when used as an outline, as it follows curves well. Two rows can be worked closely together, back to back for a feathery line, and with the heights of the vertical stitches graduated. This stitch makes an attractive outline for a circle, with the vertical stitches either inside of the shape, or fanning out round the edge. It is a little tricky to keep the knots of an even size at first, and some practice will be needed. The knots are made by winding the thread once round the thumb of the left hand (if you are right-handed) before passing the needle through the resulting loop, making a buttonhole stitch. The loop on the needle forms the knot at the top of the vertical stitch. Knotted buttonhole stitch looks best when worked with a rounded, heavy thread, such as pearl or soft cotton; a stranded thread will flatten the stitch.

LINE STITCHES

91 Plaited braid stitch ☆☆☆

Plaited braid stitch is a heavy line stitch used on plain-weave fabrics, which requires practice if it is to work successfully. It has been in use since the early sixteenth century, and was popular during that period and during the early seventeenth century when it was usually worked in metal threads to adorn clothes and furnishings. The effect this stitch creates is of a slightly raised, heavy braid, very rich and complex in appearance. It is essential to use a heavy, stiff thread when working plaited braid stitch, otherwise the loops will tangle and lose their shape. Always work the stitch from the top of the fabric downwards, passing the needle alternately under the threads and through the fabric. The back of the work should show small horizontal stitches, all of the same length, lying in a straight line. Study the sequence of loops and stitches carefully when trying this stitch for the first time; gradually, experience will tell you how loose to leave the loops to form an even line of stitching. Metallic threads work well with this stitch, as does a shiny, twisted thread, providing that it is heavy enough.

92 Three-sided stitch ☆☆☆
also known as **point Turc, lace stitch, Turkish stitch** *and* **Bermuda faggoting**

Three-sided stitch is a line stitch used on a finely woven, plain-weave fabric. It makes a pretty line with a triangular pattern of stitches and holes and can be used as a border, to follow curves, or as a decorative join when applying lace. It should be worked with a fine thread and a very heavy needle. The stitches should be pulled quite tightly to accentuate the holes made by the needle every time it enters the fabric, as they form an integral part of the pattern. The triangles are outlined by working two back stitches *(see page 14)* on each side, which must all be of equal size to give the correct effect.

93 Crossed Cretan stitch ☆☆☆

Crossed Cretan stitch is a decorative line stitch used on plain- and even-weave fabrics. It makes a zigzag line and is best worked in straight lines on a fairly small scale to make borders and bands. It can also be combined with a plainer line stitch, such as chain stitch *(see page 12)*. The line has a delicate, almost spidery appearance and needs a thread which will accentuate this delicacy. It consists of diagonal stitches, which make the zigzag, and two crossed slanting stitches worked where the diagonal stitches meet. The slanting stitches should be left fairly loose on the fabric. It is quite complicated to work, and the sequence of stitches shown should be followed carefully.

94 Portuguese knotted stem stitch ☆☆☆

Portuguese knotted stem stitch is a line stitch used on plain- and even-weave fabrics. It makes a knotted, rope-like line, which is accentuated when a heavy thread, such as pearl cotton, is used. The stitch is ideal for outlining shapes and working quite intricate linear designs as it follows curves well. A variation of ordinary stem stitch *(see page 9)*, it is worked in the same way, with two whipping stitches added to form the knots. The whipping stitches are worked over two consecutive stem stitches and do not pick up any ground fabric.

42 FABRIC STITCHES

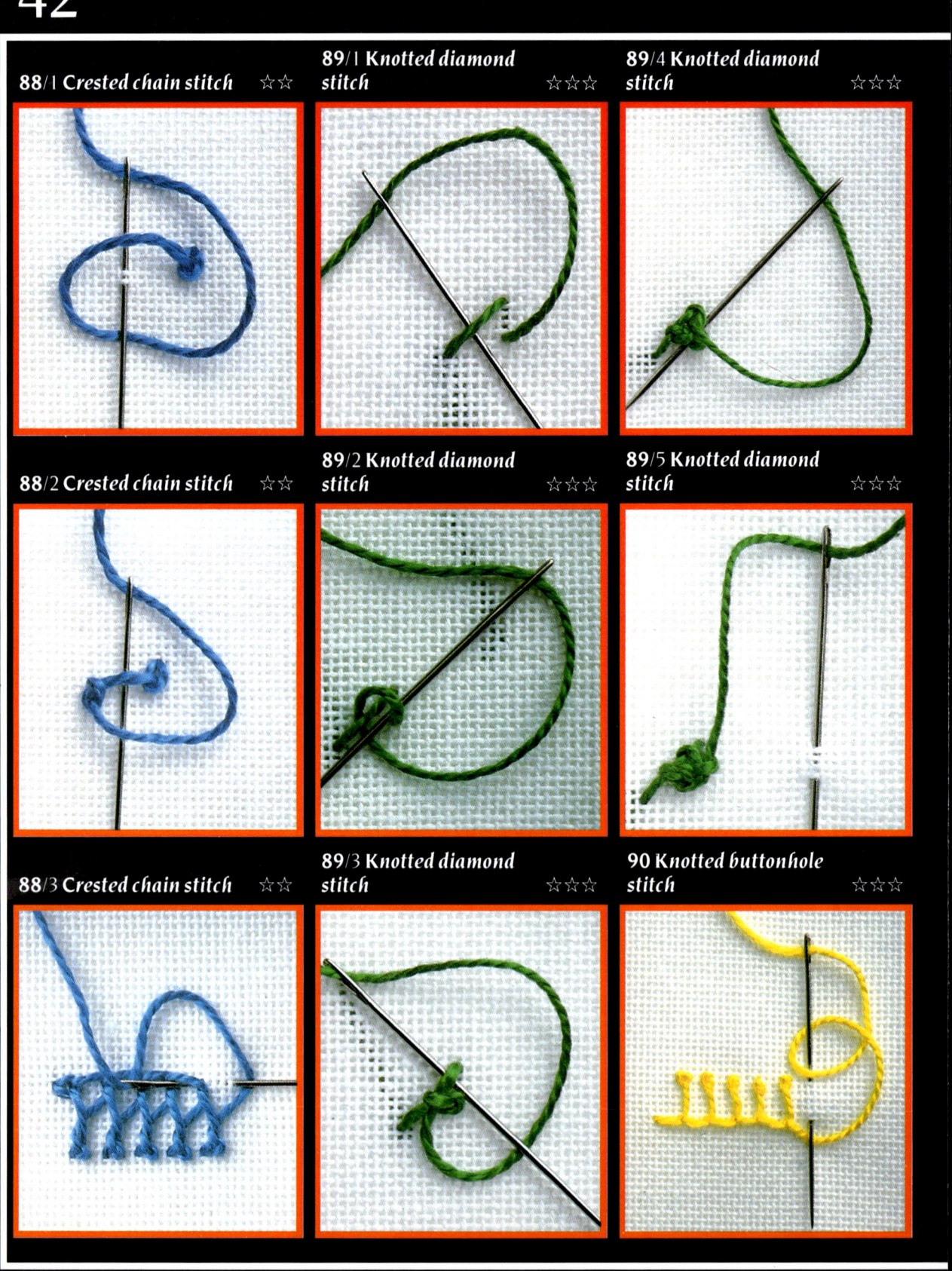

88/1 Crested chain stitch ☆☆

89/1 Knotted diamond stitch ☆☆☆

89/4 Knotted diamond stitch ☆☆☆

88/2 Crested chain stitch ☆☆

89/2 Knotted diamond stitch ☆☆☆

89/5 Knotted diamond stitch ☆☆☆

88/3 Crested chain stitch ☆☆

89/3 Knotted diamond stitch ☆☆☆

90 Knotted buttonhole stitch ☆☆☆

LINE STITCHES

43

91/1 Plaited braid stitch ☆☆☆

92 Three-sided stitch ☆☆☆

94/2 Portuguese knotted stem stitch ☆☆☆

91/2 Plaited braid stitch ☆☆☆

93 Crossed Cretan stitch ☆☆☆

94/3 Portuguese knotted stem stitch ☆☆☆

91/3 Plaited braid stitch ☆☆☆

94/1 Portuguese knotted stem stitch ☆☆☆

94/4 Portuguese knotted stem stitch ☆☆☆

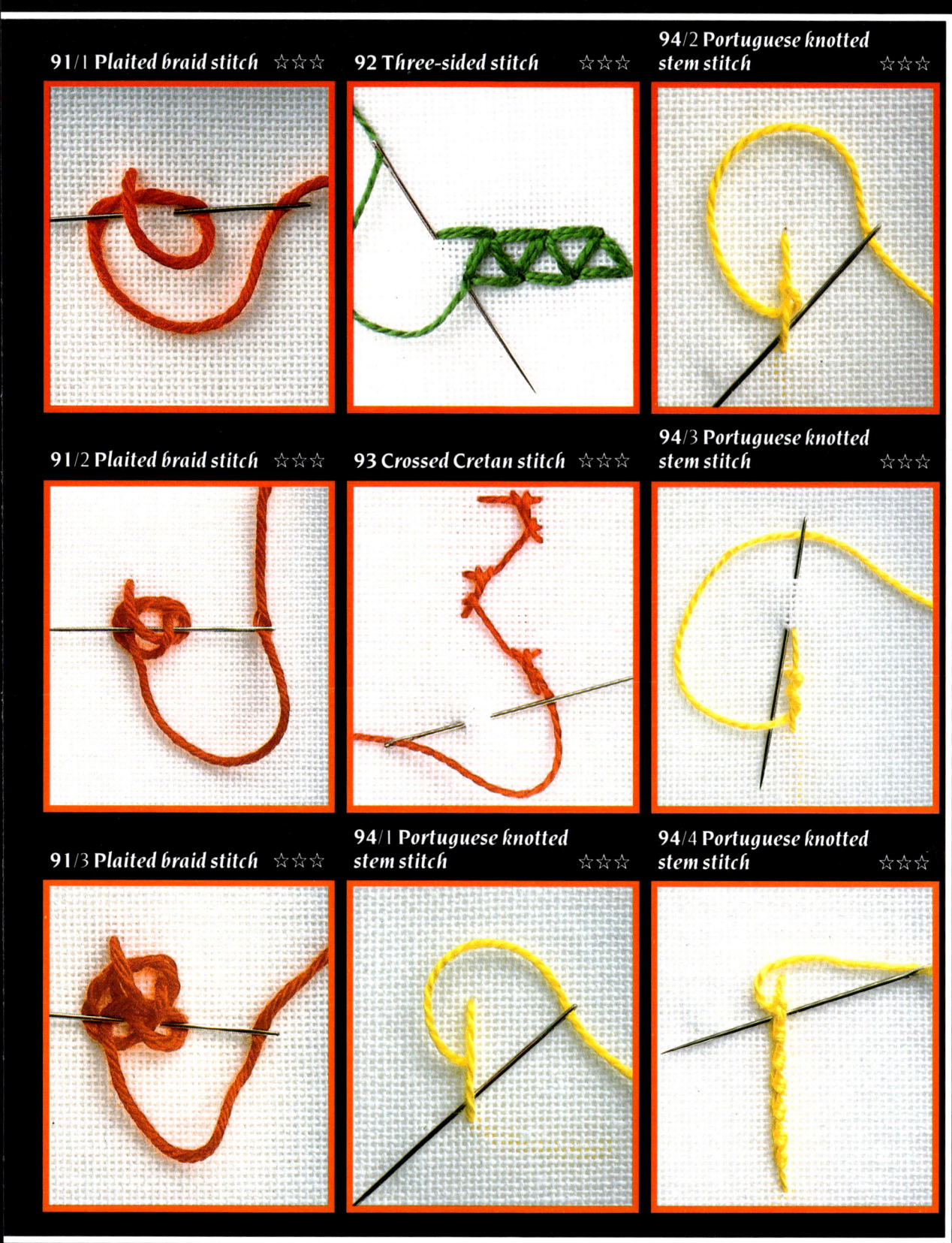

Border stitches

95 Threaded chain stitch ☆
Threaded chain stitch is a composite line stitch used on plain- and even-weave fabrics. It consists of a foundation row of spaced daisy stitches (see page 92), all facing in the same direction. These stitches are then threaded with a similar or contrasting colour thread along the row from left to right. For a more decorative line, a second threading can be made, perhaps in a third colour, with the second thread filling the spaces left on the first journey. Any type of embroidery thread is suitable for this stitch, and a metallic thread can be used for the threading. A blunt-ended tapestry needle should be used for the threading to avoid splitting the stitches on the foundation row. Extra decorative touches can be added after the threading, by working isolated French knots (see page 96) or cross stitches (see page 14) between the daisy stitches.

96 Sham hem stitch ☆
also known as *zigzag sham hem stitch*

Sham hem stitch is a line stitch used on plain- and even-weave fabrics. It was originally used to imitate a hemstitch border (see page 112) on fabric which was too fine for the threads to be removed, but it is now used as a decorative zigzag line stitch and worked in two colours. This stitch is worked in straight lines, as it does not follow curves well. To keep the row straight, guide-lines may need to be marked on the fabric if the threads cannot be counted. It is worked in two journeys. A zigzag row of diagonal straight stitches is worked first, and a second thread of contrasting colour or weight is then laced over these foundation stitches. The needle enters the fabric only at the beginning and end of each row and a blunt-ended tapestry needle should be used for the lacing to avoid splitting the foundation stitches.

97 Fancy herringbone stitch ☆
Fancy herringbone stitch is a wide, ornamental line stitch used on plain- and even-weave fabrics. It makes a rich border, particularly if a metallic thread is used for the interlacing, and it can look stunning if worked in spaced multiple rows, using a carefully chosen colour scheme. It is deceptively simple to work, in spite of its rather complex appearance. Each row is worked in three journeys. First, a foundation row of ordinary herringbone stitch (see page 8) is worked, using guide-lines marked on the fabric, unless the fabric threads can be counted, to keep the row of an even width. A row of St George cross stitch (see page 68) is then worked over the top and bottom crosses of the herringbone rows, taking care that the horizontal bar of the St George cross stitch is always worked over the vertical one. These two journeys can be worked in the same colour thread, or two contrasting threads. On the third journey, the horizontal bars are interlaced without the ground fabric being picked up. Use a blunt-ended tapestry needle for the interlacing to avoid splitting the stitches on the two preceding rows.

98 Interlaced band ☆
Interlaced band is a composite line stitch used on plain- and even-weave fabrics. Guide-lines may need to be drawn to keep the edges of the stitch straight, unless the fabric threads can be counted. This stitch can be worked in any type of thread, and looks very effective when a fairly stiff metallic thread is used for the interlacing. It makes a pretty border when two colours are used, or it can be worked in multiple rows to make a stunning filling stitch.

Each row has a foundation of vertical straight stitches placed fairly close together. A second thread is then laced through the centre of these stitches, twisting each pair in turn. This thread enters the fabric only at the beginning and end of the row, and a blunt-ended tapestry needle should be used to avoid splitting the foundation stitches. A heavier effect can be achieved by twisting four threads in two groups. If the foundation stitches are made quite long and spaced closely together, two or even three threads can be used to make a more complicated twist. The fabric will then need to be stretched in an embroidery hoop or frame to prevent it from pulling out of shape.

99 Chinese stitch ☆
also known as *Chinese cross stitch*; see also *Pekinese stitch*

Chinese stitch is a border or filling stitch used on even-weave fabrics. It is extremely simple to work and looks most effective when a loosely woven linen provides the background fabric: the loose threads of the linen are drawn together by the stitching if it is pulled quite tightly after each stitch. It can also be used as a decorative surface stitch, or the blocks can be scattered at random over a shape as a powdering. It is simply constructed in blocks and each block covers six vertical and four horizontal fabric threads. A central horizontal stitch is worked first over six vertical threads and then crossed by two vertical stitches, each worked over four horizontal threads. The next block is set with a half drop, as shown. When used as a filling stitch, the blocks can be worked solidly or can be arranged to make a chessboard pattern with rectangles of the fabric left unworked.

100 Roman stitch ☆
also known as *branch stitch*

Roman stitch is a wide line stitch used on plain- and even-weave fabrics. It makes a pretty branched line and can be used to make a border or it can be worked solidly to fill a shape. It is worked from left to right between two widely spaced parallel lines, and if the threads cannot be counted, guide-lines may need to be marked on the fabric, to keep the width of the line even. It is very simple to work: a long straight stitch is taken from the lower edge of the line to the top edge and then tied down by a short crossing stitch. The long stitches can be pulled slightly by the crossing stitches to give them a gentle curve, or they can be worked straight. The stitches should be placed close together to make a solid line and any type of embroidery thread can be used for this attractive border stitch.

BORDER STITCHES

101 Raised chevron stitch ☆
Raised chevron stitch is a heavy composite line stitch used in straight rows on plain- and even-weave fabrics. It is a variation of chevron stitch *(see page 8)* and makes a bold, raised line useful for borders and bands. It is quite simple to work but the foundation row must be worked neatly and with even spaces between the stitches for good results. A foundation row is worked first, consisting of diagonal stitches arranged in 'V' shapes. Guide-lines may need to be marked on the fabric to keep the 'V' shapes even, unless the threads of the fabric can be counted. The chevron stitch is then threaded over the foundation row, without the needle entering the fabric except at the beginning and end of the row. It is advisable to use a blunt-ended tapestry needle for the second thread to avoid splitting the stitches on the foundation row.

Raised chevron stitch should be worked with the fabric stretched in an embroidery hoop or frame to prevent the fabric from distorting when the chevron threading is worked. The chevron threading can be worked in a contrasting colour, texture or weight of thread for a more decorative effect.

102 Triangle stitch ☆
Triangle stitch is a border stitch or filling used on plain- and even-weave fabrics and has a triangular pattern. This stitch will work more successfully on a fabric where the threads can be counted, as regularity is crucial to give the correct geometric effect. A plain-weave fabric can, however, be used, but guide-lines will need to be marked on the surface.

Triangle stitch is worked in vertical rows, and two journeys are needed to complete one row. Each journey consists of a line of alternate horizontal and diagonal stitches. On the second journey, the direction of the diagonal stitches is reversed. Triangle stitch makes an attractive border, and each triangle can be decorated by working a daisy stitch *(see page 92)* or a French knot *(see page 96)* at the centre. This stitch is also used in multiple rows as a light filling. Any type of embroidery thread can be used, the choice depending on the size of the stitch being worked, and the weight of the ground fabric.

103 Sailor stitch ☆
also known as **sailor edge stitch**
Sailor stitch is a line stitch used on plain- and even-weave fabrics. It makes a delicate looped border when worked on a small scale in a fine, rounded thread such as coton à broder. It is quite an easy stitch to work, but practice is needed to keep the loops even. It is worked downwards and consists of a series of loops which are anchored by chain stitches *(see page 12)*, as shown.

Hold each loop firmly onto the fabric with your left thumb (if you are right-handed) until the anchoring stitch has been made and tightened slightly. A different effect can be made by working very large loops and anchoring them to the fabric at the centre of each loop by a daisy stitch *(see page 92)*. Sailor stitch can also be worked in multiple rows to fill a shape. Two rows can be worked along the same line, so that the chain stitches on the second row fit between those on the first. This looks very attractive if two shades of the same colour are used, or if two different weights of thread are worked and the finer thread used for the second row.

104 Interlaced buttonhole stitch ☆
Interlaced buttonhole stitch is a wide, composite line stitch used on plain- and even-weave fabrics. Simple to work, it can be made more ornate by using a rich metallic or textured thread for the interlacing. Two parallel rows of buttonhole stitch *(see page 13)*, with the stitches spaced, are worked with the looped edges facing each other and a gap lying between them. A second thread is then interlaced through these foundation rows without entering the ground fabric; a blunt-ended tapestry needle should be used to avoid splitting the threads of the foundation stitches. Stretch the fabric in an embroidery hoop or frame while working the stitch, otherwise the interlacing will pucker and distort the fabric. The tension of the second thread is also important: if it is too loose, the interlacing will lose its shape, but if it is too tight, the foundation rows will be pulled towards each other and will no longer be parallel.

105 Maidenhair stitch ☆
Maidenhair stitch is a line stitch used on plain- and even-weave fabrics. It makes a delicate, branched line and has a fern-like quality, hence the name; it is a variation of single feather stitch *(see page 12)*. This stitch looks most attractive when worked in single, straight rows, using a round thread such as pearl cotton or coton à broder. Worked downwards, groups of three stitches are placed alternately at each side of the central line. Three single feather stitches are made at the right of the line with the lengths graduated so that they line up horizontally. A similar group is then made at the left of the line, and so on down the line. Maidenhair stitch looks equally effective whether it is worked on a large or a small scale.

106 Threaded herringbone stitch ☆
also known as **barred witch stitch**
Threaded herringbone stitch is a composite line stitch used on plain- and even-weave fabrics. It makes an attractive line, which is usually worked in two contrasting colours of thread. This stitch is used as a simple, straight border, or in multiple rows as a rich, lacy filling, which can be threaded with a metallic thread to create an unusual effect. A row of ordinary herringbone stitch *(see page 8)* is worked first, and then a second thread is laced up and down through the foundation stitches. The second thread passes through the fabric only at the beginning and end of each row, and a blunt-ended tapestry needle should be used to avoid splitting the foundation stitches. When worked as a filling, the foundation rows should touch at the tips of the crosses. The colour of the lacing thread can be graduated to give a subtle colour change over the area.

46 FABRIC STITCHES

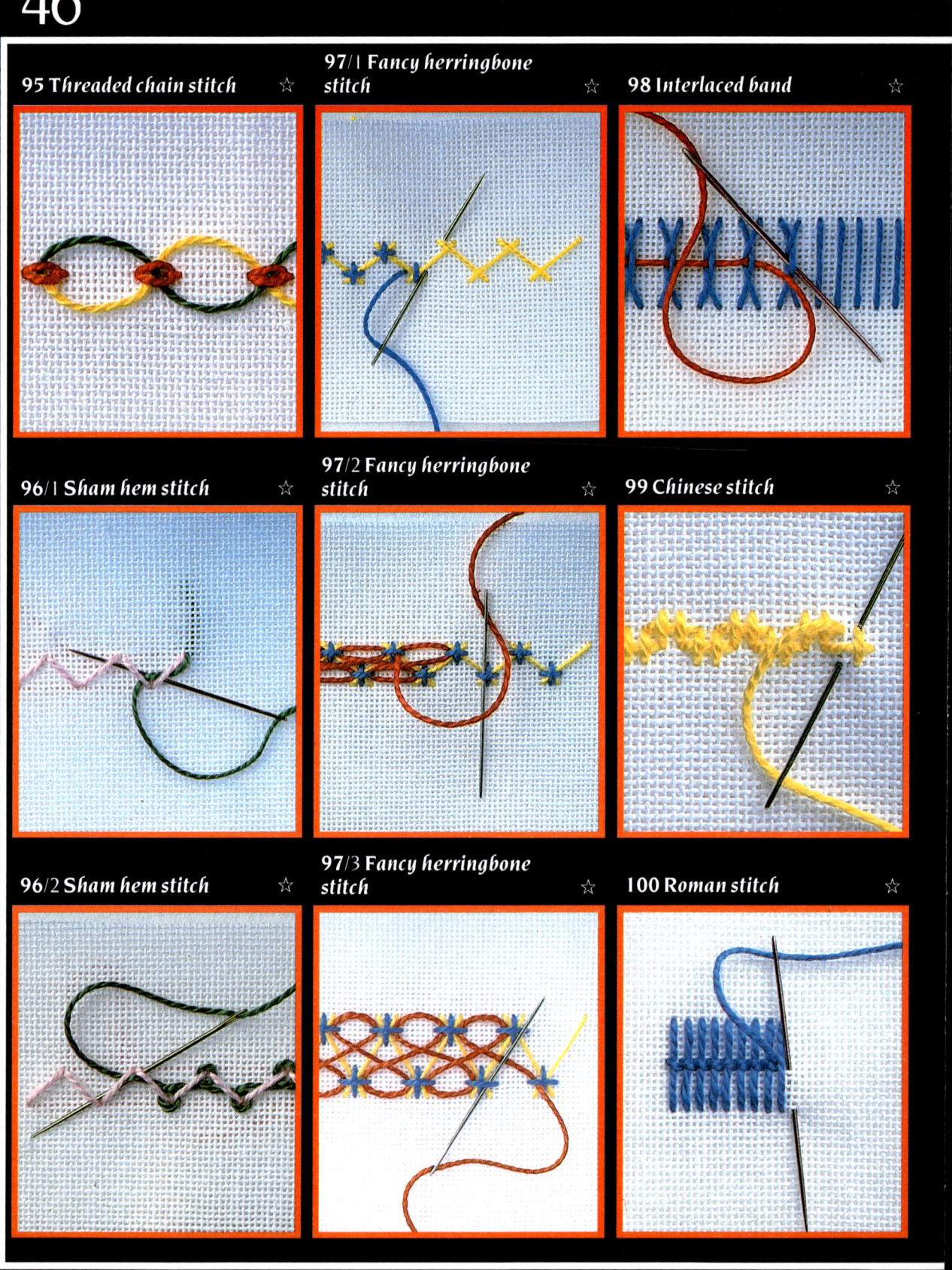

95 Threaded chain stitch ☆

97/1 Fancy herringbone stitch ☆

98 Interlaced band ☆

96/1 Sham hem stitch ☆

97/2 Fancy herringbone stitch ☆

99 Chinese stitch ☆

96/2 Sham hem stitch ☆

97/3 Fancy herringbone stitch ☆

100 Roman stitch ☆

BORDER STITCHES 47

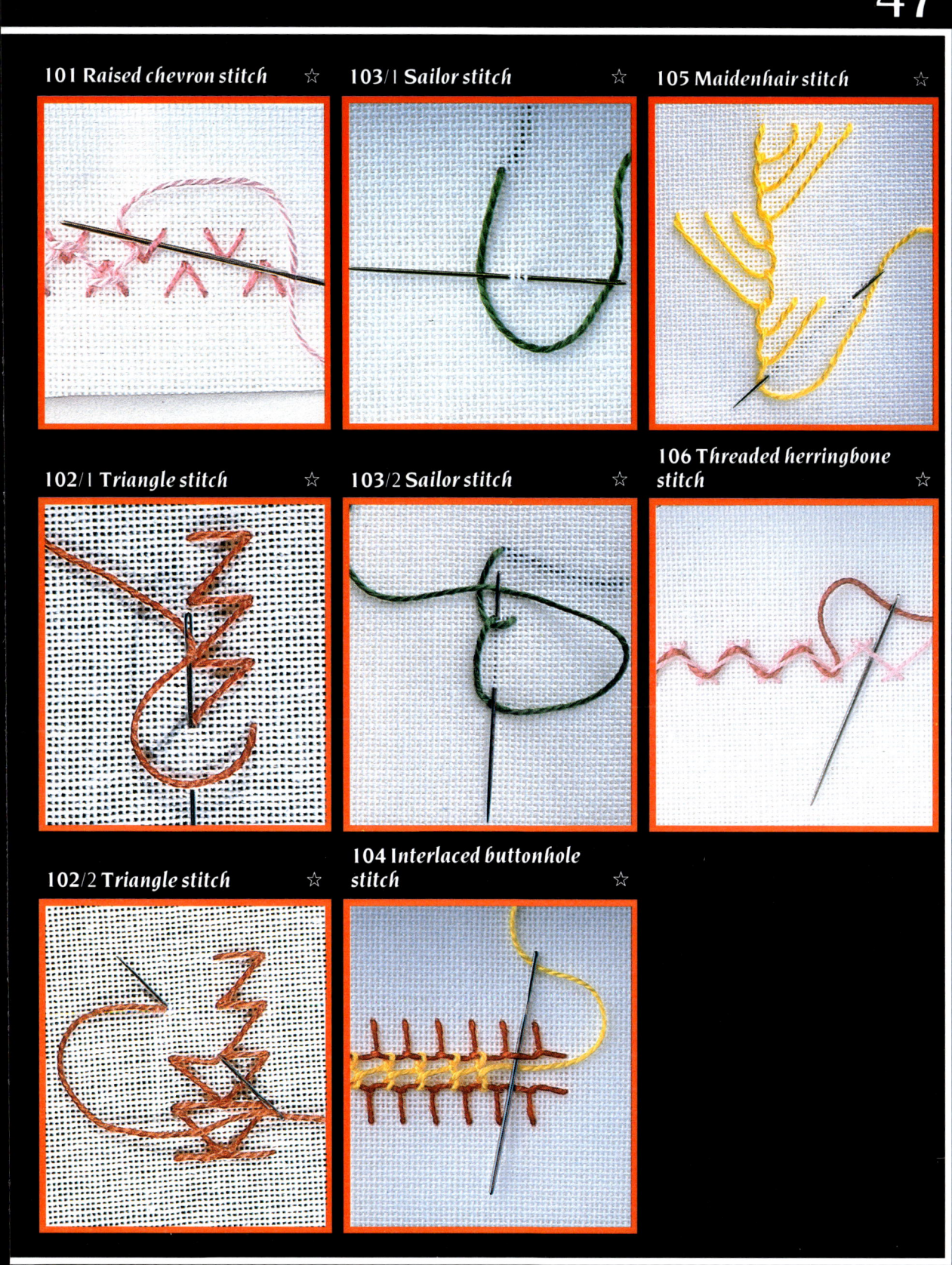

101 Raised chevron stitch ☆

102/1 Triangle stitch ☆

102/2 Triangle stitch ☆

103/1 Sailor stitch ☆

103/2 Sailor stitch ☆

104 Interlaced buttonhole stitch ☆

105 Maidenhair stitch ☆

106 Threaded herringbone stitch ☆

107 Laced buttonhole stitch

Laced buttonhole stitch is a wide, composite line stitch worked on plain- and even-weave fabrics. It is similar in construction to interlaced buttonhole stitch *(see page 45)* but the effect is simpler. Work two parallel rows of buttonhole stitch *(see page 13)* with spaced stitches; the looped edges should face each other and a gap should be left between the rows. Then, lace a second thread between the foundation rows, taking care not to enter the ground fabric. A contrasting colour or texture or a metallic finish for the second thread will make this stitch look more decorative. Use a blunt-ended tapestry needle for the lacing to avoid splitting the threads on the foundation rows.

A variation on this stitch is to work the buttonhole stitch foundation with the verticals, rather than the loops, facing each other. A second thread can then be laced across the gap and through alternate vertical stitches in the same way as a single row of cloud filling stitch *(see page 69)*. The looped edges of the buttonhole stitch can then be whipped with a contrasting colour in the same manner as whipped back stitch *(see page 16)*. This stitch should be worked with the fabric stretched in an embroidery hoop or frame, otherwise the lacing will pucker and distort the background. The lacing thread should remain fairly loose or the foundation rows will be pulled towards each other and no longer be parallel.

108 Two-sided plaited Spanish stitch

Two-sided plaited Spanish stitch is a border stitch used only on even-weave fabrics. It makes a simple pattern of 'V' shapes, pointing from left to right; the stitch is identical on both sides of the fabric. Each row requires two journeys, one immediately above the other, to complete it – both halves of the row are composed of slanting straight stitches. On the first journey, the stitches slant from the bottom left to the top right, and each stitch spans five vertical and three horizontal fabric threads. On the second journey, the stitches slant in the opposite direction, and this line is placed above the first one. If both sides of the work will be visible, break the thread off at the end of the first journey, securing it neatly, and use a second length of thread for the second journey. Any type of embroidery thread can be used, providing that it is compatible with the weight of the ground fabric, but a fine thread accentuates the delicacy of this attractive border stitch.

109 Lock stitch and lock stitch band

Lock stitch is a composite line stitch used on plain- and even-weave fabrics. It makes a delicate, laced line with a looped lower edge and is always used on the straight, never around curves. Any type of thread is suitable for this stitch and a contrasting or metallic thread can be used for the lacing. A foundation row of evenly spaced vertical stitches is made first. A second thread is then laced through the foundation stitches at the lower edge; do not pick up any ground fabric. Use a blunt-ended tapestry needle for the lacing to avoid splitting the foundation stitches.

Lock stitch band is a simple variation of lock stitch. The foundation row is made in the same way but then laced in two journeys instead of one to cover both ends of the straight stitches. Make sure that the upper and lower loops of the lacing are worked over the same two foundation stitches.

110 Butterfly chain stitch

Butterfly chain stitch is an ornamental composite line stitch used on plain- and even-weave fabrics. Each row is worked in two journeys, using either the same thread for both journeys, or two contrasting weights or colours. First work a foundation row of groups of three vertical straight stitches. The spaces between the groups of stitches should be approximately the same width as the area covered by the three stitches. On the second journey, bunch each group of stitches together with a twisted chain stitch *(see page 21)*: pull each twisted chain stitch tightly before proceeding to the next one. On the second journey, do not allow the needle to enter the ground fabric except at the beginning and end of the row.

Butterfly chain stitch should be worked with the fabric stretched in an embroidery hoop or frame to prevent it from puckering or pulling out of shape. The stitch can also be used as a light, decorative filling by working the groups of straight stitches on the second row between the groups on the first row.

111 Threaded treble running stitch

Threaded treble running stitch is a wide, composite line stitch used on plain- and even-weave fabrics. A wider version of interlaced running stitch *(see page 25)*, it makes an attractive threaded line which is best used as a border. A heavier thread is normally used for the interlacing, and a round, twisted thread, such as pearl cotton, gives a slightly raised line. The stitch can be monochrome, or contrasting colours can be used for the interlacing. A foundation of three parallel rows of ordinary running stitch *(see page 12)* is made first, and then the interlacing is worked in two journeys. This stitch can also be used in multiple rows to fill a shape, providing that a small space is left between each row.

112 Doubled herringbone stitch

Doubled herringbone stitch is a wide, decorative line stitch used on plain- and even-weave fabrics. It has an attractive, lacy, zigzag pattern, which is usually worked in a straight line. Guide-lines may need to be marked on the fabric, if the threads cannot be counted, to keep the row of an even width. It can also be worked in multiple rows to make a light filling; the rows should touch each other at the tips of the crosses. First work a row of herringbone stitch *(see page 8)* for a foundation. Then, work a second row of this stitch over the top and through the fabric, flattening the stitches so that only the tips of the crosses in the foundation row are still visible.

113 Battlement stitch ☆
Battlement stitch is a composite line stitch made up of four or more rows of evenly spaced blanket stitch *(see page 13)*. The blanket stitch rows overlap and form a heavy border with a crenellated top edge. This stitch is used on plain-weave fabrics and can be worked in more than one colour to create a more decorative border. A deeper border can be made by working two rows of parallel stitching with the straight edges facing one another. Spacing this stitch evenly is essential in order to keep the notches along the top edge an identical size and shape.

114 Threaded running stitch ☆
Threaded running stitch is a composite line stitch used on plain- and even-weave fabrics. It makes a lacy line with loops along the lower edge, and can be used alone or in multiple rows to fill a shape. A wider line can be made by working two parallel rows of the stitch with the looped edges on the outside and the inside stitches touching. This stitch does not follow curves well and should be used on the straight. It is a variation of ordinary running stitch *(see page 12)* worked on a foundation of two parallel rows. A second thread is then laced up and down each pair of stitches, linking the pairs together along the lower edge. The second thread, which enters the fabric only at the beginning and end of the row, can be of a contrasting weight, colour or texture for a more interesting effect. Use a blunt-ended tapestry needle for the second thread to avoid splitting the stitches on the foundation rows.

115 Stepped and threaded running stitch ☆
also known as laced double stitch
Stepped and threaded running stitch is a composite border stitch used on plain- and even-weave fabrics. It makes a pretty lacy line, which can also be worked solidly to fill a shape. This stitch is normally worked in straight rows as it does not follow curves well. It is a variation of ordinary running stitch *(see page 12)* and is worked on a foundation of two parallel rows of that stitch. The stitches are set alternately on the second row. A second thread is then laced from row to row without picking up the ground fabric. Use a blunt-ended tapestry needle for the threading to avoid splitting the running stitches. The second thread can be of a contrasting weight, texture and colour, or a metallic thread can be used to create a luxurious effect.

116 Siennese stitch ☆
Siennese stitch is a wide line stitch used on plain- and even-weave fabrics. It makes a pretty looped line which can be used alone as a border, or can be worked in multiple rows to fill a shape. The stitch is worked from left to right along two parallel lines, and guide-lines may need to be marked on the fabric if the threads cannot be counted to keep the row of an even width. Each stitch consists of a vertical straight stitch with a second stitch worked at the right and looped round the first stitch. The stitch can be worked with an open or closed finish, depending on the effect required and on the type of thread being used. A heavy thread, such as pearl cotton, gives this stitch a raised appearance along the central row of loops.

117 Laced double running stitch and laced treble running stitch ☆
Laced double running stitch is a composite border or filling stitch used on plain- and even-weave fabrics. It makes a simple, wide threaded line, which is normally used on the straight, although it also follows a gradual curve well. This stitch is a variation of ordinary running stitch *(see page 12)* and looks very decorative if a metallic thread is used for the lacing.

First work a foundation of two rows of evenly spaced running stitches, making sure that the stitches and the spaces between them are all of an even length. Then lace a second thread up and down the rows. The second thread can be of a heavier weight and a contrasting colour and texture to the first. Use a blunt-ended tapestry needle for the lacing to avoid picking up the ground fabric and splitting the running stitches. This stitch makes an attractive filling when worked solidly, row on row. A heavier version of this stitch can be worked by adding an extra foundation row. The stitch is then known as laced treble running stitch.

118 Eskimo edging stitch ☆
also known as Eskimo laced edge
Eskimo edging stitch is a composite line stitch used on plain- and even-weave fabrics. It is an adaptation of a reversible edging stitch, used by Eskimos to bind the edges of their sealskin clothing to make it waterproof. A simply constructed stitch, Eskimo edging stitch is worked on a foundation of running stitch *(see page 12)* and makes a looped line, which follows gradual curves well. Work evenly spaced running stitch first, from right to left. Then lace a second thread alternately through the running stitches and the ground fabric. The second thread can be of a contrasting weight and colour. This stitch looks very effective when worked as a double line, with the looped edges of each row touching.

119 Double chain stitch ☆
also known as Turkmen stitch
Double chain stitch is a line stitch and filling used on plain- and even-weave fabrics. It makes an attractive wide border when worked along two parallel lines; alternatively, the size of the stitches can be altered to fill shapes of varying widths. It can also be worked solidly, row on row, to fill larger shapes. Double chain stitch works best when used in straight lines, but it will follow a gentle curve. A simple variation of chain stitch *(see page 12)*, any type of embroidery thread can be used. The stitch consists of a fairly wide chain stitch worked downwards alternately to the left and then to the right of the line. If working double chain stitch in a straight line, guide-lines may need to be marked on the fabric to keep the width of the stitches even. The rows can be made more decorative by the addition of an isolated stitch, such as a French knot *(see page 96)* or dot stitch *(see page 92)*, worked in the centre of each chain in a contrasting thread.

50 FABRIC STITCHES

107 Laced buttonhole stitch ☆

108/1 Two-sided plaited Spanish stitch ☆

108/2 Two-sided plaited Spanish stitch ☆

109/1 Lock stitch and lock stitch band ☆

109/2 Lock stitch and lock stitch band ☆

109/3 Lock stitch and lock stitch band ☆

110 Butterfly chain stitch ☆

111 Threaded treble running stitch ☆

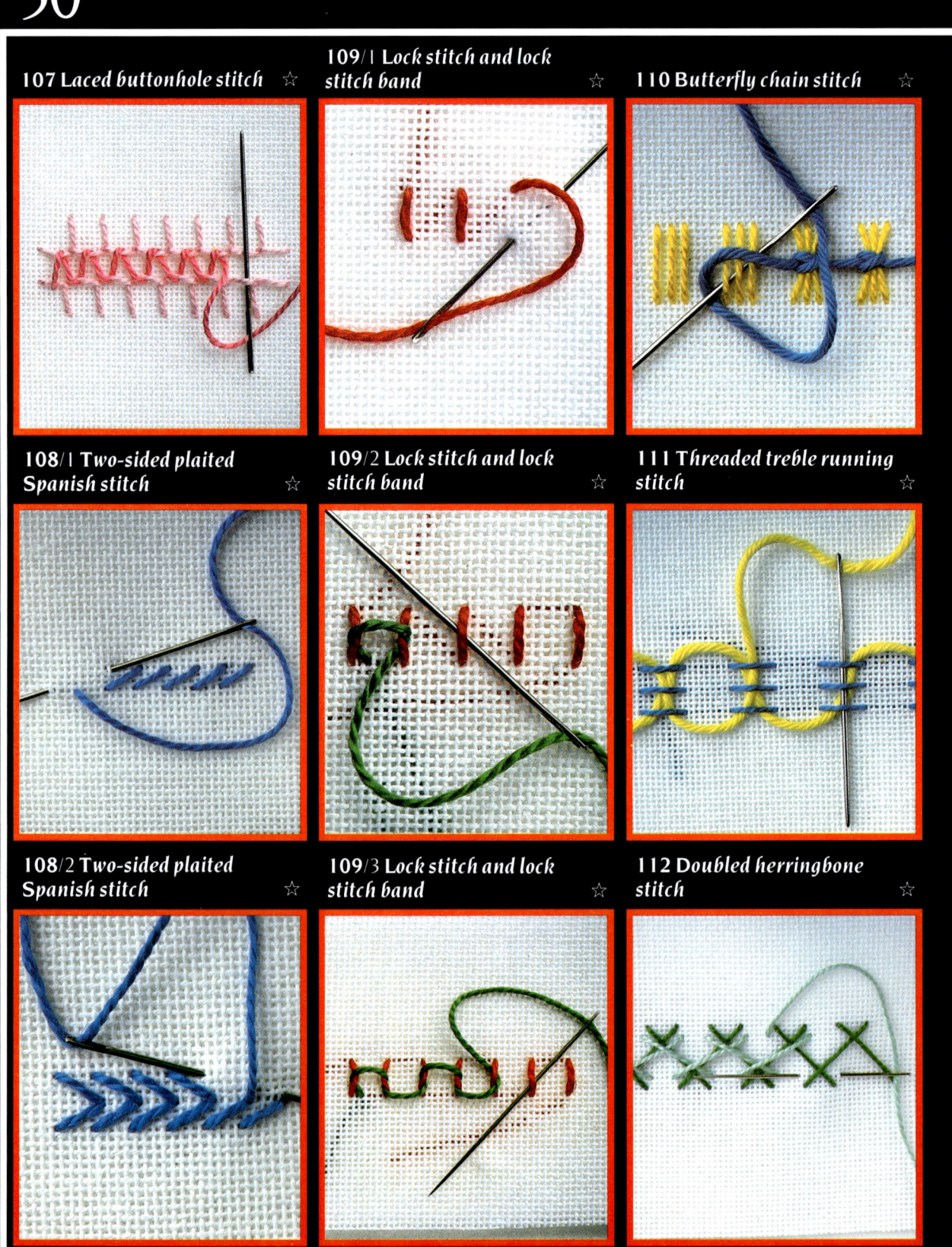

112 Doubled herringbone stitch ☆

BORDER STITCHES 51

113 Battlement stitch ☆

116/1 Siennese stitch ☆

117 Laced double running stitch ☆

114 Threaded running stitch ☆

116/2 Siennese stitch ☆

118 Eskimo edging stitch ☆

115 Stepped and threaded running stitch ☆

116/3 Siennese stitch ☆

119 Double chain stitch ☆

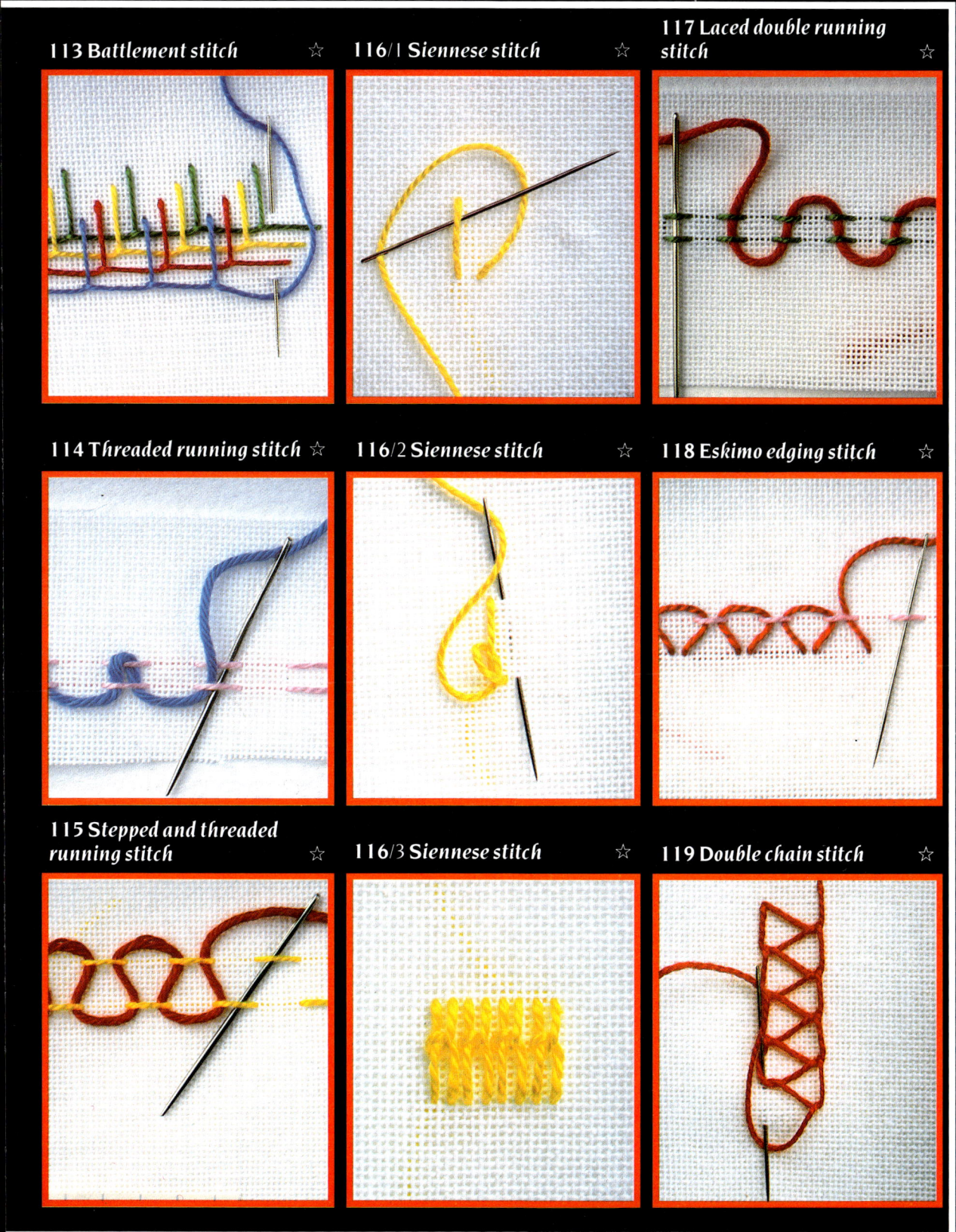

FABRIC STITCHES

120 Zigzag stitch ☆
Zigzag stitch is a line stitch or filling used on plain- and even-weave fabrics. It makes a decorative outline stitch or border and has a delicate geometric pattern. Each horizontal row is worked in two journeys. Beginning at the right, work a row of alternate vertical and diagonal staight stitches. On the return journey, the vertical stitches share the same holes as the first vertical stitches, whilst the diagonal stitches cross each other. Guide-lines may need to be marked on the fabric if the threads cannot be counted to keep the rows straight. A fine embroidery thread such as coton à broder accentuates the pattern if the stitches are worked fairly small. When used as a filling, the rows of zigzag stitch are worked close together, the vertical stitches touching, to make a lattice pattern. A different pattern can be created by arranging the rows so that the vertical stitches lie under the crossed diagonals.

121 One-sided insertion stitch ☆
Despite its name, one-sided insertion stitch is an attractive border stitch, and not a stitch to join two pieces of fabric. It can be worked on plain-weave fabrics, but a neater effect is achieved when it is used on an even-weave fabric. A decorative and intricate variation of cross stitch, it is always used in a straight line, working from right to left. One-sided insertion stitch consists of a combination of ordinary cross stitch *(see page 14)* and long-armed cross stitch *(see page 141)* and is quite easy to work; follow carefully the sequence of stitches shown.

122 Buttonholed herringbone stitch ☆☆
Buttonholed herringbone stitch is a heavy, composite line stitch used on plain- and even-weave fabrics. It makes a bold zigzag line and can be worked in multiple rows to fill a shape. Guide-lines may need to be marked on the fabric if the thread cannot be counted to keep the rows straight. This stitch should be worked on fabric stretched in an embroidery hoop or frame, otherwise the buttonhole stitch tightens the foundation row and may pucker the fabric. A foundation row of ordinary herringbone stitch *(see page 8)* is worked first and then a finer thread is used to work a row of buttonhole stitch *(see page 13)* over the foundation. At the top and bottom of the herringbone stitches, the working thread must be taken under the cross, without picking up the ground fabric. Use a blunt-ended tapestry needle for the second thread to avoid splitting the stitches on the foundation row.

123 Guilloche stitch ☆☆
Guilloche stitch is a wide, composite border stitch used on plain- and even-weave fabrics. The name is derived from an architectural term for an ornamental band containing two or more interwoven wavy lines. The stitch makes a very decorative band, which is used singly to make a border and is often worked in several colours and weights of thread. To keep these lines parallel, guide-lines may need to be marked on the fabric, unless the threads can be counted. The outer lines are worked in stem stitch *(see page 9)*, and groups of three horizontal satin stitches *(see page 24)* are then worked at regular intervals between the stem stitch lines. These groups of stitches are then threaded in two journeys, without picking up the ground fabric. Use a blunt-ended tapestry needle for the threading to avoid splitting the satin stitches. Lastly, a French knot *(see page 96)* is worked at the centre of each circle.

124 Twisted lattice band ☆☆
Twisted lattice band is a composite border stitch used on plain- and even-weave fabrics. A pretty lattice band is made by this stitch and it can be used alone to make a light border, worked in two colours or two weights of thread. Alternatively, the rows can be arranged solidly as a filling when they create an extremely decorative effect if a metallic thread is used for the lacing.

A row of double herringbone stitch *(see page 53)* is worked first, using the second method described. The foundation row should be worked quite loosely, with the fabric stretched in an embroidery hoop or frame, as the lacing will tighten the stitches. Make sure that the formation of the double herringbone stitches is correct before proceeding with the lacing. The lacing is worked in two journeys, from left to right of the area then back again; be careful not to pick up any ground fabric.

125 Raised chain band ☆☆

Raised chain band is a composite line stitch worked downwards on plain- and even-weave fabrics. It can be given a more raised appearance by working a padding of laid threads underneath the foundation stitches. The foundation of evenly spaced, short, horizontal stitches is worked first. These can vary in width to accommodate one, two or three bands of the top stitch, depending on the width of line required. The chain-like stitching is worked over the foundation threads, without picking up any of the ground fabric. Any type of thread can be used for this stitch but a blunt-ended tapestry needle should be used for the second thread to avoid splitting the foundation threads.

126 Double herringbone stitch ☆☆
also known as Indian herringbone stitch

and Triple herringbone stitch
also known as criss-cross herringbone stitch

Double herringbone stitch is a line stitch used on plain- and even-weave fabrics. It consists of a foundation row of ordinary herringbone stitch *(see page 8)* with a second row worked over it, so that the stitches interlace. This stitch has two distinct uses, for which the stitches are interlaced differently.

When this stitch is used as a decorative line on its own, it is often worked in two colours. Both rows are worked in the same manner as herringbone stitch, interlacing only where they cross each other. This version of the stitch can be composed of three rows instead of two, all spaced evenly along the line; it is then known as triple herringbone stitch. The second method of interlacing is slightly more complicated and is used as a foundation row for other stitches, such as interlaced herringbone stitch *(see page 65)*. The sequence of 'unders' and 'overs' should be followed carefully, or the interlacing will be incorrect. When used as a foundation row, this stitch is usually worked in only one colour. With both these methods, guide-lines may need to be marked on the fabric, if the threads cannot be counted, to keep the rows of an even width.

127 Striped woven band ☆☆

A striped woven band is a composite border stitch used on plain- and even-weave fabrics. It is a simply worked variation of a diagonal woven band *(see page 56)*, but in this case the stripes are horizontal rather than diagonal. The foundation stitches and the weaving are worked in the same way but, by commencing each row of weaving with the same colour of thread, the formation of the stripes is changed. The preliminary padding can be worked to give a raised band.

128 Interlaced chain stitch ☆☆

Interlaced chain stitch is a composite line stitch used on plain- and even-weave fabrics. A relatively little-known variation of chain stitch *(see page 12)*, it makes a rich, ornamental line, especially if a metallic thread is used for the interlacing. It is an old stitch, probably of French origin, and examples of it have been found on several sixteenth-century embroideries. Once the sequence of loops has been mastered it is deceptively simple to work.

Work a foundation row of fairly large chain stitch first and then interlace a second, contrasting thread through each side of the row, following the sequence shown. Always work the interlacing in two journeys, starting from the top of the foundation row each time, and without picking up any ground fabric. To avoid splitting the stitches on the foundation row, use a blunt-ended tapestry needle for the interlacing. The interlacing thread should be left fairly loose but may need to be anchored to the fabric by tiny horizontal stitches at regular intervals along the row.

This stitch should always be worked with the fabric stretched in an embroidery hoop or frame to prevent the fabric from distorting when the interlacing is worked. Rows of interlaced chain stitch alternating with ordinary chain stitch make a wide, heavy border; alternatively interlaced chain stitch can be edged on both sides with one or more rows of chain stitch.

129 Belgian cross stitch ☆☆

Belgian cross stitch is a variation of ordinary cross stitch *(see page 14)* and can be used on even-weave fabrics and canvas for borders or textured fillings. It is worked in rows from left to right, and consists of elongated diagonal stitches that cross each other. A row of horizontal straight stitches is formed along the lower edge of the stitch. When working this stitch on canvas, care should be taken when matching the weight of the thread to the gauge of the canvas to make sure that the canvas is completely covered by the stitching. On an even-weave fabric, any type of embroidery thread can be used, and the stitch can be worked with an open or closed finish, depending on the effect required.

54 FABRIC STITCHES

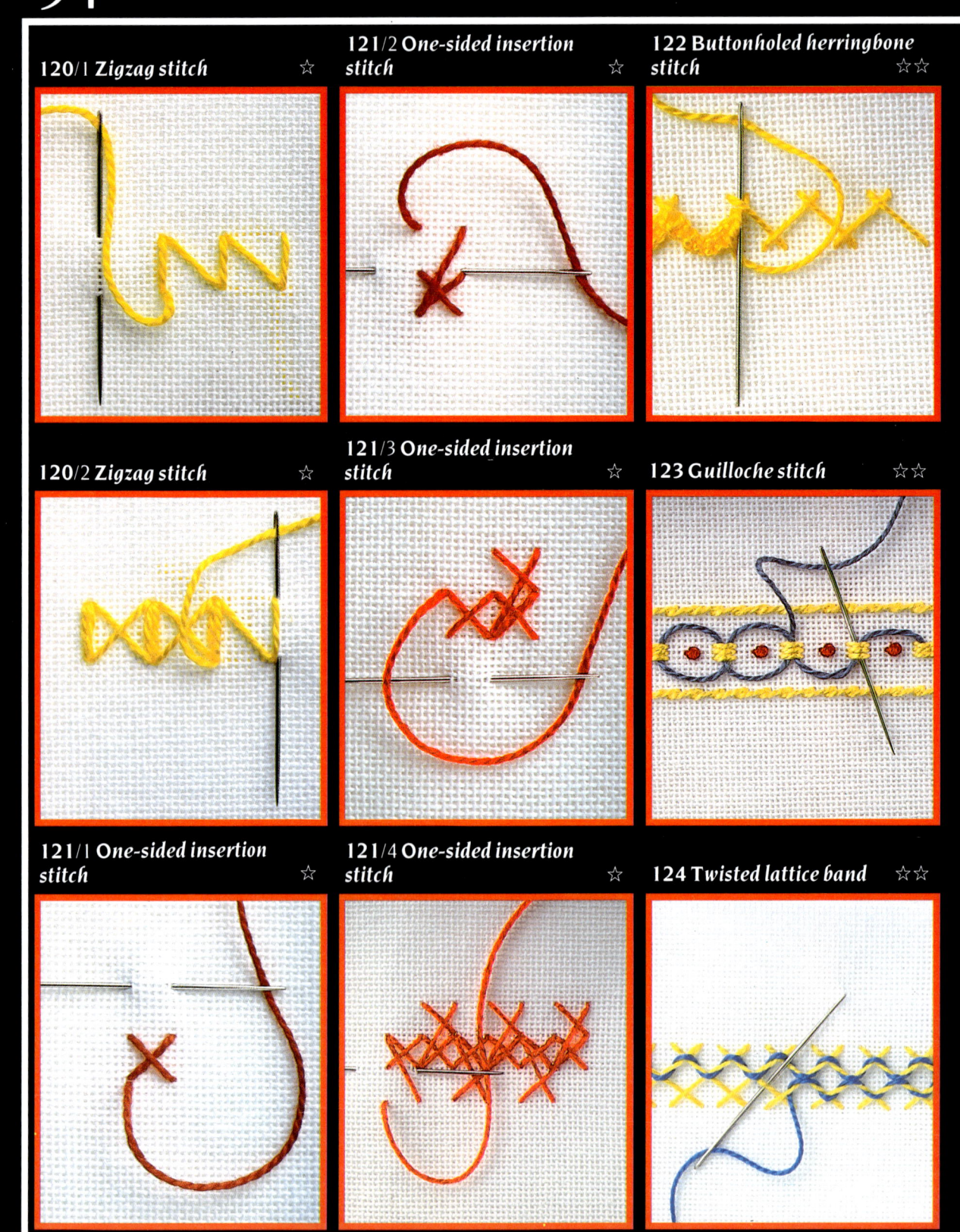

120/1 Zigzag stitch ☆

121/2 One-sided insertion stitch ☆

122 Buttonholed herringbone stitch ☆☆

120/2 Zigzag stitch ☆

121/3 One-sided insertion stitch ☆

123 Guilloche stitch ☆☆

121/1 One-sided insertion stitch ☆

121/4 One-sided insertion stitch ☆

124 Twisted lattice band ☆☆

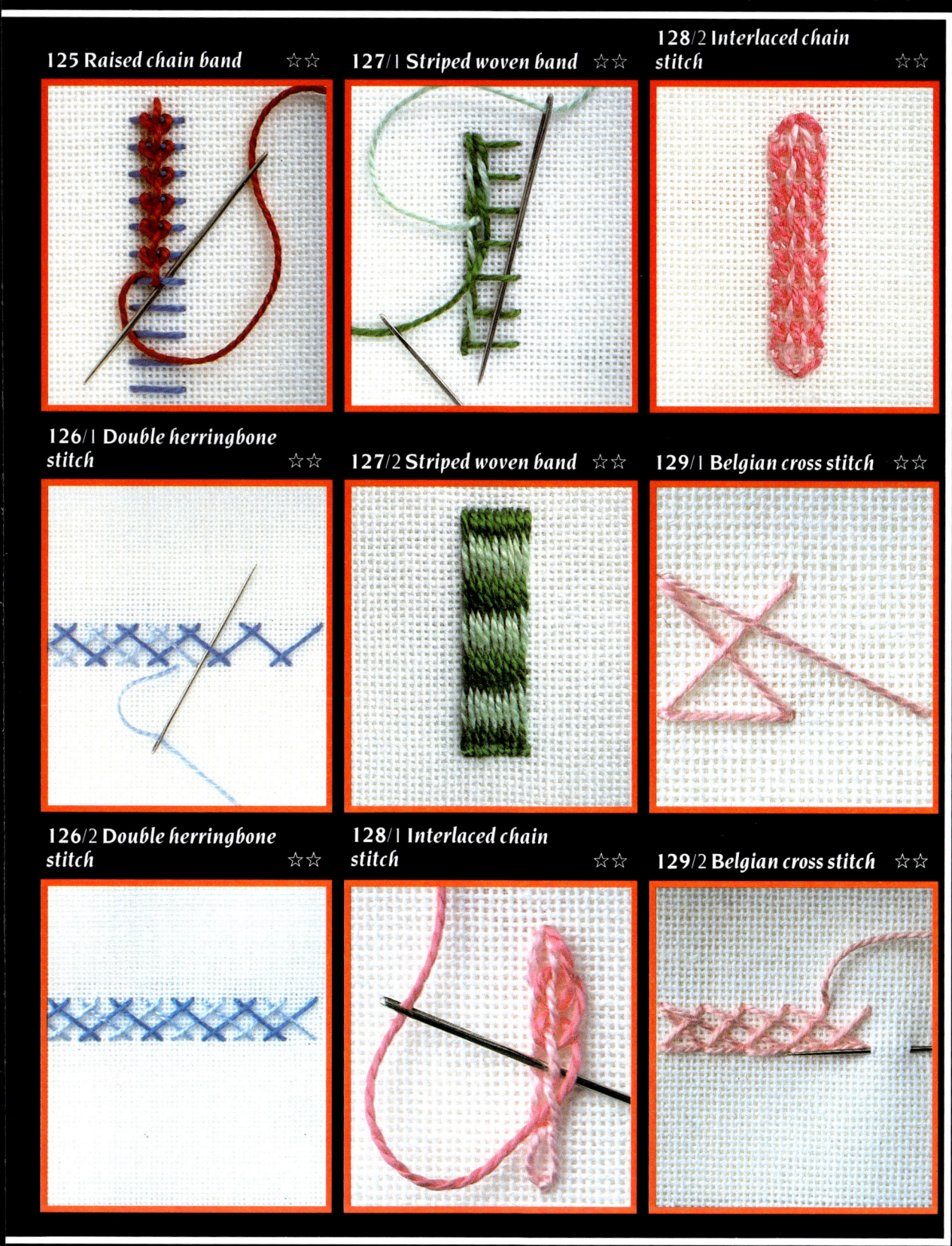

BORDER STITCHES 55

125 Raised chain band ☆☆

127/1 Striped woven band ☆☆

128/2 Interlaced chain stitch ☆☆

126/1 Double herringbone stitch ☆☆

127/2 Striped woven band ☆☆

129/1 Belgian cross stitch ☆☆

126/2 Double herringbone stitch ☆☆

128/1 Interlaced chain stitch ☆☆

129/2 Belgian cross stitch ☆☆

FABRIC STITCHES

130 French knot border ☆☆
French knot border is a composite line stitch used on plain- and even-weave fabrics. It makes an attractive knotted line, which is often used in conjunction with a plain line stitch, such as chain stitch *(see page 12)*, to make a multiple border. It is a combination of French knot *(see page 96)* and fly stitch *(see page 93)* and is easy to work once the technique of making French knots has been mastered. Each stitch consists of a fly stitch loop with a French knot instead of a straight stitch worked to anchor it. The stitches are placed close together to form a row and the rows are worked horizontally, from left to right, in one journey.

131 Step stitch ☆☆
also known as ladder stitch
Step stitch is a composite border stitch used on plain- and even-weave fabrics. It makes a very decorative wide border which looks like a ladder, and it can be worked in two colours. A fine thread should be used. Step stitch should be worked with the fabric stretched in an embroidery hoop or frame, and is always worked vertically between two parallel lines. These lines may need to be marked on the fabric if the threads cannot be counted to keep the edges of the stitch even.

First, work a foundation of two vertical rows of chain stitch *(see page 12)*, taking care to make each chain the same size, so that the chains lie directly opposite one another on the two rows. Next, work a row of horizontal straight stitches from one side of the row to the other, threading into the centres of the chains. Work these stitches through every alternate chain stitch right down the border to make the rungs of the ladder. Then use a second thread to whip along each rung, making a loop to link two rungs at the centre. The second thread should not pick up the ground fabric, and a blunt-ended tapestry needle should be used. The row of loops should lie neatly along the exact centre of the border.

132 Diagonal woven band ☆☆
A diagonal woven band is a composite border stitch used on plain- and even-weave fabrics. It is worked in two colours and makes a solid band with an attractive diagonal stripe. The stitch is worked downwards over a foundation row of evenly spaced, horizontal straight stitches. Two needles threaded with contrasting coloured threads are used for the weaving, and both threads are brought to the front of the work at the top left-hand corner of the foundation row. The threads are used alternately to weave over and under the foundation stitches. Each row of weaving commences at the top of the foundation, using the alternate colour to begin each journey. Such rows will form the diagonal stripes. The rows of weaving should be worked close together in order to completely cover the foundation stitches. The band can have a preliminary padding of long, vertical straight stitches if a raised effect is required.

133 Feather stitch raised band ☆☆
Feather stitch raised band is a composite, wide line stitch used on plain- and even-weave fabrics. It consists of a row of feather stitch *(see page 12)* worked over a padded foundation, and makes a heavy, textured line, which is always used on the straight. It can also be used as a solid filling, by working it row on row over a shape. A round, twisted thread, such as pearl cotton, gives the best results for this stitch, which is worked in three journeys. On the first journey, the padding is made of five long vertical straight stitches worked closely together. A foundation of short, horizontal straight stitches is then worked over the padding, with the stitches arranged at regular intervals. The last journey consists of a row of feather stitch worked over the foundation stitches. The needle enters the fabric only at the beginning and end of each row. Feather stitch raised band should be worked on fabric stretched in an embroidery hoop or frame to keep the padding stitches parallel.

134 Russian cross stitch ☆☆
see also herringbone stitch
Russian cross stitch is a canvas stitch used on single and double canvas. It makes a richly plaited surface and is used for borders and for filling large shapes and backgrounds. It is rather similar in construction to long-armed cross stitch *(see page 141)*, but the stitches are longer and Russian cross stitch is slightly more complicated to work. Follow carefully the arrangement of stitches shown. Any type of embroidery thread can be used, but care should be taken to match the weight of the thread to the gauge of the canvas to make sure that the canvas is completely covered by the stitching. Russian cross stitch can also be worked on an even-weave fabric using coton à broder or a fine pearl cotton for the best results.

135 Vandyke stitch ☆☆

Vandyke stitch is a border stitch and filling used on plain- and even-weave fabrics. It makes a wide line with a raised plait in the centre, and looks very attractive worked in multiple rows to create a heavy border. By graduating the length of the stitches on either side of the plait, it is also used to fill narrow shapes. It is worked downwards between two parallel lines, and guide-lines may need to be marked on the fabric if the threads cannot be counted to keep the stitch of an even width. The top stitch picks up a tiny amount of fabric at the centre to anchor the whole row. The second and subsequent stitches cross the line from left to right, passing behind the preceding stitch at the centre; no ground fabric is picked up. The stitches should be worked closely together to make a solidly stitched row that covers the fabric completely. A lustrous embroidery thread, such as stranded silk or cotton, shows Vandyke stitch to its best advantage and accentuates the central plait.

136 Singhalese chain stitch ☆☆

Singhalese chain stitch is a wide, composite line stitch worked downwards on plain- and even-weave fabrics. It looks most effective when worked in straight lines to form a border, and can be used as a narrow casing for ribbon, tape or flat cord. It is worked in the same way as open chain stitch *(see page 17)* but with contrasting threads added at the sides. Before working the open chain stitch, mark two parallel guide-lines on the fabric and pull through a contrasting thread at the top of each line. Let these threads lie loosely on the fabric, following the lines. Then work the open chain stitch over these two threads. The contrasting threads should be tightened at the end of each row and then taken to the back of the work and secured. The two extra threads give a pretty, twisted edge to the stitch.

Singhalese chain stitch is found on the traditional embroideries of Sri Lanka, and the stitch is equally effective worked with an open or closed finish. Any type of embroidery thread is suitable, but a rounded thread, such as pearl cotton, makes the stitch stand out from the background.

137 Fancy couching ☆☆

Fancy couching is the term used to describe several variations of ordinary couching stitch *(see page 8)*. Its uses are the same: outlining; linear details; covering the edges of an appliquéd shape; and making a solid filling. The variations are worked in the same way as ordinary couching, but instead of using the straight stitches, other embroidery stitches hold down the laid threads to give a more decorative effect. A number of these are suggested here, but many of the stitches which form broad bands are suitable. Fancy couching is often more striking when worked over a group of laid threads, rather than a single, thick one. Narrow ribbons, tapes or flat cords can be used instead of the laid threads, but care must be taken to secure the edges of these neatly, to prevent fraying. Buttonhole stitch *(see page 13)* and open chain stitch *(see page 17)*, arranged in a continuous row and spaced quite widely, work well as couching stitches over a single line of laid threads. Blocks of satin stitch *(see page 24)*, or a row of cross stitch *(see page 14)*, fly stitch *(see page 93)* or daisy stitch *(see page 92)* worked across the laid threads at regular intervals are also effective. Where a wide band of couching is needed, feather stitch *(see page 12)* can couch down two rows of laid threads simultaneously. The threads are arranged in parallel rows with a small gap between them.

138 Two-sided insertion stitch ☆☆

Two-sided insertion stitch is, despite its name, a decorative border stitch. Similar to one-sided insertion stitch *(see page 52)*, this stitch should be worked on an even-weave fabric to give it regularity, an essential feature of the stitch. A reversible stitch, the front of the stitch builds up plaited borders consisting of two interwoven rows of zigzag stitches of different size. On the reverse of the fabric, a lattice-work of diamond shapes is made. Each stitch is worked in five stages and the sequence of straight stitches, which are worked from left to right, should be followed carefully.

FABRIC STITCHES

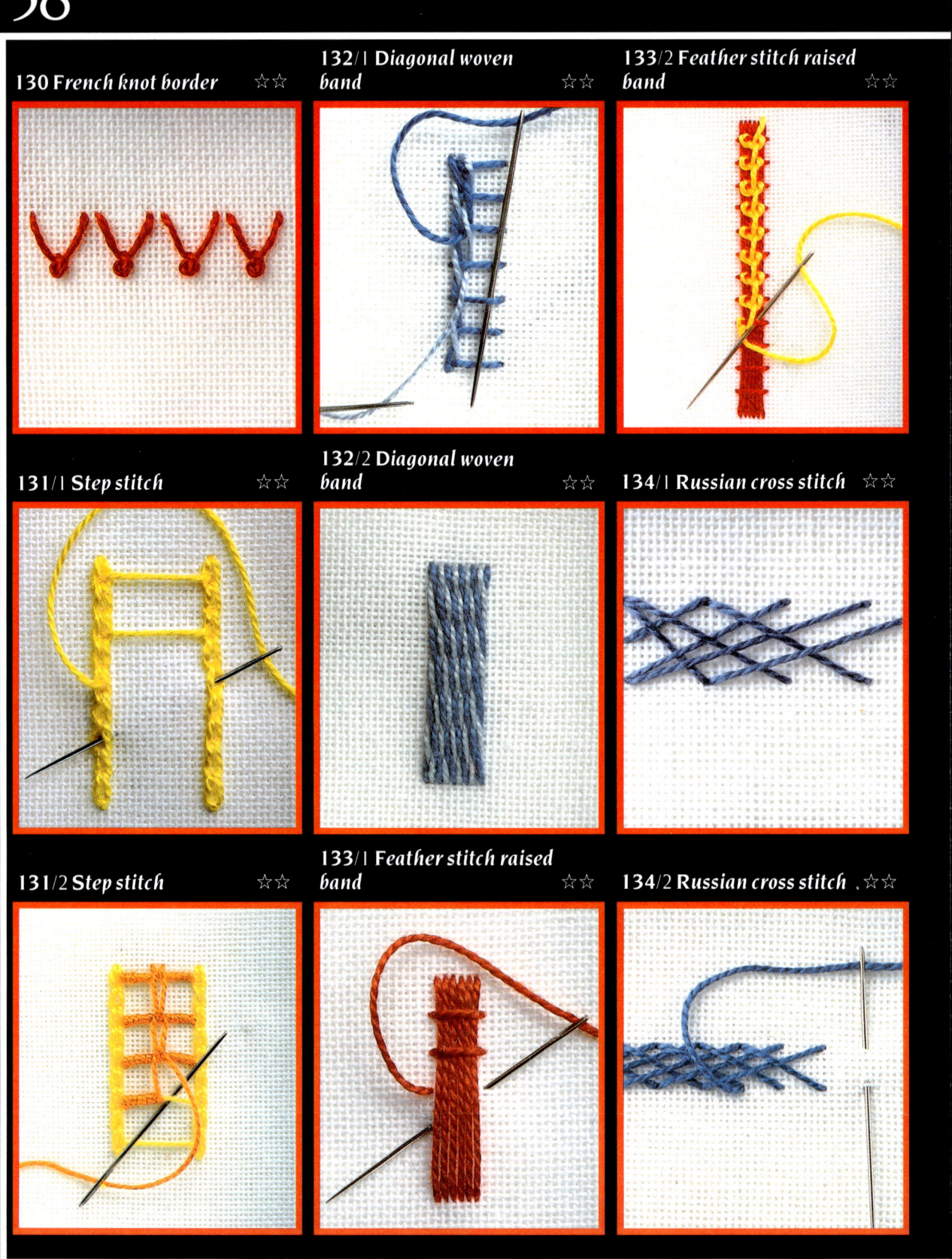

130 French knot border ☆☆

131/1 Step stitch ☆☆

131/2 Step stitch ☆☆

132/1 Diagonal woven band ☆☆

132/2 Diagonal woven band ☆☆

133/1 Feather stitch raised band ☆☆

133/2 Feather stitch raised band ☆☆

134/1 Russian cross stitch ☆☆

134/2 Russian cross stitch ☆☆

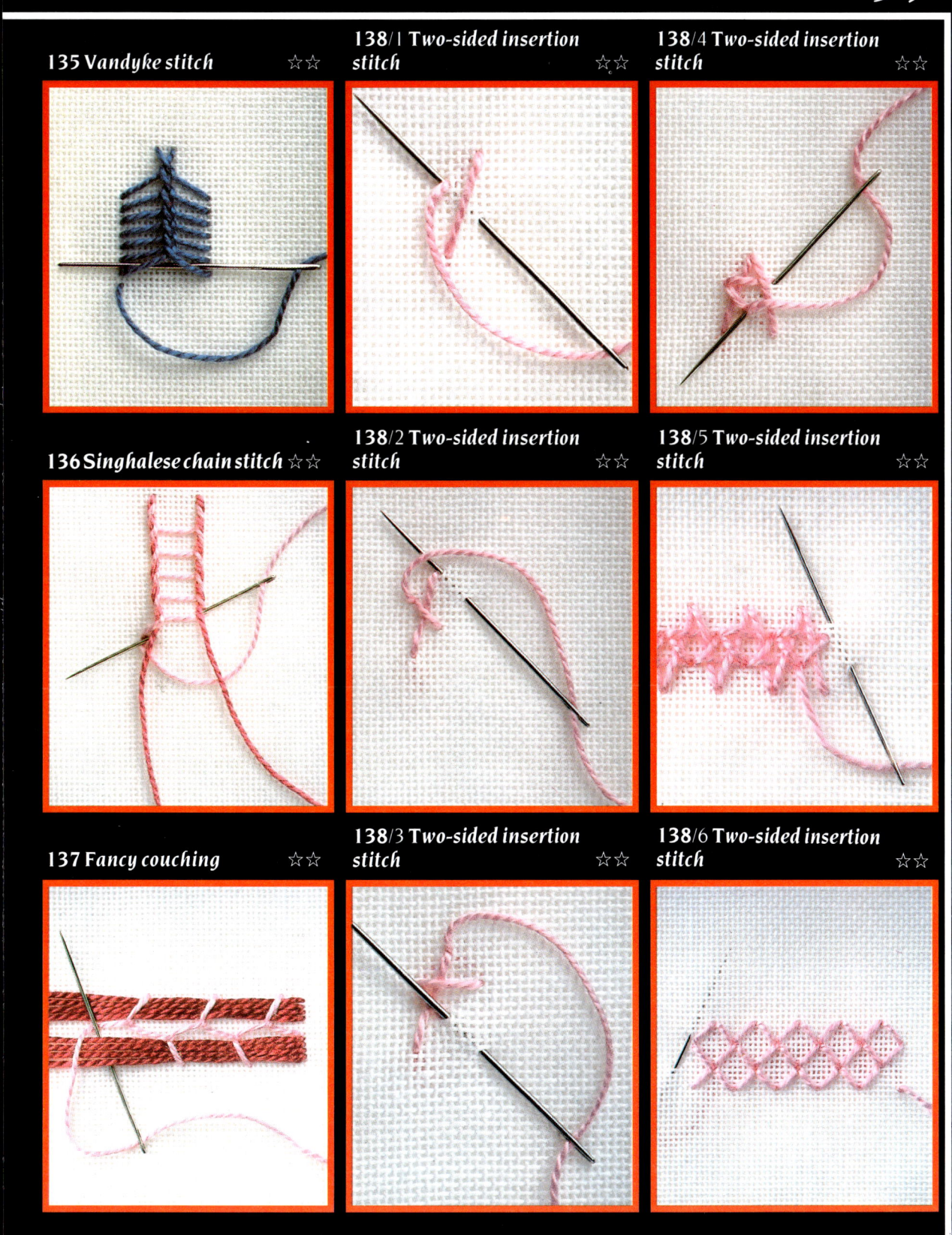

BORDER STITCHES 59

135 Vandyke stitch ☆☆

138/1 Two-sided insertion stitch ☆☆

138/4 Two-sided insertion stitch ☆☆

136 Singhalese chain stitch ☆☆

138/2 Two-sided insertion stitch ☆☆

138/5 Two-sided insertion stitch ☆☆

137 Fancy couching ☆☆

138/3 Two-sided insertion stitch ☆☆

138/6 Two-sided insertion stitch ☆☆

FABRIC STITCHES

139 Closed herringbone stitch ☆☆
also known as **shadow stitch**
Closed herringbone stitch is a dual-purpose line stitch used on plain- and even-weave fabrics. It can be worked as a border stitch when it makes a wide, plaited line. It is also used for shadow work on semi-transparent fabrics, such as organdie or voile, when it becomes an alternative way of forming double back stitch, *(see page 60)* which appears on the reverse of closed herringbone stitch. It is worked in exactly the same way as herringbone stitch *(see page 8)* but it is closed up so that the diagonal stitches touch at the top and bottom. To keep the row of an even width, guide-lines may need to be marked on the fabric if the threads cannot be counted. Closed herringbone stitch is also an attractive stitch for couching down a narrow ribbon, flat cord or group of laid threads.

140 Tied herringbone stitch ☆☆
also known as **coral knotted herringbone stitch**
Tied herringbone stitch is a composite line stitch used on plain- and even-weave fabrics. It makes a knotted zigzag line which is usually worked in two contrasting colours of thread. This stitch is used as a light border, or in multiple rows to make a lacy, knotted filling for a shape.

First, work a row of ordinary herringbone stitch *(see page 8)*, and then use a second thread to make a row of coral stitch *(see page 9)*. Work the knots over each intersection of the foundation stitches to tie them together; do not pick up any ground fabric. Use a blunt-ended tapestry needle for the coral stitch to avoid splitting the foundation threads. When used as a filling, the foundation rows should touch at the tips of the crosses. The colours of the thread used for the coral stitch can be graduated to give a subtle colour change over the area.

141 Double back stitch ☆☆
also known as **crossed back stitch**
Double back stitch is used particularly for shadow embroidery. On the front of the fabric it forms a double row of back stitch worked simultaneously along two lines, while on the reverse of the work a row of closed herringbone stitch *(see page 60)* appears. Shadow embroidery is always worked on a semi-transparent fabric, such as organdie or voile, with floss silk or stranded cotton. The rows of back stitch form the outline of the design, while the herringbone showing through the fabric forms the shadow. The two lines on the front of the fabric need not be parallel, and double back stitch is often used for leaf and petal shapes. Care should be taken with the spaces between the lines so that the herringbone on the reverse lies flat and does not sag.

142 Ladder stitch ☆☆
see also **open chain stitch**, **ladder hem stitch** *and* **step stitch**
Ladder stitch is a wide line stitch used on plain- and even-weave fabrics. It has a ladder-like appearance, hence the name, and it is used as a border stitch or to fill a long, narrow shape of varying width. This stitch should always be worked on fabric stretched in an embroidery hoop or frame to prevent it from tightening and distorting the fabric. When the stitch is worked in a straight line, guide-lines may need to be drawn on the fabric, unless the fabric threads can be counted, to keep the line straight. The rungs of the ladder can be placed close together to achieve a solid effect, or can be spaced apart to give the stitch a more lacy appearance. It is worked downwards along two parallel lines and consists of a sequence of crossing stitches, which forms the rungs, and loops which build up to create a plaited edge on each side of the row. A rounded thread, such as pearl or soft cotton, gives a raised appearance to the plaited edges.

BORDER STITCHES

143 Triple Cretan stitch ☆☆☆
also known as **French Cretan stitch**
Triple Cretan stitch is a decorative line stitch used on plain- and even-weave fabrics. It makes an attractive lacy line and can be worked with any type of embroidery thread, the choice depending on the effect required. Similar to open Cretan stitch *(see page 20)*, it has additional loops, and looks most effective when worked in a straight line; it does not follow curves well. Follow the sequence of stitches shown and be sure to tension each loop before proceeding to the next one. Triple Cretan stitch can also be worked solidly, row on row, to fill a regular shape with a very unusual lacy pattern.

144 Raised lattice band ☆☆☆
also known as **raised lace band**
Raised lattice band is a composite border stitch used on plain- and even-weave fabrics. It makes a rich padded line, which can be worked in more than one colour; a metallic thread can be used for the lacing. This stitch needs to be worked with the fabric stretched in an embroidery hoop or frame to prevent distortion.

A padding is made first: long, horizontal surface satin stitches *(see page 72)* are worked along the whole length of the row; then extra stitches are worked along the centre of the line to give a rounder effect. The padding is then covered by a foundation of closely worked, vertical satin stitches *(see page 24)* to completely cover the padding. A flat thread, such as stranded cotton or silk, gives better coverage at this stage. Care should be taken to make all the vertical stitches exactly the same length. To make the lattice pattern, a row of threaded herringbone stitch *(see page 45)* is worked over the satin stitches. The tips of the herringbones should enter the fabric just above and below the foundation line. Use a blunt-ended tapestry needle for the lacing to avoid disturbing the foundation stitches. Raised lattice band can be worked in multiple rows for a heavier border.

145 Chequered chain band ☆☆☆
Chequered chain band is a composite stitch worked downwards on plain- and even-weave fabrics. It is used as a heavy line stitch, and as a solid filling, making a chessboard pattern. A foundation of evenly spaced, short, horizontal stitches is made first, using the thread singly. Chain stitch *(see page 12)* is embroidered over these stitches, without picking up the ground fabric. They are worked in two colours of thread, using the two needles alternately on the same journey. The thread is doubled in each needle, rather than having two separate lengths threaded through it; this makes the two threads easier to manage and less likely to tangle. Blunt-ended tapestry needles should be used to avoid splitting the threads on the foundation row. The stitched examples show where to insert the two threads to begin the stitching, and how the stitches are made alternately by using one doubled thread at a time.

The horizontal bars can be made wider to accommodate three or four rows of chain stitch to make a heavier line. When this stitch is used for filling an area, lines of single, chequered chain band are worked solidly, side by side. When the colours at the top of each row alternate, a chessboard pattern emerges. A horizontal striped version is worked by making the top stitch on each row the same colour.

146 Diamond stitch ☆☆☆
Diamond stitch is a wide, knotted line stitch used as a border on plain- and even-weave fabrics. It is worked downwards between two parallel lines and, to keep the width of the stitch even, guide-lines may need to be marked on the fabric if the threads cannot be counted. It makes an attractive lacy line with a diamond pattern and can also be worked in touching rows to make a trellis filling. The stitch consists of straight, horizontal stitches placed one below the other with a knot at each end, which is worked over each straight stitch and through the fabric. A knot is also made in the centre of the row to link the straight stitches, without picking up the ground fabric. The arrangement of straight stitches and knots is shown. After completion, the line can be decorated by working an isolated stitch such as a French knot *(see page 96)* in the diamond-shaped spaces. Diamond stitch should be worked in a straight line, since it does not follow curves well.

62 FABRIC STITCHES

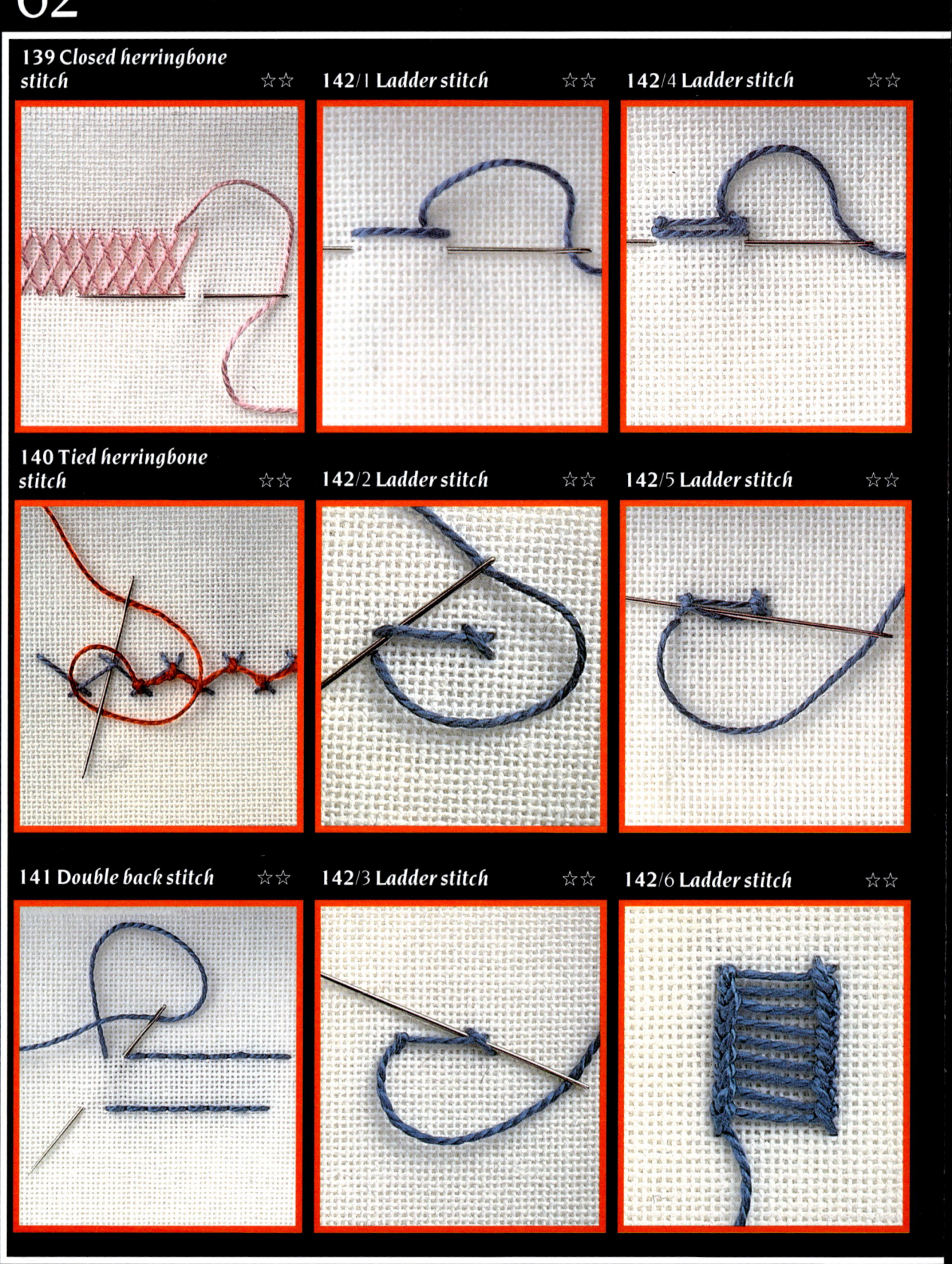

139 Closed herringbone stitch ☆☆

140 Tied herringbone stitch ☆☆

141 Double back stitch ☆☆

142/1 Ladder stitch ☆☆

142/2 Ladder stitch ☆☆

142/3 Ladder stitch ☆☆

142/4 Ladder stitch ☆☆

142/5 Ladder stitch ☆☆

142/6 Ladder stitch ☆☆

BORDER STITCHES 63

143/1 Triple Cretan stitch ☆☆☆

143/4 Triple Cretan stitch ☆☆☆

145/1 Chequered chain band ☆☆☆

143/2 Triple Cretan stitch ☆☆☆

144/1 Raised lattice band ☆☆☆

145/2 Chequered chain band ☆☆☆

143/3 Triple Cretan stitch ☆☆☆

144/2 Raised lattice band ☆☆☆

146 Diamond stitch ☆☆☆

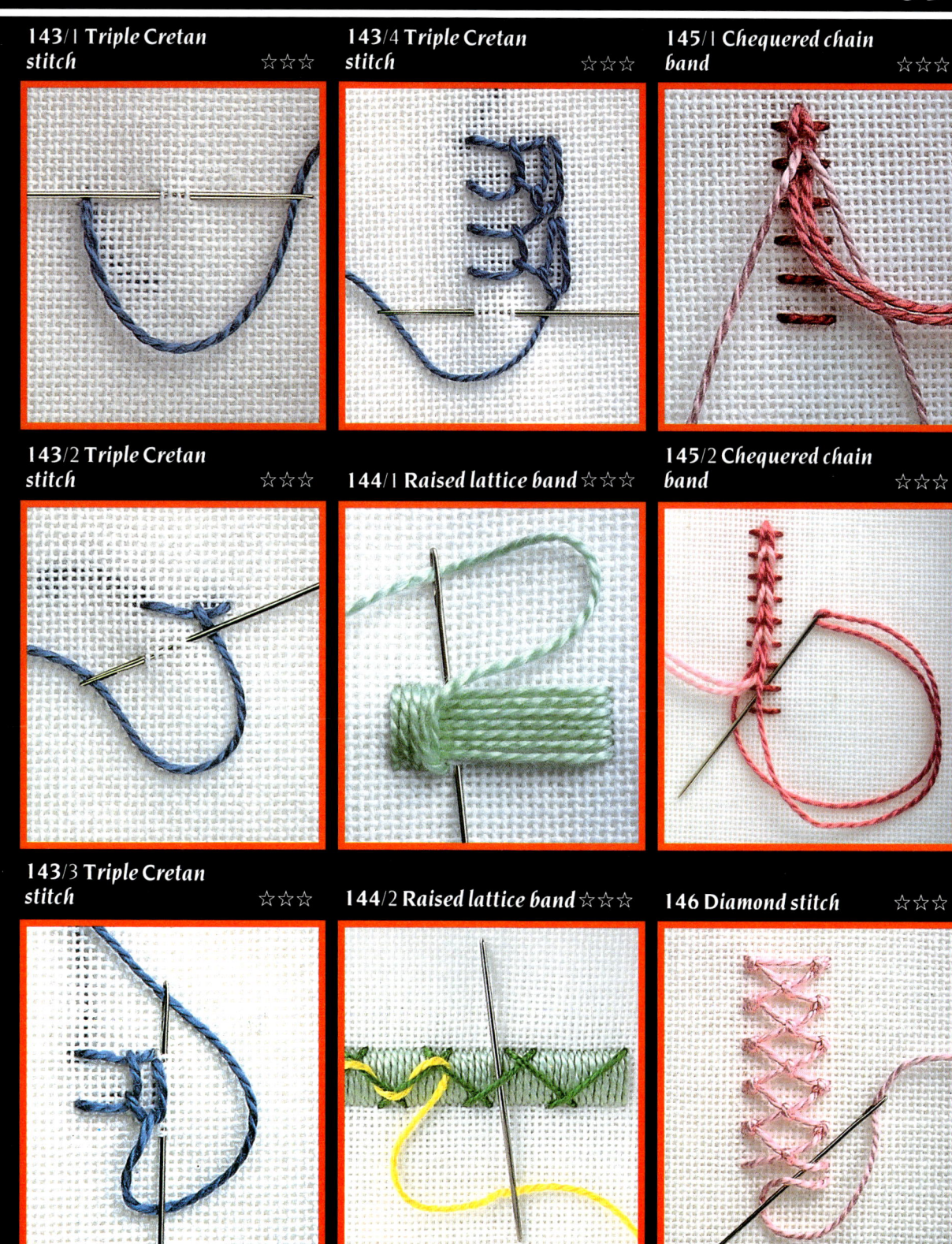

FABRIC STITCHES

147 Scottish Cretan stitch ☆☆☆
Scottish Cretan stitch is an ornamental line stitch used on plain- and even-weave fabrics. A variation of open Cretan stitch *(see page 20)*, it makes a rich, bold line, best used in a straight row to make a band or border. Any type of thread can be used, but a rounded thread, such as pearl cotton, will be easier to work with. It consists of blocks of open Cretan stitch worked closely together, and linked to form a row. After each block has been worked, the thread is passed upwards through the edge of the stitches on the left, taken over the top of the block and threaded downwards through the stitches on the right. The thread must be carefully tensioned before proceeding to the next block, and should not be pulled too tightly or the Cretan stitches will be distorted. Scottish Cretan stitch can also be worked as a motif stitch. To do this, secure the thread on the back of the fabric after each block has been threaded. The blocks can then be used to powder an area; they will look best if they are worked quite small.

148 Sheaf stitch ☆☆☆
Sheaf stitch is a composite border stitch used on plain- and even-weave fabrics. It makes a dramatic, heavy line and is always used on the straight. Sheaf stitch is a complicated stitch to work and requires some practice to master, but the end result is well worthwhile. The stitch is always worked vertically, from the bottom to the top, and three stages are needed to complete one row.

First make a foundation of pairs of horizontal straight stitches, spacing each pair evenly at a distance that matches the proposed length of the finished sheaves. (Guide-lines may need to be marked on the fabric if the threads cannot be counted.) Then bring the thread through at the bottom right-hand corner of the border, and link together the bottom two pairs of foundation stitches with a block of seven satin stitches *(see page 24)*; be careful not to pick up any ground fabric. Working upwards, link every two pairs of foundation stitches in this way, making sure that the satin stitches interlock. Then make a third journey, tying each sheaf round the centre with two satin stitches, and making rows of simple knots where the sheaves interlock. A fairly firm thread, which does not slip, is essential for working sheaf stitch successfully.

149 Spanish knotted feather stitch ☆☆☆
also known as **twisted zigzag chain stitch**
Spanish knotted feather stitch is an ornamental line stitch used on plain- and even-weave fabrics. It makes a wide, decorative line with a braided appearance and is used for bands and borders. It is worked downwards, along three parallel lines and, to keep the line straight, guide-lines may need to be marked on the fabric if the threads cannot be counted. This stitch is rather difficult to keep even at first, so some practice will be needed to achieve a good result. It consists of a series of twisted loops worked from the centre line alternately to the left and to the right. The loops create a knotted effect at the edges of the row. A round, twisted thread, such as pearl cotton, will give a bolder effect than a flat, stranded cotton or silk.

150 Raised stem stitch band ☆☆☆
Raised stem stitch band is a composite border stitch used on plain- and even-weave fabrics. It makes a wide, heavily stitched raised band, and is more successful if the fabric is stretched in an embroidery hoop or frame to prevent puckering and to keep the foundation threads parallel. A foundation is made by working long surface satin stitches *(see page 72)* along the border to the required width. Extra stitches are then added over the central portion of the row to give a more raised effect in the middle. Next, single short straight stitches are worked at regular intervals at right angles to the long stitches. Rows of stem stitches *(see page 9)* are then worked over the short stitches, without picking up the long threads underneath. Use a blunt-ended tapestry needle for the stem stitch rows to avoid disturbing the long threads. All the stem stitch rows should share a common hole at each end of the band to give a neat, rounded finish. The stem stitch rows should be packed as tightly as possible, so that none of the foundation thread shows through, and a flat, stranded thread gives good coverage.

BORDER STITCHES

151 Portuguese border stitch ☆☆☆

Portuguese border stitch is a composite stitch used on plain- and even-weave fabrics. It makes a wide, ornamental line with a raised effect, which can either be used alone as a straight border, or worked solidly to make a heavy filling. This stitch should always be worked with the fabric stretched in an embroidery hoop or frame to prevent the ground fabric from puckering. A firm thread should be used, especially for the foundation stitches so that they keep their shape. The foundation consists of horizontal straight stitches, which are evenly spaced between two parallel vertical lines. If the threads cannot be counted, guide-lines may need to be marked on the fabric to keep the foundation stitches a common length. The left-hand side of the foundation row is then threaded. Without picking up the ground fabric, a group of two satin stitches *(see page 24)* is worked over the bottom two foundation stitches; pairs of foundation stitches are then joined together by a group of two satin stitches, keeping the thread at the right. After two satin stitches have been worked, the thread is taken round the top foundation stitch of the pair to secure it, before moving upwards to the next pair of satin stitches. The right-hand side of the line is worked in the same way, starting at the bottom, but this time the thread is kept to the left of the satin stitches. The tension of the satin stitches is very important and the foundation stitches should not be pulled out of line.

152 Interlaced herringbone stitch ☆☆☆
also known as **interlacing stitch** *and* **Armenian cross stitch**

Interlaced herringbone stitch is a wide, composite line stitch used on plain- and even-weave fabrics. It makes a rich, interlaced line, which is always used on the straight. The interlacing thread is usually of a contrasting weight, texture and colour to the thread of the foundation row. This stitch looks very attractive when a metallic thread is used for the interlacing.

To keep the row of an even width, guide-lines may need to be marked on the fabric if the threads cannot be counted. A foundation row of double herringbone stitch *(see page 53)* is worked first, using the second method described. The foundation should be worked quite loosely, with the fabric stretched in an embroidery hoop or frame, as the interlacing will tighten the stitches considerably. Make sure that the formation of this row is correct before proceeding further. The interlacing is threaded in two rows, beginning at the left and completing one side before returning in the opposite direction. Follow the sequence of 'unders' and 'overs' carefully, and do not pick up the ground fabric. Use a blunt-ended tapestry needle for the interlacing to avoid splitting the foundation stitches.

153 Laced herringbone stitch ☆☆☆
also known as **woven herringbone stitch** *and* **German interlacing stitch**

Laced herringbone stitch is a decorative, composite line stitch used on plain- and even-weave fabrics. It makes an attractive border stitch and has an unusual circular threading. If the threads cannot be counted, guide-lines may need to be drawn on the fabric to keep the rows of an even width. This stitch can be worked in one or two colours: a contrasting colour, weight or texture of thread can be used for the lacing. A metallic lacing thread will also look attractive.

A foundation row of herringbone stitch *(see page 8)* is worked first, and should be at least 2cm (¾ in) wide to show the lacing to its best advantage. The work is then turned upside-down before the lacing is commenced. This will ensure that the 'unders' and 'overs' of the herringbone stitch follow in the correct sequence. The circular threading is quite complicated, so follow the sequence shown very carefully. Laced herringbone stitch should be worked with the fabric stretched in an embroidery hoop or frame, otherwise the lacing will tighten the stitch and pucker the fabric.

66 FABRIC STITCHES

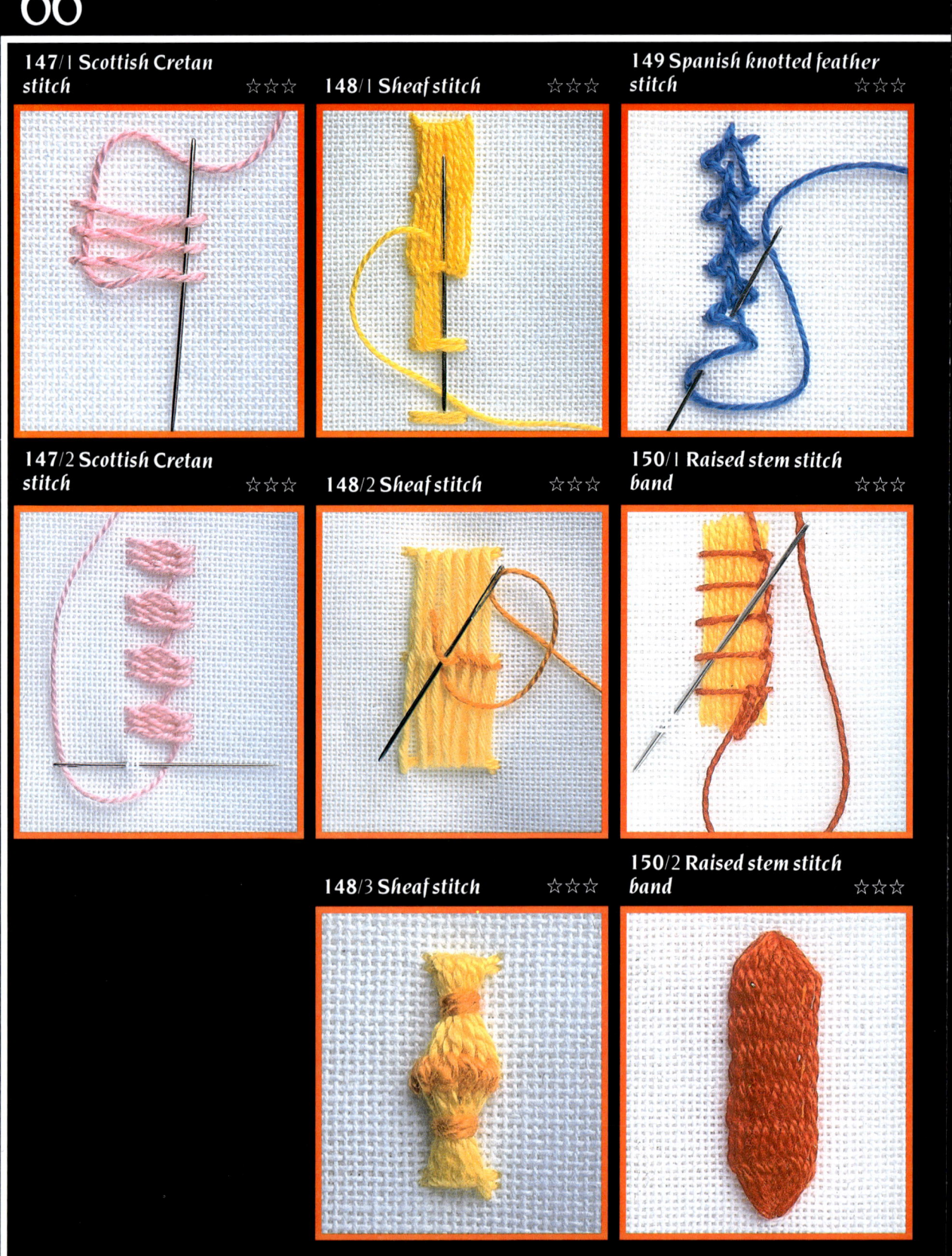

147/1 Scottish Cretan stitch ☆☆☆

148/1 Sheaf stitch ☆☆☆

149 Spanish knotted feather stitch ☆☆☆

147/2 Scottish Cretan stitch ☆☆☆

148/2 Sheaf stitch ☆☆☆

150/1 Raised stem stitch band ☆☆☆

148/3 Sheaf stitch ☆☆☆

150/2 Raised stem stitch band ☆☆☆

BORDER STITCHES
67

151/1 Portuguese border stitch ☆☆☆

152/2 Interlaced herringbone stitch ☆☆☆

153/2 Laced herringbone stitch ☆☆☆

151/2 Portuguese border stitch ☆☆☆

153/1 Laced herringbone stitch ☆☆☆

153/3 Laced herringbone stitch ☆☆☆

152/1 Interlaced herringbone stitch ☆☆☆

Filling stitches

154 Spaced buttonhole filling ☆
Spaced buttonhole filling is a quick and easy way of filling areas of plain- and even-weave fabrics. It consists of rows of buttonhole stitch *(see page 13)* in which the individual stitches are grouped together, often in pairs, with spaces in between. The first row is always worked from left to right, and the spaces on that row filled by the stitches on the next row, which is worked in the opposite direction. The number of stitches in the group can vary, as can the size of the spacing between the groups. This stitch can be worked as a detached filling, anchored through the fabric round the edges of the shape, but it is quite difficult to keep the tension of the stitches even.

155 Encroaching satin stitch ☆
Encroaching satin stitch is a filling stitch used on plain- and even-weave fabrics. It can be used over a shape of any size and is especially useful for shading and blending colours. It is worked in horizontal rows and consists of closely worked vertical satin stitches *(see page 24)*. On the second and subsequent rows, the head of each stitch is worked between the bases of the two stitches on the row immediately above. The rows of satin stitches blend into each other without a pronounced dividing line. Colours can be shaded very effectively using this stitch, and for really subtle effects the colour should be changed on every row – the colours chosen must be very similar for this to work well. Any type of embroidery thread can be used, but a lustrous thread, such as stranded cotton or silk, shows off the closely worked surface to its best advantage. Encroaching satin stitch should be worked with the fabric stretched in an embroidery hoop or frame to prevent the fabric from puckering.

156 Fly stitch filling ☆
also known as **flowing fly stitch** *and* **crossed fly stitch**
Fly stitch filling is used on plain- and even-weave fabrics for filling a shape of any size. A variation of ordinary fly stitch *(see page 93)*, it makes an attractive trellis pattern. It is worked in horizontal rows, and the tying-down stitches of each fly are very short. A row of fly stitch is worked with the 'V' shapes touching. In the second row, the fly stitches are inverted and the tying-down stitches are placed alongside those of the previous row, linking the two fly stitches to make an elongated cross. The two rows are then repeated over the space, with the rows touching. The trellis can be decorated by working a small, isolated stitch, such as a Chinese knot *(see page 96)*, or daisy stitch *(see page 92)*, in the spaces.

157 Double Algerian eye stitch ☆
Double Algerian eye stitch is a variation of Algerian eye stitch *(see page 168)*. Although it is worked in the same sequence, each stitch is drawn twice through the same hole, resulting in a heavier appearance. This effect is very useful when a textured appearance is required on a fine, even-weave fabric. This stitch is often worked in a self-coloured thread.

158 Star filling stitch ☆
Star filling stitch is used on plain- and even-weave fabrics. It has a variety of uses: as a light filling stitch, arranged either in formal rows or scattered at random over a shape; worked in a straight line to make a simple border; or used alone as an accent stitch. It is worked by making a large St George cross stitch *(see page 68)*, which is first covered by an ordinary cross stitch *(see page 14)* of approximately the same size. A tiny ordinary cross stitch is then worked at the centre to anchor both the larger crosses firmly to the fabric. Star filling stitch can be worked in one colour, or a different colour can be used for each cross, and the tiny central cross can be worked in a finer thread.

159 Seed stitch ☆
also known as **seeding stitch**, **seed filling stitch**, **speckling stitch** *and* **isolated back stitch**; *see also* **dot stitch**
Seed stitch is a filling stitch used on plain- and even-weave fabrics. It makes a light speckled powdering for an area, and is extremely quick and easy to work. Work tiny back stitches *(see page 14)* in any direction over the area to be filled. They should all be of an even length, but should be scattered irregularly and should not make a pattern. The size and spacing of the back stitches can be varied, depending on the type of thread used and the effect required. To make a similar but slightly heavier filling, use dot stitch *(see page 92)* instead of seed stitch.

160 Brick and cross filling ☆
Brick and cross filling is a simple yet attractive way of decorating an area of plain- or even-weave fabric. It is constructed by alternating square blocks of four horizontal or vertical satin stitches *(see page 24)* with single cross stitches *(see page 14)* to form a chessboard pattern; it is usually worked in vertical rows, beginning at the top and working downwards. Two or more shades of thread can be used, or it can be monochrome in appearance. A variation of this filling alternates square blocks of three vertical satin stitches with St George cross stitches *(see page 68)* worked in the centre of the spaces.

161 St George cross stitch ☆
St George cross stitch is a filling stitch used on plain- and even-weave fabrics. It is an upright cross stitch worked in two journeys. On the first journey, make a row of horizontal stitches; on the second, cross them with vertical stitches of the same length. It makes a neat, geometric filling when worked regularly over an area, and the density can be varied by altering the spaces between each cross and between the rows. Any type of embroidery thread can be used for this stitch, but a rounded thread, such as pearl cotton, will make the stitches stand out from the ground fabric better than a flat, stranded cotton or silk. St George cross stitch can also be worked individually, in the same way as ordinary cross stitch *(see page 14)*. It can then be scattered at random over a shape to make an attractive powdering, or it can be used as an accent stitch.

FILLING STITCHES

162 Double darning
also known as **pessante**
Double darning is a filling stitch best worked on an even-weave fabric as complete regularity is essential. It makes a flat, solidly stitched surface of vertical rows; no ground fabric should show through the stitching. The method of working this stitch is identical to that of Holbein stitch *(see page 9)* but double darning is always used as a filling rather than an outline stitch. Each row is worked in two journeys. On the first journey, the stitches and the spaces between them should be of equal size. On the return journey, the spaces are filled in by stitches, and the needle must enter and emerge from the fabric through the holes made on the first journey.

163 Roman filling stitch
Roman filling stitch is used on plain- and even-weave fabrics and makes an attractive and unusual filling for shapes of any size. A variation of Roman stitch *(see page 44)*, it consists of groups of seven vertical stitches of graduated length, tied down individually by tiny crossing stitches. Each group of stitches is arranged alternately over the shape with spaces between them. The groups can be worked alternately in two colours and placed with the edges touching to give a more solid effect, or they can be arranged in horizontal rows. Another variation is to work the groups so that the longest stitches touch each other at the top and bottom. Diamond-shaped areas of ground fabric then show through to add interest to the stitching.

164 Link filling stitch
also known as **link powdering stitch** *and* **detached chain filling**
Link filling stitch is used to fill shapes on plain- and even-weave fabrics. It is a simply worked filling, which can look extremely attractive, and consists of an arrangement of daisy stitches *(see page 92)* across an area. The arrangement should be very formal and the stitches worked in horizontal rows and placed so that, vertically, every other stitch aligns. This stitch is often used on crewel work, and its effect can be varied by spacing the stitches closer together or further apart. The size of the stitch depends to a large extent on the thread used. A fine crewel wool makes a smaller stitch than a heavy thread, such as pearl cotton or tapestry wool.

165 Trellis stitch
Trellis stitch is a filling stitch used on plain- and even-weave fabrics. It makes a delicate trellis pattern of laid threads, and it should be worked on fabric stretched in an embroidery hoop or frame. A foundation grid is made first, consisting of long, horizontal straight stitches, crossed by vertical stitches set at right angles. Long, diagonal stitches are then worked from top left to bottom right, crossing each intersection of the grid. The diagonal stitches are then couched down by working a tiny diagonal stitch over every intersection. Trellis stitch can be worked in one colour, or different colours can be used for each type of stitch to create a more interesting effect.

166 Cloud filling stitch
also known as **Mexican stitch**
Cloud filling stitch is a composite filling stitch used on plain- and even-weave fabrics. It is a quick and effective way of filling a shape, and it has an attractive, lacy appearance. Any type of embroidery thread can be used, the choice depending on the effect desired. A foundation of regularly spaced, vertical darning stitches *(see page 14)* is worked over the entire area to be filled. The stitches can be placed close together or be widely spaced, but they should be worked perfectly evenly. If a plain-weave fabric is used, the position of these stitches will need to be marked on the fabric before they are worked. A second thread of contrasting colour or weight is then laced through these stitches in rows. The needle enters the fabric only at the beginning and end of each row. Use a blunt-ended tapestry needle for the second thread to avoid splitting the stitches on the foundation row. The delicate trellis pattern that is made can be decorated by working an isolated knot stitch, such as French knot *(see page 96)* or Chinese knot *(see page 96)*, in the spaces. This stitch can be shaded easily by working the second and subsequent rows of threading in carefully graduated shades across the whole area.

167 Closed wave stitch
also known as **looped shading stitch**
Closed wave stitch is a solid filling stitch used on plain- and even-weave fabrics. It is an economical way of covering a shape, since nearly all the thread lies on the surface of the fabric. It is also excellent for shading, as each row, or part of a row, can be worked in a different shade. Closely packed vertical satin stitches *(see page 24)* form the top row. Then, on each subsequent row looped stitches are taken round the bases of the stitches on the preceding row. The stitches should be worked close together so that no ground fabric is visible. Stranded cotton or silk both give better coverage of the fabric than a twisted thread.

168 Stem stitch filling and stem stitch shading
Stem stitch filling is a way of using rows of stem stitch *(see page 9)* to make a very useful solid filling for a shape of any size on plain- and even-weave fabrics. It makes a closely packed filling with a woven appearance, and any type of embroidery thread can be used, from a fine crewel wool to a heavy pearl cotton. The lines of this stitch should follow the contours of the shape quite carefully, and the stem stitches should be of an even size on each row. The first stem stitch of each row should be a little shorter than the first stitch of the preceding row in order to give the effect of a pattern of diagonal lines across the surface.

Stem stitch shading is worked in exactly the same way by following the contours of the shape carefully. The colours should be evenly shaded and changed on every second or third row.

70 FABRIC STITCHES

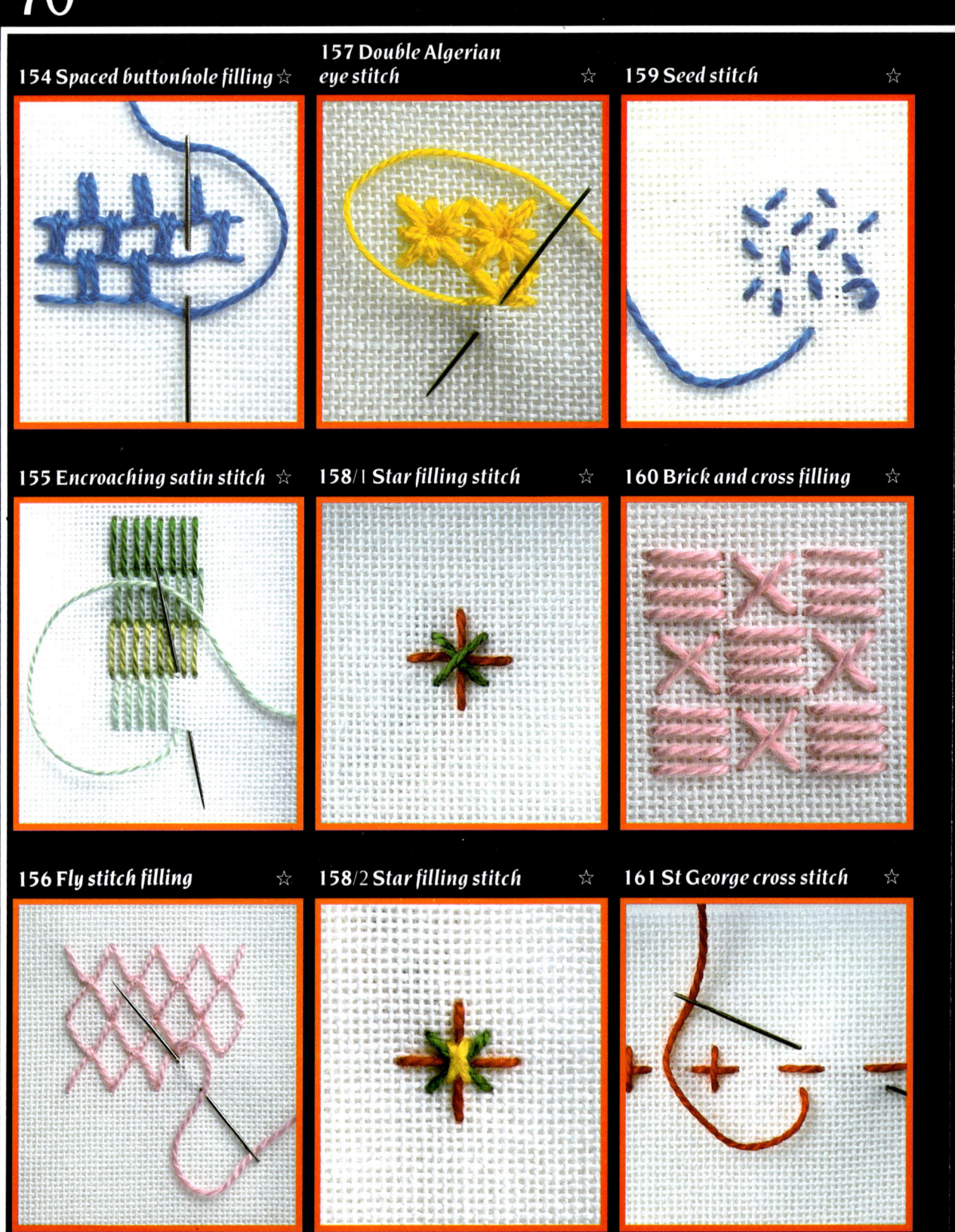

154 Spaced buttonhole filling ☆

157 Double Algerian eye stitch ☆

159 Seed stitch ☆

155 Encroaching satin stitch ☆

158/1 Star filling stitch ☆

160 Brick and cross filling ☆

156 Fly stitch filling ☆

158/2 Star filling stitch ☆

161 St George cross stitch ☆

FILLING STITCHES

71

162 Double darning

165/1 Trellis stitch

167 Closed wave stitch

163 Roman filling stitch

165/2 Trellis stitch

168 Stem stitch filling and stem stitch shading

164 Link filling stitch

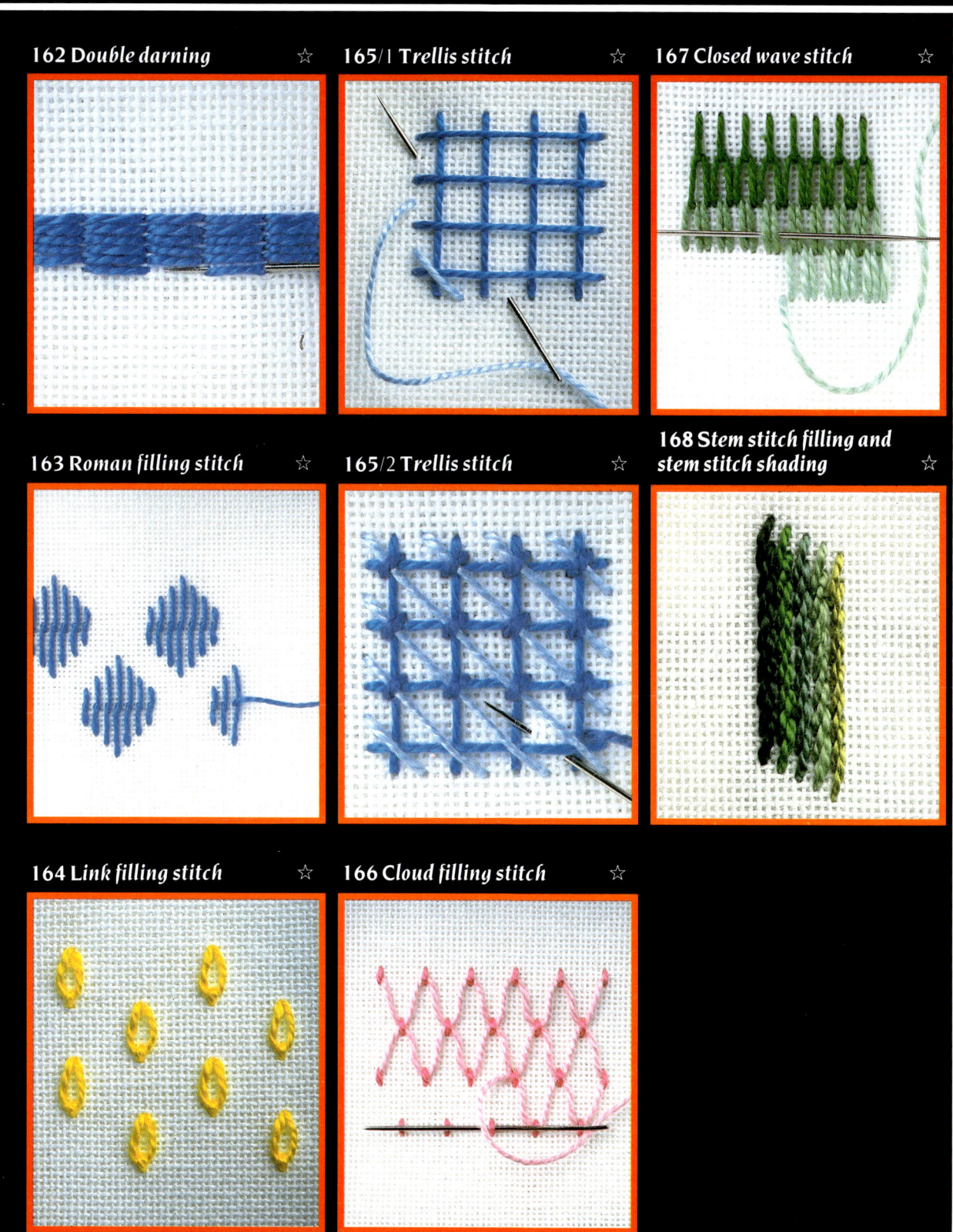

166 Cloud filling stitch

169 Colcha stitch ☆

Colcha stitch is a type of couching used on plain-weave fabrics. The stitch has its origins in New Mexico and the name refers to the 'colchas' or embroidered woollen hangings and bedcovers worked by the Spanish settlers in America.

The stitch is similar in construction to Roumanian couching *(see page 81)* and is most effective when worked with tapestry or crewel wool. Two lengths of the thread are used in the needle at the same time. A line of thread is laid across the shape and anchored at irregular intervals with slanting stitches before the next line of thread is laid. Colcha stitch gives a rough, almost woven, effect and can be used for covering large shapes, where a solid area of stitching is required.

170 Long and short stitch ☆
also known as **embroidery stitch, shading stitch, tapestry shading stitch, brick stitch, leaf stitch, Irish stitch, plumage stitch, feather-work** *and* **opus plumarium**

Long and short stitch is a variation of satin stitch *(see page 24)* which gives a gradually shaded effect and is much used in naturalistic embroidery. It is also used to fill an area that is too large or irregularly shaped to be covered neatly by satin stitch. It can be worked on all types of fabric and on single canvas. The first row is made up of alternately long and short stitches which closely follow the outline of the shape to be filled. The subsequent rows are worked in satin stitches of equal length. The stitches should lie closely together and cover the ground fabric or canvas completely.

171 Fancy stitch ☆

Fancy stitch is a modern filling stitch used on plain- and even-weave fabrics. It is worked on horizontal foundation rows, which are then threaded to make a decorative lacy filling which allows the ground fabric to show through. To keep the foundation rows straight, guide-lines may need to be marked on the fabric if the threads cannot be counted. The foundation consists of alternate rows of running stitch *(see page 12)* and short vertical stitches, commencing with a row of vertical stitches. A second thread, which can be of a constrasting weight and colour, is then threaded downwards through the foundation rows, without picking up the fabric. Each row of threading is worked separately, one row to the right and one to the left of each vertical foundation stitch. Use a blunt-ended tapestry needle for the threading to avoid splitting the stitches on the foundation rows.

172 Surface satin stitch ☆

Surface satin stitch is a way of working ordinary satin stitch *(see page 24)* on fabric, which gives the same smooth surface but is much more economical with the thread. The standard way of working satin stitch means that as much thread lies underneath the work as on the surface, which is rather wasteful, especially if an expensive silk is being used. In surface satin stitch, the needle picks up only a tiny amount of fabric at the edge of the shape, wasting very little thread. It is rather difficult to keep the stitches closely worked and even, so the shape is often covered in two journeys instead of one. On the first journey, a small space is left between each stitch, which is then filled on the return journey. This method of working satin stitch is used to make a foundation for laid-work *(see page 84)* and, except on canvas, it can be substituted for ordinary satin stitch when a large area is being worked.

173 Sheaf filling stitch ☆
also known as **faggot filling stitch**

Sheaf filling stitch is used to fill a shape of any size on plain- and even-weave fabrics. It makes an extremely attractive light filling when worked in a regular pattern, and each stitch looks like a tiny sheaf of corn. The sheaves are usually arranged in rather formal rows but they can also be scattered in all directions. Each sheaf consists of three vertical satin stitches *(see page 24)* bunched and tied round the centre by two overcast stitches *(see page 28)*. The needle should emerge from the fabric behind the satin stitches to work the overcasting, without picking up any ground fabric, before taking the needle to the back of the work. Any type of embroidery thread can be used, the choice depending on the size of sheaves required.

174 Basket filling stitch ☆
also known as **basket satin stitch**

Basket filling stitch provides a simple but effective way of filling an area of plain- or even-weave fabric with a flat, geometric pattern. It is worked in alternate blocks of four horizontal and four vertical satin stitches *(see page 24);* the blocks should be evenly spaced and regular. Although basket filling stitch is normally worked in one colour, it looks very attractive when a second colour is used for each alternate block. This stitch can also be worked on single canvas, using either wool or stranded cotton. The number of stitches in each block can vary between three stitches worked over four canvas threads, and five stitches worked over six threads, depending on the gauge of the canvas and the weight of the thread chosen.

175 Tête de boeuf filling stitch ☆

Tête de boeuf filling stitch is used on plain- and even-weave fabrics. It looks like a bull's head, complete with the horns. A fly stitch *(see page 93)* makes the horns, and a daisy stitch *(see page 92)*, anchors the fly stitch and makes the head. It is usually worked in formal rows to make an attractive light filling but the stitch can also be worked in horizontal rows to form a border.

There appears to be some confusion about exactly which embroidery stitch is called tête de boeuf filling stitch. In some modern books tête de boeuf filling stitch appears under the name of detached wheat ear stitch even though it looks exactly like a bull's head. However, the stitch described above can be found in many Victorian needlework books, including Caulfield and Saward's 1887 edition of *The Dictionary of Needlework: An Encyclopedia of Artistic, Plain and Fancy Needlework*, where a wood engraving of it and the reference 'Tête de boeuf stitch' can be seen.

FILLING STITCHES

176 Arrowhead stitch ☆
Arrowhead stitch is primarily used as a filling stitch, preferably on an even-weave fabric, as the regularity of the stitch is part of its character. It also makes a pretty line stitch when worked in pairs along a row. It can be worked horizontally or vertically, and is formed by working two straight stitches at right angles to each other. When used as a filling stitch, each row should touch the previous one. Arrowhead stitch can also be scattered in pairs at random on a plain-weave fabric for a light, powdered effect.

177 Chessboard filling stitch no. 1 ☆
Although chessboard filling stitch no.1 and chessboard filling stitch no. 2 *(see page 120)* share the same name, they create entirely different effects. Chessboard filling stitch no. 1 is used on plain- and even-weave fabrics. It makes a light, decorative filling of textured squares, and any type of embroidery thread can be used. The chessboard pattern is made by alternating stitched squares with unstitched squares. The stitched squares are usually worked in two journeys, and can be worked in two colours. Groups of four straight stitches arranged in the chessboard pattern are worked on the first journey. These groups are then overstitched on the second journey by a large cross stitch *(see page 14)*, extending from corner to corner of the group. The cross stitch is anchored in the centre by a short vertical stitch.

178 Croatian stitch ☆
Croatian stitch is a composite filling stitch used for covering small shapes on plain- and even-weave fabrics. It looks most effective worked on a small scale and using two colours which contrast boldly with the ground fabric. A thick embroidery thread, such as soft cotton, tapestry wool or the heaviest available weight of pearl cotton, accentuates the beauty of this stitch. It is extremely simple to work, but the foundation stitches must be neatly worked, and of even length. Outline the shape with a row of running stitches *(see page 12)*. Then lace a second thread of a different colour across the shape and through the running stitches to make parallel lines. Use a blunt-ended tapestry needle for the lacing to avoid picking up any ground fabric.

179 Trellis back stitch ☆
also known as **square stitch**
This trellis pattern makes an attractive filling stitch that is simple and quick to work, and can be used on both plain- and even-weave fabrics. Guide-lines need to be drawn on the surface of the fabric if the threads cannot be counted in order to keep the stitched lines evenly spaced. A totally regular grid is the main characteristic of this stitch, so care must be taken in ruling the guide-lines, which may be worked diagonally, or horizontally and vertically. To stitch the trellis, first work all the parallel lines in one direction, stitching up one and down the adjacent line. Then work the parallel lines at right angles to the first set in the same way. The trellis can be decorated in the squares with a small cross stitch *(see page 14)*, French knot *(see page 96)* or dot stitch *(see page 92)*.

180 Japanese darning ☆
Japanese darning is a light filling stitch used on plain- and even-weave fabrics. To keep the rows even, guide-lines may need to be marked on the fabric if the threads cannot be counted. Japanese darning makes an attractive geometric filling, which allows the ground fabric to show through, and it can be used for any size of shape. Spaced horizontal rows of ordinary darning stitch *(see page 14)* are worked over the shape with the stitches arranged alternately on every row. The thread is then brought through to the right of the second row to link the two rows with slanting stitches. This process is repeated over the entire shape; the linking rows should be worked from right to left. Care must be taken to make sure that the needle enters and emerges from the fabric through the holes made by the darning stitches; in this way the stitches are kept perfectly regular.

181 Open wave stitch ☆
Open wave stitch is a filling stitch used on plain- and even-weave fabrics. It makes a delicate, lacy filling and is worked in the same way as closed wave stitch *(see page 69)*, but the stitches on each row allow the ground fabric to show through. Any type of embroidery thread can be used, providing that it is compatible with the size of the stitch and the weight of the ground fabric.

182 Herringbone ladder filling stitch ☆
also known as **interlaced band stitch**, **double Pekinese stitch** *and* **laced Cretan stitch**
Herringbone ladder filling stitch is used on plain- and even-weave fabrics as both a border and a filling stitch. It has an attractive, lacy appearance and can be worked in two colours. The stitch is worked on a foundation of two parallel rows of back stitch *(see page 14)* arranged so that the stitches are placed alternately on each row. Guide-lines may need to be marked on the fabric if the threads cannot be counted to keep the rows parallel. A second thread of contrasting weight or colour is then interlaced between the two rows. The ground fabric is not picked up and a blunt-ended tapestry needle should be used for the interlacing. To use this stitch as a filling, work further parallel rows of back stitch to cross the fabric and interlace adjacent rows. This stitch can be made into a reversible border by using Holbein stitch *(see page 9)* for the foundation.

183 Brick stitch no. 1 ☆
Although both this and brick stitch no. 2 *(see page 120)* bear the same name, they give different effects. Brick stitch no. 1 is a filling stitch used on all types of fabric and on single canvas. It is constructed very simply and consists of vertical and horizontal straight stitches of an even length, fitted together to form a brick-work pattern. Any spaces left uncovered at the edge of the shape are filled in using shorter straight stitches, keeping the pattern even. It is worked in horizontal rows alternately from left to right and then from right to left.

74 FABRIC STITCHES

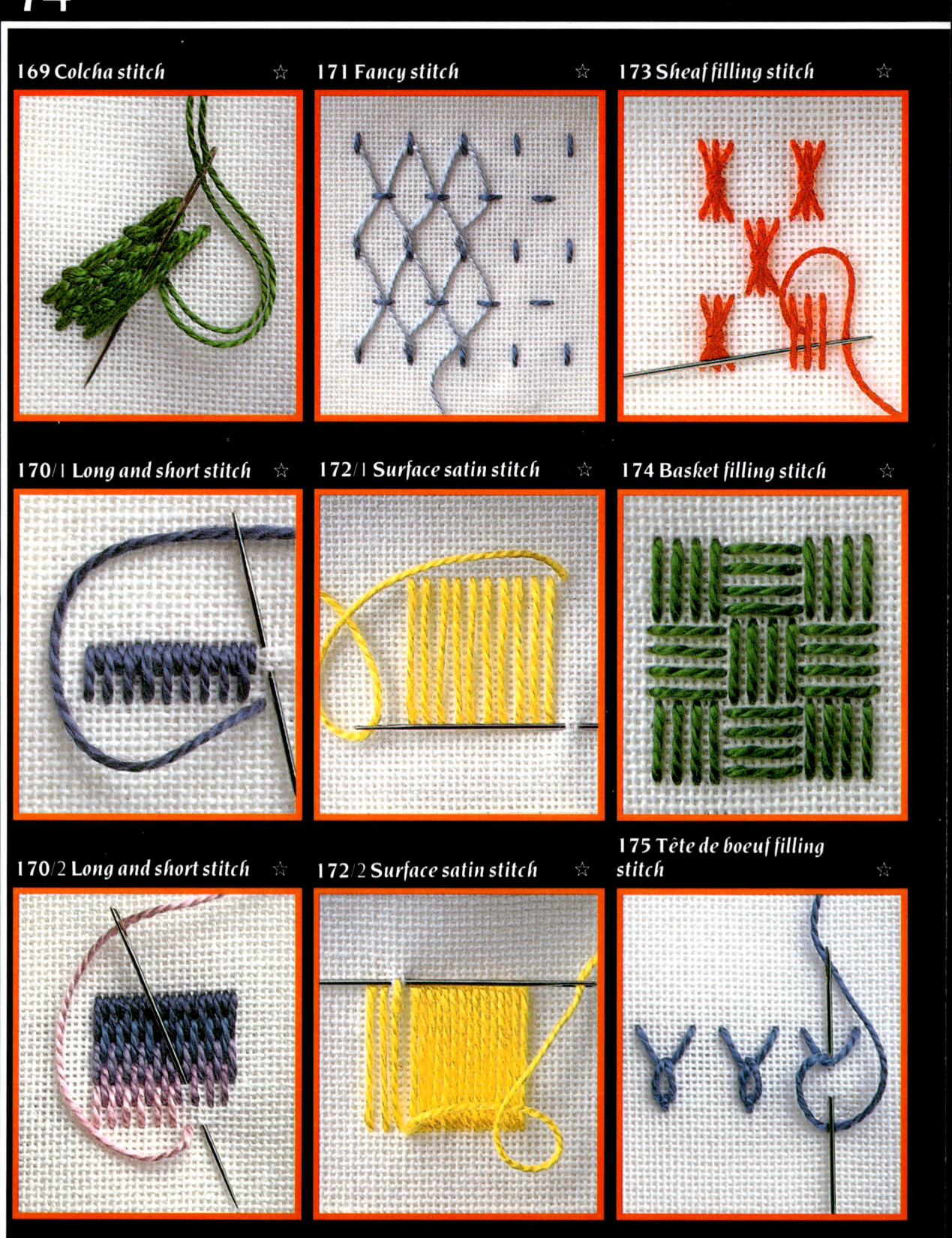

169 Colcha stitch ☆

171 Fancy stitch ☆

173 Sheaf filling stitch ☆

170/1 Long and short stitch ☆

172/1 Surface satin stitch ☆

174 Basket filling stitch ☆

170/2 Long and short stitch ☆

172/2 Surface satin stitch ☆

175 Tête de boeuf filling stitch ☆

FILLING STITCHES
75

176 Arrowhead stitch

179 Trellis back stitch

181 Open wave stitch

177 Chessboard filling stitch no. 1

180/1 Japanese darning

182 Herringbone ladder filling stitch

178 Croatian stitch

180/2 Japanese darning

183 Brick stitch no. 1

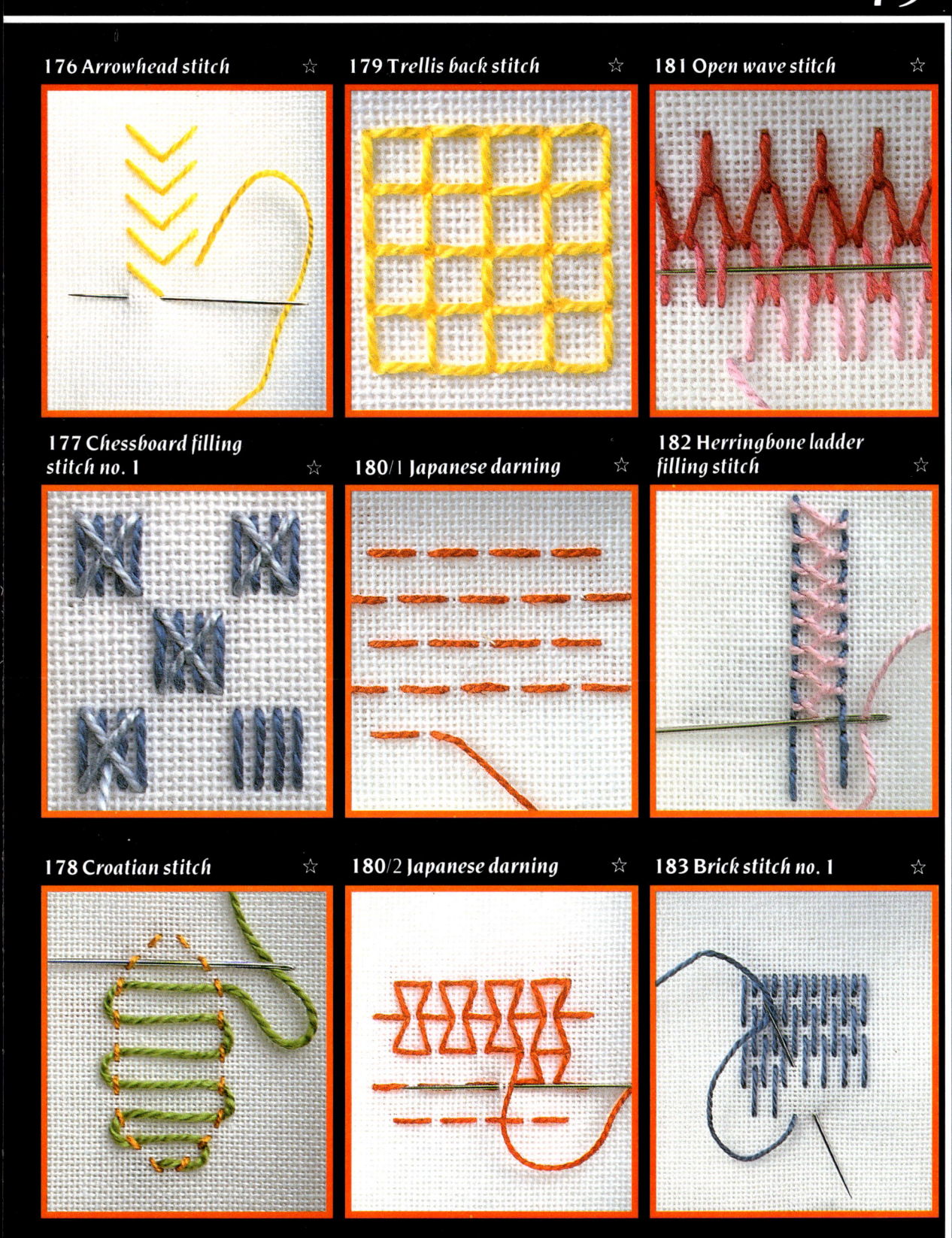

FABRIC STITCHES

184 Bosnia stitch ☆
also known as **Bosnian stitch, fence stitch** *and* **barrier stitch**
and Yugoslav border stitch
also known as **zigzag Holbein stitch**
These two stitches are grouped together because they are very similar to create and Yugoslav border stitch is probably no more than a variation of Bosnia stitch – or the other way round! Bosnia stitch is indigenous to Yugoslavia and is frequently used as a filling stitch on plain- and even-weave fabrics. It is a simply constructed stitch, worked in two journeys. On the first journey, the upright stitches are made and on the second, the spaces are filled in from bottom left to top right with slanting stitches. When it is used as a filling, the uprights of the second and subsequent rows are placed above each other in straight lines, and regularity of spacing is essential. Bosnia stitch is also found on French embroideries but the slanting stitches run from the bottom right-hand corner to the top left-hand corner and it is then known as fence or barrier stitch.

Yugoslav border stitch is probably a variation of Bosnia stitch but is always used as a line stitch rather than a filling. It is also worked in two journeys but both rows of stitches slant to form a zigzag line. This stitch is often used to decorate the national costumes of south-eastern Europe, when it is worked in multiple rows to form deep borders. It is often threaded with a second colour, in the same way as threaded herringbone stitch *(see page 45)*. The traditional colours chosen vary from village to village, although the use of a red line threaded with blue on white linen is widespread. Sometimes gold or silver threads are used, giving a rich appearance to this very simple stitch.

185 New England laid stitch ☆☆
also known as **Deerfield stitch** *and self couching*
New England laid stitch is a filling stitch used on plain- and even-weave fabrics. This stitch is an attractive variation of Roumanian stitch *(see page 77)*, worked with a longer crossing stitch, and is used for making solidly filled lines and narrow shapes. Very little thread is wasted on the back of the fabric and it is thought that the stitch was devised by the thrifty American colonial settlers when supplies of embroidery threads were extremely scarce and also expensive. New England laid stitch was used extensively on the blue and white Deerfield embroideries worked by the settlers of New England, hence its alternative name. It is very simple to work and consists of a long, horizontal straight stitch couched down by a long, slanting stitch on the return journey. The stitches should be worked closely together to cover the ground fabric completely.

186 Japanese stitch ☆☆
Japanese stitch is a solid stitch used on plain- and even-weave fabrics. Found on old Japanese embroideries, it is a traditional way of arranging satin stitch *(see page 24)* to form a wide, diagonal line. It consists of equal-sized satin stitches ranged one below another. The stitches are packed closely together so that no ground fabric shows through, and the line slants from top left to bottom right. This stitch looks most effective when worked in a lustrous thread, such as stranded cotton or, as in Japan, an untwisted silk thread. Japanese stitch is especially suitable for use on an even-weave fabric, and guide-lines may need to be marked on a fabric where the threads cannot be counted to keep the line even.

187 Open fishbone stitch ☆☆
Open fishbone stitch is a filling stitch used on plain- and even-weave fabrics. It is a variation of fishbone stitch no. 1 *(see page 80)* and is worked with an open finish to allow the ground fabric to show through. It is used to fill petal and leaf shapes where a light, open filling is needed. The stitches are worked downwards, following the outlines of the shape. The thread is taken from the left-hand side and a slanting stitch is made at the centre before the thread is taken through at the right-hand side. A lustrous embroidery thread, such as stranded cotton, will show off this stitch to best advantage, although any other type of thread can be used. Leaf stitch *(see page 80)* makes a similar open filling for a small shape.

188 Squared filling stitch no. 1 ☆☆
This and the two following stitches are all composite fillings for shapes or backgrounds, suitable for plain- and even-weave fabrics. Any type of embroidery thread and colour combinations can be used, the choice depending on personal preference. All three stitches should be worked with the fabric stretched in an embroidery hoop or frame to keep the foundation threads stable. Unless an even-weave fabric is being used, where the threads can be counted, guide-lines may need to be marked on the fabric to keep the foundation stitches evenly spaced.

Squared filling stitch no. 1 is worked on a vertical and horizontal foundation. The long vertical stitches are made first across the whole area to be covered. Then the long horizontal stitches are interwoven at right angles, exactly in the manner of darning a sock; avoid picking up the ground fabric. A second thread is then wound round the intersections of the grid on diagonal journeys from the top left to the bottom right and then back again, without picking up any ground fabric. Use a blunt-ended tapestry needle for the second thread to avoid splitting the foundation stitches.

189 Squared filling stitch no. 2 ☆☆
Squared filling stitch no. 2 is worked on a foundation grid of vertical and horizontal straight stitches which, unlike the preceding stitch, are not interwoven. First, work the horizontal stitches over the whole area to be covered, and then cross these with the vertical stitches. Couch down each intersection with a tiny diagonal stitch, before working a second diagonal grid over the entire area. The intersections of the second grid must fall over the squares of fabric showing through the first grid. Short, vertical stitches are used to couch down the second grid and anchor the filling securely.

190 Squared filling stitch no. 3 ☆☆

Squared filling stitch no. 3 is very simple to work. The diagonal foundation uses pairs of stitches to give a heavier effect. Work the diagonals that run from the bottom left to the top right first, and then cross these with a second set running in the opposite direction. Anchor each intersection to the fabric with a St George cross stitch *(see page 68)* and work a French knot *(see page 96)* or a Chinese knot *(see page 96)* in each of the diamond shapes of fabric which show through the grid.

191 Bokhara couching ☆☆

Bokhara couching is a solid filling stitch used on plain- and even-weave fabrics. Like Roumanian couching *(see page 81)*, it is a couching stitch which uses a continuous thread for both the laid and the couching stitches. It will fill any size and shape of space well and it looks best when worked with a lustrous stranded thread, either cotton or silk, to catch the light. Adjoining areas of Bokhara couching can be worked with the laid threads running in alternate directions to enhance the light and shade effect the stitch makes. It is straightforward to work but a little practice will be needed to keep the couching stitches even. This stitch should always be worked with the fabric stretched in an embroidery hoop or frame to keep the laid threads parallel. The thread is laid across the shape from left to right and then couched down on the return journey with small, slanting stitches placed at regular intervals. The slanting stitches can be arranged to form lines across the laid threads, or they can be set alternately to give a woven effect.

192 Underside couching ☆☆
also known as **invisible stitch**

Underside couching is a filling stitch used on plain- and even-weave fabrics. A very old stitch, it has been used for centuries to attach gold and silver threads to ecclesiastical vestments and church furnishings and was used extensively for this purpose during the middle ages. Many examples of 'Opus Anglicanum', as English embroidery from this period is known, still survive with much of the underside couching still intact; pieces can be seen in the Victoria and Albert Museum in London.

Underside couching is ideally suited to metal thread embroidery, as the couching stitches do not show and therefore do not conceal the metallic surface of the couched thread but it is also worked successfully with other, less precious, threads. Underside couching should be worked on a strong, finely woven ground fabric, which has been stretched tautly in an embroidery hoop or frame. The couching thread must be extremely strong and supple and it should be waxed before use. This thread lies underneath the work, and the laid thread on the surface. At regular intervals the couching thread is brought through the fabric, taken over the laid thread and then threaded back through the same hole in the fabric, when it is given a gentle pull, so that a fraction of the laid thread is taken through the fabric and secured. This stitch can be used to fill small shapes or to cover backgrounds.

193 Roumanian stitch ☆☆
also known as **Oriental stitch, antique stitch, Indian filling stitch** *and* **Janina stitch**; *see also* **Holbein stitch**

Roumanian stitch is a line and filling stitch used on plain- and even-weave fabrics. It makes an attractive wide border when worked between parallel lines and is also used to fill long, narrow shapes by graduating the width of the stitches. In either case, the tying-down stitches in the centre must be kept perfectly even and be placed in a neat line.

A long stitch is made across the line or shape to be worked and is tied down on the return journey. The construction of the stitch is similar to that of Roman stitch *(see page 44)* but the tying-down stitches are longer and slanted. The stitches should be worked closely together to cover the fabric completely and they look very effective when worked in stranded cotton or silk. A wide shape can be filled by using Roumanian couching *(see page 81)* to give a similar effect.

194 Overlapping herringbone stitch ☆☆
also known as **raised fishbone stitch** *and* **self-padded herringbone stitch**

Overlapping herringbone stitch is a raised stitch used on plain- and even-weave fabrics. It makes a closely stitched padded surface and is used for filling leaf and petal shapes and small geometric shapes where a raised effect is needed. Any type of embroidery thread can be used but a stranded cotton or silk gives a better fabric coverage. This stitch benefits from being worked in an embroidery hoop or frame although it is not essential to do so. The stitch is worked over a central straight stitch at the top of the shape and is built up with overlapping diagonal straight stitches worked from side to side and crossing in the centre. The stitches should be evenly worked and placed as close together as possible to give a smooth surface to the raised area and complete coverage of the fabric.

195 Plaid filling stitch ☆☆
also known as **tartan stitch**

Plaid filling stitch is a composite filling stitch used on plain- and even-weave fabrics. It is usually worked in three contrasting colours to give a tartan effect. It can be used to fill shapes of any size and the fabric should be stretched in an embroidery hoop or frame to keep the foundation grid perfectly even. The grid is made by working long, vertical straight stitches across the shape, which are then crossed by long, horizontal stitches; the horizontal stitches are interwoven with the verticals in exactly the same way as for darning a sock. The foundation grid should be evenly spaced and make a pattern of squares on the fabric. Two horizontal straight stitches are then worked over each square, using a second colour. Finally, two vertical stitches worked in a third colour are sewn across these to make a double cross. The crosses are placed in alternate squares to accentuate the plaid pattern.

78 FABRIC STITCHES

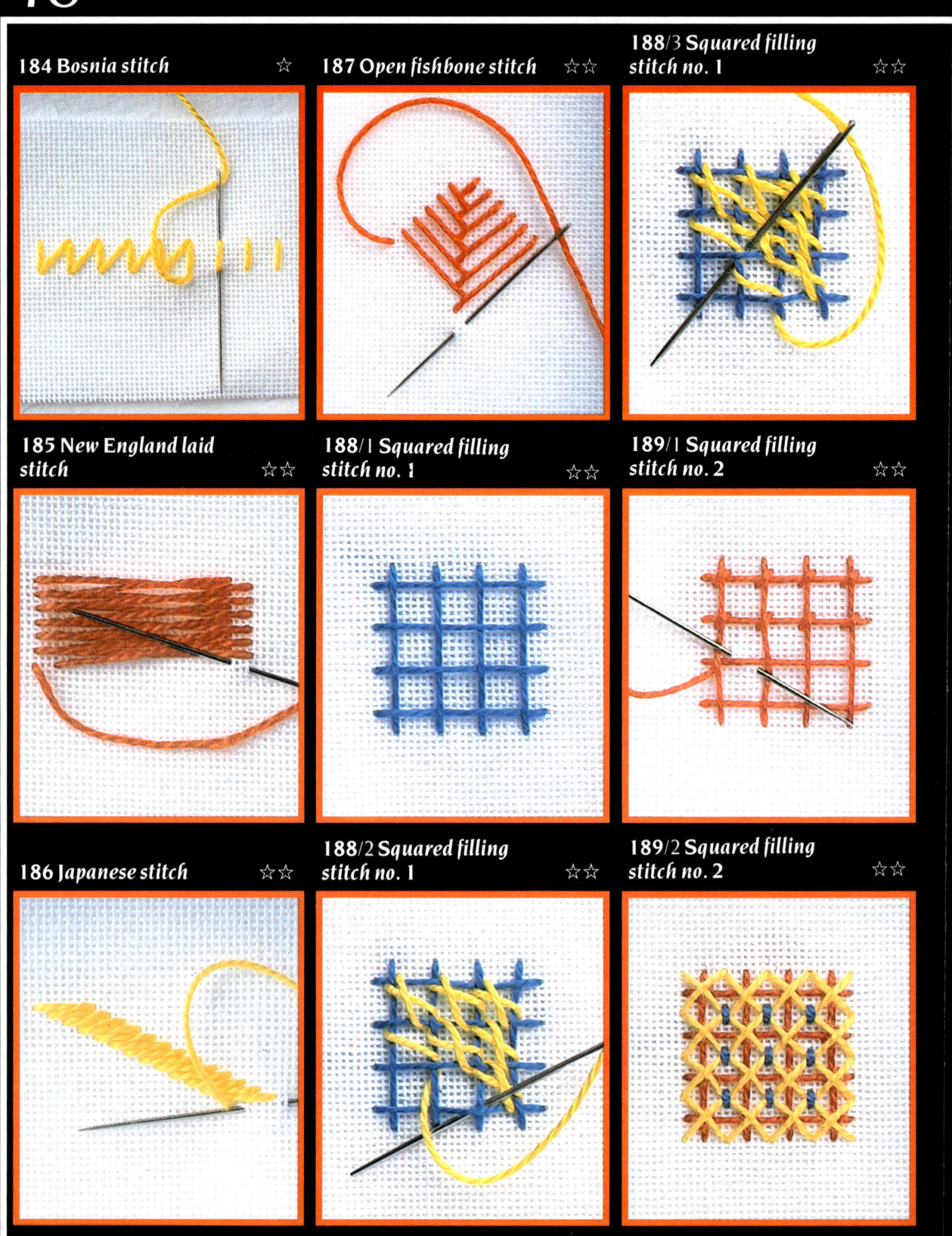

184 Bosnia stitch ☆

187 Open fishbone stitch ☆☆

188/3 Squared filling stitch no. 1 ☆☆

185 New England laid stitch ☆☆

188/1 Squared filling stitch no. 1 ☆☆

189/1 Squared filling stitch no. 2 ☆☆

186 Japanese stitch ☆☆

188/2 Squared filling stitch no. 1 ☆☆

189/2 Squared filling stitch no. 2 ☆☆

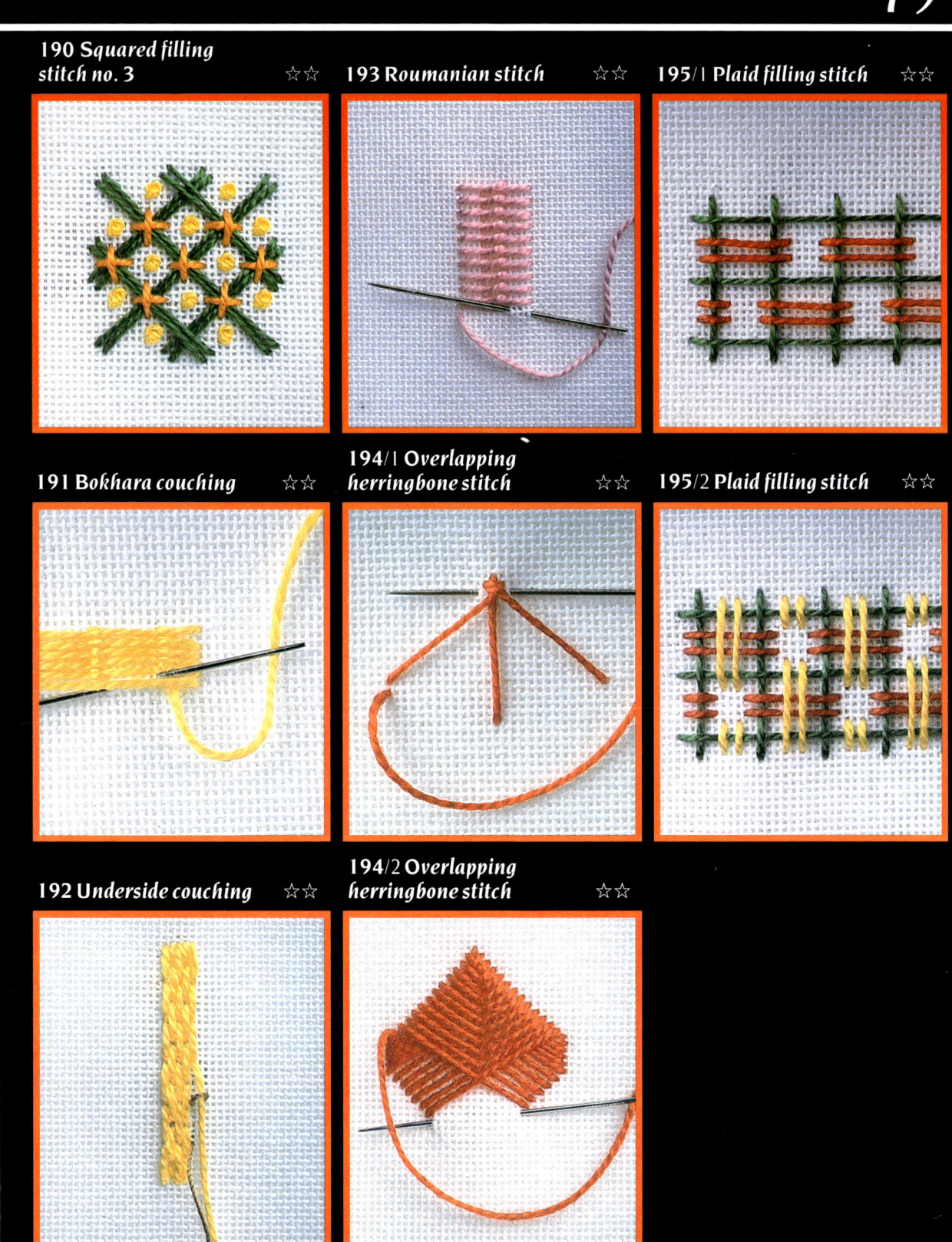

FILLING STITCHES 79

190 Squared filling stitch no. 3 ☆☆

193 Roumanian stitch ☆☆

195/1 Plaid filling stitch ☆☆

191 Bokhara couching ☆☆

194/1 Overlapping herringbone stitch ☆☆

195/2 Plaid filling stitch ☆☆

192 Underside couching ☆☆

194/2 Overlapping herringbone stitch ☆☆

196 Couched filling stitch ☆☆
also known as **Jacobean couching**
Couched filling stitch is a composite stitch used for filling shapes on plain- and even-weave fabrics. It has a pretty, lattice appearance and can be worked in two or more colours. It should always be worked with the fabric stretched in an embroidery hoop or frame to keep the foundation grid perfectly regular. The grid is worked first and consists of long horizontal stitches placed at regular intervals across the shape. Long vertical stitches are then worked to cross the first set of stitches at right angles. Keep the foundation grid as even as possible or the beauty of the stitch will be lost. These long stitches are then anchored or 'couched down' at each intersection by a tiny cross stitch *(see page 14)*, usually in a contrasting colour of thread.

197 Torocko stitch ☆
also known as **cross couched filling stitch** *and* **Hungarian cross stitch**
Torocko stitch is a quickly worked filling stitch used only on plain-weave fabrics. First a foundation grid of evenly spaced long stitches is worked to cover the whole shape. This grid is then overstitched with diagonal rows of upright crosses, and a short, diagonal stitch is worked from bottom left to top right to finish. The crosses can be worked in a second colour, with a third colour used for the anchoring diagonal stitches. Torocko stitch is most successful if worked on a closely woven ground fabric stretched in a hoop or on a frame during stitching.

198 Leaf stitch ☆☆
see also **fir stitch** *and* **long and short stitch**
Leaf stitch is a filling stitch used on plain- and finely woven, even-weave fabrics. It is a light, open stitch suitable for filling small areas, such as oval or leaf shapes. It is always worked upwards and consists of slanting straight stitches, which pass from one side of the shape to the other and make a loose plait down the centre. An outline stitch, such as back stitch *(see page 14)* or stem stitch *(see page 9)*, is often worked round the edge to define the shape more distinctly. Leaf stitch can also be worked between parallel lines to make a border and the length of the stitches can be varied to give an undulating line. A lustrous embroidery thread, such as stranded cotton, shows this stitch off to its best advantage, although any type of thread can be used. Open fishbone stitch *(see page 76)* makes a similar open filling for a small shape.

199 Honeycomb filling stitch ☆☆
also known as **net passing stitch**
Honeycomb filling stitch is used on plain- and even-weave fabrics and has a lacy, geometric appearance. It is essential to work this stitch with the fabric stretched in an embroidery hoop or frame to keep the tension even. The three sets of stitches can be worked in more than one colour and a round thread, such as pearl cotton or coton à broder, makes the stitch easier to work. Honeycomb filling stitch consists of long, horizontal and diagonal straight stitches worked so that they interlock, forming triangles. Even spacing of these stitches is crucial. The horizontal stitches are worked first across the whole shape; then one set of diagonal stitches is worked over these, from bottom left to top right. A second set of diagonal stitches is worked at right angles to the first set, passing under the horizontal and over the first diagonal stitches and interlocking all the threads, as shown.

200 Fishbone stitch no. 1 ☆☆
Although fishbone stitch no. 1 and fishbone stitch no. 2 *(see page 137)* share the same name, the effect produced from each is quite different.

Fishbone stitch no. 1 is a filling stitch used on plain- and even-weave fabrics. It is often used to fill petal and leaf shapes when the stitch lengths are graduated to follow the outline of the shape. It also makes an attractive solid border when the stitches are of equal length, and it makes a flat, solidly stitched surface in which the stitches cross one another at the centre. A central vertical straight stitch is worked at the top and then slanting straight stitches are worked alternately from the centre to each side of the shape. The stitches should be worked evenly and very close together so that no ground fabric is visible. A lustrous embroidery thread, such as stranded cotton or silk, will emphasize the different directions of the stitches. Fishbone stitch no. 1 can be striped by threading two needles with different colours and using each colour alternately.

201 Faggot filling stitch ☆☆
see also **sheaf filling stitch**
Faggot filling stitch is a composite stitch used on plain- and even-weave fabrics. It is a variation of a canvas stitch called shell stitch *(see page 160)* adapted for use on fabric. It makes a decorative row of groups of vertical stitches linked together, and it can be used as a border or to make a filling. Each row is worked in two journeys and two different threads can be used, depending on the effect required. To keep the rows even, guide-lines may need to be marked on the fabric if the threads cannot be counted. A foundation group of three vertical straight stitches is made first. Then, before proceeding to the next group, these stitches are tied down and bunched together by two short crossing stitches. After a row of bunched stitches has been made, a second thread is used to lace them together. A round, twisted thread, such as pearl cotton, shows this stitch to its best advantage.

202 Basket stitch no. 2 ☆☆
Basket stitch no. 2 is a laid filling. It is used for covering areas of ground fabric and should always be worked in an embroidery hoop or frame to prevent the fabric from puckering. The effect is like that of a woven basket and the stitch can be used on plain- or even-weave fabrics. It consists of a foundation grid of single, vertical straight stitches overlaid by double, horizontal ones. The horizontal stitches are then tied down at intervals by short, vertical stitches. The basket weave appearance of this stitch can be made more pronounced by selecting threads in three tones of one colour.

FILLING STITCHES

203 Flat stitch ☆☆
also known as **Croatian flat stitch**

Flat stitch is a filling stitch used on plain- and even-weave fabrics. It makes a flat, solidly stitched shape and is used for filling small shapes, such as leaves and petals. It can also be worked in a line to give a heavy outline to a shape, or in multiple rows to fill a large shape. It is worked downwards in slanting straight stitches, which cross in the centre of the shape. The stitches should be placed closely together so that the ground fabric is completely covered. A fairly thick thread, such as soft cotton or the heaviest available weight of pearl cotton, works best with this stitch.

204 Damask darning ☆☆
Damask darning is a solid filling stitch used on even-weave fabrics. Perfect regularity is essential for this stitch, so a plain-weave fabric is not suitable. Its appearance is of a woven fabric with a diagonal pattern and the stitch looks best when worked with a lustrous thread, such as stranded cotton or silk. The use of this type of thread will enhance the light and shade effect created by the different directions in which the thread lies. In spite of its name, this stitch is not formed by rows of darning stitches. Each diagonal row, which slants from the top left to the bottom right, is worked separately by making short, horizontal stitches. The stitch should cover the surface, allowing no ground fabric to show through, and it makes an attractive filling when used over a large area.

205 Burden stitch ☆☆
Burden stitch is named after Elizabeth Burden, the sister-in-law of the nineteenth-century designer, William Morris. Miss Burden taught at The Royal School of Needlework and revived a type of couching which dates back to the Middle Ages when it was used as a grounding stitch, particularly in Italy and Germany, and used mainly on the large ecclesiastical pieces of that period. She worked this type of couching to cover large areas in the figurative pieces she embroidered to the designs of William Morris and Walter Crane.

The stitch consists of rounded, fairly thick threads laid horizontally across the area to be covered, with an even space between each one. These laid threads are then attached to the background fabric (plain- or even-weave) by vertical straight stitches which cross them. These vertical stitches can be worked closely together or spaced out to let the colour of the fabric show through. When completed, the stitch makes a brick-like pattern, which can be shaded by the use of different colours of thread and is very effective when the laid threads are metallic. It is often used for ecclesiastical embroidery when either silk or lengths of gold and silver purl are used for the vertical stitches. The name Burden stitch is also sometimes applied to a type of darning *(see page 14)*, which makes the same brick-like pattern.

206 Buttonhole stitch shading ☆☆
A filling of closely worked rows of buttonhole stitch *(see page 13)* is ideal for shading an area when a solidly embroidered shape is required. Work the rows of buttonhole stitch from left to right, beginning at the top of the shape to be filled. The second and subsequent rows should encroach on the loops of the preceding row. The shading is effected by changing the colour of the thread very gradually row by row or once every two rows. An alternative way of shading with this stitch is to work pairs of long, horizontal stitches across the area in different colours. Then work the buttonhole stitch over each pair of laid threads, leaving spaces between the stitches. The amount of colour showing from the contrasting laid threads is controlled by the extent of the spaces between the buttonhole stitches; vary the size of the spaces until you achieve the amount of shading required. The laid threads can be all of the same colour and the buttonhole stitch worked in graduating colours to provide the shading; alternatively, the buttonhole stitch can be monochrome, with the shading created by the different colours of the laid threads.

207 Roumanian couching ☆☆
also known as **antique couching, Oriental couching, laid Oriental stitch** *and* **figure stitch**

Roumanian couching is a solid filling stitch used on plain- and even-weave fabrics. It has a continuous thread for both the laid and the couching stitches, in the same way as Bokhara couching *(see page 77)*. Roumanian couching makes a flat area of stitching without an apparent pattern and is used for filling large spaces and backgrounds. This stitch looks very effective when worked with a lustrous thread, such as stranded cotton or silk, and can be shaded over the area by choosing graduated colours. This stitch should always be worked in an embroidery hoop or frame to keep the laid threads well tensioned. The thread is laid across the area from left to right and then couched down, using loose slanting stitches arranged evenly along the row. It is straightforward to work but a little practice will be needed to achieve the correct slant and tension on the couching stitches, which should be sufficiently long and angled to be almost indistinguishable from the laid stitches.

208 Triangular Turkish stitch ☆☆
also known as **two-sided triangular Turkish stitch**

Triangular Turkish stitch is a filling stitch used on even-weave fabrics. It makes a neat, triangular pattern on both sides of the fabric. If the stitches are pulled quite tightly, the effect of a drawn fabric stitch is achieved. A fine thread, such as coton à broder or the lightest available weight of pearl cotton, is best suited to this stitch, which is worked in diagonal rows. Two journeys are necessary to complete one row and the sequence of stitches shown should be followed very carefully. Each stitch can cover three, four or five fabric threads, depending on the weight of the fabric and the effect desired, but triangular Turkish stitch does benefit from being worked on a fairly small scale.

82 FABRIC STITCHES

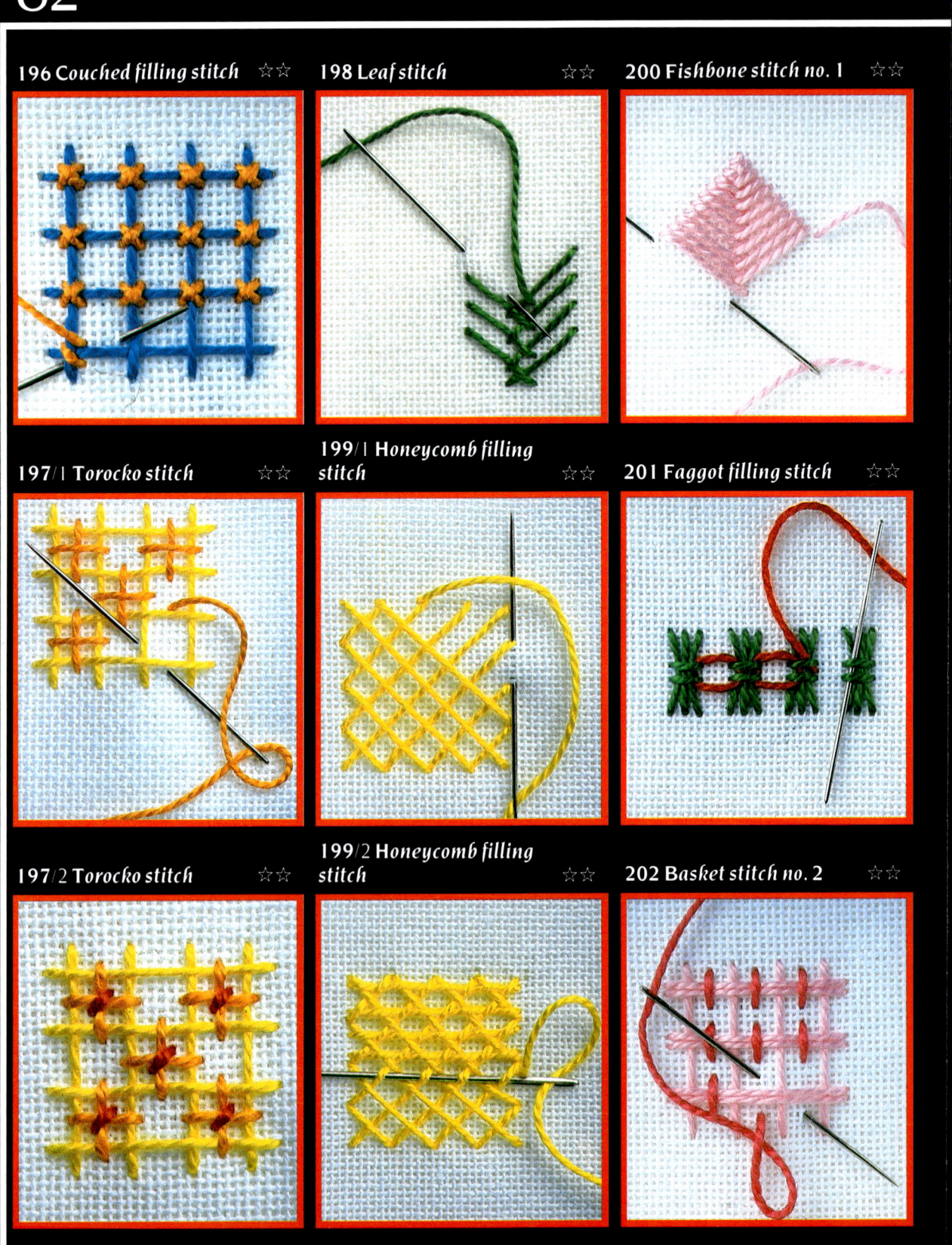

196 Couched filling stitch ☆☆

198 Leaf stitch ☆☆

200 Fishbone stitch no. 1 ☆☆

197/1 Torocko stitch ☆☆

199/1 Honeycomb filling stitch ☆☆

201 Faggot filling stitch ☆☆

197/2 Torocko stitch ☆☆

199/2 Honeycomb filling stitch ☆☆

202 Basket stitch no. 2 ☆☆

FILLING STITCHES 83

203 Flat stitch ☆☆

206 Buttonhole stitch shading ☆☆

208/2 Triangular Turkish stitch ☆☆

204 Damask darning ☆☆

207 Roumanian couching ☆☆

208/3 Triangular Turkish stitch ☆☆

205 Burden stitch ☆☆

208/1 Triangular Turkish stitch ☆☆

208/4 Triangular Turkish stitch ☆☆

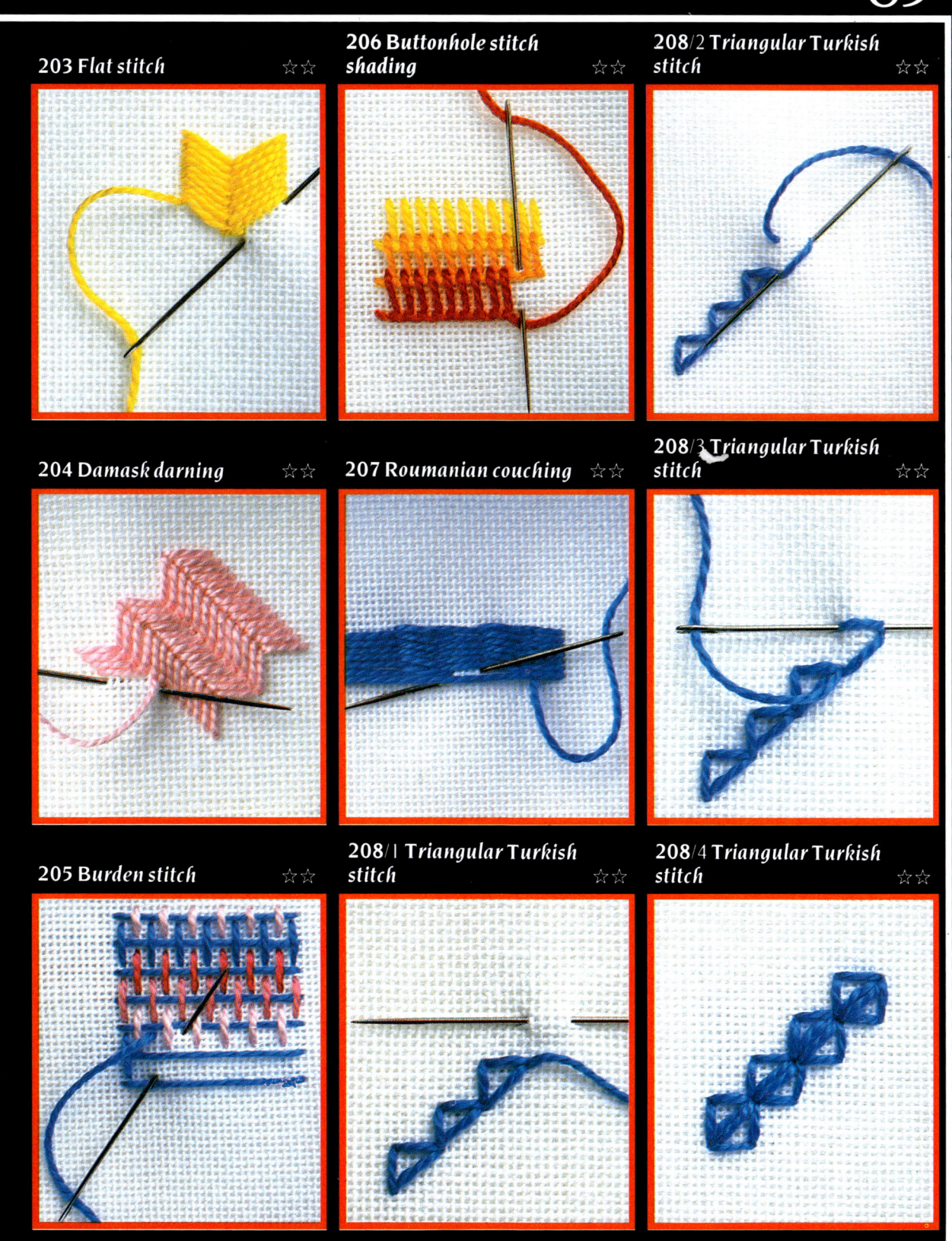

FABRIC STITCHES

209 Valerian stitch ☆☆

Valerian stitch is a filling stitch used on plain- and even-weave fabrics. It makes a trellis pattern of laid threads in the same way as trellis stitch *(see page 69)* but texture is added in the form of bullion knots *(see page 97)*. This stitch should be worked on fabric stretched in an embroidery hoop or frame to keep the foundation threads stable.

First make a grid consisting of long, horizontal straight stitches worked across the whole shape to be filled. Work vertical stitches at right angles across the horizontal stitches. Then work long, diagonal stitches from the top left to the bottom right of the shape, across each intersection of the grid. Then anchor the diagonal stitches to the fabric by working a diagonal bullion knot across every intersection. Valerian stitch can be monochrome, or a thread of contrasting colour can be used for the bullion knots.

210 Cretan open filling stitch ☆☆

Cretan open filling stitch is used on plain- and even-weave fabrics. Any type of embroidery thread can be used for this Cretan stitch. However, the foundation stitches must be worked in a firm rather stiff thread, and the fabric should be stretched in an embroidery hoop or frame. A variation of Cretan stitch *(see page 13)*, it makes an attractive chessboard pattern. First work a foundation of evenly spaced straight vertical stitches across the shape. Then take a second thread to work blocks of Cretan stitch over the foundation, without picking up any ground fabric. Work the blocks in diagonal lines, from the top right-hand corner to the bottom left-hand corner on each journey. The tension of the Cretan stitch blocks is important as they should make a neat, perfectly regular chessboard pattern.

211 Griffin stitch ☆☆☆

Griffin stitch is a laid stitch used on plain- and even-weave fabrics. It has an attractive, lacy appearance and can be used for filling shapes of any size. It is essential to work the foundation grids accurately and the fabric should be stretched in an embroidery hoop or frame to keep the stitches stable. First, cover the shape with long, vertical and horizontal straight stitches to form a squared grid. Then work a diagonal grid over the squared grid. Use vertical rows of running stitch *(see page 12)* to couch down the diagonal grid at alternate intersections, where the diagonal grid does not cross the first grid. Where the two grids cross, interlace a second thread round the intersections to make a circular shape. Do not pick up the ground fabric during the interlacing. Then, take the thread through to the back of the work so that it emerges close to the next intersection to be threaded. Use a blunt-ended tapestry needle for the interlacing to avoid splitting the stitches of the two grids.

212 Trellis couching ☆☆☆

Trellis couching is a laid-work stitch used for filling areas on plain- and even-weave fabrics. It makes a solid filling of stitches secured by a trellis pattern and is often worked in two colours. Any type of embroidery thread can be used but the stitch will look more effective if worked in a lustrous thread, such as silk. The shape is filled by a foundation of laid stitches worked in two journeys. These stitches should be worked evenly and should completely cover the ground fabric. It is essential to work this stitch in an embroidery hoop or frame, keeping the fabric stretched rather tightly. This will ensure that the foundation and trellis threads remain stable while the couching is in progress. The trellis threads are also worked in two journeys and should be placed at an angle to the foundation stitches. The trellis threads are then couched down at the intersections using a tiny straight stitch.

213 Eyelet stitch ☆☆

Eyelet stitch is a filling stitch used on plain-weave fabrics. It makes an attractive, lacy pattern and the fabric chosen should be fairly fine. Small interlocking circles are marked on the fabric and then pairs of back stitches *(see page 14)* are worked alternately along the circumference and into the centre of each circle: twelve pairs of stitches are worked into the centre, and twelve pairs around the edge. The stitches should be pulled quite firmly during the embroidery, so that small holes are created at the centre of the circles. Two stitches on one eyelet double as two stitches on an adjoining one. Eyelet stitch is often used to fill the background area, while the design itself is left unworked. A fine cotton embroidery thread should be used for this stitch.

214 Laid-work ☆☆☆

Laid-work is an extension of couching *(see page 8)* and is used for covering large and small areas of plain- or even-weave fabric. The shape is completely covered with a foundation of long threads (or laid threads), which are then anchored by a second, often contrasting, thread, which is then couched down in a pattern. It is a technique which is often used in metal thread embroidery, when the gold or silver thread is couched down over a foundation of silk or cotton laid threads. Laid-work should always be worked on fabric stretched in an embroidery hoop or frame to keep the foundation stitches even during the couching.

The simplest form of laid-work is shown. The shape is filled with vertical surface satin stitch *(see page 72)*, worked in two journeys, with the threads laid closely and evenly together. Horizontal satin stitches are worked over this foundation at regular intervals and are then couched down by a finer thread to make a simple, striped pattern. A more decorative form of laid-work is described under trellis couching *(see above)*, which makes a pretty trellis pattern. A great many different patterns can be made by the couching thread, such as swirls, scales and chevrons, but the couched threads should lie at an angle to the laid threads to ensure that they are firmly anchored.

215 Twisted lattice stitch ☆☆☆

Twisted lattice stitch is a composite filling stitch used on plain- and even-weave fabrics. It makes an attractive lattice pattern and is often worked in

FILLING STITCHES

two contrasting colours or weights of thread. Twisted lattice stitch should be worked with the fabric stretched in an embroidery hoop or frame, as the lacing will tighten the stitches and pucker the fabric if it is not. Worked on the same principle as twisted lattice band *(see page 52)*, the foundation is formed in a different way. A grid is made first by working evenly spaced, long diagonal stitches in one direction over the shape to be filled. A second set of stitches is then worked at right angles to the first set of stitches. The second set interlaces with the first, by passing over and under them in the same way as darning. Lastly, a second thread is laced through the lattice grid in the same way as for twisted lattice band.

216 Maltese cross filling stitch ☆☆☆

Maltese cross filling stitch is a complex, interlaced filling used on plain- and even-weave fabrics. It is rather similar to Maltese cross *(see page 105)* but its construction is slightly different.

A foundation grid of interlocking, diagonal straight stitches is worked first to cover the entire shape. First complete the diagonal stitches running in one direction and then work those running in the opposite direction, passing them over and under the first set in exactly the same way as for darning a sock. The spacing of the grid is important; pairs of diagonal stitches should be worked close together, making a plaid pattern on the fabric of large and small squares and rectangles. Alternatively, the foundation can be made of horizontal and vertical stitches, if preferred. The Maltese crosses are made by interlacing around the corners of the large squares and then repeating the journey, in the same sequence, to make a double interlacing. The interlacing thread can be of a contrasting weight, colour and texture to that used for the foundation, or a metallic thread can be effective. A blunt-ended tapestry needle should be used for the interlacing to avoid splitting the foundation stitches. After each square is interlaced, the needle is taken through the fabric to emerge at the next large square. The crosses can be worked on alternate squares to give a more open effect.

217 Diamond filling stitch ☆☆☆

Diamond filling stitch makes a pretty, knotted filling and is used on plain- and even-weave fabrics. It is worked on a foundation of long horizontal stitches and can be used as a detached filling. However, this stitch is difficult to keep even and a better effect is achieved if the fabric is picked up when each knot is made. To keep the rows even, guide-lines may need to be marked on the fabric if the threads cannot be counted. Each row of the filling is made in two journeys. On the first, work a horizontal foundation stitch from the right to the left of the shape, bringing the thread through the fabric just below the left-hand corner to commence the return journey. Make a coral knot *(see coral stitch, page 9)* at the corner of the shape, leaving a loop of thread; then make a second coral knot over the foundation stitch. Continue along the row, working knots at regular intervals and leaving loops between them. Then repeat the process to fill the shape, anchoring the loops of the previous row with the knots. Diamond filling stitch is a little tricky to work at first, as regularity is very important, but it is a stitch well worth practising.

218 Battlement couching ☆☆☆

Battlement couching is a type of couching used for filling areas of plain- and even-weave fabrics. The complex arrangement of differently coloured laid threads makes a bold filling for simple shapes but it should not be attempted if the shape has an intricate or sharply curved outline. It consists of a foundation of alternate vertical and horizontal threads laid on the fabric to make an overlapping lattice. Follow the sequence shown very carefully. The foundation is worked in four contrasting or toning colours of thread; a fifth thread is used to couch down the top rows of laid threads with a short diagonal stitch.

At first sight, battlement couching looks rather complicated but once the sequence of the foundation has been mastered, it will prove quite easy to effect. This stitch should always be worked with the fabric stretched tautly in an embroidery hoop or frame to keep the laid threads stable. Any type of embroidery thread can be used but the stitch will be simpler to work if the thread is twisted, rather than stranded. The secret of good battlement couching is to spend considerable time laying the foundation threads: they should have an even tension and cross each other at perfect right angles.

219 Chevron stem stitch ☆☆☆

Chevron stem stitch is a composite filling stitch used on plain- and even-weave fabrics. It is essential to work this stitch with the fabric stretched tautly in an embroidery hoop or frame to ensure that the foundation threads do not move. The foundation consists of threads laid horizontally and evenly right across the space to be covered. Stem stitch *(see page 9)* is then worked in a zigzag pattern over these threads (the needle should enter the fabric at only the beginning and end of each row). Use a blunt-ended tapestry needle for the stem stitch threading to avoid splitting the stitches on the foundation row. The rows of stem stitch should be packed closely together to completely cover the foundation threads. The pattern is made more apparent if two tones of thread are used for the zigzags. A firm thread must be used for the foundation but any type of thread can be used for the stem stitch. The small 'V' shapes at the top and bottom of the stitching should also be filled in with stem stitch, keeping the pattern correct. Chevron stem stitch can be used to fill any size shape. After the stitching is completed, the edge should be neatened by outlining the shape with another line stitch: twisted chain stitch *(see page 21)*, double knot stitch *(see page 36)* or pearl stitch *(see page 21)* would all make a neat edge.

86 FABRIC STITCHES

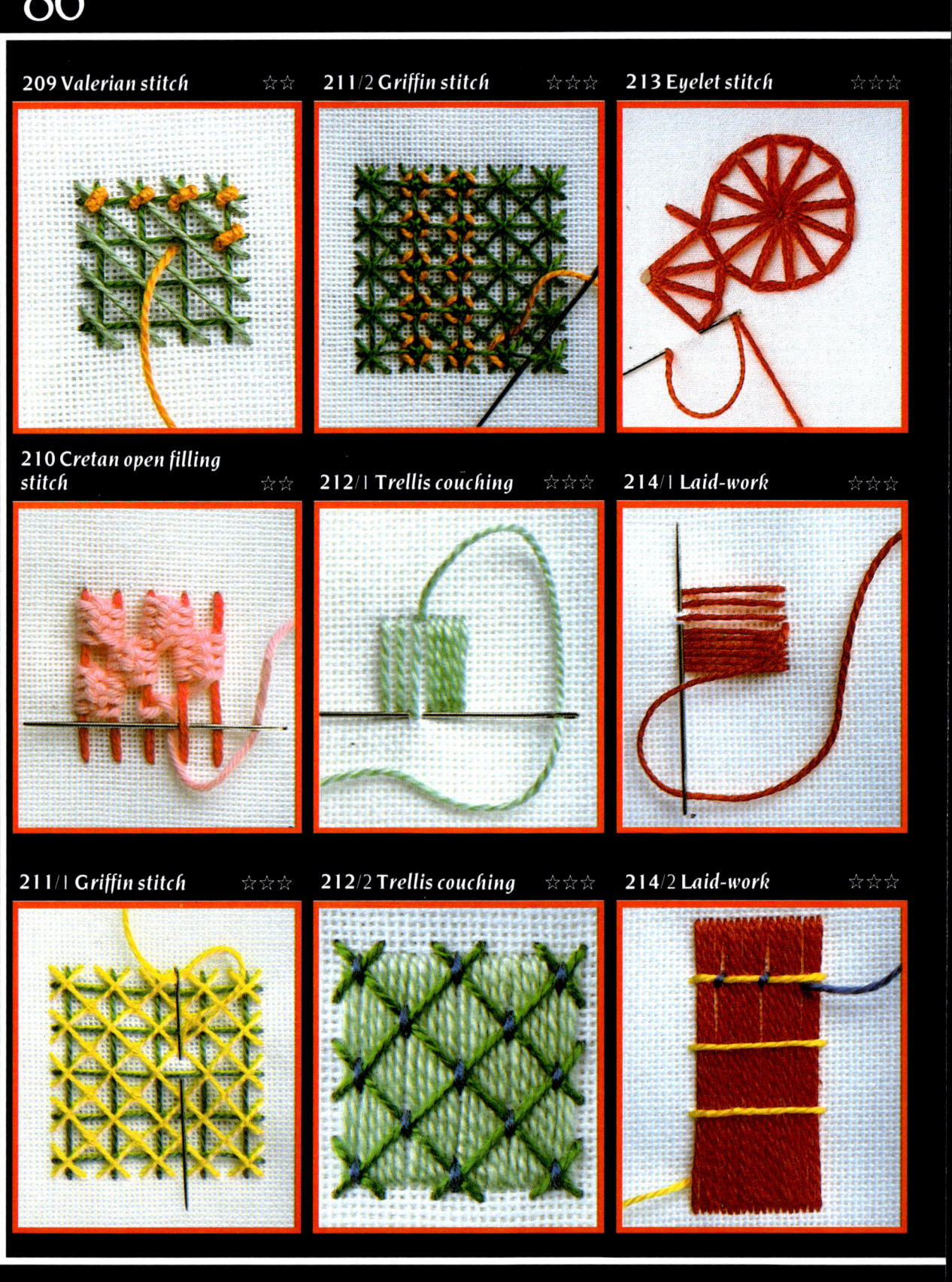

209 Valerian stitch ☆☆

210 Cretan open filling stitch ☆☆

211/1 Griffin stitch ☆☆☆

211/2 Griffin stitch ☆☆☆

212/1 Trellis couching ☆☆☆

212/2 Trellis couching ☆☆☆

213 Eyelet stitch ☆☆☆

214/1 Laid-work ☆☆☆

214/2 Laid-work ☆☆☆

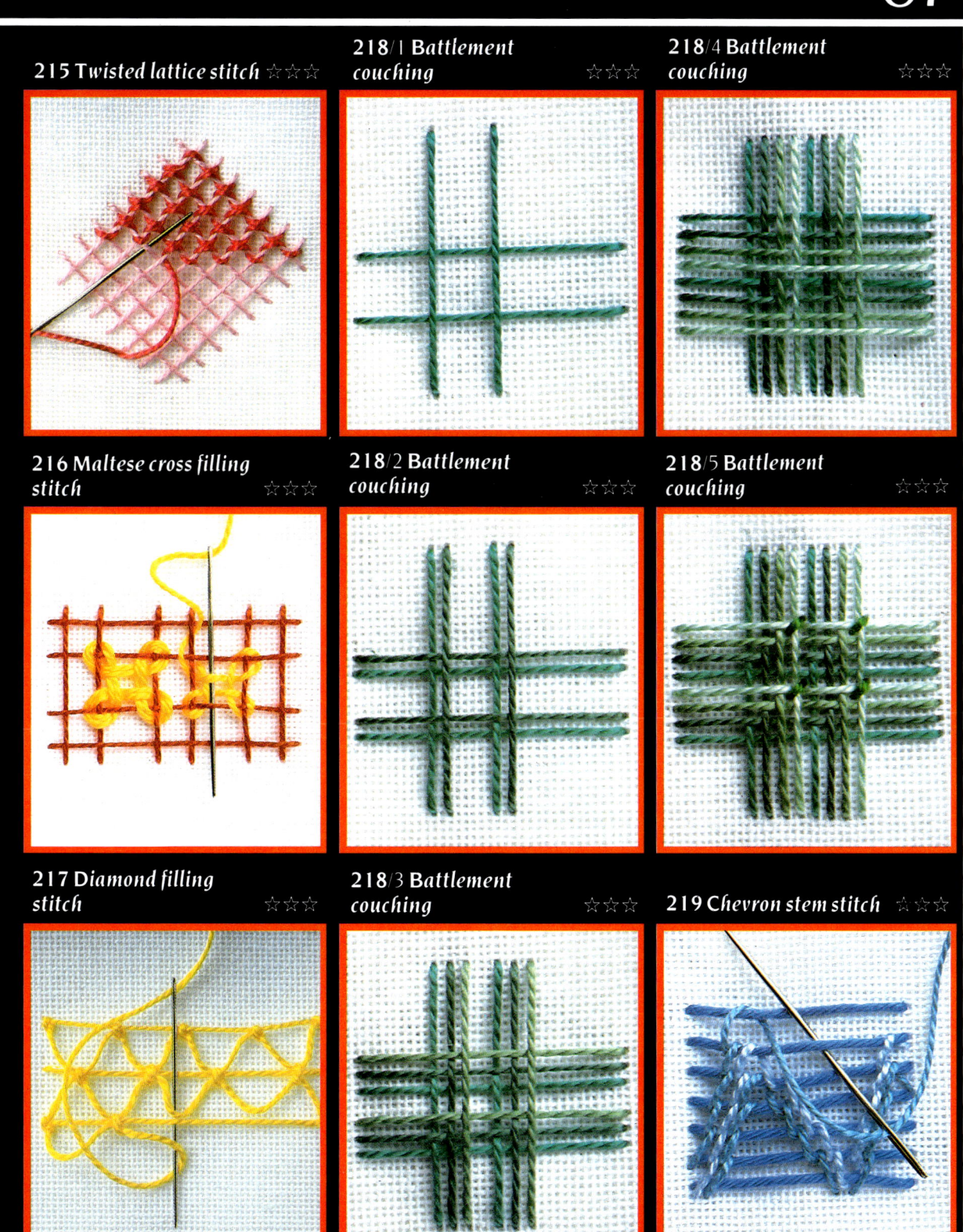

FILLING STITCHES **87**

215 Twisted lattice stitch ☆☆☆

218/1 Battlement couching ☆☆☆

218/4 Battlement couching ☆☆☆

216 Maltese cross filling stitch ☆☆☆

218/2 Battlement couching ☆☆☆

218/5 Battlement couching ☆☆☆

217 Diamond filling stitch ☆☆☆

218/3 Battlement couching ☆☆☆

219 Chevron stem stitch ☆☆☆

Detached filling stitches

220 Hollie stitch
also known as holy stitch and holy point

Hollie stitch is a detached filling stitch used on the surface of plain- and even-weave fabrics. Outline the shape to be filled with a row of chain stitch *(see page 12)* worked quite small; this makes a foundation to anchor the filling to the fabric. Work the filling rows in alternate directions, working a long, horizontal straight stitch from chain to chain from right to left across the shape. Then bring the thread through the next chain at the left-hand side to make a row of looped knotted stitches over both the thread and the chain stitch. The ground fabric should not be picked up. Continue in this way with alternate long stitches and rows of loops, working the second and subsequent rows of loops over both the long stitch and the previous row of loops. Secure the last row by working the loops through the chain stitch row at the lower edge of the shape.

221 Ceylon stitch

Ceylon stitch is a detached filling stitch used on plain- and even-weave fabrics. It can be worked to give two different effects: if the stitches are spaced widely apart, the filling appears light and lacy; if the stitches are placed close together, the filling looks like a piece of stocking stitch knitting. A horizontal straight stitch worked right across the top of the shape forms the anchoring foundation. Rows of looped stitches are then worked from left to right without picking up any fabric. At the end of each row of loops, the needle must be taken through the fabric to emerge again at the beginning of the next row; this is always at the left-hand side of the shape. This process keeps the filling anchored to the fabric at the sides. Ceylon stitch is often worked in bands of two or more colours. A round, twisted thread works well with this stitch, although a stranded thread can also look attractive.

222 Rich buttonhole stitch
also known as loop buttonhole filling stitch

Rich buttonhole stitch is a detached filling stitch with a honeycomb pattern used on plain- and even-weave fabrics. A foundation of parallel horizontal straight stitch rows is worked right across the area to be covered. A row of closely packed buttonhole stitch *(see page 13)* is then worked over the first horizontal stitch. The ground fabric must not be picked up. Buttonhole stitch is then worked over the subsequent straight stitches, and, at intervals along the rows, a longer, vertical stitch connects the row being worked to the row above. These long verticals are arranged to give a honeycomb effect.

223 Fancy buttonhole filling
also known as fancy buttonhole stitch

Fancy buttonhole filling is used as a detached filling on the surface of plain- and even-weave fabrics and also to fill a space in cut-work. When worked on the surface of the fabric, the shape must first be outlined with a row of back stitch *(see page 14)* to form a foundation to anchor the filling. The area is then covered with rows of mirrored buttonhole stitch *(see page 32)*. Work the first row of the filling from left to right into the foundation stitches without picking up any ground fabric. Then work the second and subsequent rows in alternate directions, catching each pair of stitches into the loops lying between the pairs of stitches on the first row; do not enter the fabric. When the last row is reached, the loops should be worked through the line of back stitch to anchor the filling; the filling is also anchored at the sides. When used for filling a shape in cut-work, buttonhole edging stitch *(see page 108)* serves as the anchoring foundation.

224 Knotted buttonhole filling
also known as knotted buttonhole filling stitch

Knotted buttonhole filling is used as a detached filling on plain- and even-weave fabrics and to fill spaces in cut-work. When used as a detached filling, the shape is outlined by a row of back stitch *(see page 14)* to anchor the filling. The filling rows are worked in alternate directions and consist of buttonhole stitches *(see page 13)* overstitched individually on the same journey by a second buttonhole stitch worked at an angle to the first. This second stitch forms a knot and should be pulled tight before proceeding to the next stitch. After the first row, which is worked into the back stitch foundation, the subsequent rows are worked into the loops of the previous rows. The needle should enter the fabric only at the beginning and end of the stitching. The last row is secured by working the loops through the back stitch line at the bottom. When this filling is used for cut-work, buttonhole edging stitch *(see page 108)*, worked round the raw edges, forms the anchoring foundation.

225 Trellis filling stitch

Trellis filling stitch is a detached filling used on plain- and even-weave fabrics; it has a lacy, knotted appearance. Outline the shape first with a row of evenly spaced chain stitch *(see page 12)* to make a foundation to anchor the filling. Work the first row of the filling into the chain stitch at the top of the shape by making alternate loops and knots from left to right. Tighten the knots before proceeding to the next loop by pulling the working thread to the right. When the edge is reached, and without entering the fabric, take the thread down to the next chain stitch and continue the knots and loops in the opposite direction. This row and all subsequent rows are worked into the loops on the preceding row. When the lower edge is reached, work the last row of loops through the chain stitch edge to anchor it.

226 Venetian filling stitch

Venetian filling stitch is a detached filling used on plain- and even-weave fabrics. A firm, twisted thread, such as pearl cotton, is most suitable. First, outline the shape with a row of back stitch *(see page 14)*, working each stitch quite large. Work the first row of filling from left to right over the outline. Make a loose buttonhole loop and then work a group of four buttonhole stitches *(see page 13)* into it. Continue in this way until the right-hand side of the shape is reached. Then take the thread behind the outline row to anchor it before working the return journey. On this journey, make loose loops between each group of buttonhole stitches on the preceding row by working a row of open buttonhole filling *(see below)*. These two rows alternate to form the filling, and the thread must be taken behind the outline stitches at the end of every row to anchor the filling firmly. When the lower edge of the shape is reached, pick up the outline stitches with the last row of loops.

227 Lace filling stitch ☆☆
also known as honeycomb stitch
Lace filling stitch makes a detached filling and is used on plain- and even-weave fabrics. It makes a twisted, lacy pattern and benefits from being worked in an embroidery frame or hoop, as it is rather unstable. Work the stitch with a round, twisted thread, such as pearl cotton.

Each row is worked in two journeys. On the first journey, a series of twists and loops are worked from left to right, picking up the fabric only at the right-hand side of the area to anchor the filling. On the second journey, the working thread is brought back across the shape to enter the fabric just below the point where the previous row began. This thread is then wound round each loop on the completed row. When the bottom of the shape is reached, a little fabric is picked up to secure the filling. An outline of stem stitch *(see page 9)* or back stitch *(see page 14)* is worked to define the shape.

228 Surface darning ☆☆
Surface darning is a detached filling stitch used on plain- and even-weave fabrics. It makes a closely woven surface best suited to small shapes. The fabric should be stretched in an embroidery hoop or frame to keep the foundation stitches taut while the darning is being worked. First work a foundation of surface satin stitch *(see page 72)* over the shape, placing the stitches evenly and very close together. Then weave a second thread regularly in and out of these stitches in exactly the same way as a stocking darn. With the second thread, pick up the fabric only at the sides of the shape, so that the filling is quite detached except at the edges. Any type of embroidery thread can be used but, for the foundation stitches, a round, twisted thread, such as pearl cotton, is less likely to split during the darning. The satin stitches can be darned in groups of three by working three horizontal rows below one another before changing the sequence of 'unders' and 'overs' and working the next three rows. This method gives a heavier effect and makes a close basket-work pattern.

229 Open buttonhole filling ☆☆☆
Open buttonhole filling is used as a detached filling stitch on plain- and even-weave fabrics. It can be used to fill a space in cut-work, although it is less even and stable than fancy buttonhole filling *(see page 88)* or knotted buttonhole filling *(see page 88)*. This stitch gives a very open, lacy effect and, even when worked as a surface stitch, it requires some practice to keep an even tension between the stitches. The filling consists of rows of ordinary buttonhole stitch *(see page 13)* worked in alternate directions into the loops of the previous rows. The needle enters the fabric only at the outline of the shape.

230 Detached buttonhole stitch ☆☆☆
Detached buttonhole stitch is a detached filling stitch with a rather heavy, solid appearance. It is worked on plain-weave fabrics and is useful when a raised, closely embroidered shape is needed. Work two horizontal straight stitches across the top of the area to be covered. Next, work a row of buttonhole stitch *(see page 13)* over these strands from left to right, without entering the ground fabric. The stitches should be worked closely together and a firm, quite stiff thread is needed. Work the subsequent rows of buttonhole stitch into the loops of each preceding row, alternately from side to side of the shape, with only the edge stitches passing through the fabric. The shaping is worked by increasing or decreasing stitches at the end of each row; the edge stitches should be worked with a slightly tighter tension than the detached stitches. This stitch can be made more raised by working it over a padding of felt. The felt is cut slightly smaller than the shape, but following the same contours, and then tacked in position on the ground fabric before the embroidery is started.

231 Raised honeycomb filling stitch ☆☆☆
Raised honeycomb filling stitch is a detached filling stitch used on plain- and even-weave fabrics and should be worked in an embroidery hoop or frame. It makes a very raised trellis pattern and looks its best when worked with quite a fine thread. A trellis of long vertical and horizontal straight stitches is worked over the shape first. These stitches are then overcast *(see overcast stitch, page 28)*, covering first the vertical and then the horizontal stitches. The thread is then taken round each long stitch on the trellis in a crossed spiral shape, beginning with the vertical stitches. The spirals are worked round the horizontal stitches and then overcast with a fine thread.

232 Filet stitch ☆☆☆
Filet stitch is a detached filling stitch worked on plain- and even-weave fabrics. It makes a geometric, lacy filling with raised knots and is best used for filling small shapes. It is a difficult stitch to work evenly and care must be taken to tighten each knot after it is worked. The needle enters the fabric only round the edges of the shape. Loops are made in diagonal rows from right to left and then back again, commencing at the top left-hand corner of the shape. They are then linked together by a knotted stitch. The loops can be pinned to the fabric to keep them even while the knots are being made, or held down by the thumb. Any type of embroidery thread can be used but a round thread, such as pearl or soft cotton, is easiest to work with.

90 FABRIC STITCHES

220 Hollie stitch ☆

223 Fancy buttonhole filling ☆☆

226 Venetian filling stitch ☆☆

221 Ceylon stitch ☆

224 Knotted buttonhole filling ☆☆

227 Lace filling stitch ☆☆

222 Rich buttonhole stitch ☆☆

225 Trellis filling stitch ☆☆

228 Surface darning ☆☆

DETACHED FILLING STITCHES

91

229 Open buttonhole filling ☆☆☆

231/1 Raised honeycomb filling stitch ☆☆☆

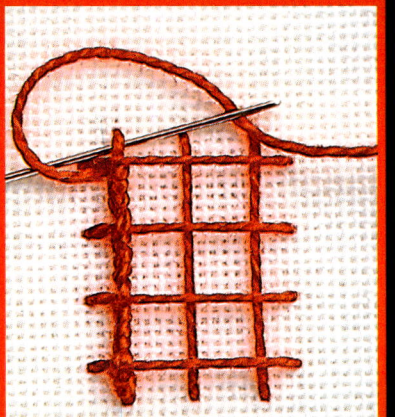

231/3 Raised honeycomb filling stitch ☆☆☆

230/1 Detached buttonhole stitch ☆☆☆

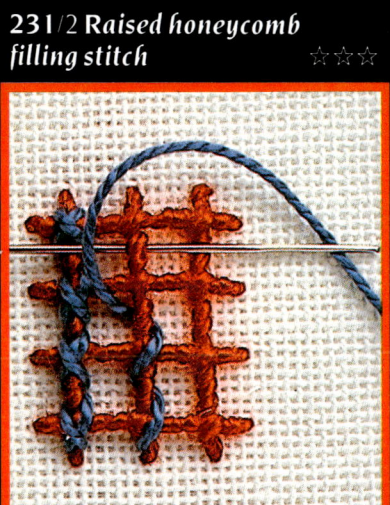

231/2 Raised honeycomb filling stitch ☆☆☆

232 Filet stitch ☆☆☆

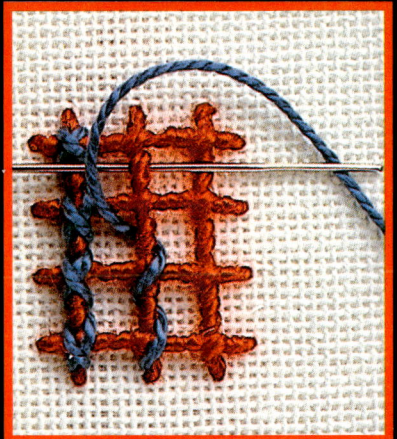

230/2 Detached buttonhole stitch ☆☆☆

Isolated stitches

233 Daisy stitch ☆
also known as **detached chain stitch, lazy daisy stitch, tail chain stitch, loop stitch, tied loop stitch, picot stitch** *and* **knotted knot stitch**
Daisy stitch is a useful isolated stitch used on plain- and even-weave fabrics. It is actually a single chain stitch *(see page 12)* and is often known by the name of detached chain stitch. This stitch is commonly used in groups to make leaf and flower shapes, hence the name 'daisy', but it also makes a pretty powdering when the stitches are scattered at random over a shape. It also makes the foundation row for threaded chain stitch *(see page 44)*. It is formed in exactly the same way as chain stitch but each loop is anchored to the fabric by a small vertical stitch before the next loop is made. The size of the stitch is determined by the weight of embroidery thread used and any type of thread will work well. An isolated knot stitch, such as a French knot *(see page 96)* or a Chinese knot *(see page 96)* can be worked in the centre of each stitch in a contrasting colour for a more decorative effect. Daisy stitch can also be worked on top of an area of flat canvas work, where an accent stitch is needed.

234 Four-legged knot stitch ☆
Four-legged knot stitch is an isolated stitch used on plain- and even-weave fabrics. It is an attractive small stitch and resembles an upright cross with a knot at the centre. It is used as an accent stitch, worked closely in a row for a narrow border, and as a powdering. The stitches can be arranged in a regular all-over pattern, or they can be scattered at random for a less formal effect. The size of the stitch varies according to the weight of the thread used but it is equally effective on any scale. First, make a vertical straight stitch; then loop a horizontal stitch round the vertical to form the knot, before making the last arm of the cross. The knot should not pick up any ground fabric.

235 Straight stitch ☆
also known as **stroke stitch**
Straight stitch is an isolated stitch which is used on plain- and even-weave fabrics. Individual satin stitches *(see page 24)* are worked to any length and in any direction to create a textured area. This stitch is particularly useful for depicting grass and other landscape details, and any type of embroidery thread can be used, depending on the weight of the ground fabric. Straight stitch should not be worked too large as the stitches then look loose and untidy. This stitch can easily be shaded and blended by using close shades of one colour, or two or three fine, contrasting threads can be used in the same needle. Lengths of differently coloured stranded thread can be split into strands and then rearranged to give a subtle blending of colours.

236 Cross and twist stitch ☆
also known as **moss stitch**
Cross and twist stitch is an isolated stitch used on plain- and even-weave fabrics. It is most effective when worked on a small scale with a fine, rounded thread, such as coton à broder, and can be used as an accent stitch or as a powdering to decorate a shape. This stitch can also be placed side by side to form a border and the top stitch can be worked in a contrasting colour or different weight of thread. An ordinary cross stitch *(see page 14)* is worked as a foundation and is then crossed by a longer vertical stitch. The vertical stitch enters the ground fabric only at the top and bottom and is looped round the centre of the cross stitch, making a twisted chain stitch *(see page 21)* with a long tail. As a variation, the vertical stitch can be made shorter.

237 Dot stitch ☆
also known as **simple knot stitch, rice grain** *and* **seed stitch**
Dot stitch is an isolated stitch used on plain- and even-weave fabrics. As the name suggests, it makes a small, raised dot, which can be used individually as an accent stitch, worked in rows as a dotted outline, or scattered at random to make a powdering. It is very simple to work and any type of thread can be used, the choice depending on the weight of the ground fabric and the size of dot required. It is made by working two back stitches *(see page 14)* into the same holes. When used as an outline, a tiny space of fabric is left between each pair of stitches. Dot stitch is often used as an accent stitch when line stitches or fillings need extra decorative spots of colour.

238 Square boss ☆
also known as **raised knot**
A square boss is a simply worked isolated stitch used on plain- or even-weave fabrics. It can be used individually, where extra colour or texture is needed, or several can be scattered over a shape to make a pretty knotted powdering.
First work a cross stitch *(see page 14)* and then cover each arm with a back stitch *(see page 14)* worked through the fabric. A round, twisted thread, such as pearl cotton, makes this stitch appear more raised than a flat, stranded thread. When used as a powdering, the crosses can all be worked on one journey and a contrasting thread can then be used for the back stitch.

ISOLATED STITCHES

239 Long-tailed daisy stitch ☆
Long-tailed daisy stitch is a simple variation of daisy stitch *(see above)* and is used on plain- and even-weave fabrics. It is worked in the same way as daisy stitch but the loop is made smaller and the anchoring stitch is elongated to form a 'tail'. It is often worked in circular groups, with either the tails or the loops at the centre. It also looks attractive as a powdering, or worked closely together in rows with the loops alternately at the top and bottom of the rows. As with daisy stitch, any type of embroidery thread can be worked easily.

240 Ermine stitch ☆
Ermine stitch is a useful isolated stitch used on plain- and even-weave fabrics. It earned its name from the ermine tail effect it makes when worked in black thread on a white fabric ground and it is often used as a filling stitch in black-work. The stitch can be used as an accent stitch or it can be worked in rows to make a delicate border. When used as a filling, it is worked regularly, often on an even-weave fabric, and it also makes a pretty powdering when scattered at random on plain-weave fabrics. It is simple to work and consists of a long, vertical straight stitch, which is then covered by an elongated cross stitch *(see page 14)* about one-third of the size of the straight stitch. The cross stitch should be placed slightly above the base of the vertical stitch.

241 Berry stitch ☆
Berry stitch can be used on any type of fabric. It can act as an accent stitch on canvas: scatter berry stitch on top of a smoothly stitched background of tent stitch *(see page 121)* or Gobelin stitch *(see page 125)*. On fabric, berry stitch can be used as a powdering, worked close together in a line, or massed together to fill a solid area. It is a very simple stitch, consisting of one large daisy stitch *(see page 92)* and one small daisy stitch worked inside the first one. A twisted thread, such as pearl or soft cotton, will help keep the circular shape of each berry stitch intact.

242 Fly stitch ☆
also known as 'Y' stitch and open loop stitch
Fly stitch is an isolated stitch often worked in rows and used on plain- and even-weave fabrics. Each stitch is worked very easily: a V-shaped loop is made and then tied down by a vertical straight stitch. The tying stitch can vary in length to produce different effects. The fly stitches can be arranged side by side to make a horizontal row, or can be worked underneath each other to make a vertical row. The stitches can touch one another or be spaced apart at a regular interval. Isolated fly stitches can be used to make a pretty powdering, either spaced evenly or scattered at random over a shape. Each stitch can be decorated by the addition of a French knot *(see page 96)* or a Danish knot *(see page 97)* in a contrasting thread. Any type of thread can be used for this stitch although the size of the stitch and the weight of the ground fabric must be taken into account.

243 Twisted satin stitch ☆
Twisted satin stitch is a useful isolated stitch worked on plain- and even-weave fabrics. It can be used alone as an accent stitch, sprinkled over a shape; worked in close rows where texture is needed in a satin stitched area; or worked solidly as a filling. Twisted satin stitches can also be arranged to make a motif, such as a flower or wheel shape. It is very simple to work and consists of an individual vertical satin stitch *(see page 24)* and a second stitch that twists round it and shares the same holes in the fabric. The second stitch passes through the fabric only at the top and bottom. Any type of embroidery thread can be used but, when the stitch is used alone, a coarse thread highlights the twists more effectively. An interesting two-colour effect can be made by working the stitches underneath first in one colour, then adding the twisted stitches in a contrasting colour on a second journey. The two-coloured effect is only possible when the stitches are spaced apart.

244 Crown stitch ☆
Crown stitch is an isolated stitch used on plain- and even-weave fabrics. It can be used as a powdering, to give a delicate texture to an area, or it can be arranged in rows, possibly combined with a line stitch to make a border. Any type of embroidery thread can be used for this stitch, the choice depending on the size of stitch required and the weight of the ground fabric. Crown stitch can be worked in two ways. The first method is to work a fly stitch *(see above)* and then add two slanting straight stitches at the base. The slanting stitches are placed at each side of the vertical line of the fly stitch and pass over the loop. The second method is to work the three bottom straight stitches, radiating from the same hole, and then work the top stitch to pass under them, without picking up any ground fabric. Whichever method you choose, the finished stitch will look exactly the same.

94 FABRIC STITCHES

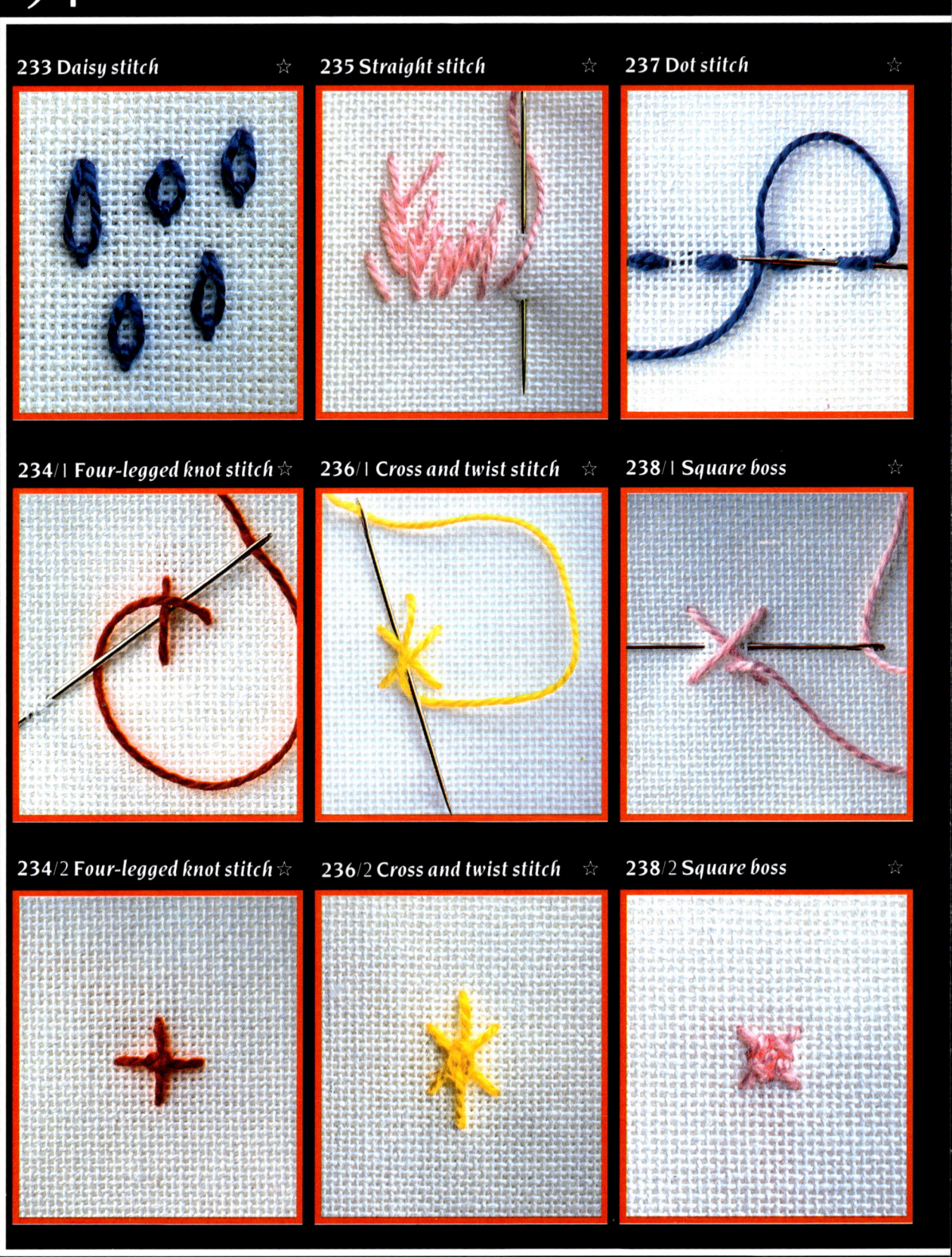

233 Daisy stitch

235 Straight stitch

237 Dot stitch

234/1 Four-legged knot stitch ☆

236/1 Cross and twist stitch

238/1 Square boss

234/2 Four-legged knot stitch ☆

236/2 Cross and twist stitch

238/2 Square boss

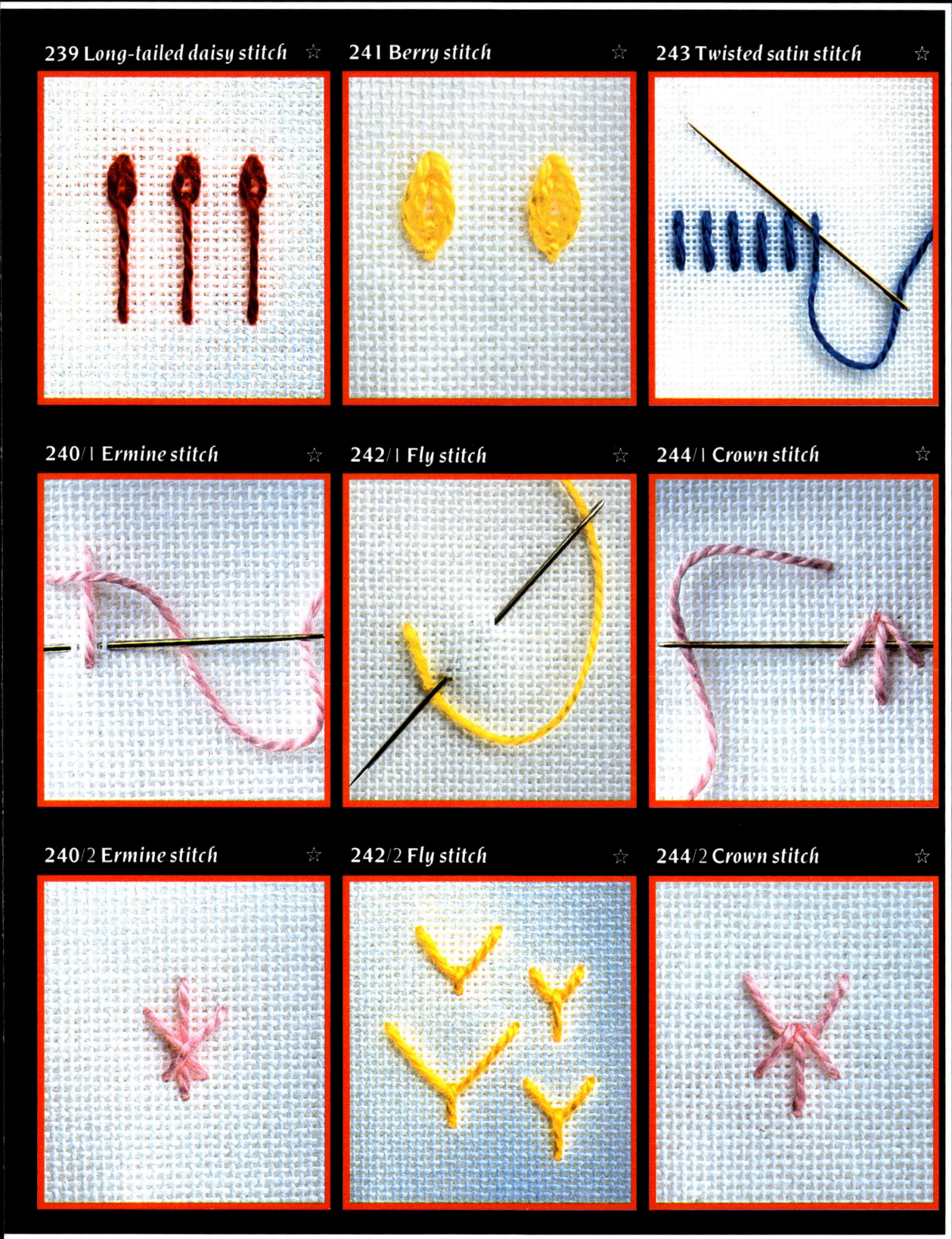

ISOLATED STITCHES 95

239 Long-tailed daisy stitch
241 Berry stitch
243 Twisted satin stitch
240/1 Ermine stitch
242/1 Fly stitch
244/1 Crown stitch
240/2 Ermine stitch
242/2 Fly stitch
244/2 Crown stitch

245 God's eye stitch ☆☆

God's eye stitch is an isolated stitch used on plain- and even-weave fabrics. It is similar in construction to ribbed spider's web *(see page 100)* and makes a bold, raised diamond shape with a long tail. It is used as an accent stitch where extra colour or texture is needed and it can be scattered over a shape to make a heavy powdering. Any type of thread can be used but a round, twisted thread, such as pearl cotton, makes the raised effect more pronounced. A foundation cross with a long lower arm is made first and then the thread is brought through at the centre where the stitches cross. A spiral line of back stitch *(see page 14)* is then worked over the four arms of the cross until they are completely covered, without picking up the ground fabric.

246 French knot ☆
also known as French dot, knotted stitch, twisted knot stitch *and* wound stitch
and long-tailed French knot
also known as long tack knot stitch *and* Italian knot stitch

A French knot is an isolated stitch used on plain- and even-weave fabrics. It is a neat, raised knot, which has many uses. It can be used as an accent stitch, as a powdering, massed together to make a solidly textured area, and worked closely in rows to make an outline. It can also be used over an area of canvas stitching, where extra texture or dots of contrasting colour are needed. Any type of thread can be used and the weight of the thread will determine the size of the finished stitch. Interesting effects can be made when French knots are massed together. To achieve this, work each knot with three or four contrasting threads placed through the needle at the same time.

A French knot is a little tricky to work and some practice will be needed to perfect the stitch. Work the knot with the fabric stretched in an embroidery hoop or frame to leave both hands free for the working. Bring the thread through the fabric and, if you are right-handed, hold it taut with the left hand, while twisting the needle round it two or three times with the right hand. Then tighten the twists, turn the needle and insert it back into the same place in the fabric, still keeping the thread taut, and pull the needle through. The thread slides through the twists to make the knot.

A long-tailed French knot is made in a similar way. The needle is held down a short distance away from the place where the thread emerges and the twists are made round it. The needle is then inserted into the fabric at the spot where it has been held; the twists are pushed down the needle, and the needle is then taken through the fabric, leaving a knot with a long tail.

247 Chinese knot ☆☆
also known as Pekin knot, forbidden knot *and* blind knot

The Chinese knot is an isolated stitch used on plain- and even-weave fabrics. It can also be used to accent areas of canvas work by stitching it onto an area already covered by embroidery. This stitch closely resembles the French knot *(see above)* but the Chinese knot is flatter and more shapely.

Chinese knots are characteristic of the rich silk embroideries of China, where they were worked very small and massed together to texture large areas. They were often worked in rows to create beautiful borders, with each row set close to the next one. Subtle colour variations in the silk thread resulted in a delicate shading. The name blind knot reputedly derives from the fact that Chinese embroiderers stitched this knot on such a minute scale over large areas of fabric that eventually their eyesight was affected.

The Chinese knot is easy to work, especially if the fabric is stretched in an embroidery hoop or frame. A simple, loose loop is made round the needle and tightened after the needle has entered the fabric but before it is pulled right through. Hold the loop down on the fabric with the left thumb, while pulling the needle through the fabric. This stitch works well with any type of embroidery thread; choose the thread according to the effect required. A stranded cotton or silk will give a flatter knot, while a rounded thread, such as pearl cotton or tapestry wool, will make a raised knot.

248 Sword-edging stitch ☆☆

Sword-edging stitch is an isolated stitch used on plain- and even-weave fabrics. It makes an elongated cross and is used as a powdering or worked close together to make a soft outline stitch. It is very quick and easy to work and consists of a loose straight stitch, which is pulled into a 'V' shape by a second stitch. The choice of thread depends on the size of the stitch and the effect desired. A round thread, such as soft or pearl cotton, makes sword-edging stitch stand out more from the background than a flat, stranded thread.

ISOLATED STITCHES

249 Swedish split stitch ☆☆
also known as **detached split stitch**
Swedish split stitch is an isolated stitch used on plain- and even-weave fabrics. It can be used in different ways: as an accent stitch; arranged to form a flower shape; scattered over a shape to make a powdering; or used as a solid filling stitch in the same way as long and short stitch *(see page 72)*. It is like split stitch *(see page 9)* in construction but two threads are used at once in the needle, so the same thread restrictions do not apply. A long straight stitch is made, which is then split with the needle between the two threads, and a downward slanting stitch anchors it to the fabric. Different effects can be created by using two contrasting threads in the needle, or by working the straight stitches on one journey and using a second colour for the splitting stitches.

250 Danish knot ☆☆
also known as **Danish knotted stitch** *and* **double knot**
A Danish knot is an isolated stitch used on plain- and even-weave fabrics. It is made by first working a foundation of short diagonal stitches from bottom right to top left; the knot will be made over this. The needle is then brought through the fabric close to the diagonal stitch and two looped stitches are made over the foundation, without picking up any ground fabric. The needle then re-enters the fabric before the next stitch is made. This stitch makes quite a raised, robust knot, which is accentuated by the use of a round, twisted thread, such as pearl cotton. It can be worked as an accent stitch, as a powdering or massed together to create a densely textured area. When it is worked solidly, different weights and colours of thread can be used to make an interesting surface.

251 Bullion knot ☆☆☆
also known as **bullion stitch, caterpillar stitch, coil stitch, knot stitch, post stitch, worm stitch, Porto Rico rose** *and* **grub knot**
A bullion knot is an isolated stitch used on plain- and even-weave fabrics. It is a long, coiled knot which can be used as an accent stitch; as a powdering; massed together to make a densely textured filling; worked close together to make a heavy outline; or used on top of an area of flat canvas work, where extra texture or splashes of colour are needed. Any type of embroidery thread can be used; the weight of the thread determines the size of the finished knot. Three or four contrasting fine threads can be threaded through the needle at the same time to create some interesting effects with this stitch.

A bullion knot is a little tricky to work and some practice will be needed to perfect it. It is better to work bullion knots on fabric which is stretched in an embroidery hoop or frame, thus leaving both hands free to work the knot. Bring the thread to the surface and insert the needle a short distance away, so that the point emerges at the same place as the thread. The distance between the point where the needle is inserted and the place where the thread emerges determines the length of the knot. Coil the thread round the needle six or seven times and then pull the needle carefully through the coil, which should be firmly held down on the fabric with the left thumb (if you are right-handed). Gently pull the working thread in the opposite direction to tighten the coils and insert the needle in exactly the same place as before. The coil of thread should now lie neatly on the surface. A rather thick needle with a small eye should be used so that it will pass easily through the coil. By coiling the thread many more times round the needle a different type of bullion knot can be created. The coil will be too long to lie flat on the fabric and will make a small hump instead of a long knot.

252 Turk's head knot ☆☆☆
A Turk's head knot is an isolated stitch used on plain- and even-weave fabrics. It makes a large, complex knot, which should be worked in a firm, twisted thread for maximum effect. Bring the thread to the surface of the fabric and work the sequence of loops. Then pass the needle in and out of these loops in the order shown. Pull the working thread through gently to tighten the knot before returning through the fabric directly below the knot. Turk's head knots are normally worked alone where an accent of colour and texture is needed but they can be massed together to fill a shape. They can also be used to decorate canvas work, by working them on top of previously stitched areas.

98 FABRIC STITCHES

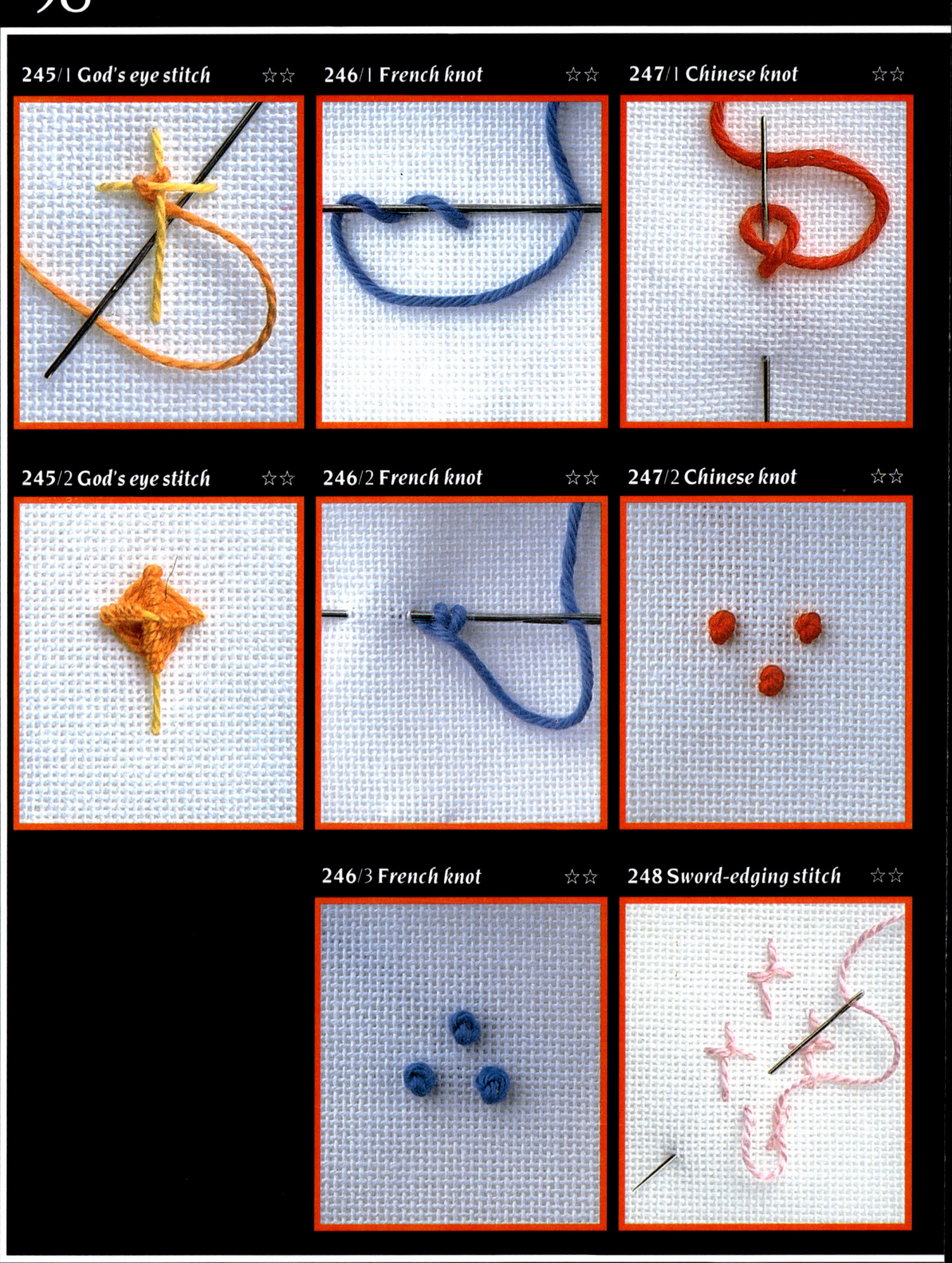

245/1 God's eye stitch ☆☆

246/1 French knot ☆☆

247/1 Chinese knot ☆☆

245/2 God's eye stitch ☆☆

246/2 French knot ☆☆

247/2 Chinese knot ☆☆

246/3 French knot ☆☆

248 Sword-edging stitch ☆☆

ISOLATED STITCHES

99

249 Swedish split stitch ☆☆

251/1 Bullion knot ☆☆☆

252/1 Turk's head knot ☆☆☆

250/1 Danish knot ☆☆

251/2 Bullion knot ☆☆☆

252/2 Turk's head knot ☆☆☆

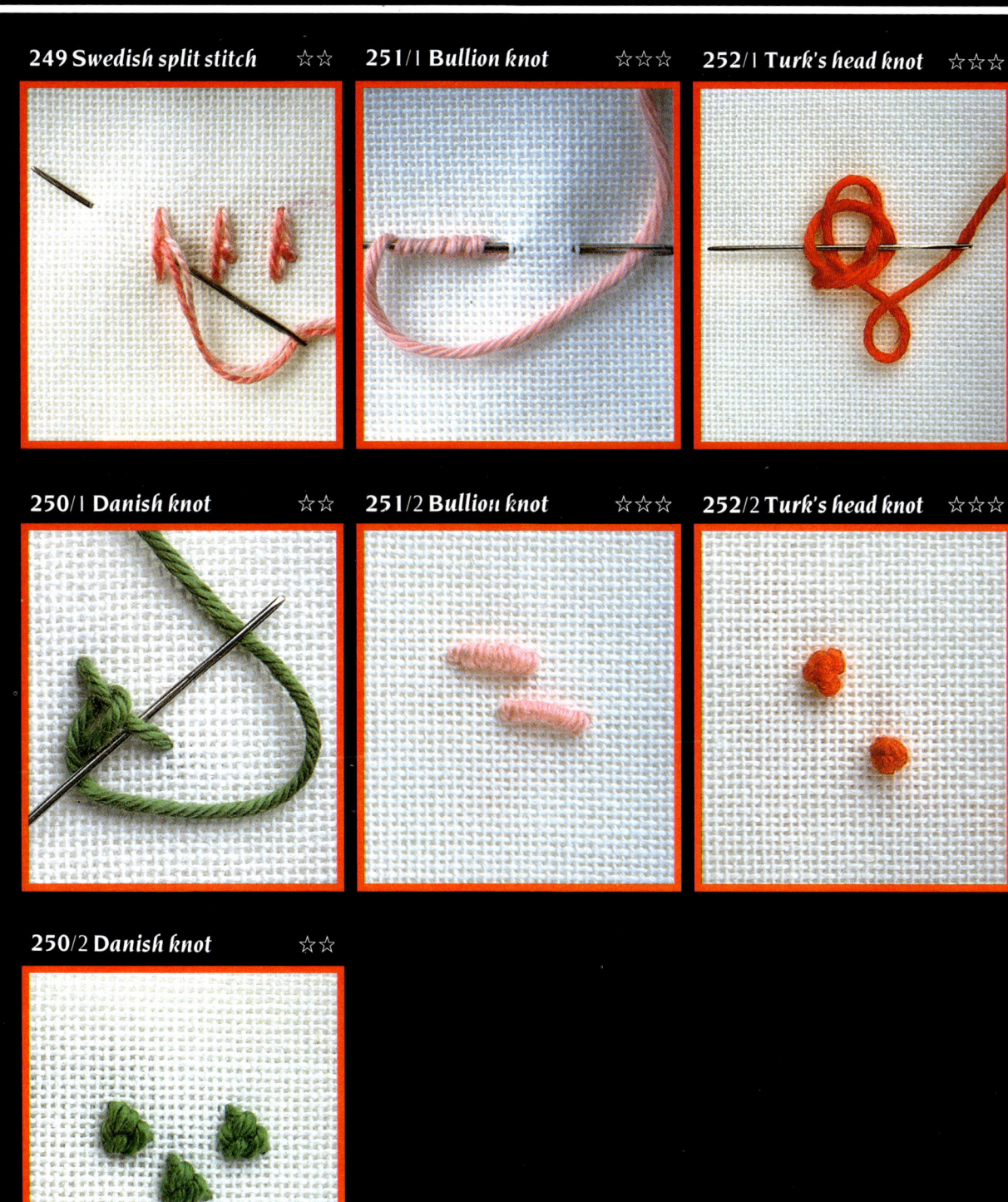

250/2 Danish knot ☆☆

Motif stitches

253 Russian chain stitch ☆
also known as **three chain stitch**
Russian chain stitch is a motif stitch which can also be used as a lightweight border. Always used on plain- and even-weave fabrics, it is suitable for use with any type of embroidery thread, depending on the size of the stitch and the weight of the background fabric. As indicated by its name, this stitch is found on Russian embroideries, often in conjunction with rows of ordinary chain stitch. The stitch is composed of three daisy stitches *(see page 92)* grouped together. Work the top daisy stitch first and then work the bottom stitches at an angle into the first stitch. When worked as a horizontal border, the Russian chain stitches are worked side by side, with the top daisy stitch pointing upwards. When used vertically, they are placed underneath each other, the top daisy stitch again pointing upwards.

254 Spider's web ☆
also known as **woven wheel, woven spot** *and* **woven spoke stitch**
A spider's web is a motif stitch used on plain- and even-weave fabrics. It makes a raised, circular shape like a spider's web and can be used alone as an accent stitch, or worked in a number of different sizes to powder a shape. A foundation of spokes is made first: these should be of an odd number and should radiate from the central point of the circle. The stitched example shows how to make a five-spoke wheel by using a fly stitch *(see page 93)* combined with two straight stitches. A seven- or nine-spoke wheel can be made by working evenly spaced straight stitches from the circumference of the circle to the centre point. After completion of the foundation, a second thread is woven under and over the spokes, beginning at the centre and working outwards; be careful not to pick up any ground fabric. The second thread can be of a contrasting colour and a round thread, such as pearl cotton, makes the spider's web stand out more from the background than a flat, stranded thread. Use a blunt-ended tapestry needle for the second thread to avoid splitting the foundation stitches.

255 Ribbed spider's web ☆
also known as **ribbed wheel** *and* **backstitched spider's web**
A ribbed spider's web is a motif stitch used on plain- and even-weave fabrics. It makes a ribbed, circular shape, which is heavier in appearance than an ordinary spider's web *(see above)*. It can be used alone as an accent stitch of colour or texture, or can be scattered over a shape to make a powdering. First, a foundation of spokes is made and these should be of an even number. The stitched example shows how to make a foundation of eight spokes by working a cross stitch *(see page 14)* over a St George cross stitch *(see page 68)*. A larger or smaller number of spokes can be made by working evenly spaced straight stitches from the circumference of the circle to the centre point. After the foundation has been completed, a spiral of back stitch *(see page 14)* is worked over the spokes from the centre outwards. The second thread passes through the fabric only at the beginning and end of the spiral, and a blunt-ended tapestry needle should be used to avoid splitting the foundation stitches. A round thread, such as pearl or soft cotton, accentuates the ribbed appearance of this stitch better than a flat, stranded thread.

256 Vell stitch ☆
Vell stitch is a motif stitch used on plain- and even-weave fabrics. It makes an attractive barred cross which can be used in a variety of ways. The stitch can be used individually to provide an accent of colour; it can be worked as a border, either horizontally or vertically; or it can be scattered over an area to make an unusual powdering. It is extremely quick and simple to work and consists of a vertical straight stitch crossed by three shorter, horizontal straight stitches. Any type of embroidery thread can be used, providing that it is compatible with the size of stitch required and the weight of the ground fabric.

257 Point Russe stitch ☆
Point Russe stitch is a motif stitch used on plain- and even-weave fabrics. It is a quick and simple stitch to work and makes a pretty fan-shaped pattern. They can be used individually as accent stitches, or be arranged in vertical or horizontal rows to make a filling over shapes of any size. Any type of embroidery thread can be used, the choice depending on the weight of the ground fabric and the size of the stitch required. The stitch consists of four diagonal straight stitches arranged in pairs at both sides of a vertical straight stitch. These stitches should touch at the bottom and fan out evenly at the top. Point Russe stitch looks very attractive when worked in a colour which contrasts strongly with that of the background fabric.

258 Buttonhole wheel ☆
also known as **wheel stitch**

A buttonhole wheel is a circular form of buttonhole stitch *(see page 13)*. Stitched on plain- and even- weave fabrics, it works best on a fabric with quite a loose weave. Work buttonhole stitches in a circle, passing each vertical stitch through the same central space. The fabric threads are pulled back by the stitching and a neat circular hole forms at the centre. If the fabric weave is too close for this to happen easily, the hole may have to be started with the help of a stiletto.

A variation of this wheel, used on a very open, heavy fabric, is worked in the same way but a pair of cross threads are left in the centre of the hole, forming a cross at the centre of the wheel.

259 Cup stitch ☆

Cup stitch is a raised motif stitch used on plain- and even-weave fabrics. It can also be used to decorate and add depth to an area of canvas which has already been covered by a flatter stitch. It makes a circular, raised band rather like a cup and is best worked in a fairly firm thread to make it stand out well from the background. A foundation of three straight stitches, which forms a triangle, is first worked – this can vary in size depending on the size of cup being worked. The thread is then brought back to the surface of the fabric just outside the triangle and looped stitches are made over the foundation, without entering the ground fabric. The looped stitches are worked closely together right round the triangle and the more closely they are packed, the more three-dimensional the effect will be. A second row of looped stitches can be worked into the loops on the first round to make a higher cup.

260 Point à la minute ☆

Point à la minute is a motif stitch used on plain- and even-weave fabrics. It makes a heavy, raised, upright cross, which can be used as an accent stitch where extra colour or texture is needed, or scattered at random over a shape to make an impressive powdering. A rounded thread, such as pearl or soft cotton, shows this stitch off to its best advantage; a stranded thread, however, gives a flatter appearance. This stitch should be worked with the fabric stretched in an embroidery hoop or frame to prevent puckering.

A foundation of four vertical and four horizontal straight stitches is made forming a cross. Each of these stitches is then whipped very closely, using the same thread and without picking up any ground fabric *(see whipped back stitch, page 16)*. For added emphasis point à la minute can also be worked on top of an area of smoothly stitched canvas work.

261 Star of David ☆

Similar to star darn *(see below)*, Star of David is an interwoven six-pointed star. Used on plain- and even-weave fabrics, the star can be used alone where an accent of colour or a different weight of thread is needed, or several stars can be scattered over an area to make a light powdering. It consists of two interlocking triangles made of straight stitches. Any type of embroidery thread can be used to make a Star of David, providing that it is compatible with the size of the stitch and the weight of the ground fabric. To emphasize the shape, the central hexagon could have a solid filling made of massed Chinese knots *(see page 96)* or closely worked satin stitches *(see page 24)* in a contrasting colour or weight of thread.

262 Star darn ☆
also known as **woven star**

A star darn is a simple motif stitch used on plain- and even-weave fabrics. It makes an interwoven five-pointed star shape which can be used alone or scattered over a shape to form a rather attractive powdering. It consists of five straight stitches, arranged as shown. Any type of embroidery thread can be used for a star darn, providing that it is compatible with the size of stitch and the weight of the ground fabric.

A star darn can be decorated by working an isolated stitch, such as a Danish knot *(see page 97)* or daisy stitch *(see page 92)*, in the centre.

263 Tulip stitch ☆

Tulip stitch is a motif stitch used on plain- and even-weave fabrics. The stitch makes a pretty floral motif, as its name suggests, and can be worked in any type of embroidery thread. The motifs can be used alone to add a splash of colour; worked in a straight line to make a border; or scattered over a shape as a powdering. This stitch is quick and easy to work. First work a large daisy stitch *(see page 92)* with quite a long tail. Then make three stitches of different lengths from one side of the daisy stitch to the other, passing under the tail; do not pick up any fabric.

102 FABRIC STITCHES

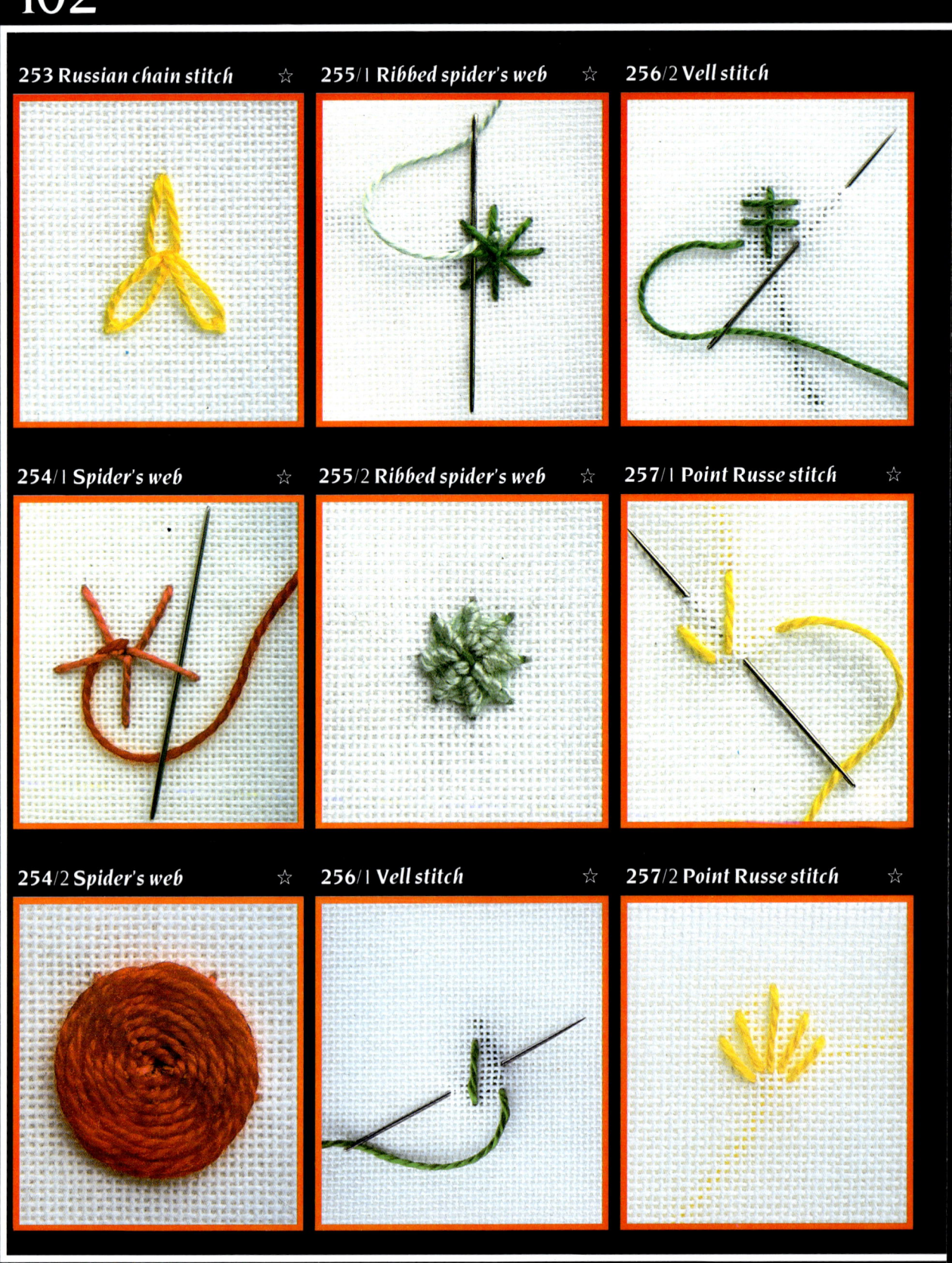

253 Russian chain stitch

255/1 Ribbed spider's web

256/2 Vell stitch

254/1 Spider's web

255/2 Ribbed spider's web

257/1 Point Russe stitch

254/2 Spider's web

256/1 Vell stitch

257/2 Point Russe stitch

MOTIF STITCHES **103**

258 Buttonhole wheel
260/1 Point à la minute
262 Star darn
259/1 Cup stitch
260/2 Point à la minute
263/1 Tulip stitch
259/2 Cup stitch
261 Star of David
263/2 Tulip stitch

264 Star ☆☆

A star is, strictly speaking, a tailoring finish which is worked to strengthen a garment where there is a point of stress; for example, at the top of a pleat on a skirt. This stitch is, however, a highly decorative way of arranging satin stitches *(see page 24)* and it can be used in embroidery where a solidly stitched geometric motif is needed. Care should be taken to make the points of the star perfectly even. The stitches should cover the star shape completely: no ground fabric should show through. Any type of embroidery thread can be used for this stitch, but a lustrous thread, such as stranded cotton, enhances the light and shade effect created by the positioning of the satin stitches. Similar stitches are the crow's foot *(see below)* and the sprat's head *(see below)*.

265 Rose stitch ☆☆

Rose stitch is a motif stitch used on plain- and even-weave fabrics. It makes a raised flower shape, which can be used as an accent stitch to provide extra colour and texture in the same way as cup stitch *(see page 101)*, although the effect is flatter. This stitch can also be used to make an unusual powdering to decorate a shape. A round, twisted thread, such as pearl cotton, makes the flowers stand out more from the background than a flat, stranded cotton.

First make a French knot *(see page 96)* to form the centre of the flower. Then work concentric circles of overlapping straight stitches around the French knot. The number of circles necessary depends on the size of rose stitch required; they can be in a different colour from the central knot.

266 Wrapped cross stitch ☆☆

Wrapped cross stitch is a motif stitch used on plain- and even-weave fabrics. It is very simple to work and has a very raised, distinctive appearance. Interesting effects can be achieved by using a textured or heavy metallic thread for the wrapping. This stitch should be worked with the fabric stretched in an embroidery hoop or frame to prevent the wrapping from distorting and puckering the ground fabric. A large ordinary cross stitch *(see page 14)* forms the foundation, and this is then wrapped by the same or a second thread, without picking up the ground fabric. A fairly substantial thread should be used for the foundation cross but a supple thread is preferable for the wrapping.

267 Sprat's head ☆☆

A sprat's head is, strictly speaking, a triangular tailoring finish which is worked to strengthen part of a garment where there is a point of stress; for example, at the top of a pleat on a skirt. This stitch is, however, highly decorative and can be used in embroidery where a small, heavily stitched, geometric shape is needed. Follow the method of working shown, taking care to make the two outside stitches the same length. The remaining stitches should be worked closely together and should completely cover the triangular shape. Any type of embroidery thread can be used to work a sprat's head but a lustrous thread, such as stranded cotton, or a shiny one like pearl cotton, enhances the light and shade effect created by the positioning of the different slants of the stitches. A similar stitch is a crow's foot *(see below)*.

268 Crow's foot ☆☆

A crow's foot is, strictly speaking, a triangular stitch used in dressmaking to strengthen a garment where there is a point of stress, for example, at the top of a pleat on a skirt. The stitch is, however, very decorative and can be used in embroidery where a small, heavily stitched geometric shape is needed. Care should be taken to make the three outside stitches equal in length. The remaining stitches should be worked closely together and should completely cover the triangular shape without revealing the fabric beneath. Any type of embroidery thread can be used to work a crow's foot but a lustrous thread, such as stranded cotton, or a shiny one like pearl cotton, will enhance the light and shade effect made by the different directions of the stitches. A similar stitch is a sprat's head *(see above)*.

MOTIF STITCHES

269 Interlaced cross stitch ☆☆☆
Interlaced cross stitch is a composite motif stitch used on plain- and even-weave fabrics. It looks very attractive when worked adjacent to or combined with a simpler stitch, such as ordinary cross stitch *(see page 14)* or herringbone stitch *(see page 8)*, to make a border. A foundation of four interlocking straight stitches, which make a diamond shape, is worked first. A second thread, often of a contrasting weight or colour, is then interlaced through the foundation, without picking up any ground fabric. A blunt-ended tapestry needle should be used for the second thread to avoid splitting the foundation stitches. A rounded embroidery thread, such as pearl cotton, should be used for the straight stitches but any type of thread can be used for the interlacing stitches. Use a metallic thread for the interlacing to make this stitch look rich and decorative.

270 Catherine wheel ☆☆☆
This stitch is a modern interpretation of an open needlepoint filling used during the nineteenth century for whitework, particularly on Ayrshire embroidery. The stitch was originally used as an open filling but is now used as a surface stitch on plain- and even-weave fabrics. The appearance of the new stitch is similar to the nineteenth-century version, but the structure is rather different. A circle of blanket stitch *(see page 13)*, with the loops facing inwards, is worked first, in a heavy thread. A second row is then worked inside the first in a thinner thread through the loops of the first circle; this row is detached from the ground fabric. Four straight stitches are then worked through the fabric and span the centre space to make eight 'spokes'. Finally, two rings of back stitch *(see page 14)* are worked over the spokes to form the 'hub' of the wheel, without picking up the ground fabric. The central portion of the wheel is anchored to the fabric at the beginning and end of the back stitch. This stitch needs a firm thread to make it stand out from the fabric. Two thicknesses should be used: a heavy thread for the outside circle, and a lighter one for the remainder of the stitching.

271 Square-laced herringbone stitch ☆☆☆
Square-laced herringbone stitch is a large, isolated stitch used on plain- and even-weave fabrics. It is used as a heavy accent stitch, worked side by side for a border, or worked solidly to fill a rectangular shape. It is a development of interlaced cross stitch *(see above)* although the finished effect is much heavier. This stitch should be worked with the fabric stretched in an embroidery hoop or frame to avoid puckering. It is worked in one colour and weight of thread throughout but the needle should be changed to a blunt-ended tapestry needle for the lacing to avoid picking up any threads of ground fabric. First, work a square foundation of herringbone stitch *(see page 8)*: bring the thread through at the bottom left-hand corner of the area and lace the square tightly together. This tightening gives the stitch quite a different look from interlaced cross stitch. After the lacing is completed, take two vertical stitches over the centre, without picking up the fabric, and then cross these with two horizontal stitches. Pass the thread through the fabric behind the interlacing to anchor the stitch to the fabric at the centre.

272 Maltese cross ☆☆☆
Maltese cross is a motif stitch used on plain- and even-weave fabrics. It makes an intricate, interlaced cross shape, which can be used alone or as a rich, heavy border. When used as a border, the motifs can be joined at the corners or placed edge-to-edge for a more solid effect.

A foundation grid of crossed straight stitches is made first; the stitches must pass over and under each other in the sequence shown. The interlacing tightens up the grid, so work the stitches quite loosely on fabric that has been stretched in an embroidery hoop or frame and make sure that the grid is correctly worked before proceeding to the interlacing. The interlacing is worked in a similar way to interlaced herringbone stitch *(see page 65)*, and either the same thread or one of a contrasting weight, colour or texture is used; a metallic thread also looks very decorative. Use a blunt-ended tapestry needle for the interlacing to avoid splitting the foundation stitches. The motif can also be worked as a square by making the foundation stitches run vertically and horizontally, rather than diagonally.

106 FABRIC STITCHES

264 Star ☆☆

266/1 Wrapped cross stitch ☆☆

267/2 Sprat's head ☆☆

265/1 Rose stitch ☆☆

266/2 Wrapped cross stitch ☆☆

268/1 Crow's foot ☆☆

265/2 Rose stitch ☆☆

267/1 Sprat's head ☆☆

268/2 Crow's foot ☆☆

MOTIF STITCHES **107**

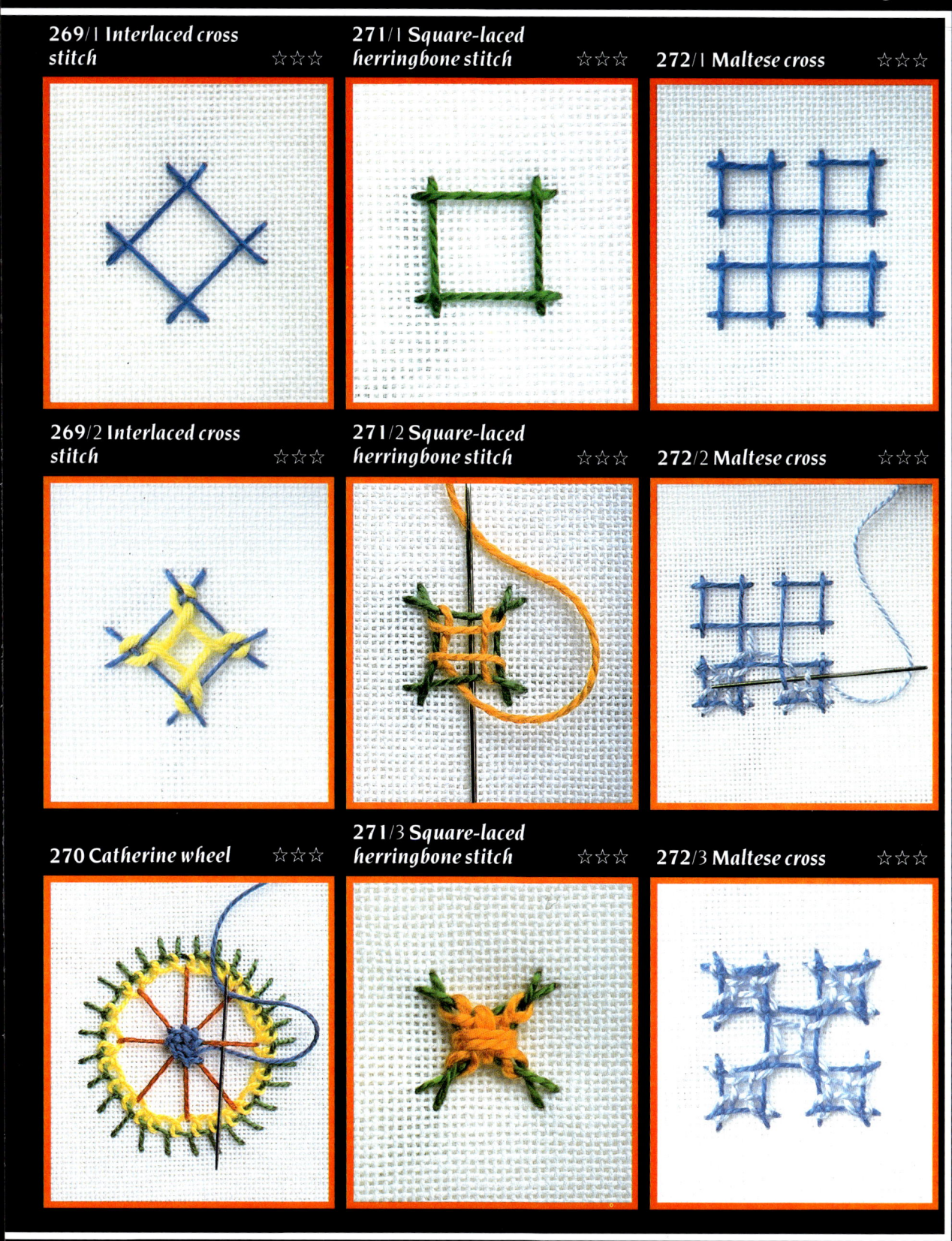

269/1 Interlaced cross stitch ☆☆☆

271/1 Square-laced herringbone stitch ☆☆☆

272/1 Maltese cross ☆☆☆

269/2 Interlaced cross stitch ☆☆☆

271/2 Square-laced herringbone stitch ☆☆☆

272/2 Maltese cross ☆☆☆

270 Catherine wheel ☆☆☆

271/3 Square-laced herringbone stitch ☆☆☆

272/3 Maltese cross ☆☆☆

Edging stitches

273 Looped edging stitch no.1 ☆
Looped edging stitch no.1 is worked on plain- and closely woven even-weave fabrics. It makes a neat, firm edging to a piece of fabric and is stronger than buttonhole edging stitch *(see below)*, although the appearance of both stitches is similar. It is often used in cut-work as it makes a good anchoring foundation for a lace filling stitch. Work from left to right over a tiny turned edge. Make a simple looped stitch along the edge and tighten each stitch by pulling the thread away from the body; this movement ensures that the loops fit neatly along the edge. Work the stitches close together. Any cotton embroidery thread can be used, providing that the weight of the thread is compatible with the fabric.

274 Loop picot ☆
also known as pinned picot
Loop picot is one of the simplest forms of picot and a firm, rounded thread should be used. It is worked from right to left of the area, which makes the buttonhole edging stitch *(see below)* to which it is usually attached a little more difficult to work but the picots much easier to effect. Once the place where the picot is to be worked is reached, insert a dressmaking pin into the fabric close to the last buttonhole stitch. Loop the thread under the pin, take a stitch into the fabric and adjust the loop for size. Secure the loop by passing the needle under it. Then tighten the working thread and continue with the edging stitch. The pin can be removed at this stage.

275 Ring picot ☆
Ring picots are easy to work and have a heavier appearance than other picot stitches. Any type of embroidery thread can be used but a flat stranded cotton gives a flatter picot than a rounded thread, such as pearl cotton. Buttonhole edging stitch *(see below)* is worked from right to left, as the picot is easier to work in this direction. Once the place is reached where the picot is to be worked, make a loop of working thread through a buttonhole loop three or four stitches back along the edging. This loop should be made fairly tight as the subsequent buttonholing enlarges it considerably. Then work close buttonhole stitches over the loop of thread until the edge of the fabric is reached. The resulting ring is then secured by the next buttonhole edging stitch.

276 Buttonhole edging stitch ☆
Buttonhole edging stitch is used to finish the edges of all types of cut-work, particularly Renaissance and Richelieu embroidery. Traditionally executed in white thread on a white fabric, cut-work is the term applied to work which has portions of the background fabric cut away around the stitched motifs; strengthening bars are then worked across the created spaces. Three or four straight stitches span the gap and are then covered by a row of buttonhole edging stitch to form a bar. This type of embroidery was popular during the sixteenth and seventeenth centuries and is probably the forerunner of needlemade laces. Cut-work appears to have originated in Italy or Flanders and examples of the technique were exported to the rest of Europe during the sixteenth century. By the seventeenth century, cut-work was found on most of the whitework samplers being produced in England. Broderie anglaise is another example of cut-work where buttonhole edging stitch can be used to make an edge before parts of the ground fabric are cut away. In this type of embroidery, the centre of the motifs (usually small circles or ovals), rather than the background around them, is cut away.

Buttonhole edging stitch consists of a row of closely packed buttonhole stitch *(see page 13)*, worked with the looped edge of the stitch next to the area to be cut away. If the fabric shows no sign of fraying, the shape is first outlined with running stitch *(see page 12)*, the fabric cut away close to this stitched line, and then the buttonhole edging stitch worked over the raw edge. For a fabric which looks as though it will fray, work the running stitch line and buttonhole edging stitch before cutting away the surplus fabric; always use very sharp scissors and cut very carefully. This method is also used for working a scallop-shaped edging on a piece of fabric.

277 Armenian edging stitch ☆☆
Armenian edging stitch is used as a decoration on the plain, hemmed edge of a piece of plain-weave fabric. Work from left to right and pull the working thread quite tight after each knot is completed. Like most edging stitches, Armenian edging stitch is most effective when the stitches are small and evenly spaced along the edge and when a smooth thread is used.

278 Plaited edge stitch ☆☆
Plaited edge stitch is worked on plain- and even-weave fabrics. It makes a decorative finish on the hemmed edge of a piece of fabric and is often used to ornament items of household linen. It is worked from left to right and makes a neat, knotted edge which can be worked with an open or closed finish. It can also be used to finish a raw edge, if the stitches are worked close together. A rounded thread, such as pearl or soft cotton, gives plaited edge stitch a heavier appearance than a flat, stranded thread.

279 Buttonhole picot ☆☆
also known as **Venetian picot**
Buttonhole picot makes a larger picot than bullion picot *(see below)* and a firm, rounded thread should be used. It is worked from right to left, which makes the buttonhole edging stitch *(see page 108)* which it usually decorates a little difficult to work but the picots themselves much easier to effect. When the place where the picot is to be worked is reached, insert a dressmaking pin into the fabric close to the last buttonhole stitch; this will anchor the next loop of thread while the buttonhole stitch is worked over it. Insert the needle through the loop and over the pin, making sure that the point of the needle passes over the working thread. Pull the needle through and tighten the resulting stitch well, as it forms the end of the picot. Then work closely packed buttonhole stitches along the loop until the edge of the fabric is reached, when buttonhole edging stitch is resumed. Remove the pin after the picot is completed.

280 Bullion picot ☆☆
Picot is an embroidery term referring to a small loop of twisted thread attached to an edging. This stitch and the following picots can be used in a variety of ways: to decorate a plain buttonhole stitch edge *(see page 13)*; for ornamenting a bar in cut-work and needlemade laces; or to add to a row of buttonhole stitch worked on the surface of the fabric, such as in appliqué. With the exception of woven picot *(see below)*, which is worked directly into the fabric, the picots are worked into the buttonhole stitch loops without entering the ground fabric.

Bullion picot is one of the easiest picots to work and a firm, rounded thread, such as pearl cotton, is very suitable. Work buttonhole stitches *(see page 13)* close together along the edge until the place where the picot is to be made is reached. Insert the needle into the upright of the previous buttonhole stitch and twist the thread five or six times round the point of the needle in exactly the same way as for a bullion knot *(see page 97)*. Place the left thumb over the coils (if you are right-handed) and pull the needle through completely before tightening the coils. The bullion is then secured by the next buttonhole stitch, which must be worked very close to the previous one.

281 Antwerp edging stitch ☆☆
also known as **knot stitch** *and* **knotted blanket stitch**
Antwerp edging stitch adds a decorative finish to the plain, hemmed edge of a piece of plain-weave fabric and is often used to ornament items of household linen, such as tablecloths and napkins. Work the stitch from left to right along the turned edge, using a fairly heavy, smooth thread. Additional rows of the stitch can be added for a deeper, lacy edging, or the outer row of loops can be whipped with a contrasting colour *(see whipped back stitch, page 16)*. Antwerp edging stitch can also be used as a lacy line stitch on the surface of the fabric.

282 Braid edging stitch ☆☆☆
Braid edging stitch makes a useful edging on the plain, hemmed edge of a piece of plain-weave fabric. It can be used to finish the edges of items of household linen, such as a tablecloth or napkin. This stitch is more difficult to work than Antwerp edging stitch *(see above)* or Armenian edging stitch *(see page 108)*, as the stitch is worked from right to left along the edge, which is itself facing away from the stitcher. The secret of working this stitch well is to leave the knot slack while the size of the loop is adjusted. After this has been done, tighten the knot firmly by pulling the thread outwards at right angles to the edge of the fabric. As with the two edging stitches mentioned above, the knots and loops should be evenly spaced and of a regular size, and some practice will be needed to achieve this. Care should also be taken in selecting thread: a firm thread is needed to keep the loops in shape. A fringe can be attached to the loops after the edging has been worked *(see fringed Antwerp edging stitch, page 29)*.

283 Woven picot ☆☆☆
Woven picots are rather large and, unlike other picots, are worked directly into the fabric edge. A firm, quite stiff, thread should be used for this stitch. Hold the edge of the fabric away from the body and make a loop of thread. Then insert a dressmaking pin over the loop and into the fabric to keep the loop firm. Slip the thread through the loop and tighten it to form the top of the picot. Then make a series of weaving movements until the edge of the fabric is reached. Each stitch should be tightened quite firmly to make the picot solidly worked and rather stiff. The end of the thread should be finished off as invisibly as possible and the pin removed.

110 FABRIC STITCHES

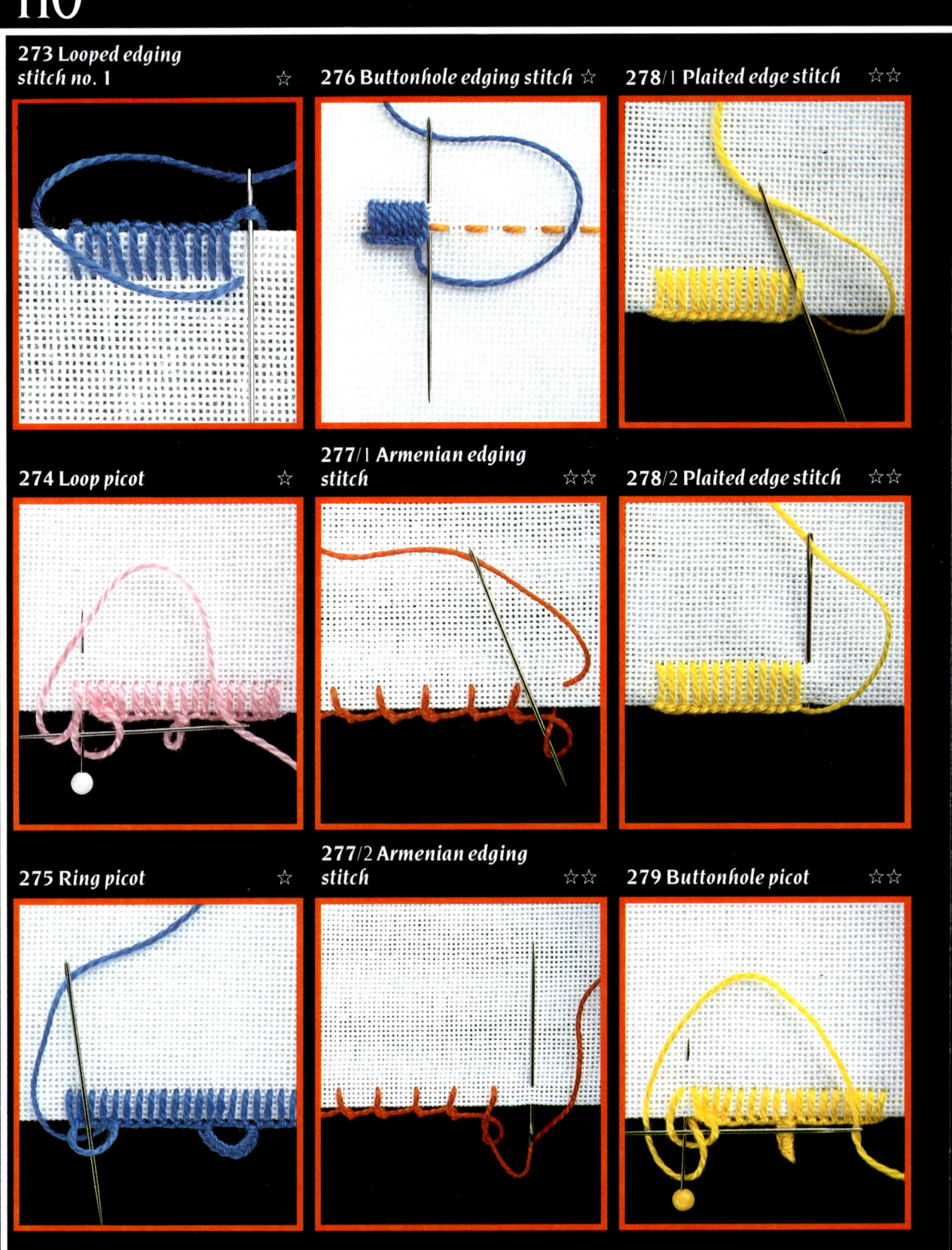

273 Looped edging stitch no. 1 ☆

274 Loop picot ☆

275 Ring picot ☆

276 Buttonhole edging stitch ☆

277/1 Armenian edging stitch ☆☆

277/2 Armenian edging stitch ☆☆

278/1 Plaited edge stitch ☆☆

278/2 Plaited edge stitch ☆☆

279 Buttonhole picot ☆☆

EDGING STITCHES

111

280 Bullion picot ☆☆

281/1 Antwerp edging stitch ☆☆

281/2 Antwerp edging stitch ☆☆

282 Braid edging stitch ☆☆☆

283/1 Woven picot ☆☆☆

283/2 Woven picot ☆☆☆

283/3 Woven picot ☆☆☆

283/4 Woven picot ☆☆☆

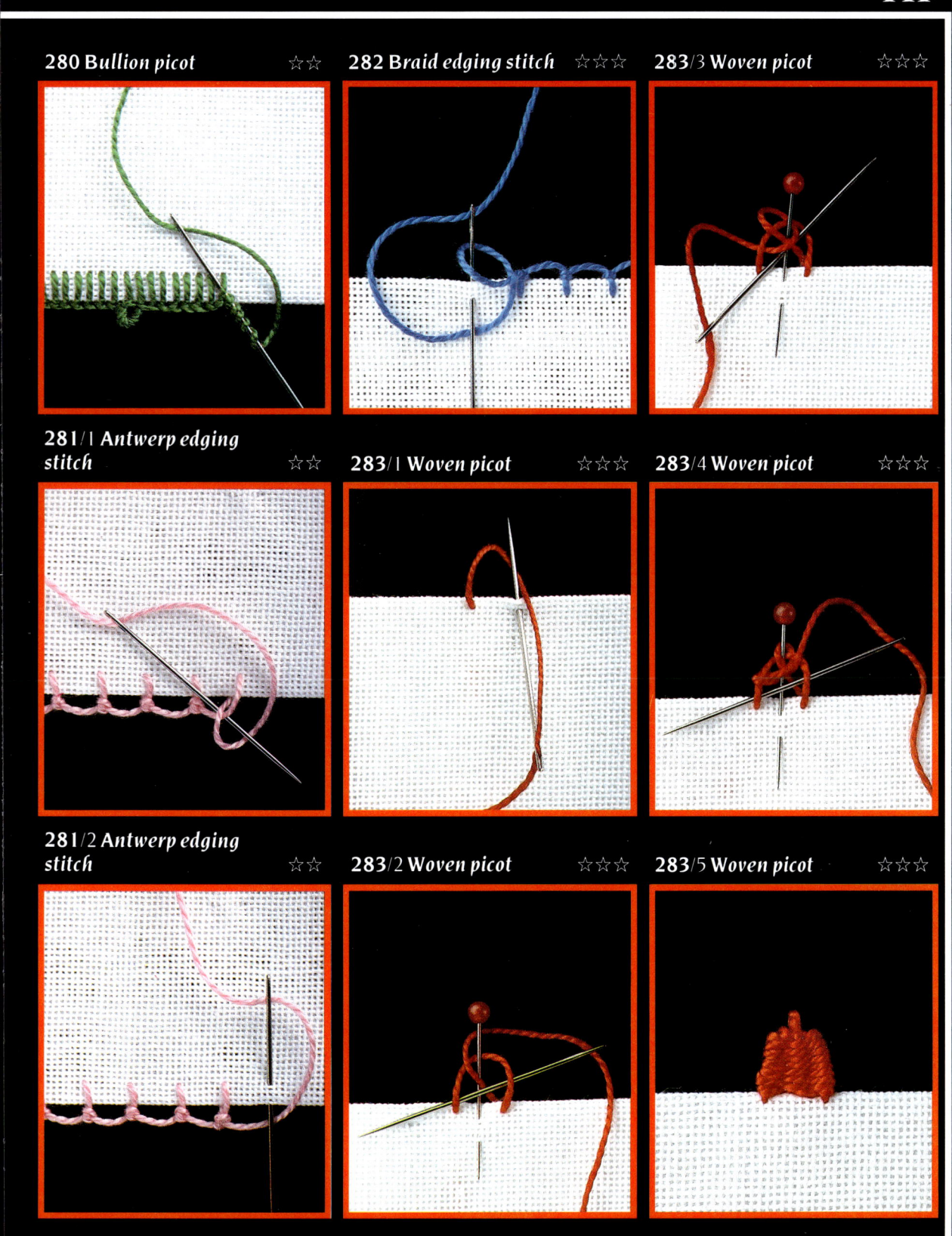

283/5 Woven picot ☆☆☆

Hem stitches

284 Hem stitch ☆

Hem stitching is a technique used to decorate and secure a hem. It is used for items of household linen and decorative hems and borders on clothes. Ordinary hem stitch is used for this purpose and is traditionally worked in white thread on white fabric. This technique can only be worked on a fabric with a fairly loose weave, such as linen, since three or four of the horizontal threads are removed from the fabric before the embroidery takes place. The threads are withdrawn and then the hem is turned in, just up to the edge of the drawn threads, and tacked in position. The embroidery stitches, which group the remaining vertical threads into clusters, are then worked. After the embroidery is completed, the tacking thread is removed. Any type of fine embroidery thread can be used, providing that it is compatible with the weight of the fabric.

Ordinary hem stitch is the simplest and easiest to work of all the hem stitches. It is worked from left to right, with the right side of the work facing the stitcher. The embroidery thread should be secured neatly inside the hem at the beginning and end of the length. Follow the sequence of stitches shown, grouping the threads into fours, and pull each stitch quite tightly to make the cluster. Care must be taken to make sure that the needle picks up the hem at the back of the work on the downward stroke so that it is secured in position.

285 Antique hem stitch ☆

Antique hem stitch is a variation of ordinary hem stitch *(see above)*. It is worked on the wrong side of the fabric and gives a much neater finish than ordinary hem stitch, as only the horizontal stitches that secure the clusters are visible on the right side of the work. It is worked in the same way as ordinary hem stitch but the needle is slipped between the hem instead of picking it up.

286 Serpentine hem stitch ☆☆
also known as **trellis hem stitch**

Serpentine hem stitch is a variation of ladder hem stitch *(see below)* and makes a pretty zigzag border. It is worked in the same way as ladder hem stitch and consists of a row of ordinary hem stitch *(see above)* worked at the top and bottom of the withdrawn threads. The vertical threads are bunched together in groups of four (or any even number) along the lower line and then divided and regrouped when the upper edge is worked.

287 Ladder hem stitch ☆☆
also known as **ladder stitch**

Ladder hem stitch is an attractive variation of ordinary hem stitch *(see above)* and makes a border with a ladder pattern. It consists of a single row of hem stitch worked along the lower edge in the usual way, bunching three vertical threads into each cluster. The fabric is then inverted and another row is worked on the opposite side of the drawn out threads. Make sure that the same three vertical threads are bunched together as on the preceding row. The number of horizontal threads which are withdrawn can be greater than that for ordinary hem stitch.

288 Italian hem stitch ☆☆☆
also known as **double hem stitch**, **Roumanian hem stitch** *and* **double-rowed open-work**

Italian hem stitch is a wider, more decorative hem stitch than the preceding two and is worked in two journeys. Work a row of ordinary hem stitch *(see above)* just above the hem, grouping three threads into each cluster. Leave three or four horizontal threads intact and withdraw the next group of horizontal threads – these should be of the same number as the threads which were drawn out originally. Work the second row of embroidery along the band of intact horizontal threads to form the vertical threads above and below this band into clusters. Follow the sequence of stitches shown, making sure that the clusters are formed from the same three vertical threads which were grouped together by the ordinary hem stitch.

Insertion stitches

289 Buttonhole insertion stitch ☆
also known as buttonhole faggot stitch
Insertion stitches are used to make open-work seams; the technique is also known as faggoting. It was originally developed as a way of joining two pieces of narrow hand-woven fabric to make large items of household linen, such as sheets, and the effect is very decorative. Traditionally, insertion stitches were worked in white, on white. With the exception of one-sided insertion stitch *(see page 52)*, and two-sided insertion stitch *(see page 57)*, insertion stitches are all used for this purpose on plain- and even-weave fabrics. The method of preparing the fabric is the same for each version, although the space left between the two pieces of fabric varies depending on the width of the stitch. The fabric pieces are hemmed first, and then tacked on top of a strip of firm brown paper, leaving a gap between them. The paper ensures that the gap remains even, and that the stitches are of equal size. The paper is removed after the insertion stitch has been completed. Any type of cotton thread can be used, providing it is fairly strong and compatible with the weight of the fabric.

Buttonhole insertion stitch is a simple insertion stitch, which is worked over a fairly narrow space. Groups of three buttonhole stitches *(see page 13)* are worked alternately from edge to edge. The stitch commences at the right-hand side of the row and the central stitch of each group is made slightly longer than the others.

290 Twisted insertion stitch ☆
also known as faggoting
Twisted insertion stitch is one of the simplest forms of insertion and it makes a pretty, twisted zigzag line. Make a simple twisted stitch alternately from one edge of the fabric to the other, ensuring that the needle always emerges from the back of the fabric. *(See buttonhole insertion stitch for details on preparing the fabric.)*

291 Knotted insertion stitch ☆☆
also known as knotted faggot stitch
Knotted insertion stitch makes a fairly narrow insertion with an attractive knotted appearance. It is quite simple to work and consists of Antwerp edging stitch *(see page 109)* worked so that the stitches are made alternately on the top and bottom edges of the fabric, as shown. *(See buttonhole insertion stitch for advice on preparing the fabric.)*

292 Plaited insertion stitch ☆☆☆
also known as interlaced faggot stitch
Plaited insertion stitch is a wide, ornate insertion stitch and should be worked in a firm, heavy thread. Often used on Victorian bed linen and ecclesiastical vestments, this stitch makes a bold plaited zigzag line across an area. The stitch consists of diagonal stitches taken from one side of the space to the other in sequence. The stitches are grouped to make a heavy line of three threads and each stitch is interwoven with the adjacent one. *(See buttonhole insertion stitch for details on preparing the fabric.)*

293 Interlacing insertion stitch ☆☆☆
also known as interlaced faggot stitch and interlaced insertion stitch
Interlacing insertion stitch makes a very decorative wide insertion and is worked in exactly the same way as interlaced herringbone stitch *(see page 65)*. Work a row of double herringbone stitch *(see page 53)* into the edges of the fabric, using the second method described. Make sure that the stitches pass over and under each other in the correct formation before beginning the interlacing; follow the sequence shown. *(See buttonhole insertion stitch for advice on preparing the fabric.)*

294 Laced insertion stitch ☆☆☆
also known as laced faggot stitch
Laced insertion stitch is a wide, lacy insertion stitch, often worked in two colours. Unlike other insertion stitches, some of the embroidery is worked before the two pieces of fabric are tacked to the brown paper. *(See buttonhole insertion stitch for advice on preparing the fabric.)* A row of braid edging stitch *(see page 109)* is worked along each edge of the fabric before the fabric is tacked down; the loops on the top edge should alternate with those on the bottom. The two rows of loops are then laced together, as shown.

Although this stitch makes a very pretty join, it is not particularly stable and it is therefore not advisable to use it on an item that is to be laundered. However, instead of the lacing, a row of knotted insertion stitch *(see above)* can be worked to join the rows of loops; this makes the join much stronger.

114 HEM STITCHES

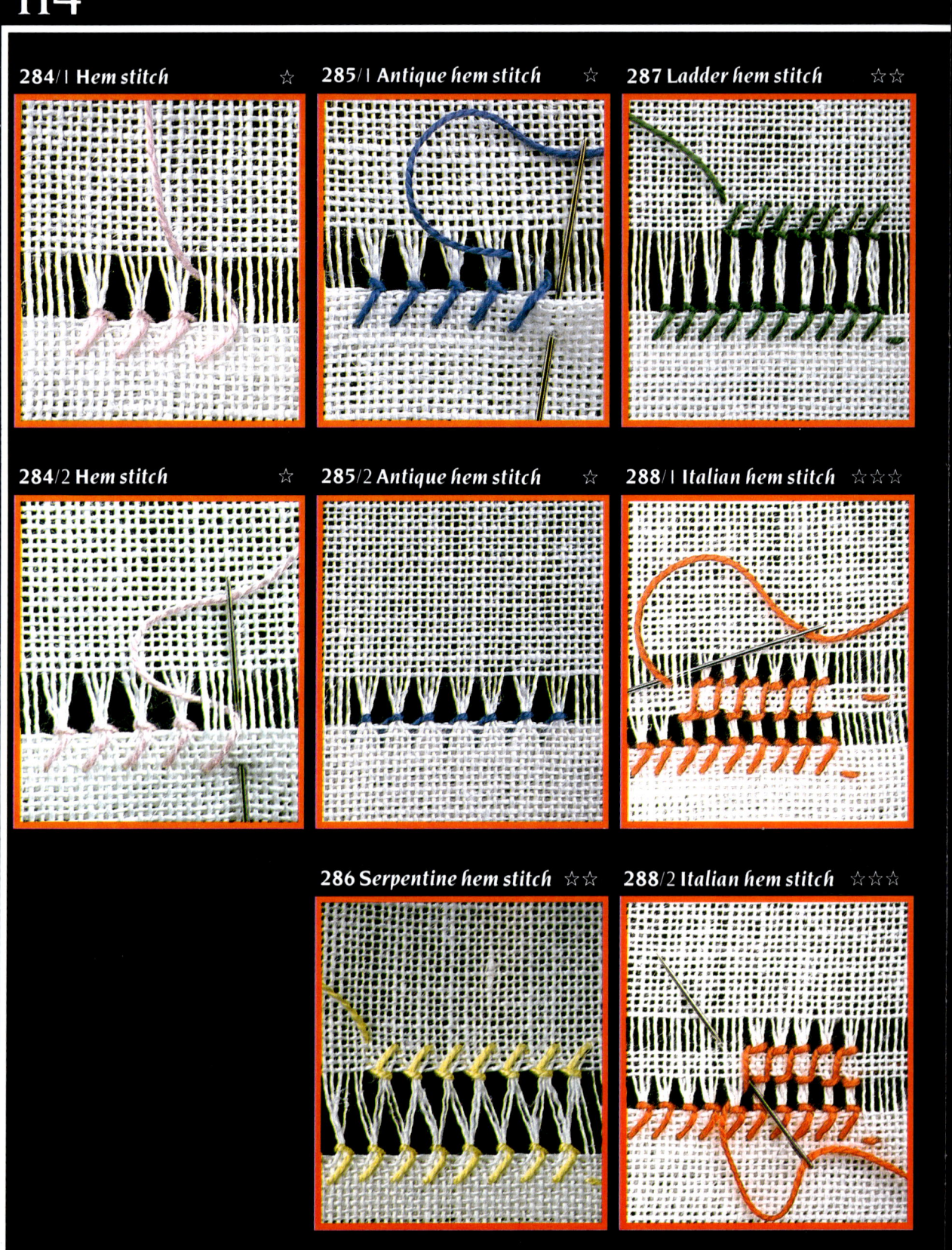

284/1 Hem stitch ☆

285/1 Antique hem stitch ☆

287 Ladder hem stitch ☆☆

284/2 Hem stitch ☆

285/2 Antique hem stitch ☆

288/1 Italian hem stitch ☆☆☆

286 Serpentine hem stitch ☆☆

288/2 Italian hem stitch ☆☆☆

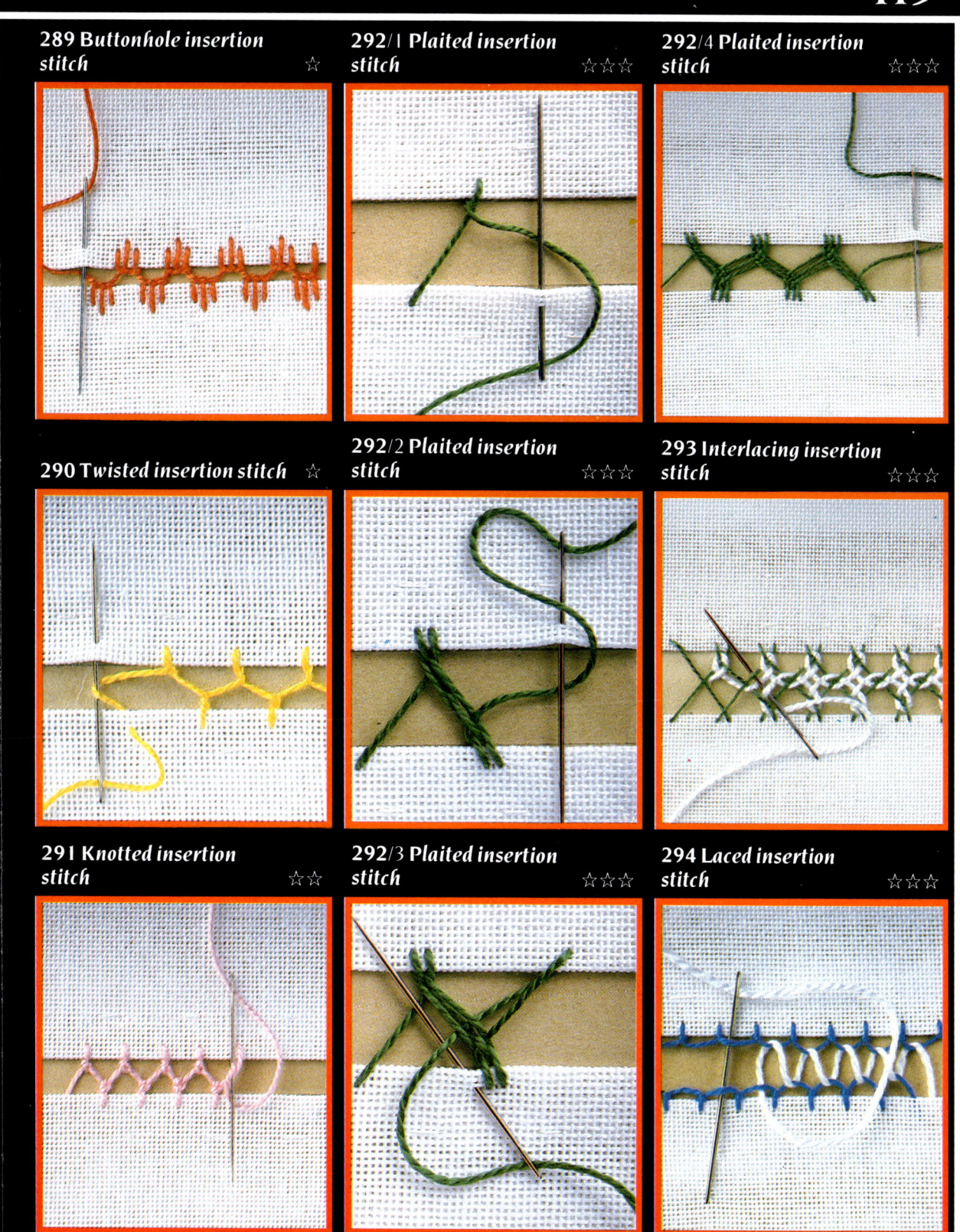

INSERTION STITCHES 115

289 Buttonhole insertion stitch ☆

292/1 Plaited insertion stitch ☆☆☆

292/4 Plaited insertion stitch ☆☆☆

290 Twisted insertion stitch ☆

292/2 Plaited insertion stitch ☆☆☆

293 Interlacing insertion stitch ☆☆☆

291 Knotted insertion stitch ☆☆

292/3 Plaited insertion stitch ☆☆☆

294 Laced insertion stitch ☆☆☆

Other fabric stitches

295 Lazy squaw stitch ☆
Lazy squaw stitch is a stitch used to attach beads to a plain-weave fabric. This stitch, as its name implies, is used extensively by North American Indians when they attach beads to items of clothing. It is a quick and easy way of beading an area, as several beads are attached at once, but a very strong thread should be used, possibly even a button thread. The thread should enter the bead easily and an embroidery hoop or frame should be used to keep the fabric taut.

This stitch is worked downwards between two parallel lines, which should be marked on the fabric. Several beads are threaded and then a horizontal straight stitch is made from one side of the row to the other, as shown. A small stitch is taken through the fabric at one side to anchor the beads and the process is repeated until the bottom of the line is reached. Work several bands of this stitch to fill the required area. For an alternative method of attaching beads, refer to spot stitch *(see below)*.

296 Spot stitch ☆
also known as bead couching and overlay stitch
Spot stitch provides a way of attaching beads to plain- or even-weave fabrics which is much quicker than sewing each one on individually. It is a variation of couching *(see page 8)* used by the North American Indians, particularly those of the Blackfoot, Crow and Shoshone tribes, for decorating items of clothing.

The beads are threaded onto a fairly strong thread, which is also fine enough to pass easily through the hole in the beads. The end of this thread is secured and the threaded beads are laid along the line to be covered. A second thread is then used to couch the first thread by making a tiny slanting stitch after every group of four beads. This method can be used for outlines or to make a solidly beaded shape, either worked in straight rows, or spiralling outwards from the centre of the shape. See lazy squaw stitch *(above)* for an alternative method of attaching beads.

297 Corded bar stitch ☆
Corded bar stitch is a detached stitch used on plain- and even-weave fabrics. Simple to work, it is used as an accent stitch in conjunction with other stitches where a raised effect is needed. It can also be scattered over a wide area to make an unusual powdering. Stretch the fabric in an embroidery hoop or frame to prevent distortion when the stitch is whipped. A foundation bar is worked first, consisting of six horizontal threads packed closely together; this bar should be kept fairly small. When a line is needed, work several small bars with the ends touching. A second thread is used to whip these foundation threads together. The second thread enters the fabric at only the beginning and end of each bar and a blunt-ended tapestry needle should be used to avoid splitting the foundation stitches. Corded bar stitch will have a more raised appearance if a round twisted thread, such as a heavy pearl cotton, is used.

298 Victorian tufting ☆
Victorian tufting is a ridged pile stitch used on plain- and even-weave fabrics. It can be worked in a straight line or in multiple rows to fill a shape. This stitch is simple to work and consists of rows of closed herringbone stitch *(see page 60)* worked one on top of the other. The first row, which makes the centre of the line of pile, is quite narrow but the second and subsequent rows should gradually become wider. Each row should overlap the previous row by a tiny amount. Work as many overlapping rows as possible until the required depth of line is reached. Using an extremely sharp pair of embroidery scissors, cut through each row of stitches carefully along the centre. The resulting pile will be quite short at the centre of the line, becoming higher towards the edges. A soft wool thread, such as Persian wool, gives the best pile but a stranded thread can also be used, or even a mixture of the two. The rows of closed herringbone stitch can be worked in alternate colours, creating an unusual striped pile.

299 Cord stitch ☆☆
Cord stitch is a decorative joining stitch used on plain- and even-weave fabrics. It makes a neat, plaited line, which covers the fabric completely, and is often used to finish cushion covers. The raw edges of the two pieces of fabric to be joined are first turned in and pressed. The pieces are then placed with the wrong sides facing each other and are tacked together to hold them in place. The thread is secured neatly between the two layers and then brought to the right side of the front piece of fabric. The stitch is worked with a forwards and backwards motion and builds up until the edges are covered with a plaited line. When the embroidery is completed, the tacking thread should be removed, and the join pressed open from the wrong side. Press carefully to avoid flattening the embroidery. Any type of thread can be used but a flat thread, such as stranded cotton, will give better cover.

300 Eyelet hole ☆☆

Eyelet holes are worked on finely woven, plain-weave fabrics and are chiefly used for broderie anglaise, worked in a white thread on a white fabric. They are normally circular but oval and triangular shapes can be made in the same way. The circle is first traced on the fabric and outlined by tiny running stitches *(see page 12)*. The centre of the fabric is then snipped vertically and horizontally. The surplus fabric is turned to the back and a row of closely packed overcast stitches *(see page 28)* is worked round the circle. When forming a triangle, make the overcast stitches slightly longer at the points to prevent fraying. The surplus fabric is then trimmed away on the back of the work. Tiny eyelet holes are worked in the same way, although the fabric is pierced by a stiletto to make the hole.

301 Shisha stitch no. 1 ☆☆

Shisha embroidery is the ancient Indian technique of attaching discs of mirror or tin to a piece of fabric by means of an embroidered surround. The word 'shisha' actually means 'little glass'. The origins of shisha embroidery are found in the seventeenth century: the Taj Mahal in Agra, India, was built by Shah Jahan as a permanent monument to his wife, Mumtaz Mahal, who is believed to have developed the use of mirrors in embroidery *circa* AD 1630. The technique is still in use today, notably in the provinces of Kutch and Sind in India, and also in Pakistan and Afghanistan; the modern methods are practically identical to the old ones. Indian embroiderers still use this technique for traditional purposes: to decorate skirts and bodices; as ceremonial trappings for animals; and on torans. Torans are embroidered friezes using shisha mirrors, which hang over doorways or windows on festive occasions. They are richly embroidered and have a row of pointed pendant shapes along the lower edge. Shisha mirrors are made in India and Pakistan and are available in this country through specialist needlework suppliers. They are made in a variety of colours: silver, which is the traditional colour, amber, green and blue. The mirrors are hand cut and have irregular edges, which are covered by the embroidery. An alternative to the genuine shisha mirror for this type of work is a large round sequin but use the type which has a hole near the edge, rather than in the centre.

The three shisha stitches in this book not only give different effects, but they show alternative methods of making the basic framework of stitches that hold the mirror in place while the decorative edge is worked. A snug framework is essential to prevent the mirror from being dislodged. Take care when stitching the framework to insert the needle vertically as close to the mirror as possible and also to tighten the stitches during working.

Shisha stitch no. 1 shows the traditional method of attaching the mirror, probably similar to that devised by Mumtaz Mahal. The framework is made by four straight stitches, two horizontal and two vertical. The vertical stitches are threaded over and under the horizontal stitches where they cross. When the mirror is firmly attached, the decorative twisted edging is then worked, as shown. A variation of this technique uses the same framework, but a row of tightly packed buttonhole stitches *(see page 13)* is worked round the edge to give a plainer effect. Any type of smooth, strong thread can be used but stranded cotton with either six or twelve strands, depending on the size of the mirror, produces a good edge.

302 Shisha stitch no. 2 ☆☆

This method uses eight straight stitches, interwoven in pairs, to anchor the mirror to the fabric. If a large mirror is being used, twelve stitches spaced in groups of three may be needed for extra security. After the framework has been completed, a band of stitches is worked round the circumference. The stitches can be all the same length, or alternately long and short for a more decorative finish. Buttonhole stitch *(see page 13)* also works successfully as a border with this framework.

303 Shisha stitch no. 3 ☆☆

This method of attaching the mirror differs from the previous two in that the framework is left uncovered and forms part of the decoration. It is a modern American interpretation of the technique and is much simpler to work than the preceding stitches. It is only successful, however, if a regularly shaped mirror or large sequin is used, as the edges are not covered by the border. Three vertical straight stitches are worked across the mirror, and then three horizontal stitches are woven through them, creating a mesh across the surface of the mirror; four vertical and four horizontal stitches will be needed if the mirror is large. These stitches must be placed centrally across the mirror and worked firmly. To finish, an outline of chain stitch *(see page 12)* is then worked through the fabric as close to the mirror as possible.

118 FABRIC STITCHES

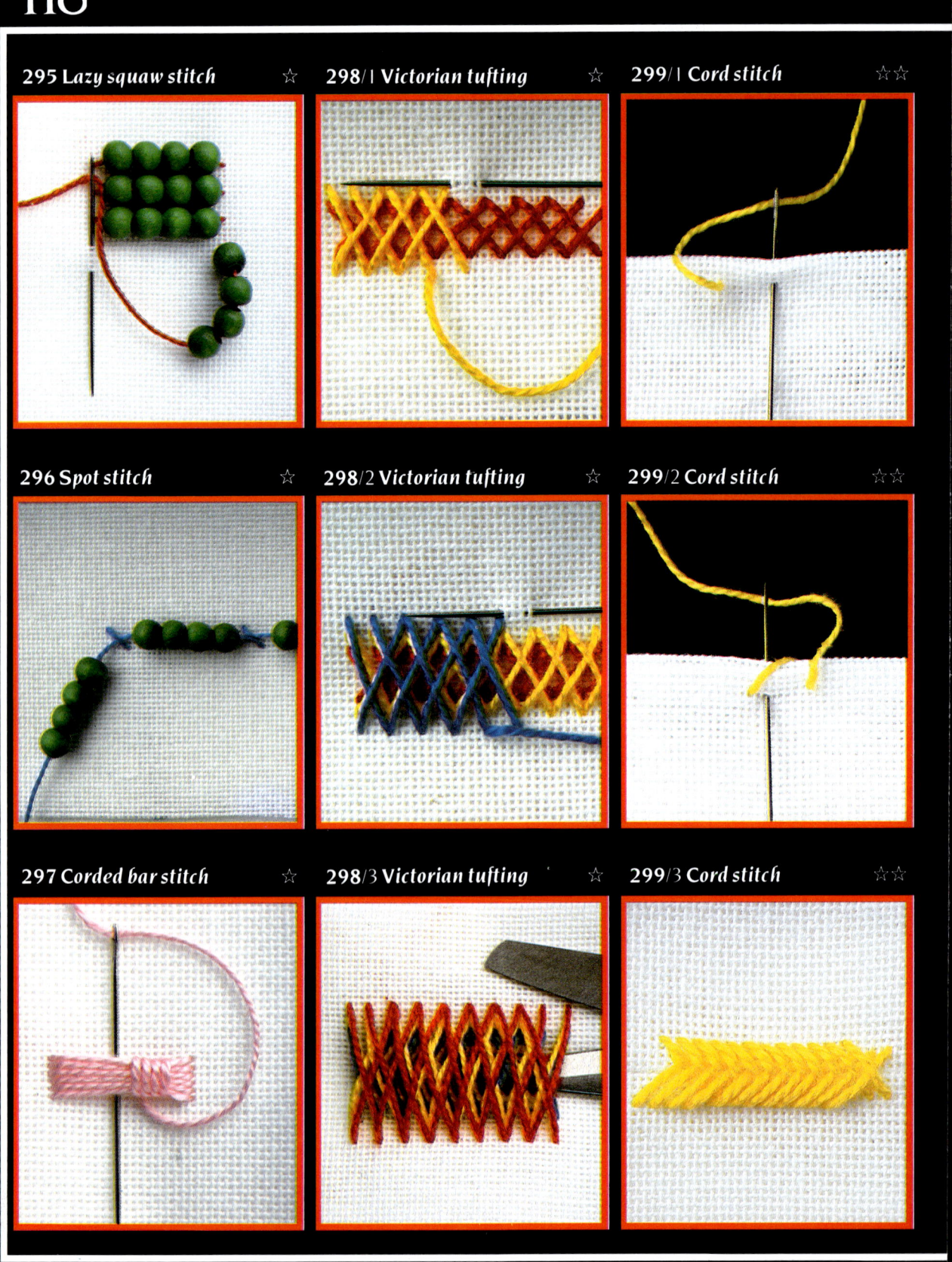

295 Lazy squaw stitch ☆

298/1 Victorian tufting ☆

299/1 Cord stitch ☆☆

296 Spot stitch ☆

298/2 Victorian tufting ☆

299/2 Cord stitch ☆☆

297 Corded bar stitch ☆

298/3 Victorian tufting ☆

299/3 Cord stitch ☆☆

OTHER FABRIC STITCHES 119

300/1 Eyelet hole ☆☆

301/2 Shisha stitch no. 1 ☆☆

302/2 Shisha stitch no. 2 ☆☆

300/2 Eyelet hole ☆☆

301/3 Shisha stitch no. 1 ☆☆

302/3 Shisha stitch no. 2 ☆☆

301/1 Shisha stitch no. 1 ☆☆

302/1 Shisha stitch no. 2 ☆☆

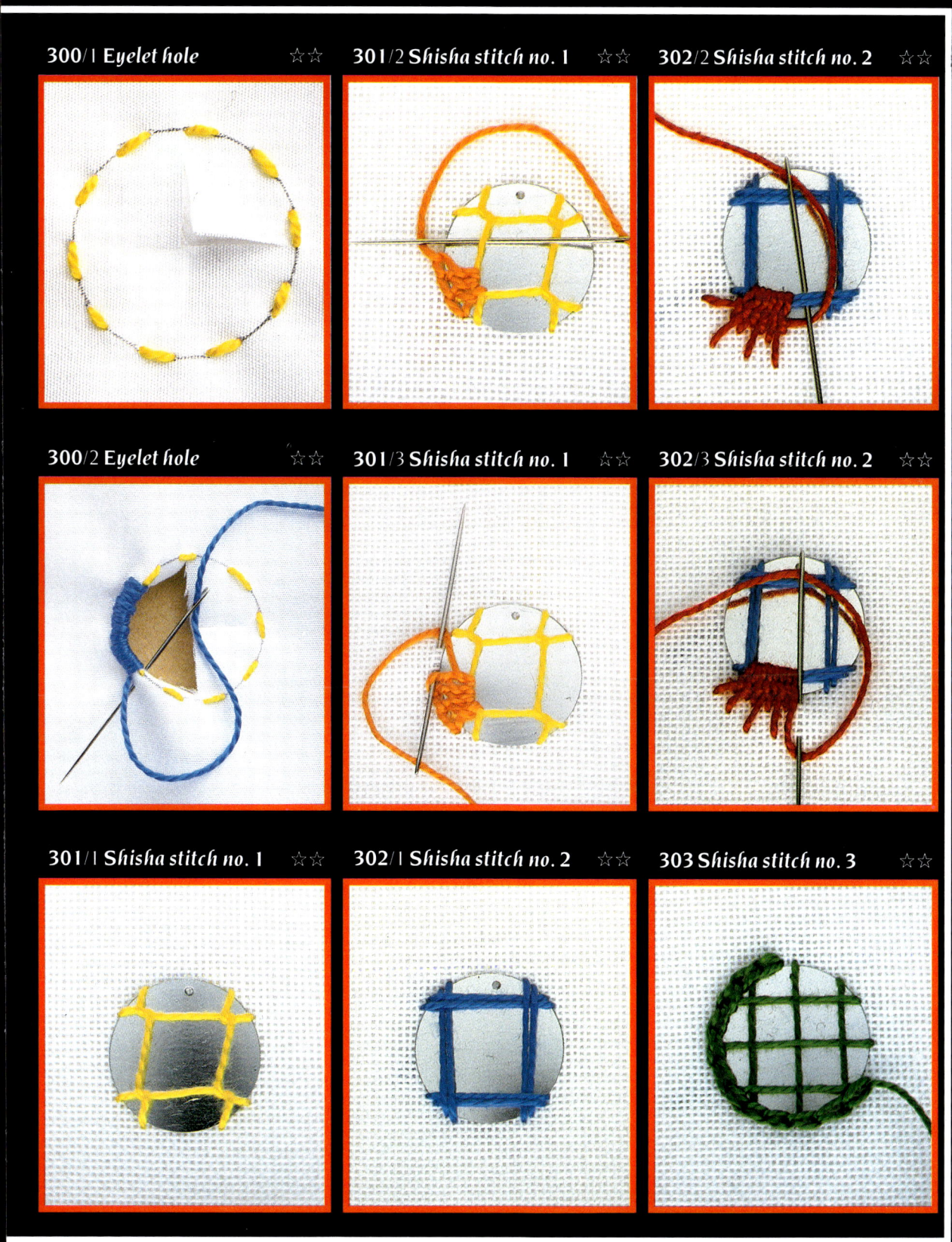

303 Shisha stitch no. 3 ☆☆

CANVAS STITCHES
Straight and slanted stitches

304 Reversed cushion stitch ☆
Reversed cushion stitch is a canvas stitch used on single canvas. It is a variation of cushion stitch *(see page 152)* worked without the framing of tent stitch. It makes a small-scale squared pattern over the canvas and is used for filling shapes and for background areas. The stitch consists of blocks of graduated diagonal straight stitches worked over squares of three canvas threads. The direction of these stitches is reversed on every alternate block.

An attractive light and shade effect is made by the positioning of the stitches, and this effect can be enhanced by choosing an embroidery thread with a sheen, such as stranded cotton. However, this stitch also looks attractive if it is worked with tapestry or Persian wool. When used over a large area, reversed cushion stitch can be shaded by the use of several tones of thread.

305 Algerian filling stitch and Algerian filling stitch with bar ☆
Algerian filling stitch is worked on single canvas in vertical blocks of three satin stitches taken over four canvas threads. The blocks are worked diagonally with a half drop from top left to bottom right of the area to be covered. The stitch covers the canvas ground quickly, giving an even, slightly textured effect and is primarily used for background areas.

Algerian filling stitch with bar is a variation of Algerian filling stitch, in which a horizontal satin stitch is worked at the base of each block of vertical stitches. This extra stitch is worked either in the same thread or in a thread of contrasting colour or texture.

306 Chessboard filling stitch no.2 ☆
Chessboard filling stitch no. 2 is a canvas stitch adapted from a drawn fabric stitch. It is used on single canvas and has a regular geometric pattern which fills a large area quickly. Care should be taken when using it, as the pattern produced can be rather dominant unless it is worked on a small scale. It looks most attractive when worked with a lustrous thread, such as stranded cotton or silk, as the light and shade effect created by the different directions of the stitches are enhanced by these. Chessboard filling stitch no. 2 consists of blocks of horizontal or vertical straight stitches. Each block is composed of three bands of ten straight stitches over three threads of canvas. The blocks are usually worked in diagonal rows, from top left to bottom right of the canvas.

307 Mosaic stitch ☆
Mosaic stitch is a canvas stitch used on single and double canvas. It makes a tiny, squared pattern and can be used to build up intricate patterns by using many different colours for the tiny squares (mosaics are made in the same way). Any type of thread can be used for this stitch, providing that it is compatible with the gauge of the canvas selected, but a smooth, non-hairy thread is essential to keep the pattern crisp. The stitch can also be used to work a monochrome area, as the smooth surface makes a good foil for the more raised and textured canvas stitches. It is composed of short and long diagonal straight stitches, and two horizontal journeys are needed to complete a row of squares. When working a complicated, multicolour design, work all the areas in the main colour first, and then go back and fill in the spaces with the other colours.

308 Florentine stitch ☆
also known as **bargello stitch, cushion stitch, flame stitch, Irish stitch** *and* **Hungary stitch**
Florentine stitch is a canvas stitch used on single canvas. This stitch is used for a type of canvas work called Florentine work or bargello and makes a characteristic flame-shaped pattern. This type of canvas work is often used for cushion covers and upholstery, and should be worked in a hard-wearing thread, such as tapestry wool. The stitch consists of vertical straight stitches, usually placed over four horizontal canvas threads, worked in a step sequence to form zigzag rows. The stitches can be arranged in different formations to create curves and pinnacles as well as zigzags. One row is worked across the canvas, and the following lines of stitches are worked in different colours to fill the canvas above and below the first line, always following its contours. The stitches are the same length on the second and subsequent rows. This stitch is always worked using different colours or different shades of one colour and the pattern is created by the use of colour.

309 Brick stitch no. 2 ☆
Brick stitch no. 2 is used only as a canvas stitch. Again it takes its name from the brick-work pattern that it produces but is used mainly for filling background areas. It is a quick and easy stitch to work and looks equally effective worked in wool or stranded cotton, depending on the gauge of the canvas. It consists of blocks of three horizontal straight stitches worked over six vertical threads of the canvas, which run side by side across the canvas. Below this row of blocks are two rows of short horizontal stitches, which are worked over two threads. This stitch looks best when worked in monochrome or in two very close tones of one colour; one tone for the blocks and the other for the small stitches.

310 Long stitch ☆
Long stitch is a canvas stitch used on single canvas. It makes a triangular pattern and has the appearance of a brocaded fabric when worked in a lustrous embroidery thread, such as stranded cotton or silk. Each horizontal row is worked in two journeys, and consists of groups of graduated vertical straight stitches, arranged in triangles. On the second journey, the triangles are reversed and fill in the spaces left on the first journey. Each journey can be made using a different colour and the stitch looks very effective when two shades of the same colour are used. Each double row of triangles is worked over five horizontal threads but the stitch can be made deeper by adding extra graduated stitches to each triangular group.

311 Parisian stitch ☆

Parisian stitch is a canvas stitch used on single canvas. It is quick and easy to work and makes a fairly smooth surface, which is ideal for filling large areas and backgrounds. Any type of embroidery thread can be used for this stitch, but care should be taken to match the weight of the thread to the gauge of the canvas to ensure complete coverage of the surface. It is composed of long, vertical straight stitches worked over six horizontal canvas threads and short straight stitches worked over two horizontal threads, alternating across the canvas. The second and subsequent rows overlap the row immediately preceding them by two horizontal threads. This stitch is very useful where a gradually shaded area is needed, as it can be attractively blended in bands by using very similar shades of colour.

312 Double Parisian stitch ☆
also known as **old Parisian stitch**

Double Parisian stitch is a canvas stitch used on single canvas. A simple variation of Parisian stitch *(see above)*, it is worked in a similar way, except that the stitches are longer and arranged in pairs. The long stitches are nine threads high and the short stitches cover three canvas threads. A fairly coarse thread, such as tapestry or Persian wool, will probably be needed to cover the canvas adequately but a small sample can be stitched first to check if another thread would be suitable. This stitch is used for large areas and backgrounds, which can be shaded in bands, but it gives a less even blend of colours over an area than ordinary Parisian stitch.

313 Moorish stitch ☆

Moorish stitch is a canvas stitch used on double canvas. The flat surface produced has an attractive zigzag pattern, which is usually worked in two colours of thread and can be worked in a combination of wool thread and cotton thread. Any type of embroidery thread can be used but care should be taken when matching the weight of the thread to the gauge of the canvas selected to ensure complete coverage of the canvas.

The stitch is worked diagonally from the top left to the bottom right of the area, in alternate rows. One row consists of groups of four graduated diagonal stitches, which form squares, and the other is made up of tiny diagonal stitches running in the same direction as those on the preceding row.

314 Tent stitch ☆
also known as **needlepoint stitch, petit point, canvas stitch, perlen stitch, cushion stitch** *and* **continental stitch**
and reversed tent stitch

Tent stitch is a tiny canvas stitch used on single canvas. It is known to have existed as long ago as the sixteenth century and was probably in use much earlier than that. It is a stitch which appears never to have gone out of fashion, which is probably due to its versatility.

A small, diagonal stitch, it can be worked in vertical, horizontal or diagonal rows to give a fairly smooth, flat surface; the stitches should all lie in the same direction. When filling large areas with this stitch, work the stitch diagonally, as this method is less likely to distort the canvas. The small size of the stitches allows figurative designs to be intricate and full of detail. The designs are often followed from a coloured chart, or from a painting on the canvas itself. Commercially produced canvas work kits are usually worked in this stitch.

Tent stitch combines well with the heavier, more textured canvas stitches and accentuates their raised appearance. It is used to fill in the gaps of unworked canvas when a larger stitch does not totally cover the shape; in this case a matching thread should be used. It also frames square blocks of stitches, using a contrasting colour or weight of thread; Scottish stitch *(see page 156)* is a good example of this use. Tent stitch can be trammed to make a hard-wearing, slightly ridged surface which, when a durable thread is used, is ideal for covering chair seats. Trammed tent stitch is worked on double canvas, so that the tramming stitches can be worked between the pairs of canvas threads.

Reversed tent stitch gives a slightly more textured surface. It is mainly used for covering a solidly coloured shape, giving a contrasting area to a textured stitch. It is worked in the same way as tent stitch but in this case the rows are horizontal and the direction of the stitches is reversed on every alternate row.

315 Jacquard stitch ☆

Jacquard stitch is a canvas stitch used on single or double canvas. It is used for covering large shapes and background areas, and has the appearance of a woven or brocaded fabric. It is quick and easy to work and can be sewn in more than one colour and weight of thread, when it makes a diagonal, striped zigzag pattern. It is worked diagonally from the top left to the bottom right of the area to be covered. Rows of satin stitches *(see page 24)*, each covering two vertical and two horizontal canvas threads, are arranged in steps of six stitches, as shown. The satin stitch rows alternate with rows of tent stitch *(see above)*. Any type of embroidery thread can be used but a combination of wool for the satin stitch and stranded or pearl cotton for the tent stitch looks attractive.

316 Knitting stitch ☆
also known as **tapestry stitch** *and* **kelim stitch**

Knitting stitch is a canvas stitch used on single canvas. It has a closely worked, almost woven, surface and the effect varies depending on the weight of the thread and the gauge of the canvas used. A fine thread on small-gauge canvas gives the stitch the appearance of woven tapestry and the stitch can be used for tiny shapes and fine details. A bolder effect like that of knitting is made by using a coarse thread, such as tapestry wool, on a larger gauge of canvas; the stitch can then be used for large shapes and background areas. Knitting stitch is similar to chain stitch *(see page 12)* but each vertical row of knitting is worked in two journeys. Each row consists of slanting straight stitches, worked upwards first and then downwards, with a reverse slant.

122 CANVAS STITCHES

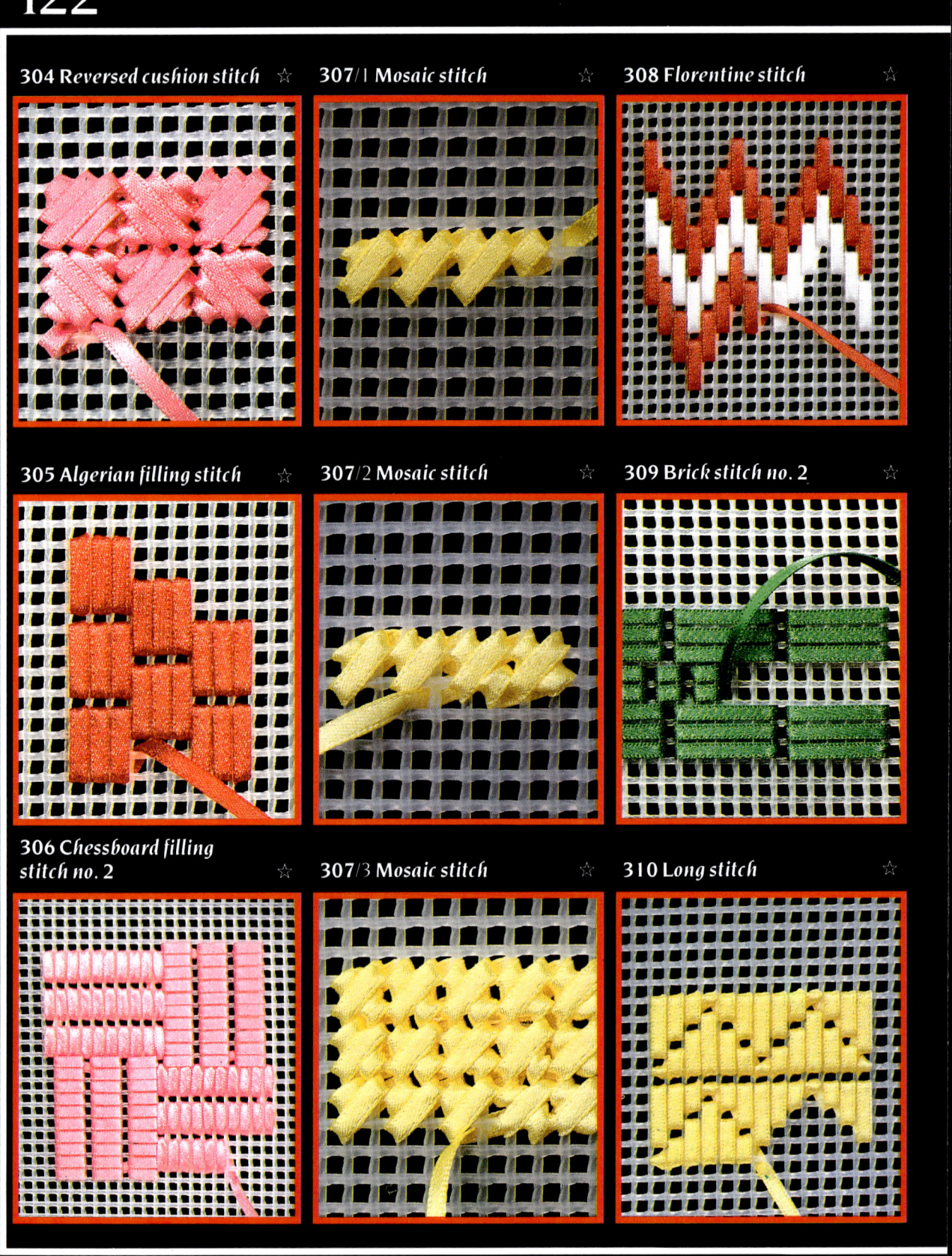

304 Reversed cushion stitch ☆

307/1 Mosaic stitch ☆

308 Florentine stitch ☆

305 Algerian filling stitch ☆

307/2 Mosaic stitch ☆

309 Brick stitch no. 2 ☆

306 Chessboard filling stitch no. 2 ☆

307/3 Mosaic stitch ☆

310 Long stitch ☆

STRAIGHT AND SLANTED STITCHES

123

311 Parisian stitch ☆

314/1 Tent stitch ☆

315 Jacquard stitch ☆

312 Double Parisian stitch ☆

314/2 Tent stitch (back) ☆

316/1 Knitting stitch ☆

313 Moorish stitch ☆

314/3 Tent stitch (diagonal) ☆

316/2 Knitting stitch ☆

317 Cashmere stitch ☆
Cashmere stitch is a canvas stitch worked on single canvas. Quick to work and with good covering power, it is useful for stitching large areas of background. It makes a small, neat pattern with a steep slant and consists of a series of groups of three diagonal stitches which form slanting rows. The stitching usually starts in the top left-hand corner of the area and the first row is worked downwards to the bottom right-hand corner; the second row is then worked upwards, parallel to the first; the third downwards, and so on. Any type of thread is suitable for this stitch but the weight of the thread used must be compatible with the gauge of the canvas.

318 Straight Cashmere stitch ☆
Straight Cashmere stitch is a canvas stitch used on single canvas for covering large background areas. It is a relatively easy stitch to work and quickly covers the canvas. A variation of Cashmere stitch *(see above)*, it forms neat, rectangular blocks of slanting stitches. The blocks are fairly small and consist of four diagonal straight stitches which fill an area comprising two vertical canvas threads by three horizontal threads. The blocks can be worked in either horizontal or vertical rows to cover the area and, if worked in two colours or tones of thread, will make a tiny chessboard pattern. As with Cashmere stitch, any type of embroidery thread is suitable but the weight of the thread must be compatible with the gauge of the canvas.

319 Fancy brick stitch ☆
also known as fancy bricking
Fancy brick stitch, as its name implies, is a more complicated version of brick stitch no. 2 *(see page 120)*. It is a canvas stitch used on single canvas and has a textured appearance. The stitch is constructed in a similar way to brick stitch no. 2 but the blocks in the first strip are smaller since they are made up of three horizontal straight stitches over three canvas threads. In the next strip, the small straight stitches are interspersed with pairs of vertical stitches. Fancy brick stitch is used for filling shapes and for a background of textured brick pattern.

320 Twill stitch ☆
Twill stitch is a canvas stitch used on single canvas. It is quick and easy to work and makes a small woven pattern with a strong diagonal feel. It is used to fill a shape of any size and is ideal for a background area. It is worked in diagonal rows from the top left to the bottom right of the area to be covered. The rows consist of vertical straight stitches worked over three horizontal canvas threads. Wool or cotton embroidery threads are equally well suited to this stitch but a stranded cotton or silk enhances the smoothly stitched surface beautifully. The rows can be worked in two colours to give a diagonally striped effect.

321 Hungarian stitch ☆
Hungarian stitch is used on single and double canvas. It makes tiny diamond shapes, which can be worked alternately in two colours or used to create a more complex geometric design, using several colours. It also makes a good background stitch when worked in monochrome. When making a complicated pattern, first work all the stitches of one colour, then all the stitches of the second colour, and so on. Each stitch consists of three vertical straight stitches of different lengths to cover two, four and then two horizontal threads of the canvas.

322 Diamond straight stitch ☆
Diamond straight stitch is used on single canvas. It is used for filling large or small shapes and for background areas and has a small, regular, diamond-shaped pattern. It consists of diamond shapes made of five vertical straight stitches of graduating length, surrounded by small vertical stitches worked over one canvas thread. Work the diamonds in horizontal rows over the area, so that each row fits neatly into the one above. With the same thread, fill the remaining spaces with the small stitches.

323 Diagonal stitch ☆
Diagonal stitch is used on single canvas for filling large shapes and backgrounds. It makes a flat, patterned surface with the appearance of a woven or brocaded fabric, which can be made more striking by using a lustrous thread, such as stranded cotton. It is worked in diagonal rows from the top left-hand corner to the bottom right-hand corner of the shape and consists of graduated diagonal stitches. The stitches on each row fit neatly into the stitches on the preceding row and the largest stitches are worked on a line with the smallest stitches so that no gaps are created. Diagonal stitch can be worked in two or more colours to make a bold, diagonally striped pattern. Work back stitch *(see page 14)* in a different colour between the rows of diagonal stitch to enhance the striped effect.

324 Reversed mosaic stitch ☆
Reversed mosaic stitch is used on single and double canvas. Like mosaic stitch *(see page 120)*, it makes a tiny squared pattern, although the diagonal stitches run in the opposite direction every alternate square. Each square is completed before moving on to the next one and they are worked in horizontal rows across the shape, and then back again. The light and shade effect created by the slanting stitches is enhanced by the use of a lustrous thread, such as stranded or pearl cotton.

325 Linked stitch ☆
Linked stitch is used on single canvas and is extremely quick and simple to work. Suitable for backgrounds, it makes a brick-work pattern of square, barred blocks, worked in horizontal rows. The blocks can be worked in vertical rows with a half drop and the number of vertical stitches in each block can be altered to form a rectangle. Each block consists of five vertical straight stitches worked over six horizontal canvas threads and overstitched by one horizontal straight stitch over six vertical threads.

326 Double twill stitch ☆

Double twill stitch is a canvas stitch used on single canvas. A simply worked variation of twill stitch *(see page 124)*, it has a bold diagonal pattern useful for filling large shapes and background areas. It is worked in diagonal rows, from the top right to the bottom left of the area to be covered. Rows of large vertical straight stitches, worked over four horizontal canvas threads, alternate with rows of shorter vertical straight stitches, worked over two horizontal threads. The rows can be worked in two contrasting or toning colours to give a diagonally striped effect. Any type of embroidery thread can be used but care should be taken to match the weight of the thread to the gauge of the canvas to make sure that the canvas is completely covered by the stitching.

327 Byzantine stitch ☆

Byzantine stitch is a canvas stitch used on single canvas. It is useful for large background areas because it is easy to work and covers the canvas rapidly. The regular zigzag pattern made by this stitch is similar to the formal geometric patterns found in Byzantine art and architecture; hence its name. The Byzantine Empire existed in Eastern Europe and parts of Africa and Asia during the period between AD 330 and AD 1453 when it was conquered by the Turks. The textiles of the Byzantines embodied the characteristic blend of classical traditions and Eastern influences found in all the visual arts of that civilization. In AD 552, the Emperor Justinian acquired the secrets of silk cultivation and Byzantium (present-day Istanbul) became the first centre outside China to produce silk thread and fabrics. Byzantine pattern weaving became greatly admired for its stylized designs of animals and birds and for its complex geometric patterns. The technical skill of the weavers was also widely recognized. Silk production continued in Byzantium as a jealously guarded monopoly almost until the time of the Turkish conquest.

Byzantine stitch produces the effect of a woven or brocaded fabric, especially when worked on a small-gauge canvas with a stranded silk or cotton thread. The zigzag pattern is made by arranging groups of five diagonal straight stitches in equal-sized steps. The rows are worked diagonally, beginning at the top left-hand corner of the area to be covered. Any small spaces at the edge of the shape that are not covered by the diagonal rows are filled in with shorter diagonal stitches, always keeping the pattern correct.

328 Gobelin stitch ☆☆
also known as **oblique Gobelin stitch**

Gobelin stitch is a canvas stitch used on single canvas. It makes a smooth surface, which is useful where a flat area of canvas work is needed to accentuate a more textured stitch. It is very similar to tent stitch *(see page 121)* in appearance and consists of horizontal rows of small slanting stitches. The rows are worked from the bottom of the area to be covered and run alternately from left to right and from right to left. The stitches are two canvas threads tall and slant diagonally over one thread. It is very important to follow this method closely in order to keep the 'pull' of the stitch correct, otherwise the surface will become uneven.

329 Encroaching Gobelin stitch ☆☆
also known as **interlocking Gobelin stitch**

Encroaching Gobelin stitch is a canvas stitch used on single canvas and is a variation of Gobelin stitch *(see above)*. It makes a flat surface and is an ideal stitch to use if you wish to shade and blend colours over large areas. It is worked in close horizontal rows, starting at the top of the area to be covered, and the rows are worked in alternate directions. The stitches are longer than ordinary Gobelin stitches: they are worked over five horizontal canvas threads and slant diagonally over one thread. The stitches in each row overlap the stitches in each previous row by one horizontal thread, causing the rows to interlock. Any type of embroidery thread can be used but care should be taken to match the weight of the thread to the gauge of the canvas.

330 Gobelin filling stitch ☆☆

Gobelin filling stitch is used on single canvas and is used both for filling shapes and for backgrounds. It makes a fairly flat surface, and it is important to match the weight of the thread to the gauge of the canvas to ensure that the canvas is completely covered by the stitching. A very quick stitch to work, it lends itself very well to shading and blending different colours, as the rows of stitches overlap each other by three canvas threads. To prevent an obvious break between rows, the shades of the colours used should not be dramatically different. The rows are worked horizontally in alternate directions, beginning from the left. Each row consists of spaced, vertical straight stitches worked over six horizontal canvas threads into alternate holes in the canvas. Each row overlaps the preceding row by three canvas threads and fills in the spaces.

331 Square satin stitch ☆☆
also known as **flat square**

Square satin stitch is a canvas stitch used on single canvas primarily for filling large shapes and backgrounds. It makes a pattern of diamond shapes, which in turn makes a pattern of large squares when four diamonds are set together. Each diamond shape consists of eleven satin stitches *(see page 24)* of graduating lengths, with the satin stitches worked either vertically or horizontally. Follow the arrangement of the diamonds and the direction of the stitches shown carefully. This stitch looks extremely attractive when worked on a small scale, using a pearl or stranded cotton to accentuate the light and shade effect created by the different directions of the stitches. The diamonds can also be striped in alternating colours: this creates a strong bold pattern on the surface if two contrasting colours are used, or a much more subtle effect if two close shades of one colour are used.

126 CANVAS STITCHES

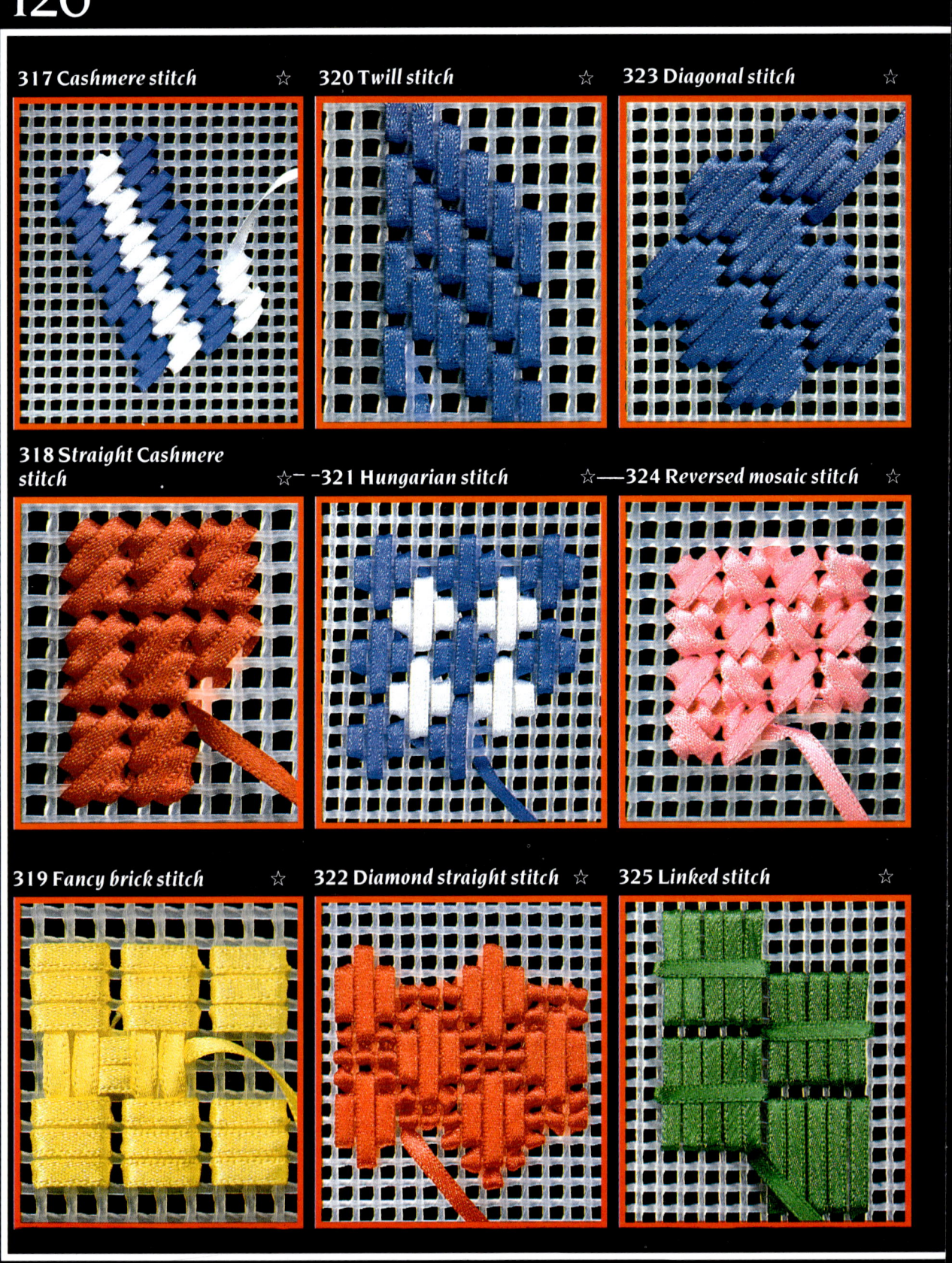

317 Cashmere stitch ☆

320 Twill stitch ☆

323 Diagonal stitch ☆

318 Straight Cashmere stitch ☆

321 Hungarian stitch ☆

324 Reversed mosaic stitch ☆

319 Fancy brick stitch ☆

322 Diamond straight stitch ☆

325 Linked stitch ☆

326 Double twill stitch ☆

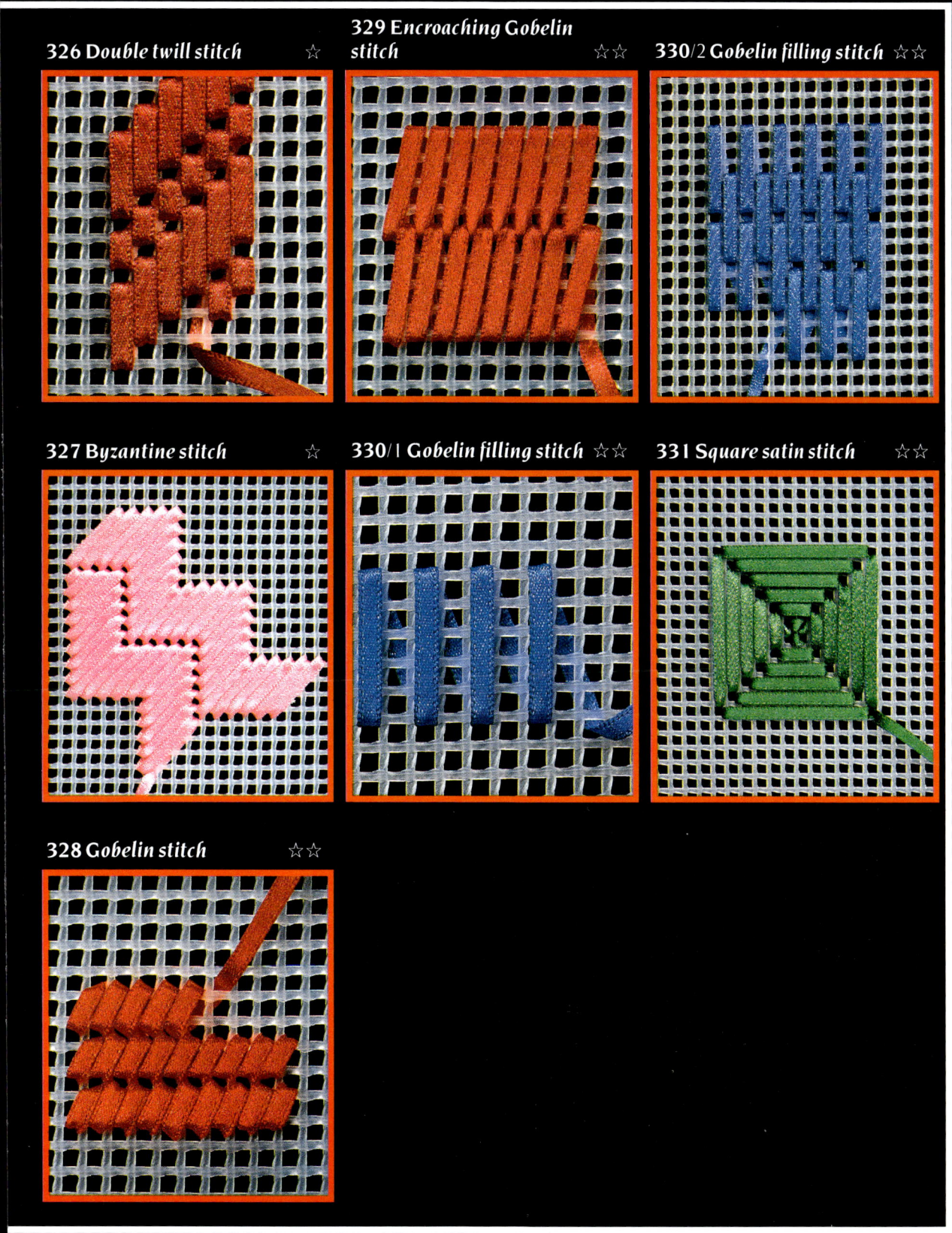

329 Encroaching Gobelin stitch ☆☆

330/2 Gobelin filling stitch ☆☆

327 Byzantine stitch ☆

330/1 Gobelin filling stitch ☆☆

331 Square satin stitch ☆☆

328 Gobelin stitch ☆☆

CANVAS STITCHES

332 Wide Gobelin stitch ☆☆
also known as **oblique Slav stitch**
Wide Gobelin stitch is a canvas stitch used on single canvas. A larger version of Gobelin stitch *(see page 125)*, it makes a flat surface, which is useful to contrast with the more textured canvas stitches. It is worked in horizontal rows in the same way as Gobelin stitch but the slanting straight stitches are larger and each cover three horizontal canvas threads. They also have a more angled slant, running across two vertical canvas threads instead of one. Wide Gobelin stitch looks very effective when worked in closely shaded bands and any type of embroidery thread can be used, providing that it is compatible with the gauge of the canvas.

333 Balloon satin stitch ☆☆
Balloon satin stitch is a canvas stitch used on single canvas for filling large shapes and backgrounds. The pattern of balloon shapes is made with ordinary satin stitches. The horizontal stitches are worked in vertical rows from the top of the shape and the second and subsequent rows interlock closely. A lustrous thread, such as stranded cotton or silk, is well suited to this stitch and enhances the smooth, even surface of each balloon shape but a wool thread can also be used with good results. To add texture to this stitch, an isolated knot stitch, such as a small bullion knot *(see page 97)* or a French knot *(see page 96)*, can be worked between the balloons.

334 Upright Gobelin stitch ☆☆
also known as **straight Gobelin stitch**
Upright Gobelin stitch is a canvas stitch used on single canvas. It is simple and very quick to work and makes a close, ridged surface, which lends itself well to working small, intricate shapes, as well as backgrounds. The upright variation of Gobelin stitch *(see page 125)*, it is worked in horizontal rows, in alternate directions, from the top of the area to be covered. The rows consist of small vertical straight stitches, each worked over two horizontal canvas threads and worked close together, filling every hole along the rows. Upright Gobelin stitch can be trammed to give a hard-wearing surface suitable for upholstery.

335 Linen stitch ☆☆☆
Linen stitch is a canvas stitch used on single and double canvas. As its name suggests, this stitch creates a neatly woven surface reminiscent of linen fabric. It provides an unusual way of covering large areas and backgrounds and looks equally effective worked in tapestry wool, soft cotton or stranded cotton, providing that the gauge of the canvas is compatible with the weight of the thread. The rows are worked diagonally from bottom left to top right and then back again. A neatly interlocking pattern of straight stitches is made; each vertical and horizontal stitch covers two canvas threads.

336 Plaited Gobelin stitch ☆☆☆
Plaited Gobelin stitch is a canvas stitch worked on a double canvas. It makes an attractive plaited surface and is used for filling large areas and backgrounds. Quite quick to work, it covers the canvas well, providing that the weight of the thread used is compatible with the gauge of the canvas chosen. It is a variation of Gobelin stitch *(see page 125)* and the stitches are all the same size, covering two double canvas threads and slanting diagonally over one thread. However, the rows are arranged in a different way from Gobelin stitch. They are worked in horizontal rows, from right to left and then back again, starting at the top right-hand corner of the area. The stitches on the first row slant to the left, while those on the second and every alternate row thereafter slant to the right and overlap the stitches on each preceding row by one horizontal double thread.

337 Rep stitch ☆☆☆
also known as **Aubusson stitch**
Rep stitch is a canvas stitch that must be worked on double canvas. A very small diagonal stitch with a ridged texture, it is used for working finely detailed designs and tiny shapes. This stitch takes its name from the fabric, rep, which it resembles when worked closely, using a heavy thread. Rep stitch should cover the canvas completely, and a small sample should be worked to check the compatibility of the weight of the thread with the gauge of the canvas. It is worked in the same way as tent stitch *(see page 121)* but in this case the rows are always worked downwards and the stitches are less slanted. Each vertical row covers one vertical double thread of the canvas, and the stitches are worked not only in the wider spaces but also between the double threads, giving a very closely stitched appearance.

338 Milanese stitch ☆☆☆
Milanese stitch is used on single and double canvas. It makes an attractive, triangular pattern, with a brocaded appearance and flat surface, and is excellent for backgrounds. This brocaded effect is enhanced when the stitch is worked in a lustrous thread, such as stranded or pearl cotton, and also looks effective when worked in a wool thread.

The triangles consist of four stitches of graduated lengths, arranged so that they point alternately up and down. Instead of working satin stitch blocks, as is usual when producing this type of pattern, Milanese stitch is worked entirely in back stitch *(see page 14)*. Begin at the top left of the area to be covered and work the rows diagonally up and down the shape, ensuring all the time that the triangular formation is retained.

339 Straight Milanese stitch ☆☆☆
Straight Milanese stitch is a canvas stitch used on single and double canvas. It is a simply worked variation of ordinary Milanese stitch *(see above)* but in this case the triangles are arranged in horizontal rather than diagonal rows. It is worked in back stitch *(see page 14)* in exactly the same way as Milanese stitch but the rows run alternately from left to right, and from right to left.

340 Oriental stitch ☆☆☆
see also Roumanian stitch
Oriental stitch is a canvas stitch used on single and double canvas. It is a variation of Milanese stitch *(see above)*, which makes a larger pattern with a definite zigzag look to the flat surface. It is quick and easy to work, and is used for large areas and backgrounds. This stitch is worked in the same way as Milanese stitch: back stitch *(see page 14)* is worked in diagonal rows across the shape from the bottom left-hand corner to the top right-hand corner of the shape and back in the opposite direction, keeping the pattern correct. Any type of embroidery thread can be used for this stitch but care should be taken when matching the weight of the thread to the gauge of the canvas selected to ensure complete coverage of the canvas.

341 Lozenge satin stitch ☆☆☆
Lozenge satin stitch is used on single canvas for filling large shapes and backgrounds. The bold, lozenge-shaped pattern is made by arranging ordinary satin stitches *(see page 24)* in the pattern shown. The vertical stitches are worked in horizontal rows, beginning at the left-hand side of the area to be covered. The central group of three stitches can be left unworked on the first journey, to be filled in later, using a contrasting colour of thread. A lustrous thread, such as stranded cotton or silk, enhances the smoothly stitched surface of the lozenges but tapestry or Persian wool is also suitable.

342 Renaissance stitch ☆☆☆
Renaissance stitch is used on single and double canvas. It makes a flat, closely worked surface of tiny vertical stitches arranged in horizontal rows and is used for a shape of any size. This stitch can be used to work small details and complex geometric patterns can be built up using many different colours of thread. This stitch makes a very hard-wearing surface when worked in a durable thread, such as tapestry wool, and it can be used for upholstery. It is similar in appearance to upright Gobelin stitch *(see page 128)* but the methods of working are entirely different.

Each Renaissance stitch consists of two vertical stitches worked over two canvas threads and a horizontal stitch of the same length. The stitch is worked in vertical rows, and each pair of vertical stitches is worked under the preceding pair; the rows should always be worked downwards. Any type of embroidery thread can be used but care should be taken to make sure that the canvas is completely covered by the stitching, especially when using double canvas.

343 Web stitch ☆☆☆
Web stitch is a canvas stitch used only on double canvas. It has a closely woven surface and is used for filling shapes or backgrounds of any size. It is a form of couching *(see page 8)*, and consists of long, diagonal straight stitches tied down at regular intervals by short, diagonal straight stitches. The short stitches should lie at right angles to the long stitches and be set alternately on each row to create a woven surface. The long stitches are worked into the holes between the double threads but the short stitches pass into the tiny holes between the threads. Any type of embroidery thread can be used but care should be taken to match the weight of the thread to the gauge of the canvas to make sure that the canvas is completely covered by the stitching.

130 CANVAS STITCHES

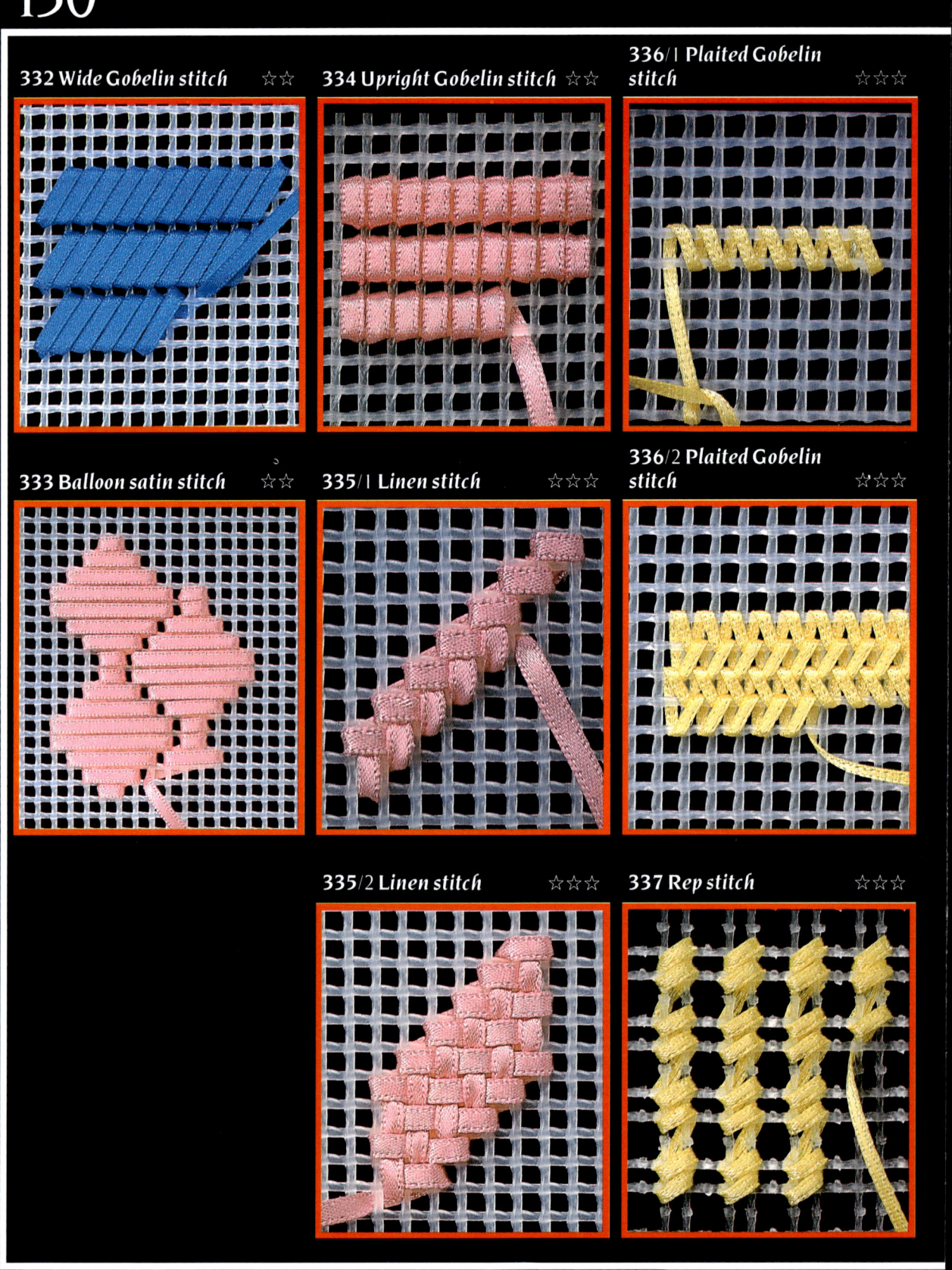

332 Wide Gobelin stitch ☆☆

334 Upright Gobelin stitch ☆☆

336/1 Plaited Gobelin stitch ☆☆☆

333 Balloon satin stitch ☆☆

335/1 Linen stitch ☆☆☆

336/2 Plaited Gobelin stitch ☆☆☆

335/2 Linen stitch ☆☆☆

337 Rep stitch ☆☆☆

STRAIGHT AND SLANTED STITCHES

131

338 Milanese stitch ☆☆☆

341 Lozenge satin stitch ☆☆☆

342/3 Renaissance stitch ☆☆☆

339 Straight Milanese stitch ☆☆☆

342/1 Renaissance stitch ☆☆☆

343 Web stitch ☆☆☆

340 Oriental stitch ☆☆☆

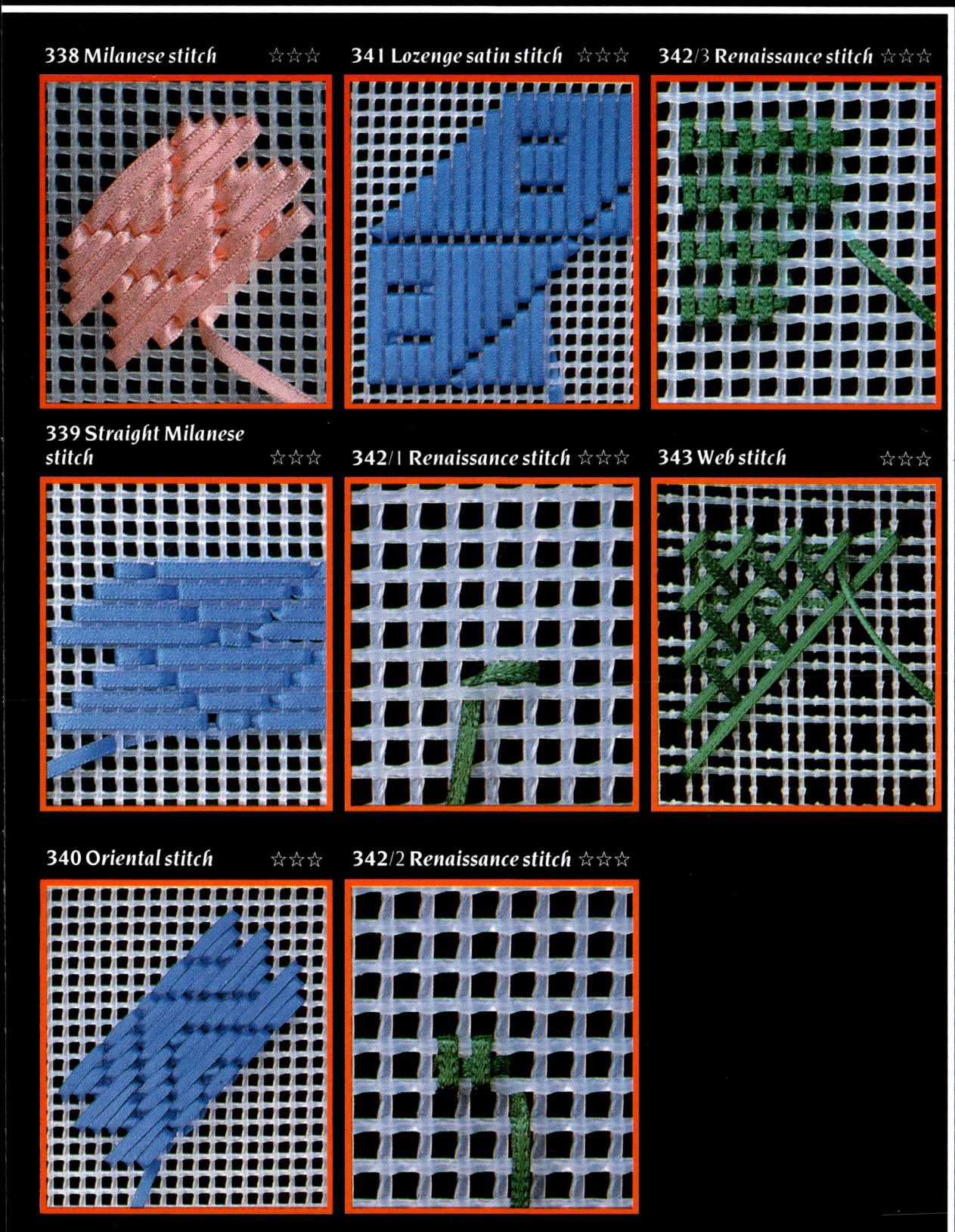

342/2 Renaissance stitch ☆☆☆

Crossed stitches

344 Canvas fern stitch ☆
Canvas fern stitch is used on double canvas. It makes a striking ridged surface and is used for filling shapes and for backgrounds. It consists of vertical rows of top-heavy crosses which are worked downwards to make ridges. The ridged effect can be accentuated by the use of two or more toning or contrasting colours of thread. Any type of embroidery thread can be used but care should be taken to match the weight of the thread to the gauge of the canvas to make sure that the canvas is completely covered by the stitching. Rows of canvas fern stitch can be worked alternately with rows of broad stem stitch *(see page 9)* to make an attractive striped pattern.

345 Double stitch ☆
also known as **alternating cross stitch**; *see also* **stepped and threaded running stitch**
Double stitch is a composite canvas stitch and is used on single canvas. It makes a good background stitch as it is quite quick to work and covers the canvas well. It can be worked in two colours by working the differently sized crosses on two journeys instead of one. It looks most attractive when the two threads chosen are close to each other in tone.
 Double stitch consists of interlocking horizontal rows of cross stitch *(see page 14)* alternating with oblong cross stitch *(see page 133)*. The rows are arranged so that the oblong cross stitches fit neatly under the ordinary cross stitches of the previous row. The oblong cross is worked over two vertical and six horizontal threads, while the ordinary cross stitch covers a square of two threads. Any type of embroidery thread can be used but care should be taken to match the weight of the thread to the gauge of the canvas to ensure that the canvas is completely covered by the stitching.

346 Cross stitch plus two ☆
Cross stitch plus two is primarily a canvas stitch used on single canvas but it can also be worked successfully on an even-weave fabric. When worked on canvas, this stitch makes a distinctive woven surface and is useful for filling large shapes and background areas since it is quite quick to work. It consists of a large, slightly elongated cross stitch worked over four vertical and six horizontal canvas threads with the addition of a vertical straight stitch across the centre of the cross. A horizontal straight stitch is then worked at the base of the cross. Any type of embroidery thread can be used, providing that it covers the canvas well but the woven pattern will be most effective if a thick thread, such as tapestry wool, is used. When working this stitch on an even-weave fabric, it makes a pretty, lacy pattern if a fine pearl cotton or coton à broder is used.

347 Broad diagonal cross stitch ☆
also known as **diagonal broad cross**
Broad diagonal cross stitch is a canvas stitch used for filling large shapes and background areas and is usually worked on single canvas. It is worked in the same way as broad cross stitch *(see page 133)* and makes a raised geometric pattern with a bold, diagonal appearance. Although worked in the same way as broad cross stitch, the blocks are arranged on the diagonal rather than the straight. Each block consists of three straight stitches, slanting from the top right-hand corner to the bottom left-hand corner and crossed by three straight stitches, which slant in the opposite direction. The rows are worked diagonally, from the top left-hand corner to the bottom right-hand corner of the area to be covered and all the rows of blocks interlock as shown. Any type of embroidery thread is suitable for broad diagonal cross stitch but care should be taken when matching the weight of the thread to the gauge of the canvas to make sure that the canvas is completely covered by the stitching.

348 Double Dutch stitch ☆
also known as **Dutch double cross stitch**
Double Dutch stitch is a canvas stitch used on single canvas. A variation of Dutch stitch, it is used for filling large areas and for backgrounds. It makes a textured surface with strong vertical lines and is worked downwards. This stitch uses oblong cross stitches *(see page 133)* worked horizontally over four vertical and two horizontal canvas threads. They are worked in vertical rows, and each alternate cross is tied down with a vertical stitch over three canvas threads. Each row is arranged so that the tied crosses line up next to each other. A second journey of stitching is then begun, using either the same thread, or one of a contrasting colour and weight. This journey consists of rows of back stitch *(see page 14)*, worked quite large and covering four horizontal threads, placed between the rows of crosses. Double Dutch stitch gives better coverage of the canvas than Dutch stitch and any type of embroidery thread can be used, providing that it is compatible with the gauge of the canvas.

349 Oblong cross stitch with back stitch and double tied oblong cross stitch ☆
Oblong cross stitch with back stitch is a simply worked variation of oblong cross stitch *(see page 133)*. It is used on single canvas and can be worked in two colours. It has the same uses as oblong cross stitch and is worked in exactly the same way, over two vertical and four horizontal threads of the canvas. After the required area has been stitched, a row of back stitch *(see page 14)* is worked over the centre of each row of oblong cross stitch. The back stitch row can be worked in a contrasting colour or a different weight of embroidery thread.
 Double tied oblong cross stitch is similar in appearance to oblong cross stitch with back stitch but the method of working is different and it is worked in one colour. Each oblong cross stitch, worked over two vertical and seven horizontal threads, is tied down by two short straight stitches before proceeding to the next cross stitch. This stitch has a more textured appearance than oblong cross stitch or oblong cross stitch with back stitch and has a pronounced ridge running along the centre of each row.

CROSSED STITCHES

350 Broad cross stitch ☆
also known as **broad cross**
Broad cross stitch is a canvas stitch used for filling large shapes and background areas and is usually worked on single canvas. Quite a large stitch, it covers a square of six vertical and six horizontal canvas threads, making a raised geometric pattern, which is bold and striking in appearance. It is very straightforward to work and the blocks consist of three vertical straight stitches, which are then crossed by three horizontal stitches of the same length. It is worked in horizontal rows, beginning at the top left-hand corner of the area to be filled. The blocks in one row fit into the spaces at the bottom of the preceding row. Any type of embroidery thread is suitable for broad cross stitch, but care should be taken when matching the weight of the thread to the gauge of the canvas to make sure that the canvas is completely covered by the stitching. A variation of this stitch can be made by working the horizontal stitches first and the vertical stitches last.

351 Canvas herringbone stitch ☆
Canvas herringbone stitch is used on single canvas for filling large shapes and backgrounds. It makes a dense, plaited texture and is worked in exactly the same way as ordinary herringbone stitch. Each crossed diagonal stitch covers four vertical and four horizontal canvas threads and the rows interlock closely. Any type of thread can be used, but a soft wool thread, such as tapestry or Persian wool, gives the best coverage of the canvas. Canvas herringbone stitch can be striped in two or more colours to make an attractive chevron pattern.

352 Underlined stitch ☆
Underlined stitch is a canvas stitch used on single and double canvas to fill a shape or background of any size. A variation of cross stitch *(see page 14)*, it can also be used on an even-weave fabric, provided that a fairly fine thread is used. It is worked in horizontal rows and each cross stitch is underlined by a horizontal straight stitch before the next cross stitch is formed. Any type of embroidery thread can be used but care should be taken to match the weight of the thread to the gauge of the canvas to make sure that the canvas is covered by the stitching.

353 Half cross stitch ☆
also known as **half stitch**
Half cross stitch is a line or filling stitch used on even-weave fabrics and double canvas. It is a small, diagonal stitch, always worked in the same direction, which can be used as a filling stitch to fill shapes with a flat area of stitching, or as a line stitch. As its name suggests, half the stitch consists of half an ordinary cross stitch *(see page 14)*. When worked on canvas, half cross stitch looks identical to tent stitch *(see page 121)*. However, the method of working the two stitches is different and they should never be used together, as the different stitches created on the back of the work will result in an uneven, distorted surface. Half cross stitch is very easy to work and the rows should run horizontally from the left to right of the area. When worked on canvas, this stitch can be trammed *(see Glossary)* to give better coverage. Any type of thread can be used on an even-weave fabric but care should be taken when using half cross stitch on canvas to select a thread which will cover the canvas adequately.

354 Oblong cross stitch ☆
also known as **long cross stitch**, **economic long cross** *and* **czar stitch**
Oblong cross stitch is a variation of ordinary cross stitch *(see page 14)* and is used on single and double canvas. It is used for lines and for filling large areas and backgrounds, since it is extremely quick to work. Each row is worked in two journeys and the stitch makes a neat, ridged texture. Almost the same as ordinary cross stitch in construction, the stitches of oblong cross stitch are elongated. One set of diagonals is worked from right to left on the first journey and the crosses are completed on the second journey in the opposite direction. This stitch can be worked over four, or six or more horizontal canvas threads but it is usually kept at the width shown. Any type of embroidery thread can be used but care should be taken, especially when using double canvas, to match the weight of the thread to the gauge of the canvas to ensure that the canvas is completely covered by the stitching.

355 Double cross stitch ☆
also known as **double straight cross stitch**; *see also* **leviathan stitch**
Double cross stitch is a canvas stitch used on single canvas. It is a very decorative stitch and forms large, raised diamond shapes. The diamonds comprise a row of large, upright cross stitches *(see page 137)* worked over four vertical and horizontal canvas threads, and then over-stitched by a row of smaller ordinary cross stitch *(see page 14)*. Follow the sequence of stitches shown and start stitching from the top left-hand corner of the canvas, working the rows first from left to right, and then from right to left. Any type of embroidery thread can be used but care should be taken to match the weight of the thread to the gauge of the canvas to ensure that the canvas is completely covered.

356 Knotted stitch ☆
also known as **Persian cross stitch** *and* **Pangolin stitch**; *see also* **coral stitch** *and* **French knot**
Knotted stitch is used on double canvas. It has a closely packed ridged appearance and is quick and easy to work, which makes it suitable for backgrounds and large areas. This stitch can be used with any type of embroidery thread, providing it is compatible with the gauge of the canvas but a soft wool thread, such as tapestry or Persian wool, gives better coverage. The stitch consists of a long, slanting stitch over one vertical and three horizontal double threads of canvas, which is tied down by a short, diagonal crossing stitch. The rows of stitching overlap each other by one horizontal double thread, and a pretty, broken striped pattern is created if alternate rows are worked with a contrasting thread.

//134 CANVAS STITCHES

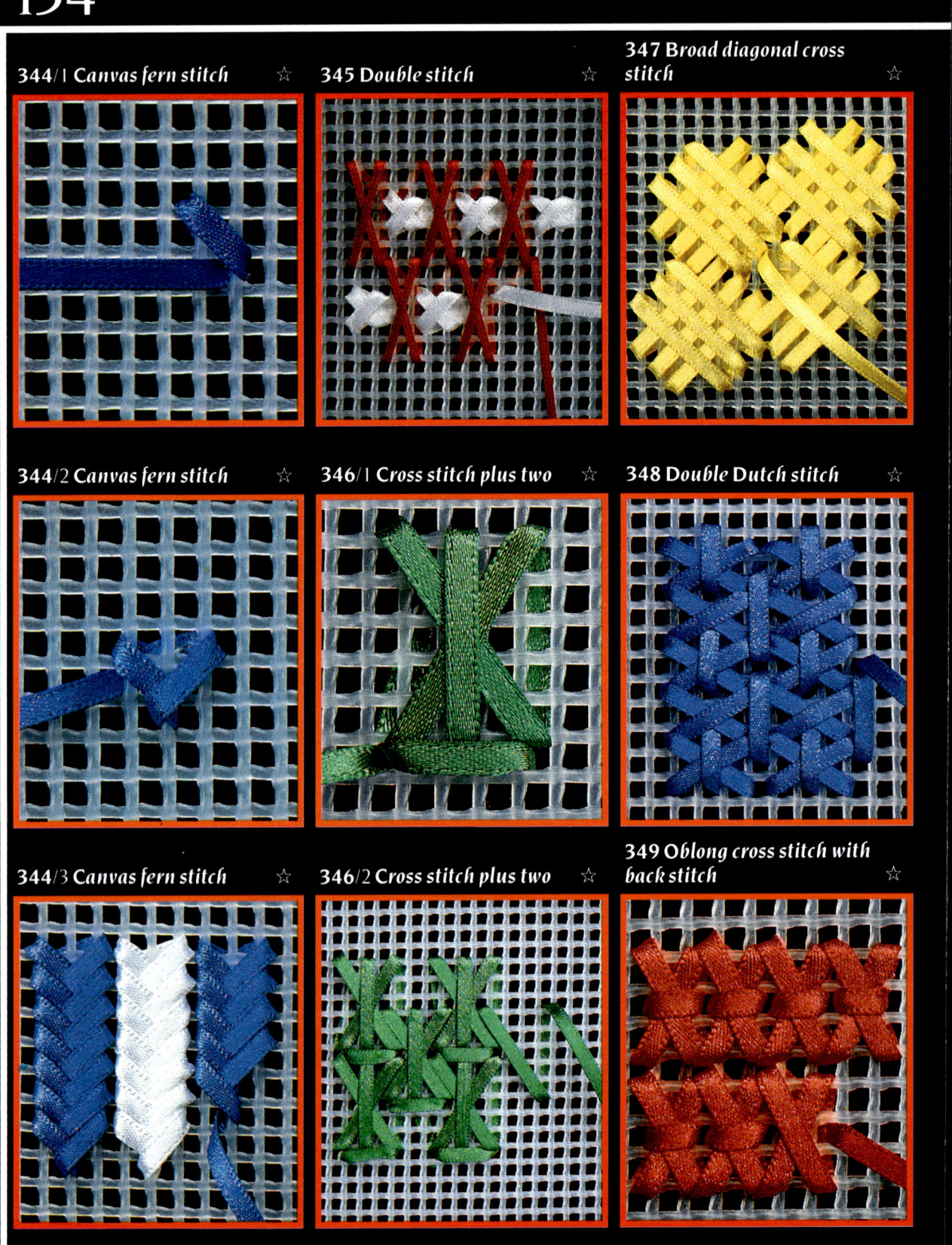

344/1 Canvas fern stitch

345 Double stitch

347 Broad diagonal cross stitch

344/2 Canvas fern stitch

346/1 Cross stitch plus two

348 Double Dutch stitch

344/3 Canvas fern stitch

346/2 Cross stitch plus two

349 Oblong cross stitch with back stitch

CROSSED STITCHES

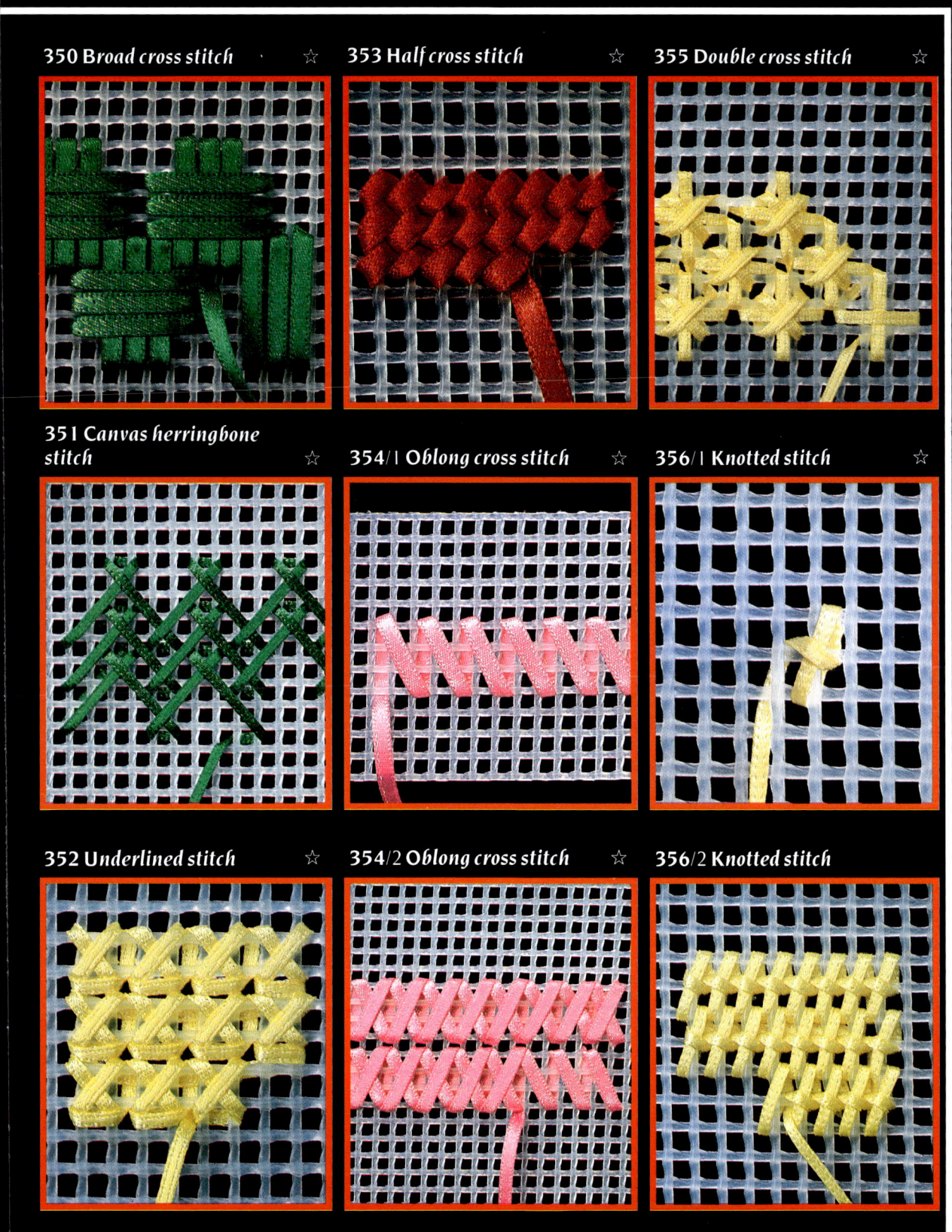

135

350 Broad cross stitch

353 Half cross stitch

355 Double cross stitch

351 Canvas herringbone stitch

354/1 Oblong cross stitch

356/1 Knotted stitch

352 Underlined stitch

354/2 Oblong cross stitch

356/2 Knotted stitch

CANVAS STITCHES

357 Leviathan stitch ☆
also known as **double cross stitch,** **Smyrna cross stitch** *and* **railway stitch**

Leviathan stitch is a canvas stitch which can also be used on even-weave fabrics provided that a fine thread is used. It consists of an upright cross stitch *(see page 137)* worked over a basic cross stitch *(see page 14)* and usually covers four horizontal and four vertical canvas threads. Each stitch forms a neat, raised square unit and these units can be worked in alternate colours to give a chessboard effect. Leviathan stitch worked in tapestry wool makes an extremely hard-wearing surface, suitable for chair seats and cushion coverings.

358 Crossed Gobelin stitch ☆
Crossed Gobelin stitch is a canvas stitch used on single canvas. A decorative variation of Gobelin filling stitch *(see page 125)*, it has a more textured effect. Each row consists of spaced vertical straight stitches worked over six horizontal canvas threads into alternate holes in the canvas. After each stitch is formed, an ordinary cross stitch *(see page 14)* is worked over the centre. The rows are worked horizontally, in alternate directions. Each row overlaps the preceding row by two horizontal threads to fill in the spaces. As with Gobelin filling stitch, it is important to choose an embroidery thread that will cover the canvas adequately.

359 Rice stitch ☆
also known as **cross corners cross stitch** *and* **William and Mary stitch**

Rice stitch is used on single or double canvas and has a rather dense texture. It covers the canvas ground well and can be used for small areas and for backgrounds. It can be worked in two colours or two thicknesses of thread. Work the large crosses first and then stitch the corner diagonals with a second thread. If using two thicknesses of thread, use a thick thread for the large crosses and a thinner one for the corner stitches. Rice stitch looks very effective when stitched with a combination of tapestry or Persian wool with pearl cotton for the corner stitches. Interesting shaded effects can be achieved by working an area of large crosses in one colour and varying the colours of the second thread.

360 Reversed cross stitch ☆
Reversed cross stitch is a composite canvas stitch worked on single canvas, usually in two colours. It is a filling stitch worked in three journeys, which can be shaded by choosing graduating colours for the last journey. It has a dense, closely worked texture and is equally useful for filling any size of shape or for backgrounds. Reversed cross stitch is a combination of ordinary cross stitch *(see page 14)* and upright cross stitch *(see page 137)* worked in two journeys. These stitches are then repeated in reverse sequence on the third journey and worked over the existing crosses. On the third journey, the stitching is usually completed with a contrasting, finer thread, perhaps metallic. The underneath stitches can be worked in any type of embroidery thread, as long as it is compatible with the gauge of canvas chosen.

361 Ridge stitch ☆
Ridge stitch is a canvas stitch used on single canvas. It makes a distinctive vertically ridged pattern and is used for filling shapes of any size and for background areas. It is most attractive when worked in a fairly heavy wool thread, such as tapestry or Persian wool, as these threads accentuate the ridged appearance of the stitch. This stitch is worked vertically in rows from the top of the area to be covered, beginning at the left-hand side. It consists of an oblique cross stitch worked over four vertical canvas threads. Each vertical row overlaps the preceding row by one canvas thread so that the rows interlock. Ridge stitch can be striped by using two colours in alternate rows.

362 Horizontal fishbone stitch ☆
Horizontal fishbone stitch is a canvas stitch used on double canvas. It is a variation of fishbone stitch no. 2 *(see page 137)* and forms a strong diagonal pattern. The stitches are worked in diagonal rows from the bottom left to the top right of the canvas and the stitches are all set horizontally. Any type of embroidery thread can be used but care should be taken to match the weight of the thread to the gauge of the canvas to make sure that the canvas is completely covered by the stitching.

363 Upright rice stitch ☆
Upright rice stitch is used on single and double canvas. It is a simply worked variation of ordinary rice stitch *(see above)* and makes a pattern of diamonds on the surface. It is worked exactly like rice stitch but the foundation stitch is an upright cross stitch *(see page 137)* worked over four vertical and four horizontal threads of the canvas. The corners are then crossed by short vertical and horizontal straight stitches over two canvas threads. Any type of embroidery thread can be used but care should be taken to match the weight of the thread to the gauge of the canvas to make sure that the canvas is completely covered by the stitching. Upright rice stitch can be attractively shaded by varying the colours of the short crossing stitches.

364 Dutch stitch ☆
also known as Dutch cross stitch

Dutch stitch is a canvas stitch used on single canvas. It is used for filling large shapes and for background areas, and makes a raised pattern of crosses. It is worked in two journeys and a contrasting thread can be used for the vertical stitches worked on the second journey. This stitch looks very attractive when tapestry or Persian wool is used for the first set of stitches and a stranded cotton or silk thread is used for the overstitching. The area is first covered by oblong cross stitches *(see page 133)* worked horizontally over four vertical and two horizontal canvas threads. The crosses fit neatly into each other and are arranged as shown. A second journey is then worked to overstitch the crosses with vertical straight stitches over four horizontal canvas threads.

365 Plaited stitch ☆
see also herringbone stitch

Plaited stitch is used on double canvas. It makes an attractive, ridged surface and is used for filling shapes and backgrounds. It consists of overlapping vertical rows of top-heavy crosses, and the method of working is very similar to that of canvas fern stitch *(see page 132)*. In that stitch the vertical rows are set side by side but in plaited stitch they overlap; each row overlaps the previous row by one vertical double thread of canvas. A soft wool thread, such as tapestry or Persian wool, looks best with this stitch and gives good canvas coverage.

366 Fishbone stitch no. 2 ☆
Unlike fishbone stitch no.1 *(see page 80)*, which is only worked on fabric, fishbone stitch no. 2 is used on double canvas for filling large areas and for backgrounds. It makes an attractive chevron pattern and can be worked in more than one colour. It consists of vertical rows of diagonal straight stitches crossed at the end by a shorter stitch, and is worked alternately up and down over the area. The slant of the diagonal stitches alternates on each row to form the chevrons. Any type of embroidery thread can be used for this stitch but care should be taken to match the weight of the thread to the gauge of the canvas to ensure that the canvas is completely covered by the stitching.

Fishbone stitch makes an attractive pattern when worked in alternate rows with tent stitch *(see page 121)*. When worked like this, the long diagonal stitches of the fishbone rows should all point in the same direction.

367 Diagonal fishbone stitch ☆
also known as stepped fishbone stitch

Diagonal fishbone stitch is a canvas stitch used on double canvas. It is a variation of fishbone stitch no. 2 *(see above)* and any type of embroidery thread can be used but care should be taken to match the weight of the thread to the gauge of the canvas to make sure that the canvas is completely covered by the stitching. The stitches are identical to those of fishbone stitch no. 2 but the arrangement of them over the canvas is different and they make a strongly diagonal pattern on the surface. The stitches are worked in diagonal rows with the stitches set horizontally or vertically in alternate rows. The rows run from the bottom left to the top right of the canvas. Diagonal fishbone stitch makes a good background stitch as it is fairly quick and easy to work.

368 Upright cross stitch ☆
also known as straight cross stitch

Upright cross stitch is a canvas stitch used on double canvas. The stitch makes a neat, crunchy texture on the surface and it is useful for filling small areas because of the small scale of the stitches. Each stitch is worked over two vertical and two horizontal double threads of the canvas; it is worked diagonally in two journeys, from the bottom right-hand corner to the top left-hand corner of the canvas, and then back again. The vertical stitches are worked first and then crossed by horizontal stitches of the same length. Any type of embroidery thread can be used but care should be taken to match the weight of the thread to the gauge of the canvas to make sure that the canvas is completely covered by the stitching.

369 Triple rice stitch ☆☆
and multiple rice stitch

Triple rice stitch is used on single and double canvas. As the name implies, this stitch is a complex variation of ordinary rice stitch *(see page 136)* and gives a heavier effect. It can be worked in two contrasting colours but looks equally attractive when worked in one. Any type of embroidery thread can be used with this stitch, providing that it is compatible with the gauge of the canvas but a lustrous thread, such as stranded cotton, enhances the light and shade effect created by the stitch. Each unit consists of six vertical and six horizontal canvas threads, and each corner is over-stitched by three graduated diagonal stitches.

The ordinary cross stitch *(see page 14)* can be made larger, with more diagonal stitches crossing the corners; it is then known as multiple rice stitch. This can be given a pretty striped pattern by working the alternate diagonal stitches in a contrasting colour of thread.

138 CANVAS STITCHES

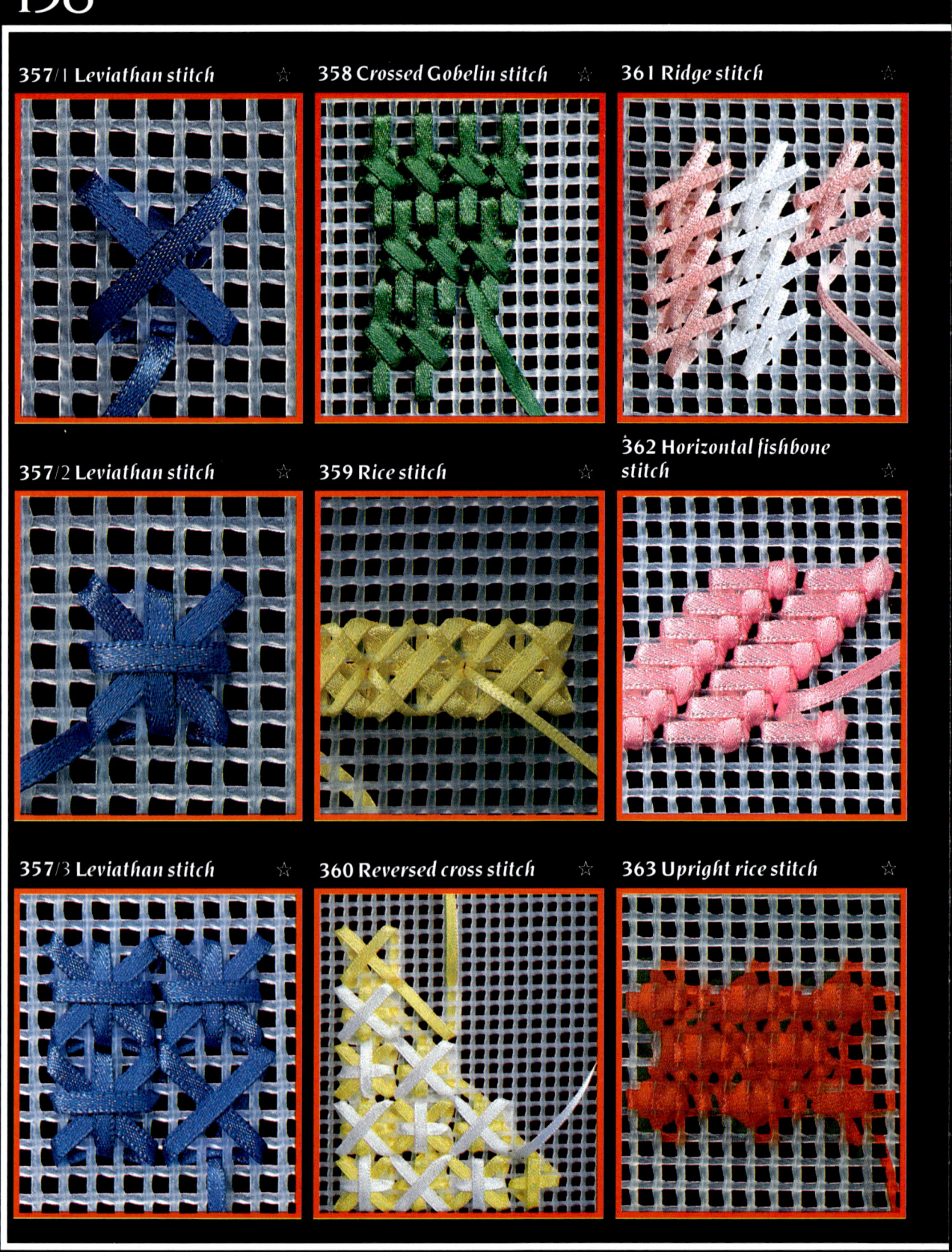

357/1 Leviathan stitch

358 Crossed Gobelin stitch

361 Ridge stitch

357/2 Leviathan stitch

359 Rice stitch

362 Horizontal fishbone stitch

357/3 Leviathan stitch

360 Reversed cross stitch

363 Upright rice stitch

CROSSED STITCHES **139**

364 Dutch stitch ☆

366/1 Fishbone stitch no. 2 ☆

367 Diagonal fishbone stitch ☆

365/1 Plaited stitch ☆

366/2 Fishbone stitch no. 2 ☆

368 Upright cross stitch ☆

365/2 Plaited stitch ☆

366/3 Fishbone stitch no. 2 ☆

369 Triple rice stitch and multiple rice stitch ☆☆

370 Chained cross stitch ☆☆

Chained cross stitch is a composite canvas stitch used on single or double canvas. It is a small stitch worked in rows to make a neat, regular texture and is used for filling shapes or background areas. An extremely hard-wearing stitch, it is very suitable for covering chair seats and church kneelers, provided that a durable thread has been used. It is straightforward to work and covers a square of four vertical and four horizontal canvas threads. A cross stitch *(see page 14)* is worked across this square, which is then over-stitched horizontally with a twisted chain stitch *(see page 21)*. The loop of the twisted chain stitch is anchored by a tiny diagonal stitch and the rows are worked from left to right of the area to be filled. Any type of embroidery thread is suitable for chained cross stitch, but care should be taken to match the weight of the thread to the gauge of the canvas to ensure that the canvas is completely covered by the stitching.

371 Diagonal cross stitch ☆☆

Diagonal cross stitch is a canvas stitch used for filling large shapes and background areas on single canvas. It is relatively quick to work and covers the canvas well. Worked upwards in diagonal rows from the bottom right-hand corner to the top left-hand corner of the area to be filled, it can be stitched in two or more colours to give a pretty, diagonally striped pattern. Each row consists of upright cross stitches *(see page 137)* worked over four vertical and four horizontal canvas threads and separated by diagonal straight stitches. Any type of embroidery thread can be used with diagonal cross stitch, but care should be taken to match the weight of thread to the gauge of canvas to ensure that the canvas is completely covered by the stitching. Diagonal cross stitch can also be used to fill shapes on an even-weave fabric.

372 Italian cross stitch ☆☆
also known as **two-sided Italian cross stitch, arrowhead cross stitch** *and* **Italian stitch**

Italian cross stitch is primarily a canvas stitch used on single or double canvas. It gives a dense texture and can also be used on even-weave fabrics if the thread is fairly fine. When this stitch is worked on a very loosely woven, even-weave fabric, the stitches can be pulled together tightly to produce an open-work effect. It consists of a cross stitch *(see page 14)* which covers a square of three vertical and three horizontal canvas or fabric threads, and four straight stitches arranged in a square around the cross stitch. Any type of fine embroidery thread can be used on an even-weave fabric but care should be taken, when using Italian cross stitch on canvas, to select a thread that will allow the stitching to completely cover the canvas.

CROSSED STITCHES

373 Long-armed cross stitch ☆☆
*also known as **long-legged cross stitch**, **plaited Slav stitch**, **Portuguese stitch** and **twist stitch***
Long-armed cross stitch is a canvas stitch used primarily on single and double canvas, although it can also be worked successfully on even-weave fabrics. It can be used both as a border and as a textured filling when it has a pretty, plaited appearance. It is worked in rows from left to right and consists of long diagonal stitches crossed by short diagonal stitches; the long stitches are worked over twice the number of threads as the short stitches. Long-armed cross stitch is straightforward to work and looks equally effective on fabric or canvas. Any type of embroidery thread can be used with this stitch, providing that the weight of the thread is compatible with the fabric or canvas.

374 Woven cross stitch ☆☆
*also known as **plaited cross stitch***
Woven cross stitch is a canvas stitch used on single and double canvas. This stitch forms square blocks that have a textured, woven appearance. It is used for large areas and backgrounds where a geometric stitch is needed. It can be worked in two contrasting or toning colours and the blocks arranged to make a chessboard pattern; a further colour can be introduced to frame the blocks with a border of back stitch *(see page 14)*. The blocks consist of a large ordinary cross stitch *(see page 14)* worked over four vertical and four horizontal canvas threads and overstitched by four diagonal straight stitches. These diagonal stitches are woven over and under each other as they are worked, and the sequence of stitches should be followed carefully. Any type of embroidery thread can be used with this stitch, but a soft wool thread, such as tapestry or Persian wool, will accentuate the woven appearance more than a cotton thread.

375 Double cross ☆☆
Double cross is a composite canvas stitch used on single canvas. It makes a heavy, squared pattern of raised blocks, which can be worked in two colours to make a chessboard pattern. Careful choice of thread and gauge of canvas is important, as this stitch looks its best when worked on quite a small scale; otherwise the pattern can be rather dominant. The blocks cover a square of seven canvas threads and each block is worked in two stages. The square is first crossed by two horizontal and two vertical straight stitches to make an upright cross figure. A second cross, made up of four diagonal straight stitches, is then worked: two run from top right to bottom left and two in the opposite direction. To complete the stitch, a tiny upright cross stitch *(see page 137)* is worked over two vertical and two horizontal canvas threads, where the corners of the blocks meet. Once completed, the blocks can be framed by vertical and horizontal straight stitches.

142 CANVAS STITCHES

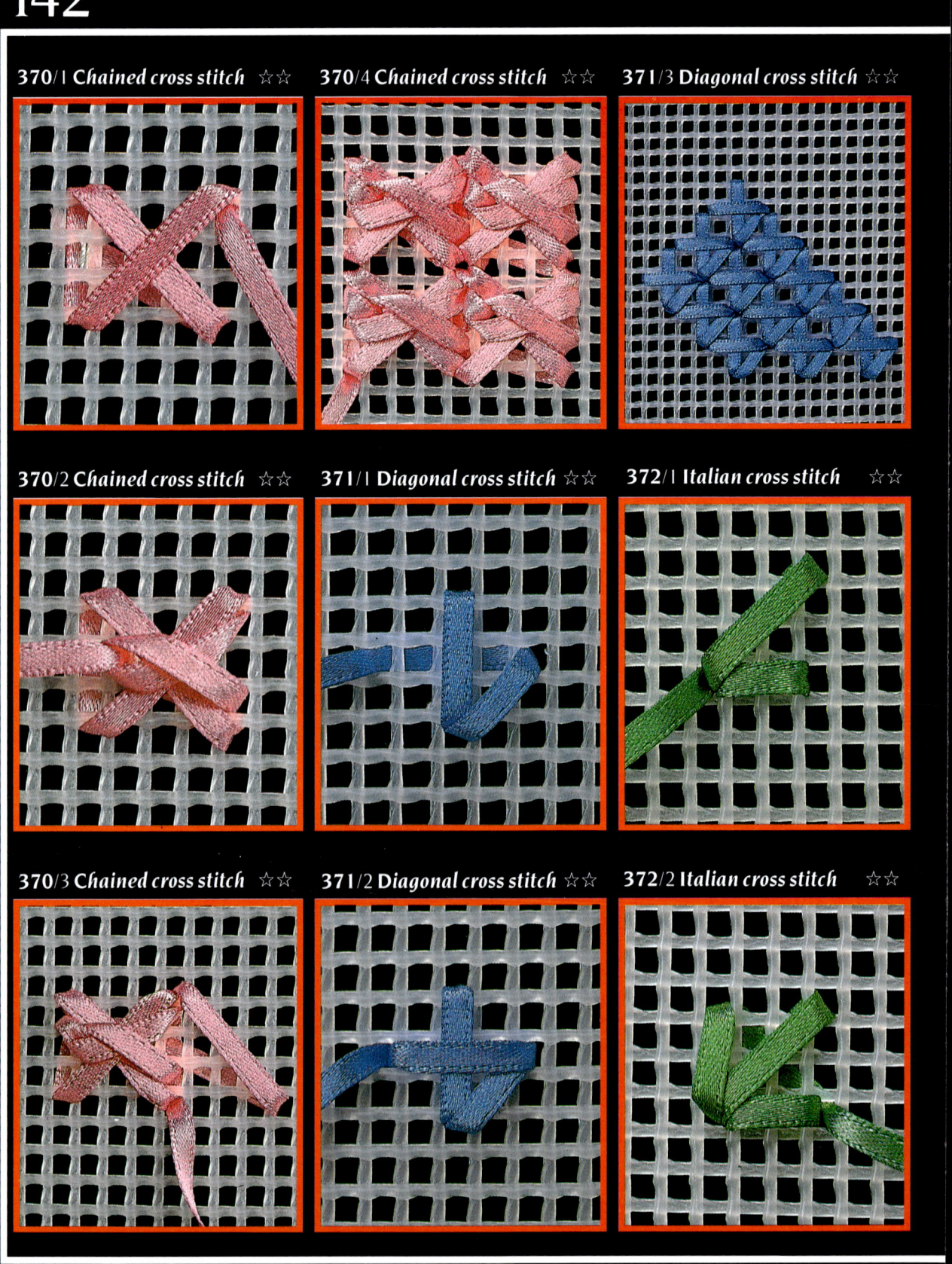

370/1 Chained cross stitch ☆☆

370/4 Chained cross stitch ☆☆

371/3 Diagonal cross stitch ☆☆

370/2 Chained cross stitch ☆☆

371/1 Diagonal cross stitch ☆☆

372/1 Italian cross stitch ☆☆

370/3 Chained cross stitch ☆☆

371/2 Diagonal cross stitch ☆☆

372/2 Italian cross stitch ☆☆

CROSSED STITCHES **143**

372/3 Italian cross stitch ☆☆

373/2 Long-armed cross stitch ☆☆

375/1 Double cross ☆☆

372/4 Italian cross stitch ☆☆

374/1 Woven cross stitch ☆☆

375/2 Double cross ☆☆

373/1 Long-armed cross stitch ☆☆

374/2 Woven cross stitch ☆☆

375/3 Double cross ☆☆

376 Plaited Algerian stitch ☆☆
Plaited Algerian stitch is used on double canvas and is worked in a similar way to closed herringbone stitch *(see page 60)*, forming neat channels of back stitch on the reverse of the canvas. On the surface, this stitch closely resembles plait stitch *(see below)* but its use of working thread is more economical. Plaited Algerian stitch is most effective when worked on a small-gauge canvas with a smooth thread, such as pearl cotton. It gives a dense, plaited texture and is used for working small areas in one colour.

377 Greek stitch ☆☆
also known as Greek cross stitch
Greek stitch is a canvas stitch used on single and double canvas. It should always be worked in a fairly thick thread, such as tapestry or Persian wool. Used for filling large shapes and background areas, it makes a raised, plaited pattern arranged in horizontal bands. It is worked rather like herringbone stitch *(see page 8)* but the crosses are spaced asymmetrically and are usually two double canvas threads tall. It is worked in horizontal rows with the crosses slanting in the opposite direction on every alternate row.

378 Montenegrin stitch ☆☆
also known as Montenegrin cross stitch and two-sided Montenegrin cross stitch
Montenegrin stitch is a canvas stitch used on single or double canvas. Similar in appearance to long-armed cross stitch *(see page 141)* and worked in a similar way, it has additional vertical bars. It is quick to work and can be used for filling large shapes and backgrounds; use a heavy thread so that the canvas is completely covered.

Work Montenegrin stitch upwards in horizontal rows, beginning each row at the left-hand side of the area to be filled. First make an irregular cross, in which the longest stitch is twice the length of the shortest stitch, and then make a vertical stitch. When worked in the correct sequence, this stitch is reversible, as the back builds up a pattern of ordinary cross stitches *(see page 14)*, alternating with vertical stitches. Montenegrin stitch can also be worked on an even-weave fabric, providing that a fairly fine thread is used.

379 Plait stitch ☆☆
also known as Spanish stitch
Plait stitch is a canvas stitch used on double canvas. It makes a dense, slightly raised and plaited surface, which is rather similar in appearance to plaited Algerian stitch *(see above)* but the method of working is different. This stitch should be worked in a fairly heavy thread, such as tapestry or Persian wool, to accentuate the raised surface and to cover the double threads of the canvas adequately. It can be used for outlines or for filling large areas and backgrounds, and it is quick and easy to work.

The horizontal rows are worked from left to right over two horizontal double threads of the canvas. A series of irregular cross stitches are made; the needle must always be inserted vertically through the canvas. Every row should begin at the left of the area to be covered and the second and subsequent rows should be worked directly underneath the preceding rows.

380 Rhodes stitch ☆☆
Rhodes stitch is a canvas stitch used on single canvas. The stitch makes a pattern of raised square blocks and is used for large areas and backgrounds. It can be worked over different sizes of square but is usually worked over six canvas threads. Any type of embroidery thread can be used but care should be taken to match the weight of the thread to the gauge of the canvas to make sure that the canvas is completely covered by the stitching.

Each block consists of straight stitches worked across the square, following each other in an anti-clockwise direction, so that they all cross over the same central point. Begin each square by working the first stitch from the bottom left-hand corner to the top right-hand corner and fill every hole round the square. After the block has been covered, work a short vertical stitch in the centre over two horizontal threads. This central stitch should be omitted if the stitch is worked over an odd number of threads. When a Rhodes stitch is worked very large, perhaps over ten canvas threads, a neater way of tying it down is to work a straight stitch over each corner, from the mid-point of one side of the square to the mid-point of an adjacent side. The blocks are arranged in horizontal rows, and can be worked in two contrasting colours to give a chessboard effect.

381 Half Rhodes stitch ☆☆
Half Rhodes stitch is a canvas stitch used on single canvas. It makes an attractive textured surface, which is used for filling large shapes and background areas; it is a variation of Rhodes stitch *(see above)*. This stitch

is worked in diagonal rows from the top left to the bottom right of the area to be covered, and the stitches on each row interlock with those on the preceding row. Each stitch consists of a half-worked Rhodes stitch, worked over six vertical and six horizontal canvas threads. Form the first stitch in the same way as Rhodes stitch and continue round in an anti-clockwise direction until all the holes at the top and bottom of the square are filled. Any type of embroidery thread can be used, but care should be taken to match the weight of the thread to the gauge of the canvas to make sure the canvas is completely covered by the stitching.

Half Rhodes stitch can also be worked in horizontal rows with the edges of the stitches touching. A series of diamond shapes of canvas are left showing through and these are filled in with a matching thread, using tent stitch *(see page 121)*.

382 Plaited Rhodes stitch ☆☆

Plaited Rhodes stitch is a canvas stitch used on single canvas. It makes an attractive plaited surface and is a variation of half Rhodes stitch *(see page 144)*, which is used for filling shapes of any size and for backgrounds. The stitches are worked in horizontal rows and each row interlocks with the preceding row. The direction of the stitches changes on alternate rows from anti-clockwise to clockwise and the size of each plaited Rhodes stitch is quite small, covering four vertical and four horizontal canvas threads. Any type of embroidery thread can be used with this stitch, providing it is compatible with the gauge of the canvas, but a lustrous thread, such as stranded cotton or silk, shows it off to better advantage than a hairy woollen thread.

383 Captive rice stitch ☆☆

Captive rice stitch is a canvas stitch used on single or double canvas. A variation of ordinary rice stitch *(see page 136)*, it makes a strongly textured geometric pattern and is used for large areas and backgrounds. Any type of embroidery thread can be used, but care should be taken to match the weight of the thread to the gauge of the canvas to make sure that the canvas is completely covered by the stitching. The stitch consists of a rice stitch surrounded by groups of straight stitches to make a framed block. The second and third straight stitches are worked into the same holes, making a raised bar, and they cover six canvas threads. The blocks are arranged side by side, and a small area is left where the corners of four blocks meet. This can remain unworked, or a tiny ordinary cross stitch *(see page 14)* can be worked to fill it. Captive rice stitch looks very effective when the framing straight stitches are worked in a thread of contrasting colour to that of the rice stitch.

384 Star stitch ☆☆

see also Algerian eye stitch

Star stitch is a canvas stitch used on single canvas. It makes an attractively textured pattern of stars and can be used to fill a shape of any size or for background areas.

Work a grid of large, upright cross stitches *(see page 137)* over six vertical and six horizontal canvas threads to cover the whole shape. They should be worked in horizontal rows and the four adjoining arms of the crosses should share the same holes in the canvas. Next, work a small cross stitch *(see page 14)* over two canvas threads over the upright crosses on every other horizontal row. Then overstitch the upright crosses on the remaining rows with a larger cross stitch worked over four canvas threads. Any type of embroidery thread can be used but care should be taken to match the weight of the thread to the gauge of the canvas to make sure that the canvas is completely covered by the stitching. The cross stitches can be worked in a contrasting colour or weight of thread.

385 Square herringbone stitch ☆☆

also known as multiplait

Square herringbone stitch is a canvas stitch used on single canvas. It makes a large, bold, dramatic pattern, which can be rather dominant, and is used for background areas. The stitch makes a plaited diamond shape, which can be altered in size by increasing or decreasing the number of rows worked. It consists of a central ordinary cross stitch *(see page 14)* enclosed by rows of herringbone stitch *(see page 8)*. The diamond shapes are worked in horizontal rows, so that the rows interlock. The gaps between the edges of the diamond shapes are filled by two straight stitches of commensurate lengths. A soft wool thread, such as tapestry or Persian wool, is the most suitable for this stitch.

146 CANVAS STITCHES

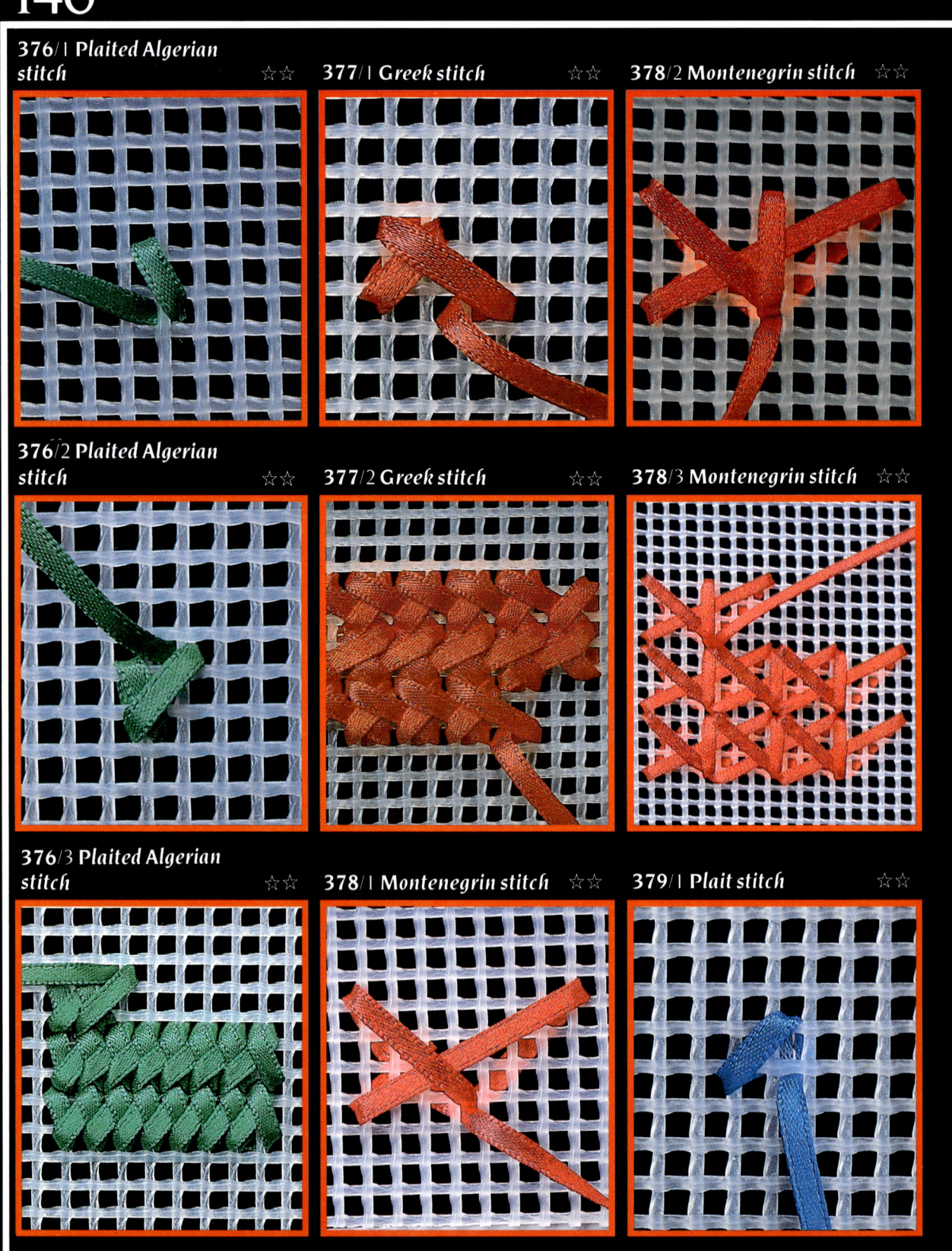

376/1 Plaited Algerian stitch ☆☆

377/1 Greek stitch ☆☆

378/2 Montenegrin stitch ☆☆

376/2 Plaited Algerian stitch ☆☆

377/2 Greek stitch ☆☆

378/3 Montenegrin stitch ☆☆

376/3 Plaited Algerian stitch ☆☆

378/1 Montenegrin stitch ☆☆

379/1 Plait stitch ☆☆

CROSSED STITCHES **147**

379/2 Plait stitch

381/1 Half Rhodes stitch

383 Captive rice stitch

379/3 Plait stitch

381/2 Half Rhodes stitch

384 Star stitch

380 Rhodes stitch

382 Plaited Rhodes stitch

385 Square herringbone stitch

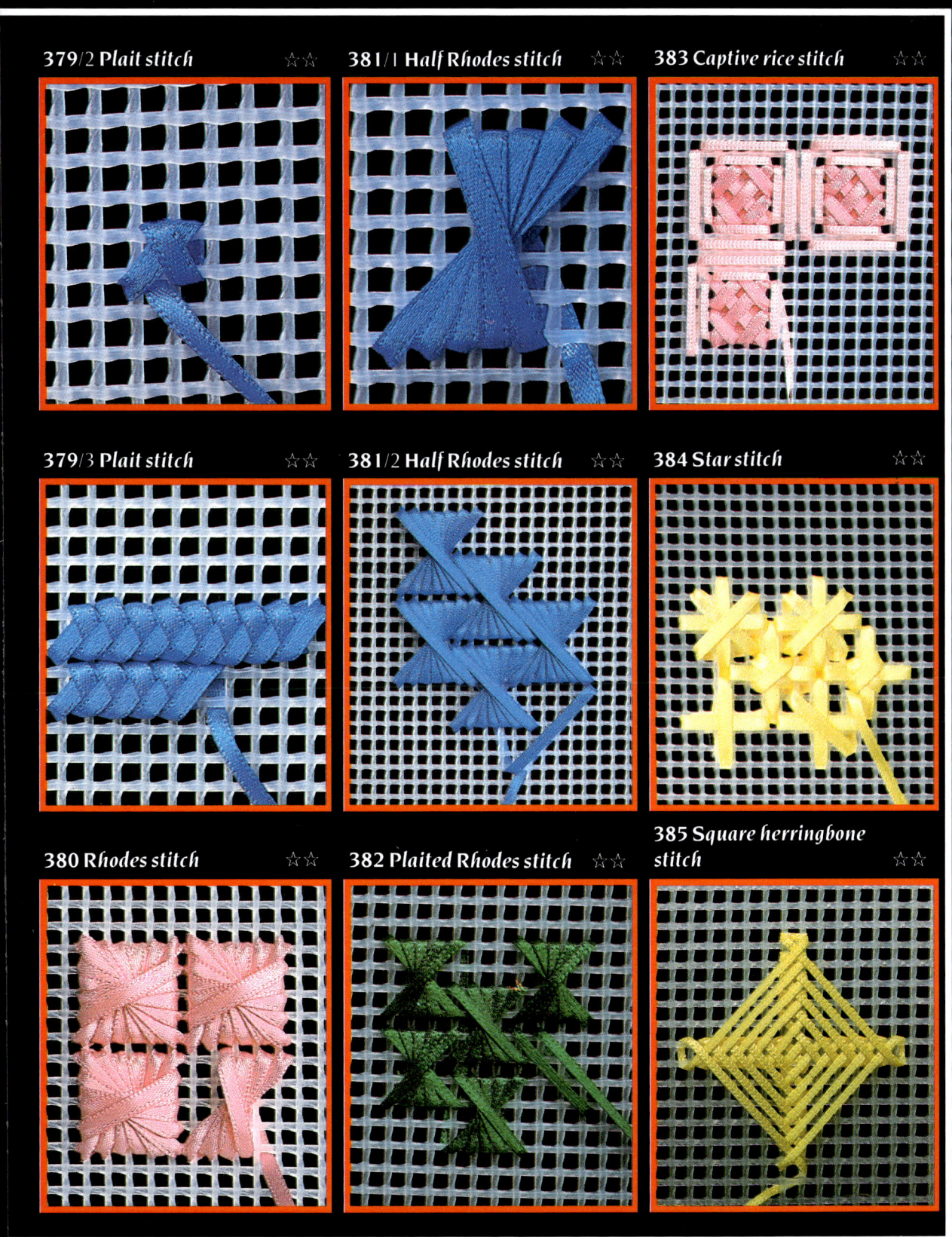

386 Velvet stitch ☆☆
also known as rug stitch, tassel stitch, raised stitch, Astrakhan stitch, plush stitch and Berlin plush stitch

Velvet stitch resembles the pile of a carpet and is worked only on double canvas. It became very popular during the Berlin woolwork craze in Europe and America during the middle to late nineteenth century. It was used to give a three-dimensional quality to animals, birds and flowers, against a flat cross stitch background. When working velvet stitch, use one strand of a thick, soft wool or several strands of a fine wool. Cut and trim the loops to length after the stitching has been completed. If the stitches are worked very closely together on the canvas and a thick wool is used, the resulting pile will be dense enough to be sculptured with a sharp pair of scissors.

387 Waffle stitch ☆☆☆
also known as Norwich stitch

Waffle stitch is a large canvas stitch used on single canvas. It makes a pattern of square blocks with superimposed raised diamonds, and is used to fill large shapes and background areas. The blocks can be worked in various sizes, but the squares must contain an odd number of canvas threads. The photograph shows a waffle stitch worked over a square of nine threads: eighteen diagonal straight stitches are worked across the square, following the sequence shown. The second and subsequent straight stitches are worked over each preceding stitch until seventeen have been completed. The eighteenth stitch is taken under the last stitch that it crosses, rather than over it. Any type of embroidery thread can be used with waffle stitch, providing that the weight of the thread is compatible with the gauge of the canvas selected.

388 Octagonal Rhodes stitch ☆☆☆
Octagonal Rhodes stitch is a canvas stitch used on single canvas. A variation of Rhodes stitch *(see page 144)*, it makes a very raised surface of octagonal blocks, and the spaces in between are filled by individual Rhodes stitches; it is used for filling large areas and for backgrounds. It is worked in the same way as Rhodes stitch, with the stitches following each other in an anti-clockwise direction, so that they all cross over the same central point, but the outline shape followed is an octagon rather than a square. Follow the sequence of stitches carefully and arrange the octagons so that they touch at the vertical and horizontal edges. The squares of canvas remaining should be covered with an ordinary Rhodes stitch in a matching thread. Care should be taken when deciding where to use this stitch, as the pattern can be very dominant and may swamp a smaller, more delicate, stitch. Any type of embroidery thread

389 Criss-cross stitch ☆☆☆

Criss-cross stitch is a large-scale canvas stitch used on single canvas. A complicated stitch to work, it gives a dense, unusual texture. It is used over large areas or backgrounds, as it covers the canvas well. Any type of embroidery thread can be used, but care should be taken when matching the weight of the thread to the gauge of the canvas selected. As with other complex canvas stitches, a small sample should be worked to test the compatibility of the thread and canvas: if the thread is too fine, the canvas ground will show through; if it is too heavy, the resultant stitch will be too bulky and distorted to give a pleasing appearance.

Criss-cross stitch consists of five slanting stitches radiating from the bottom left-hand corner and crossed by four slanting stitches from the bottom right-hand corner. They are worked alternately, and make a woven surface. Follow the sequence shown carefully, as accuracy is crucial to the formation of the stitch. The completed stitches are arranged in horizontal rows, and are always worked from left to right of the area to be covered.

390 Plaited double cross ☆☆☆

Plaited double cross stitch is a composite canvas stitch and is used on single canvas. It is a more complex version of double cross stitch *(see page 141)* and has the same raised square pattern but with a woven effect. It is worked in a similar way: first the blocks are made in two stages, and then the small upright crosses are worked. The difference lies in the arrangement of the straight stitches that make the square blocks as they are plaited over and under each other. The sequence

can be used, but care should be taken to match the weight of the thread to the gauge of the canvas to make sure that the canvas is completely covered by the stitching.

of stitches shown should be followed very carefully. As with double cross, choice of thread and gauge of canvas is important, as the pattern can be rather dominant when worked on a large scale.

391 Double leviathan stitch ☆☆☆

Double leviathan stitch is a canvas stitch used on single or double canvas. It is a more complex variation of leviathan stitch *(see page 136)* and makes a larger, more raised pattern of square blocks. These blocks can be worked in two colours to give a chessboard pattern. A large cross stitch *(see page 14)* worked over four canvas threads is stitched first, followed by further crossing stitches and, lastly, a large upright cross stitch *(see page 137)*. Follow the sequence of stitches carefully. The raised, almost crunchy surface of double leviathan stitch looks best when worked in a fairly thick thread, such as tapestry or Persian wool.

150 CANVAS STITCHES

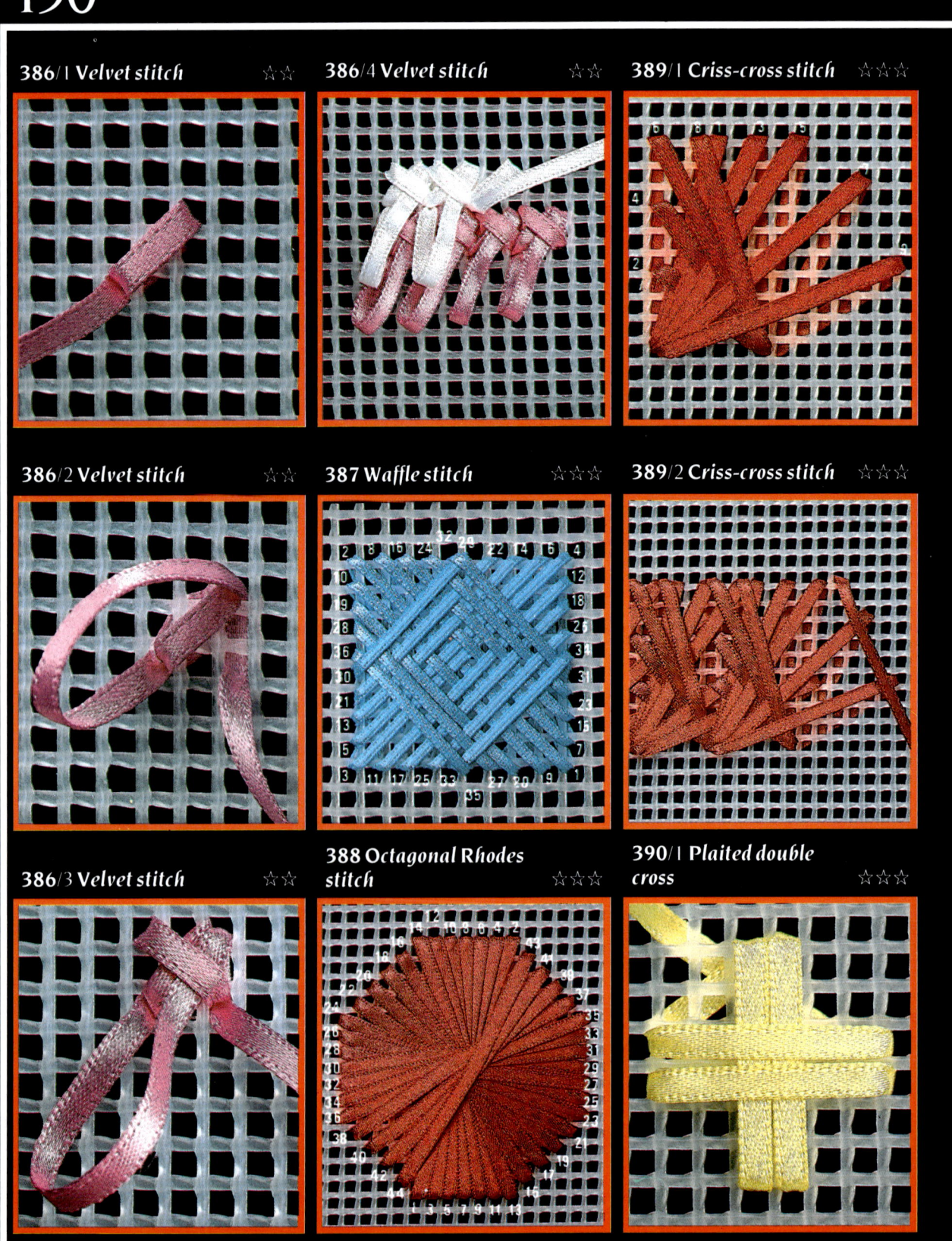

386/1 Velvet stitch ☆☆

386/4 Velvet stitch ☆☆

389/1 Criss-cross stitch ☆☆☆

386/2 Velvet stitch ☆

387 Waffle stitch ☆☆☆

389/2 Criss-cross stitch ☆☆☆

386/3 Velvet stitch ☆☆

388 Octagonal Rhodes stitch ☆☆☆

390/1 Plaited double cross ☆☆☆

CROSSED STITCHES **151**

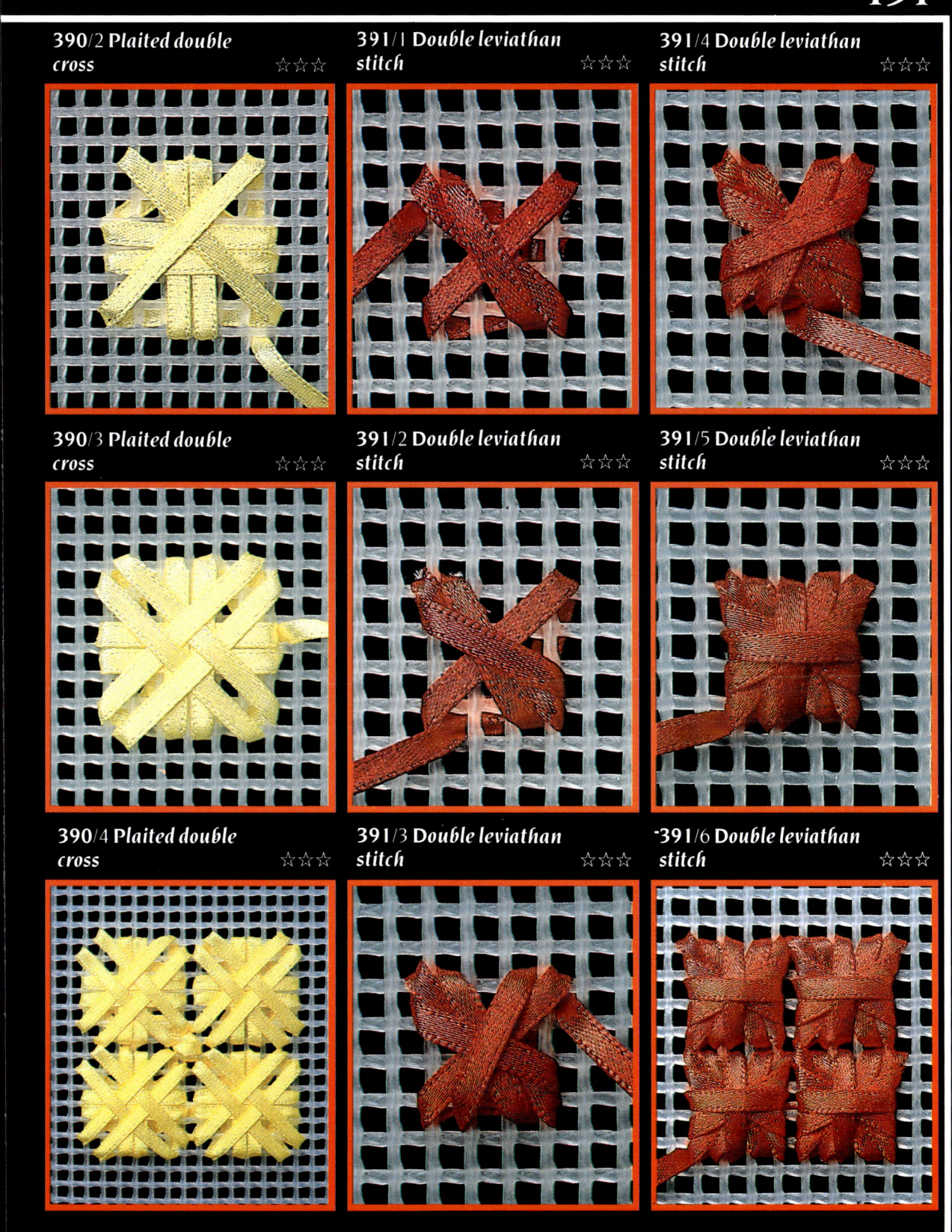

390/2 Plaited double cross ☆☆☆

391/1 Double leviathan stitch ☆☆☆

391/4 Double leviathan stitch ☆☆☆

390/3 Plaited double cross ☆☆☆

391/2 Double leviathan stitch ☆☆☆

391/5 Double leviathan stitch ☆☆☆

390/4 Plaited double cross ☆☆☆

391/3 Double leviathan stitch ☆☆☆

391/6 Double leviathan stitch ☆☆☆

Composite stitches

392 Balcony stitch ☆
Balcony stitch is a canvas stitch that is very quick to work over a large area. It is not suitable for cushions or upholstery, as the stitches are quite long and will snag and catch easily. Single canvas should be used, and consideration should be given to the gauge of canvas and the weight of thread used in order to cover the canvas ground successfully. If the crossing threads are too long, they will sag and spoil the geometric basketweave appearance of the stitch. Work the five vertical straight stitches first, and then cross them with five horizontal stitches of the same length. Work these groups of stitches diagonally across the area to be covered and fit them together. Balcony stitch can also be used to shade an area if graduated tones of thread are chosen for the horizontal crossing stitches.

393 Chained stitch ☆
Chained stitch is a canvas stitch used on single canvas. It can also be worked on an even-weave fabric, where the threads can be counted to keep the stitches even. On canvas, it is used for filling shapes and backgrounds since it creates an unusual texture and is quite quick to work. It is similar to cross stitch *(see page 14)* except that the second diagonal is made by a chain loop instead of a straight stitch. Each stitch is worked over an area two canvas threads wide and two threads deep. Care should be taken when matching the weight of the thread to the gauge of the canvas to ensure that the canvas will be completely covered by the stitch.

394 Chequer stitch ☆
Chequer stitch is a composite canvas stitch used on single canvas. When worked in one colour, the stitch has the look of a woven or brocaded fabric, enhanced by the use of a light-catching flat thread, such as stranded cotton or silk. It looks equally attractive worked in two tones or two contrasting colours of tapestry, Persian or crewel wool, to make a chequered pattern. It is often used for backgrounds when a geometric pattern is needed. Relatively quick to work, it covers the canvas well. The pattern is arranged in squares, each square covering an area of four vertical and four horizontal canvas threads. Squares of sixteen tent stitches *(see page 121)* alternate with squares composed of seven diagonal straight stitches of graduating lengths. These squares should be worked in diagonal rows from top left to bottom right of the area to be filled.

395 English stitch ☆
English stitch is a modern stitch used on single canvas. It makes a bold, textured surface and is most effective when worked in tapestry or Persian wool. It is used for filling large shapes and backgrounds since it covers the canvas well. Work the stitch in rectangular blocks in either horizontal or vertical rows. Each block should cover an area of six vertical and four horizontal canvas threads. First cover the block with five vertical straight stitches. Then overstitch the corners of the block with two diagonal straight stitches of different lengths. The size of the blocks can be altered, if required, but the threads in the block must always be of an even number.

396 Foliage stitch ☆
Foliage stitch is a canvas stitch worked on single canvas. Since it is relatively quick to work and covers the canvas well, it is used for filling shapes of any size and for backgrounds. It makes a regular geometric pattern of square blocks and each block looks rather like a diagonal leaf. Each block is worked over four canvas threads, and the blocks are repeated in horizontal rows. Each block consists of three vertical and three horizontal straight stitches of graduating lengths, divided by a long diagonal stitch worked over the square from the bottom left-hand corner to the top right-hand corner. Foliage stitch can be worked in any type of embroidery thread, providing that it is compatible with the gauge of the canvas, but it probably looks most attractive when worked with a soft wool thread, such as Persian wool.

397 Cushion stitch ☆
see also Florentine stitch and tent stitch
Cushion stitch is a composite canvas stitch used on single canvas. It is worked in two stages with the same thread and has the appearance of a woven or brocaded fabric. It has a neat, geometric pattern and is used for filling background areas. It is relatively quick and simple to work and any type of thread can be used, providing that it is compatible with the gauge of the canvas. However, this stitch will look more striking if it is worked in a lustrous thread, such as stranded cotton.

On the first journey, small squares of graduated diagonal stitches are worked over three vertical and three horizontal canvas threads; the stitches should all fall in the same direction. A gap of one canvas thread separates each square and each row of squares. The squares are then framed by a border of tent stitch *(see page 121)* worked in the same thread and with the stitches facing in the same direction. Strictly speaking, the name 'cushion' refers only to the square blocks, which can be worked without the border of tent stitch.

398 Crossed corners cushion stitch ☆
Crossed corners cushion stitch is a geometric canvas stitch used on single canvas. It is a very effective stitch for covering backgrounds as it is quick to work and covers the canvas well. The pattern consists of square blocks, which can be worked to any size, arranged in fours so that a square motif is formed. Each block is filled by graduated diagonal straight stitches, running in one direction. Half the square is then overstitched in the opposite direction. Any type of embroidery thread can be used, but care should be taken to match the weight of the thread to the gauge of the canvas to ensure that the canvas is completely covered by the stitching. However, this stitch looks most effective when a lustrous thread, such as stranded cotton, is used to enhance the light and shade effect made by the arrangement of the stitches.

COMPOSITE STITCHES

399 Beetle stitch and barred beetle stitch ☆

Beetle stitch is a canvas stitch best worked on single canvas and with a thick thread, such as tapestry or Persian wool. It forms slightly padded oval shapes, hence its name, and is used for filling backgrounds. It consists of a padding layer of three vertical straight stitches worked in the centre three spaces of the oval; and eight horizontal stitches varying in length worked over the padding. If any canvas threads are still visible after the beetle shapes have been worked, the gaps can be filled in with tent stitch *(see page 121)*, or the ovals can be outlined with back stitch *(see page 14)*, using the same thread.

Barred beetle stitch forms the same oval shapes, but the horizontal straight stitches are worked before the vertical ones. The three vertical stitches are then added, with the base of each stitch sharing the same central hole in the canvas; these three stitches make a V-shaped bar across the beetle shape. As with beetle stitch, gaps between the shapes can be filled with either tent stitch or back stitch.

400 Flower stitch ☆

Flower stitch is a canvas stitch used on single or double canvas. It has a similar appearance to floral stitch *(see below)* but the regular pattern created by flower stitch is slightly larger. It can be used to fill any size of shape or background area, and looks most effective when worked in a soft wool thread, such as tapestry or Persian wool. The pattern is worked in two horizontal rows, which alternate as they fill the area. The first row consists of blocks of two horizontal straight stitches worked over four vertical canvas threads, and alternating with a small cross stitch *(see page 14)* worked over one thread. The second row consists of blocks of two vertical straight stitches worked over four horizontal canvas threads and alternating with a larger cross stitch worked over two threads and surrounded by four straight stitches, each worked over two threads.

401 Floral stitch ☆

Floral stitch is a composite canvas stitch used on single or double canvas. It makes an attractive regular pattern, which can be used to fill any size of shape or background area. Any type of thread can be used for this stitch, provided that it is compatible with the gauge of the canvas selected, but a soft wool thread, such as tapestry or Persian wool, is particularly suitable. The pattern is formed by two horizontal rows of stitching, which are worked alternately to cover the shape. The first row consists of blocks of three horizontal straight stitches worked over three vertical canvas threads, alternating with cross stitch *(see page 14)* worked over three threads. The second row consists of blocks of three vertical straight stitches worked over three horizontal canvas threads alternating with a smaller cross stitch worked over two threads. The crosses and the blocks of straight stitches alternate.

402 Chessboard stitch ☆

Chessboard stitch is a canvas stitch used on single canvas. It gives a ridged effect overstitched by crosses, and provides a quick and easy way to fill large areas of canvas. Any type of embroidery thread is suitable for this stitch, providing that it is matched to the gauge of canvas being used. It is worked in alternate squares: one kind of square is worked over the canvas first, then the spaces are filled in by the second kind of square. The first squares consist of four vertical straight stitches worked in a group over four horizontal threads of the canvas. This group of stitches is then overstitched by a large cross stitch *(see page 14)*, extending diagonally across the group; the centre of the cross stitch is anchored by a small, horizontal straight stitch. The spaces left uncovered on the canvas after the first set of squares have been completed are filled in by groups of four vertical straight stitches. Although usually worked in monochrome, chessboard stitch can look very effective if two contrasting colours or two tones of the same colour are used.

403 French stitch ☆
also known as tied Renaissance stitch

French stitch is a canvas stitch worked on double canvas. It makes a closely worked, slightly textured surface and is ideal for filling large shapes and backgrounds. It looks most attractive when worked with a soft, thick thread, such as tapestry or Persian wool, and it covers the canvas well. The stitches are arranged in horizontal rows and worked from right to left and then left to right, alternately. Each stitch consists of two vertical straight stitches worked over four double canvas threads, which are worked in the same holes at the ends. The long stitches are tied down at each side over the double threads by two short horizontal stitches. The two long stitches bow slightly when they are anchored. The stitches on the second row interlock with those on the first, and so on. If preferred, French stitch can also be worked in diagonal rows from the top left to the bottom right of the shape but the finished results are identical.

154 CANVAS STITCHES

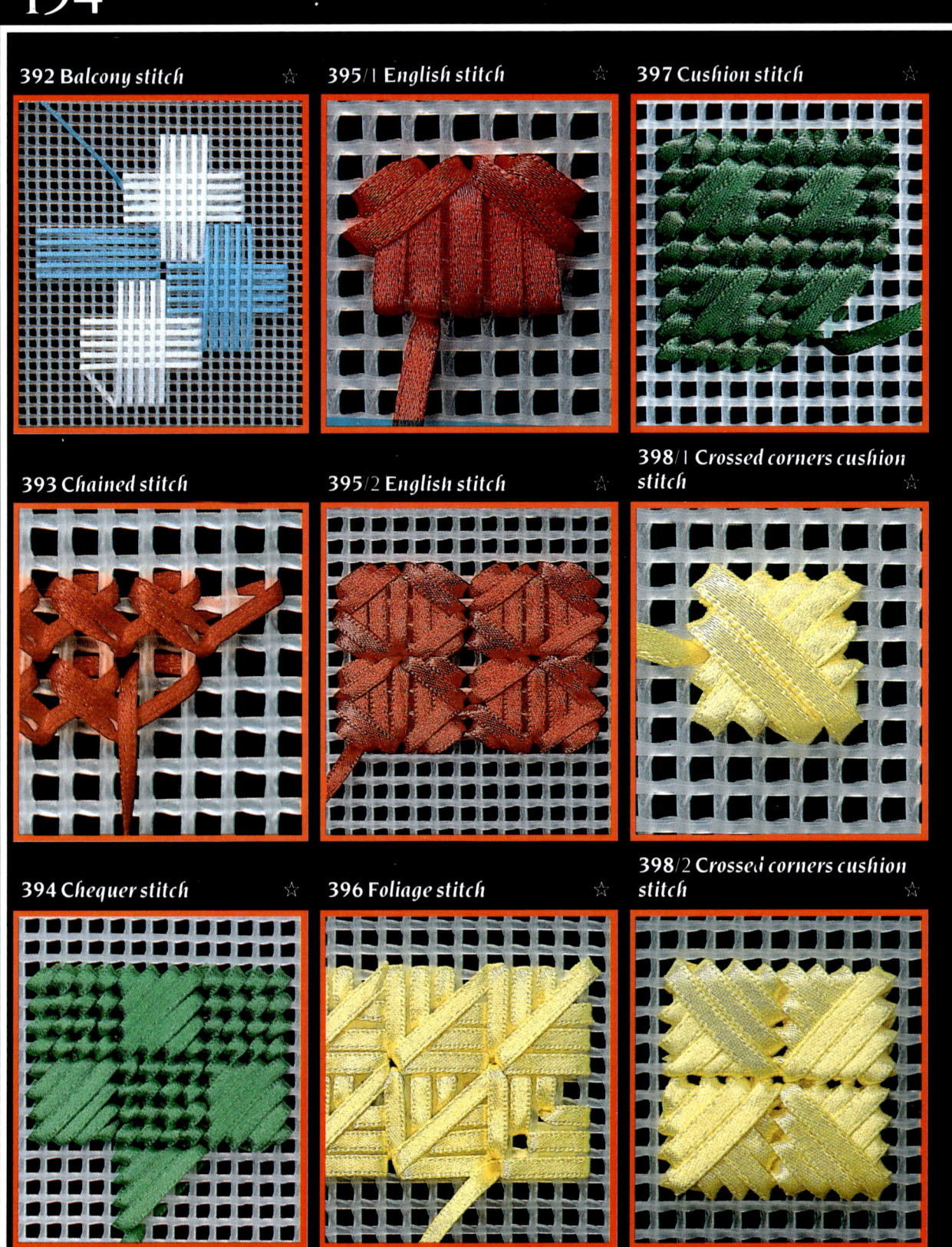

392 Balcony stitch

395/1 English stitch

397 Cushion stitch

393 Chained stitch

395/2 English stitch

398/1 Crossed corners cushion stitch

394 Chequer stitch

396 Foliage stitch

398/2 Crossed corners cushion stitch

COMPOSITE STITCHES 155

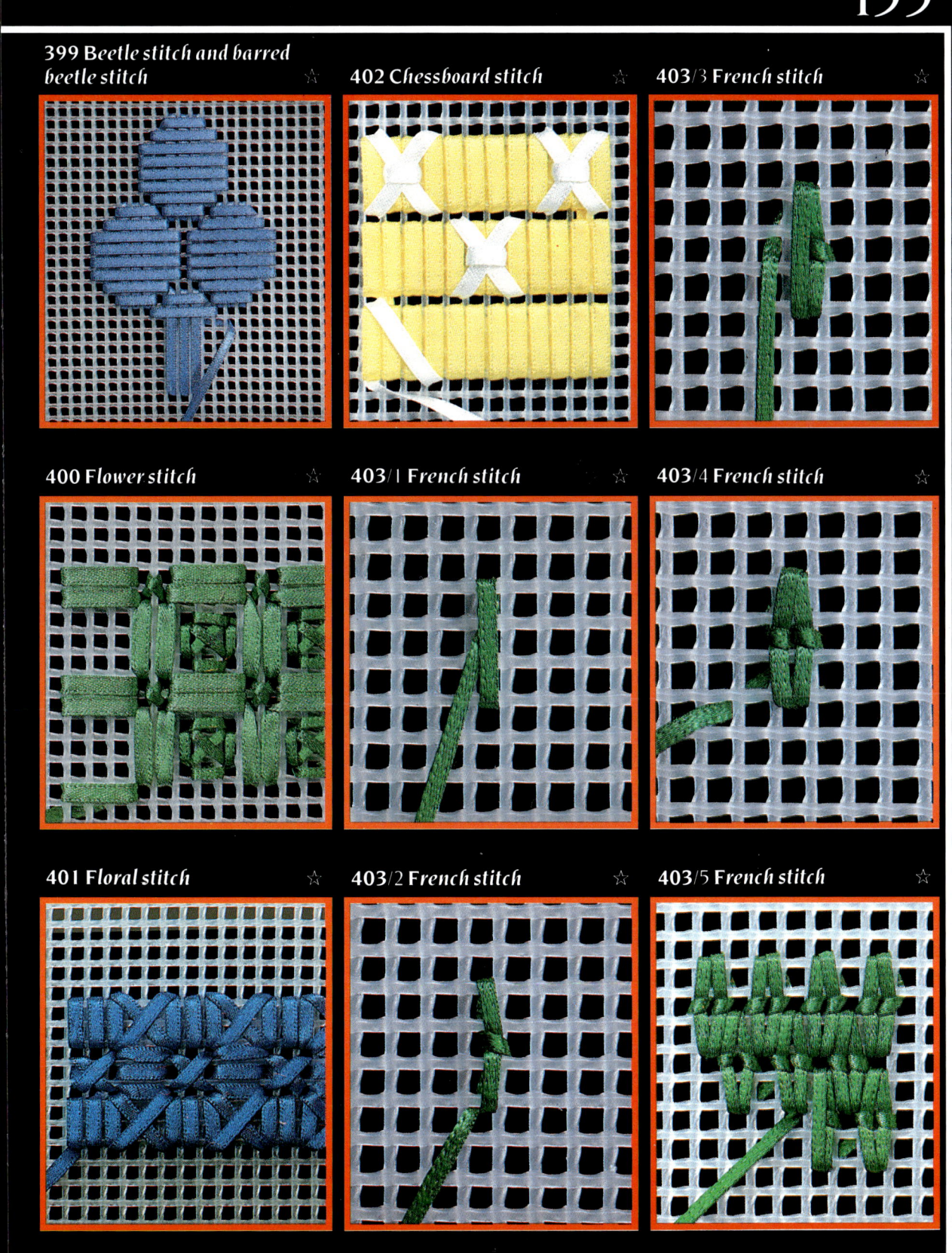

399 Beetle stitch and barred beetle stitch

402 Chessboard stitch

403/3 French stitch

400 Flower stitch

403/1 French stitch

403/4 French stitch

401 Floral stitch

403/2 French stitch

403/5 French stitch

CANVAS STITCHES

404 Wheat sheaf stitch ☆
Wheat sheaf stitch is a canvas stitch used on single canvas for filling a shape of any size. It consists of three vertical straight stitches tied down by a tiny horizontal stitch to make a shape like a sheaf of corn. The sheaves can be worked over four or six horizontal canvas threads; if they are to be worked solidly over the canvas, the corners of the sheaves should touch each other. This stitch looks very attractive if the sheaves are spaced two or three canvas threads apart over the entire shape. The unworked canvas can then be covered by tent stitch *(see page 121)* worked in a matching thread. The sheaves can also be worked with a half drop. Any type of embroidery thread can be used to work wheat sheaf stitch, providing that the weight of the thread is compatible with the gauge of the canvas selected.

405 Rapid stitch ☆
Rapid stitch is a canvas stitch used on single canvas. As its name indicates, rapid stitch is extremely quick to work; it is used for filling shapes of any size and backgrounds. Any type of embroidery thread can be used with this stitch, but care should be taken to match the weight of the thread to the gauge of the canvas to make sure that the canvas is completely covered by the stitching. A soft wool thread, such as tapestry or Persian wool, gives the best coverage, and is preferable to a firm cotton thread. Rapid stitch makes a textured surface. Each stitch covers an area of four vertical and four horizontal canvas threads. An ordinary cross stitch *(see page 14)* is first made across the square and then four slanting stitches are worked across it with one pair at the right and one at the left. If any canvas is still showing, an extra stitch can be made in the centre, running from the top to the bottom of the square, and each square can be framed with back stitch *(see page 14)* to give a more closely worked effect. The back stitch can be worked in a matching or contrasting colour, or in a lighter weight of thread than the rest of the stitching.

406 Quodlibet stitch ☆
Quodlibet stitch is a canvas stitch used on single canvas. It is suitable for covering large areas and backgrounds and makes a closely worked surface with a pattern of arrowheads. Any type of embroidery thread can be used, although the gauge of the canvas should be taken into consideration. This stitch will benefit from being worked in a fairly flat thread, such as stranded cotton or silk. It is quite easy to work and consists of large lozenge-shaped units which contain two arrowheads, one pointing upwards and one downwards. First work a central vertical stitch over twelve horizontal canvas threads. Then make the bottom arrowhead, which consists of four slanting stitches radiating from the same hole. Tie down the long stitch with a short, horizontal stitch before making the top arrowhead in exactly the same way. The lozenges are arranged side by side in horizontal rows, each row interlocking with the preceding one, as shown. Quodlibet stitch makes an interesting pattern when alternate rows are worked in a contrasting colour.

407 Seven stitch ☆
Seven stitch is a canvas stitch used on single and double canvas. It is very quick to work and is useful for filling large areas and backgrounds. The stitch makes a regular pattern of lightly textured blocks, each one consisting of seven stitches. Four vertical straight stitches are worked first, covering four horizontal canvas threads. These are then covered by three horizontal straight stitches. The blocks are worked in horizontal rows, and two colours can be used to make a chessboard pattern. The two threads left uncovered at the corners of the blocks can have an ordinary cross stitch *(see page 14)* worked over them, or, alternatively, a row of small back stitches *(see page 14)* can be worked to frame each block and cover these threads. Any type of embroidery thread can be used, but care should be taken to match the weight of the thread to the gauge of the canvas to ensure that the canvas is completely covered by the stitching.

408 Pineapple stitch ☆
Pineapple stitch is a canvas stitch used on single canvas. It makes a pattern of textured blocks, which are worked with a half drop, and, as its name indicates, it looks very much like the skin of a pineapple. This stitch is very quick and easy to work and is suitable for covering large shapes and background areas. It can be worked in two colours by using a second thread for the superimposed cross and the tying stitch. Any type of embroidery thread can be used, but care should be taken to match the weight of the thread to the gauge of the canvas to ensure that the canvas will be completely covered by the stitching.

Each block is first covered by four vertical straight stitches worked over four horizontal canvas threads. Work an ordinary cross stitch *(see page 14)* over four threads, making sure that the top diagonal stitch crosses from the bottom right-hand corner to the top left-hand corner. Then tie down the cross in the centre by working a short, diagonal stitch over the central vertical thread of the canvas.

409 Tied stitch ☆
Tied stitch is a canvas stitch used on single canvas. It makes a neat pattern of barred rectangular blocks arranged with a half drop. It is very quick and easy to work and is ideal for covering large shapes and background areas rapidly. Each stitch consists of two long, vertical straight stitches worked over six horizontal canvas threads and tied down by a short crossing stitch in the centre. The stitch is worked diagonally across the area to be filled, working from the top left to the bottom right. Any type of thread can be used, but care should be taken to match the weight of the thread to the gauge of the canvas to ensure that the canvas is completely covered by the stitching.

410 Scottish stitch ☆
Scottish stitch is a canvas stitch worked on single canvas in two colours of thread. It makes a neat pattern of framed squares and is very similar to cushion stitch *(see page 152)*, except that cushion stitch is

COMPOSITE STITCHES

worked in only one colour. Scottish stitch consists of small blocks of five diagonal straight stitches worked over three vertical and three horizontal canvas threads. Each square is framed by a border of tent stitch *(see page 121)* worked in a contrasting colour of thread. The diagonal and tent stitches should always fall in the same direction – from bottom left to top right. Any type of embroidery thread can be used, providing that it is compatible with the gauge of the canvas, but a combination of a lustrous, stranded cotton with a wool yarn can look extremely effective.

411 Roman filling ☆
Roman filling is a canvas stitch used on single canvas. It makes an attractive diamond pattern and is used for filling large shapes and backgrounds. An adaptation of a fabric stitch called Roman stitch *(see page 44)* for use on canvas, it can be worked with any type of embroidery thread, providing that it is compatible with the gauge of the canvas selected. However, this stitch is shown off to best advantage when pearl or stranded cotton is used, and when it is worked on a small scale. Each diamond shape spans seven vertical and eight horizontal threads of canvas, and they are worked in diagonal rows from the top left to the bottom right of the area to be covered. Seven Roman stitches are worked in the centre of each diamond shape. Roman filling can be worked in more than one colour to give pretty zigzag stripes across the entire shape.

412 Crow's foot stitch ☆☆
Crow's foot stitch is a canvas stitch used on single canvas. It makes an attractive filling or background stitch and it is fairly quick to work. It is worked in two journeys; the first journey must cover the whole area before the second journey can commence. On the first journey, groups of straight stitches, radiating from a central hole, are worked over three or four horizontal canvas threads, depending on the size of stitch required. A single vertical straight stitch is worked alternately with the groups on the same journey. The rows are worked horizontally, from left to right and then back again. After the shape has been covered, rows of back stitch *(see page 14)* are worked over four vertical canvas threads to divide the rows with horizontal lines. The back stitch rows are worked in a matching or contrasting colour of thread. Any type of embroidery thread can be used, but care should be taken to match the weight of the thread to the gauge of the canvas to ensure complete canvas coverage.

413 Fir stitch ☆☆
also known as leaf stitch
Fir stitch is a canvas stitch used on single canvas. It is a bold stitch used for making large shapes and for background areas and makes a lozenge-shaped pattern, which looks rather like a row of fir trees. It can create a shaded background by using threads in graduated shades of one colour. Each lozenge is made up of a central vertical straight stitch worked over six horizontal canvas threads, with five slanting stitches worked at each side. The slanting stitches fan out, beginning five spaces below the vertical stitch and, to complete the lozenge, another central stitch is worked over these spaces. Any type of embroidery thread can be used, but care should be taken to match the weight of the thread to the gauge of the canvas to make sure that the canvas is completely covered by the stitching.

414 Large petal stitch ☆☆
Large petal stitch is a composite canvas stitch used on single canvas. It makes large square units which have four petal shapes radiating from a central hole to the corners of the area. This stitch has a heavy, textured appearance and careful consideration should be given before using it, as its dominant pattern might swamp a more delicate canvas stitch if the two were used together. Any type of thread can be used, but a smooth, non-hairy thread is preferable. As with other complex canvas stitches, such as perspective stitch *(see page 161)* and sunburst stitch *(see page 165)*, a small sample should be worked first to check the compatibility of the weight of the thread to the gauge of the canvas.

Although at first sight large petal stitch looks rather complicated, it is fairly simple to work. Each square unit covers ten vertical and ten horizontal canvas threads. The four petals are made by first working five slanting straight stitches of graduated lengths from each corner of the area into a common hole at the centre of the square. The thread is brought back through the canvas under one of the petals to a position one canvas thread away from the central hole. It is then wound round in a spiral, passing under the four petals and making five complete rings round the centre, as shown. The outer ring is tied down by four tiny straight stitches to complete the unit. A second, contrasting, thread can be used for the circular threading. The units are worked in horizontal rows, and a framework of back stitch *(see page 14)* can be worked to fill any gaps between them.

415 Fan stitch ☆☆
also known as expanded ray stitch and fantail stitch; see also ray stitch
Fan stitch is a canvas stitch used on single canvas. A pattern of fan shapes is made over the canvas, set alternately on the second and subsequent rows. When a patterned background is needed, fan stitch is a very effective stitch to use. The fan shapes cover an area of ten vertical and five horizontal canvas threads and are made up of fifteen straight stitches of varying lengths, radiating from the same hole. A smaller group of five radiating stitches is worked directly underneath, with the central stitch covering three canvas threads. Below this is added a single straight stitch over two horizontal threads. The photograph shows how the two groups of stitches and the single stitch are arranged. Any type of thread can be used but care should be taken to match the weight of the thread to the gauge of the canvas to ensure that the canvas is completely covered by the stitching.

158 CANVAS STITCHES

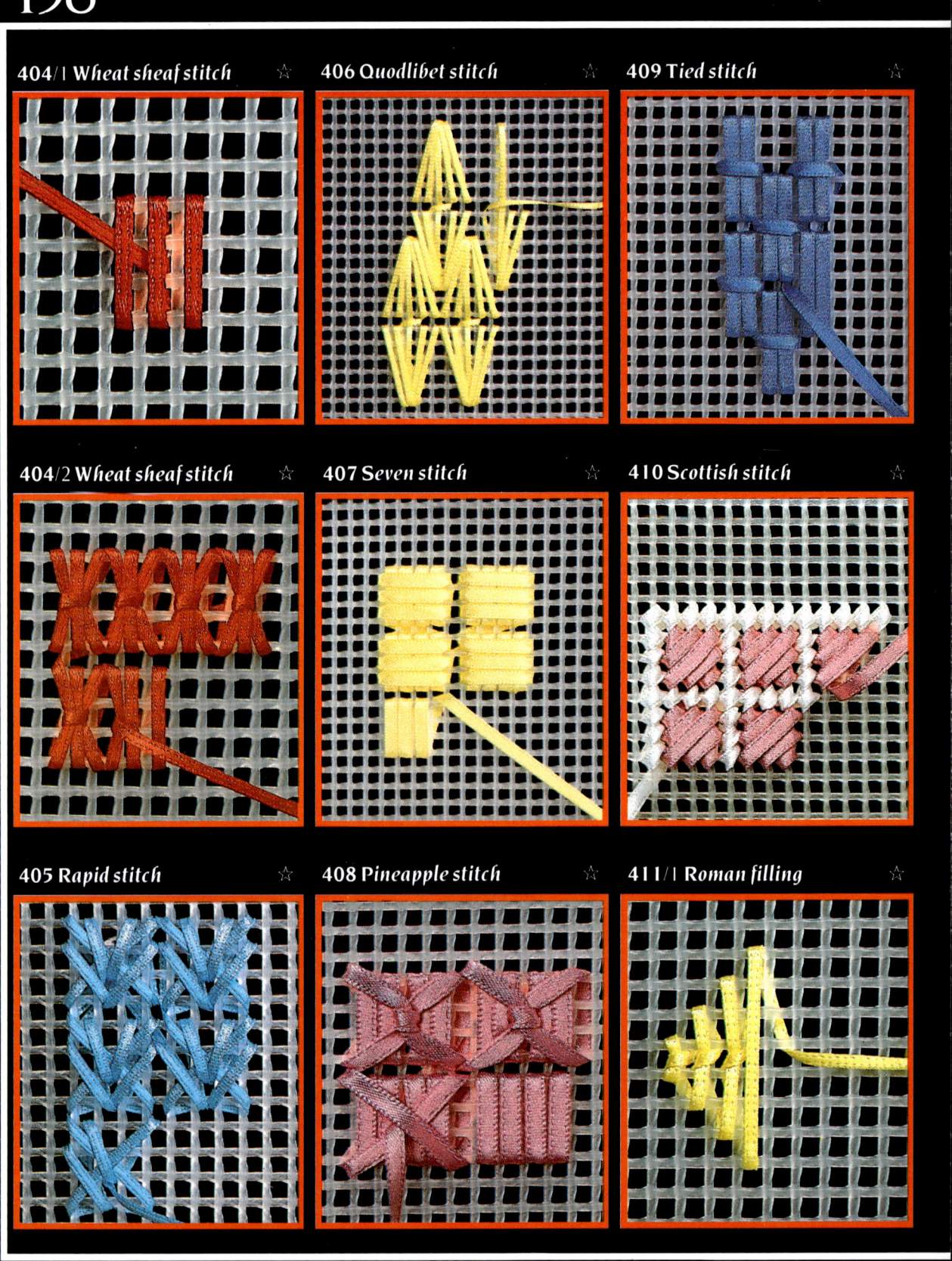

404/1 Wheat sheaf stitch	406 Quodlibet stitch	409 Tied stitch
404/2 Wheat sheaf stitch	407 Seven stitch	410 Scottish stitch
405 Rapid stitch	408 Pineapple stitch	411/1 Roman filling

COMPOSITE STITCHES # 159

411/2 Roman filling ☆

413/1 Fir stitch ☆☆

414/1 Large petal stitch ☆☆

412/1 Crow's foot stitch ☆☆

413/2 Fir stitch ☆☆

414/2 Large petal stitch ☆☆

412/2 Crow's foot stitch ☆☆

413/3 Fir stitch ☆☆

415 Fan stitch ☆☆

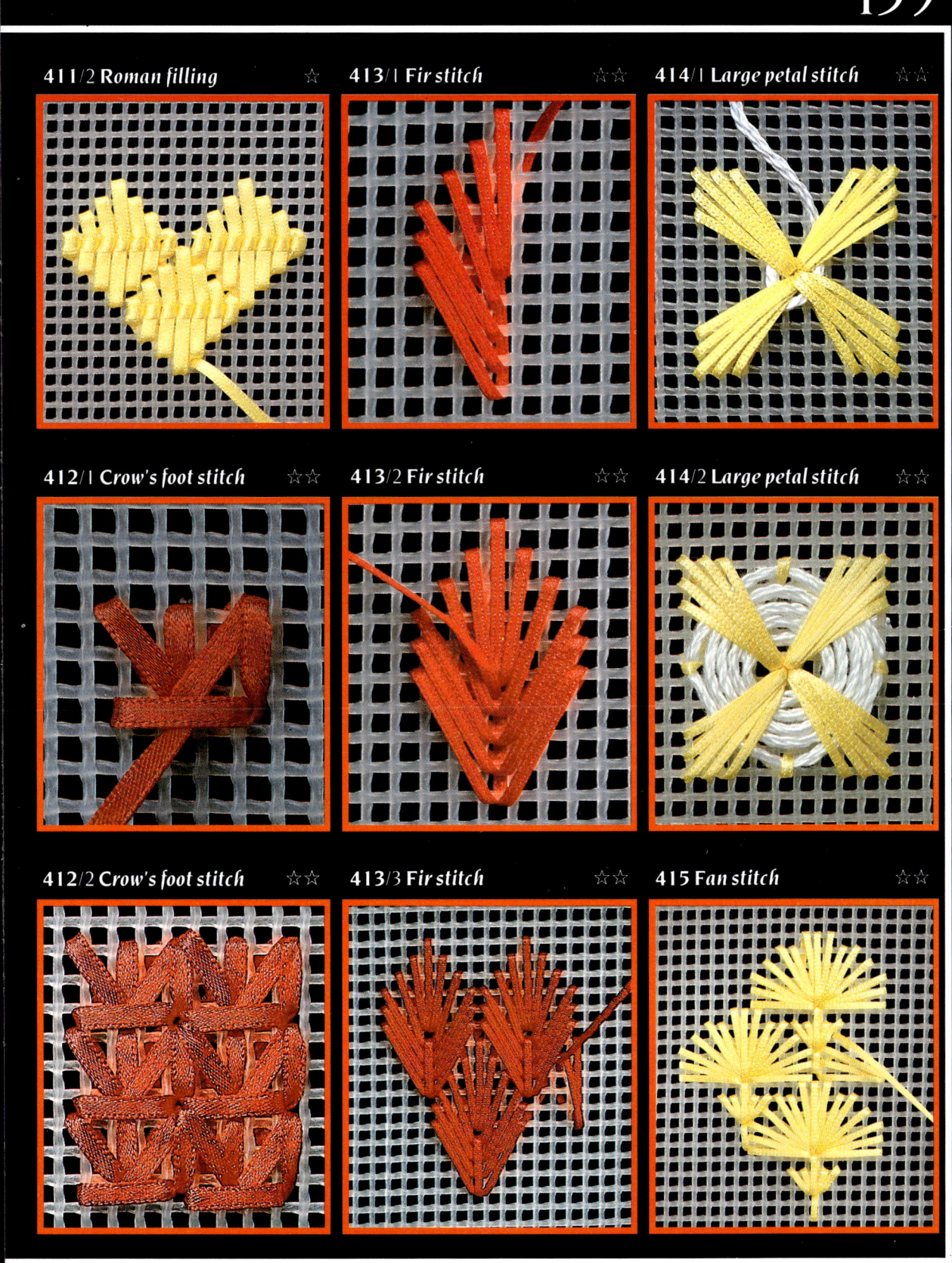

CANVAS STITCHES

416 Vault stitch ☆☆
also known as **fan vaulting**
Vault stitch is a canvas stitch used on single canvas for filling large shapes and background areas. It makes a regularly textured surface, which is enhanced by the use of a soft wool thread, such as tapestry or Persian wool. The stitch forms a pattern of alternating vertical and horizontal rectangles, each worked individually. A central straight stitch is worked over eight threads and an oblong cross stitch *(see page 133)* of the same height is superimposed. A shorter, wider oblong cross stitch is worked over the previous stitches to complete the rectangle. Small areas of canvas may be visible between each rectangle at this stage, depending on the weight of the thread being used. These can be filled in with a tent stitch *(see page 121)*, or a tiny ordinary cross stitch *(see page 14)* worked in either a matching thread or a tweed of contrasting colour or weight.

417 Brighton stitch ☆☆
Brighton stitch is a composite canvas stitch used on single canvas. Normally worked in wool as a geometric background stitch, it looks effective on small-gauge canvas, stitched with pearl or stranded cotton. The sheen of these threads accentuates the light and shade effect made when blocks of slanting stitches, in alternate directions, are placed side by side.

The stitch consists of blocks of five slanting stitches worked in rows. The direction of the slant changes on every alternate block and each row of blocks is the mirror image of the row above, thus creating a pattern of diamond shapes. After the blocks have been worked over the desired area, an upright cross stitch *(see page 137)* is worked in the space between each block; it can be the same or a contrasting colour.

418 Tile stitch ☆☆
Tile stitch is a canvas stitch used on single canvas. It makes a textured surface with a square pattern, and is used for filling shapes and background areas. Work a cross stitch *(see page 14)* over two canvas threads and then surround it with four straight stitches to make a small block. Frame each block with a border of tent stitch *(see page 121)*, as shown; leave one canvas thread unworked round the blocks. Then fill this space with a smaller frame of tent stitch worked in a slightly finer thread. This second frame can be of a contrasting colour to the larger frame. Any type of embroidery thread can be used, but care should be taken to match the weight of the thread to the gauge of the canvas to ensure that the canvas is completely covered by the stitching.

419 Padded satin stitch ☆☆
Padded satin stitch is a canvas stitch used on single canvas for filling large shapes and background areas. It makes a pattern of raised diamond shapes which are padded individually after they have been stitched. Each diamond consists of two triangular shapes, each made up of ten satin stitches *(see page 24)* of varying lengths. The same thread is then brought out of the canvas at the top of the left-hand triangle and threaded under the right-hand triangle and back up under the left to the point where the thread emerged. This thread should pass under the satin stitches only and no canvas threads should be picked up. This process is then repeated until the padding reaches the required height and the thread is taken back through the canvas to the place where it originally emerged. A soft wool thread, such as tapestry or Persian wool, is preferable for working padded satin stitch.

420 Hound's tooth ☆☆
Hound's tooth is used on single or double canvas and needs a fairly thick thread, such as tapestry or Persian wool, to cover the canvas well. It makes a neat square surface that is quite textured and can be used for both large and small areas. The squares can be worked over any number of canvas threads, providing that the weight of the threads matches the size of the stitches. The squares are worked over four canvas threads. A diagonal straight stitch is worked from the bottom left-hand corner to the top right-hand corner of the square. Interlocking loops are then worked, one at each of the remaining two corners, encircling the diagonal stitches. The squares are worked in horizontal rows and are set directly underneath each other. This stitch can be worked in two colours to create a chessboard pattern.

421 Shell stitch ☆☆
Shell stitch is a canvas stitch used on single canvas as a decorative border and is also worked solidly to fill shapes. It is worked in horizontal rows from right to left in two journeys, using a contrasting colour or weight of thread for the second journey. On the first journey, groups of four vertical straight stitches worked over six horizontal canvas threads are tied together at the centre by a short horizontal stitch worked over two threads to form bundles. On the second journey each bundle of stitches is linked together by a second thread, which is laced through the short, tying stitches. The second thread passes through the canvas only at the beginning and end of each row. The rows of bundles are worked underneath each other and can be divided by rows of back stitch *(see page 14)*. An adaptation of this stitch for use on plain- and even-weave fabrics is faggot filling stitch *(see page 80)*.

COMPOSITE STITCHES

422 Arrow stitch ☆☆
Arrow stitch is a canvas stitch usually worked on single canvas with tapestry or Persian wool. Three vertical straight stitches are worked over four threads of the canvas and pulled tightly to one side with a small horizontal stitch. Worked side by side, the stitches form textured rows, which are ideal for filling geometric shapes. If small gaps occur at the edge of a filled shape, cover the exposed canvas threads with tent stitch *(see page 121)*, using the same yarn. Arrow stitch can be used to create an attractive background pattern: make a half drop between adjoining groups of stitches and pull them alternately to the left and to the right.

423 Gate stitch ☆☆
Gate stitch is a modern canvas stitch used on single canvas. It makes a regular pattern of textured rectangular blocks worked with a half drop. It can be worked in vertical, horizontal or diagonal rows, depending on preference; in each case the finished effect is the same. It is used for filling large shapes and background areas and looks best when a soft, thick thread, such as tapestry or Persian wool, is used. Each block covers an area of five vertical and six horizontal canvas threads and is worked in three stages before proceeding to the next block. Four vertical straight stitches are worked first over six horizontal threads; an elongated cross stitch *(see page 14)* is then worked over these stitches. Then, a horizontal straight stitch covering five vertical threads is worked over the cross, two threads from the top or bottom. Both the blocks with the crossing stitch near the top and the blocks with the crossing stitch near the bottom are worked directly underneath each other.

424 Tudor rose stitch ☆☆
Tudor rose stitch is a canvas stitch used on single canvas to fill large shapes and background areas. It makes a large, stylized, floral pattern, which looks extremely attractive when worked in more than one colour. The stitch is worked in two stages. Alternate horizontal rows of cross stitch *(see page 14)* and rice stitch *(see page 136)* cover the area first. Each of these stitches occupies a square of four canvas threads, and unworked squares of the same size lie between them. These unworked areas are then filled by five straight stitches of graduating lengths. Any type of embroidery thread can be used, but care should be taken to match the weight of the thread to the gauge of the canvas to make sure that the canvas is completely covered by the stitching.

425 Bouclé stitch ☆☆
Bouclé stitch is a square canvas stitch used on single canvas, and has a tight, knobbly texture reminiscent of bouclé fabric. It can be used either to fill small areas or for backgrounds. It is worked over a small square of canvas and consists of two slanting stitches worked side by side in the same holes, each one anchored by a loop. Work the top left-hand portion of the stitch first, taking care to keep the diagonal stitch taut. Then work the bottom right section in the same way. The anchoring loops should be left quite loose and not tensioned in the way that the diagonal stitches are, in order to create the knobbly texture. Bouclé stitch can be worked over different numbers of threads on the canvas, depending on the size of the shape to be filled, but care should be taken when matching the weight of the yarn to the size of the stitch; the yarn should cover the canvas threads without being too bulky.

426 Perspective stitch ☆☆
Perspective stitch is a canvas stitch used on single canvas. It makes a bold pattern of three-dimensional boxes and is usually worked in two shades of the same colour. The pattern of this stitch can be rather dominant and careful consideration must be given when choosing it as it could swamp a more delicate stitch if placed next to it. However, it can make a very attractive background when the colours used are subdued. It is quite simple to work once the sequence of stitches has been mastered, but follow the sequence shown carefully.

One complete pattern is worked in four stages, and each stage consists of vertical groups of three diagonal straight stitches. Each diagonal stitch is worked over two vertical and two horizontal canvas threads. The slant of the stitches alternates from group to group. Each stage should be worked in alternate colours to give the correct sequence, and the stitches made in stages two and four should overlap the stitches made in the previous stages. Perspective stitch looks equally effective worked with stranded cotton on a small-gauge canvas or on a larger scale with a heavier thread, such as Persian wool.

162 CANVAS STITCHES

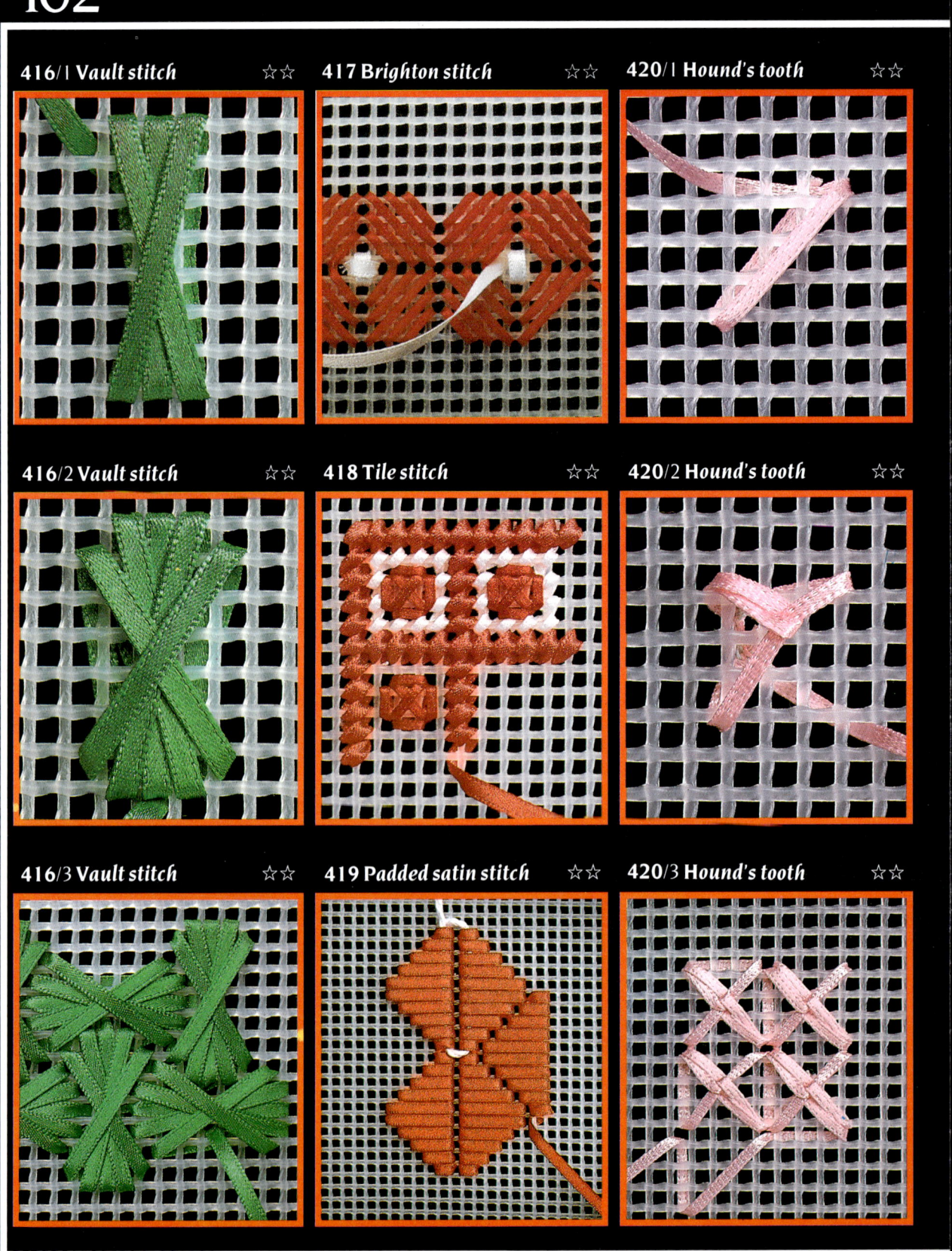

416/1 Vault stitch ☆☆

417 Brighton stitch ☆☆

420/1 Hound's tooth ☆☆

416/2 Vault stitch ☆☆

418 Tile stitch ☆☆

420/2 Hound's tooth ☆☆

416/3 Vault stitch ☆☆

419 Padded satin stitch ☆☆

420/3 Hound's tooth ☆☆

COMPOSITE STITCHES 163

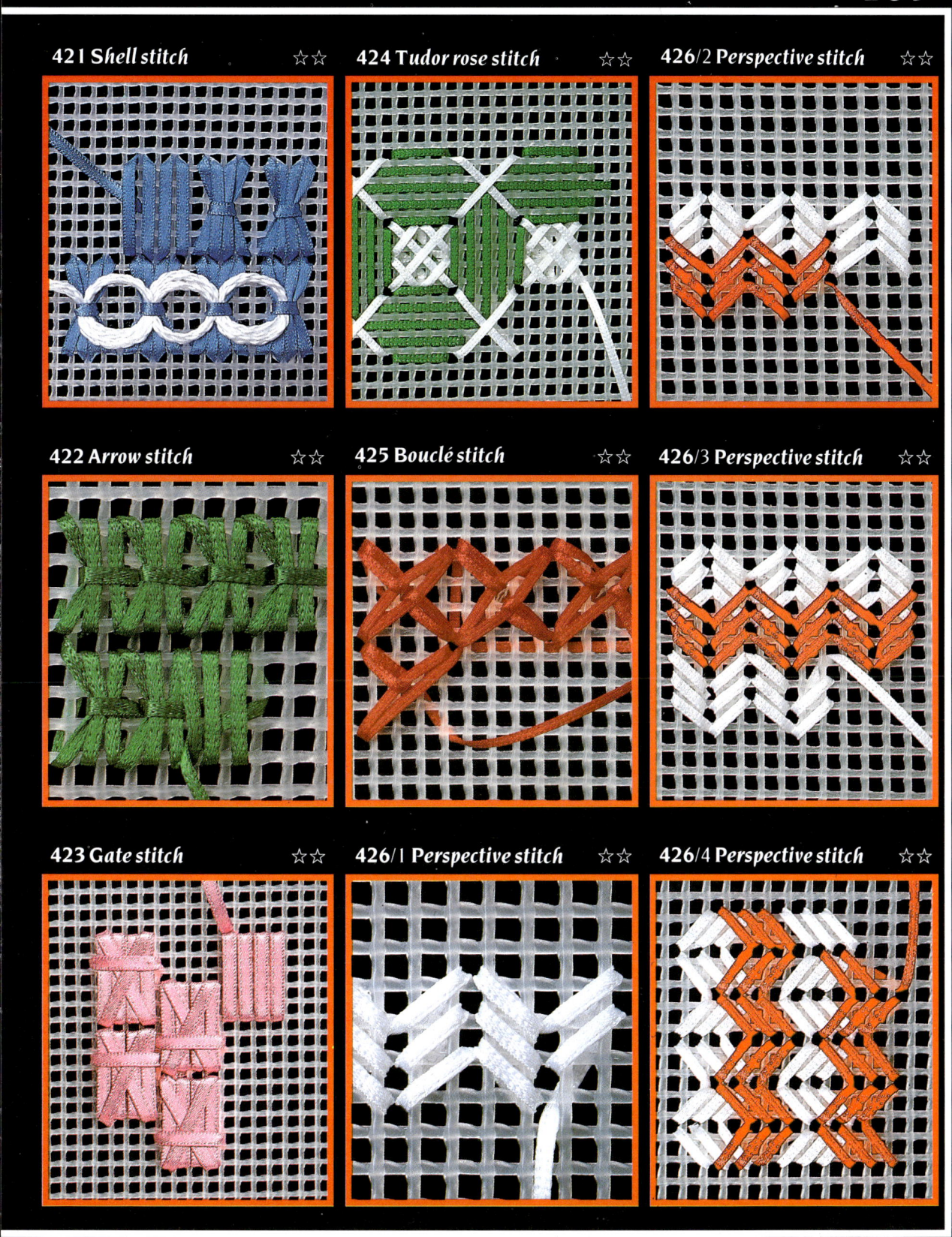

421 Shell stitch ☆☆
424 Tudor rose stitch ☆☆
426/2 Perspective stitch ☆☆
422 Arrow stitch ☆☆
425 Bouclé stitch ☆☆
426/3 Perspective stitch ☆☆
423 Gate stitch ☆☆
426/1 Perspective stitch ☆☆
426/4 Perspective stitch ☆☆

427 Vee stitch ☆☆
Vee stitch is a canvas stitch used on single canvas for filling large shapes and background areas. It makes a vertically striped pattern which can be worked in two or more colours; a soft wool thread, such as tapestry or Persian wool, is needed to give adequate coverage of the canvas. The stripes are worked downwards, and each stitch overlaps the stitch immediately preceding it. Each vee stitch is quite large, spanning ten vertical and eight horizontal canvas threads, and overlaps the previous stitch by four horizontal threads. A vertical straight stitch covering four threads is worked in the centre and four slanting stitches radiate at each side from the base hole of the vertical stitch.

428 Compact filling stitch ☆☆
Compact filling stitch is a canvas stitch used on single canvas. As its name suggests, it gives a compact textured finish and is ideal for filling small areas or backgrounds. It is quite quick to work once the spacing of the stitches is mastered, and it covers the canvas well. This stitch looks equally attractive when worked in a wool or a cotton embroidery thread.

The stitch consists of two straight stitches, one vertical and one horizontal, worked over three canvas threads and set at right angles to each other. Two diagonal stitches are then worked at the bottom right of these stitches. The stitch is usually worked in diagonal rows, from the top left-hand corner to the bottom right-hand corner of the area to be covered.

429 Spring stitch ☆☆
also known as **coiled stitch**
Spring stitch is a modern canvas stitch used on single canvas. It makes an attractive pattern of springs or coils over the surface and has a strong diagonal feel; it looks most effective when worked with tapestry or Persian wool on a compatible gauge of canvas. It is used for filling large areas or backgrounds as it has quite a large pattern; the diagonal effect is lost if it is worked over a small area.

Each stitch covers a long rectangle of three vertical and twelve horizontal canvas threads. A large, oblong cross stitch *(see page 133)* is worked over the rectangle, then seven horizontal straight stitches over three vertical threads are worked over the cross. The rectangles are worked in diagonal rows from the top left to the bottom right of the area to be covered; the second and subsequent rectangles on each row are dropped by three threads. The small oblong cross stitch at each end of the springs is worked on a separate journey after all the rectangles are complete.

430 Broad stem stitch ☆☆
also known as **canvas stem stitch**
Broad stem stitch is a composite canvas stitch used on double canvas; it is not a variation of the stem stitch used on fabric, despite its name. It makes an attractive ridged surface and can be used as a border or to fill a shape of any size or a background area. This stitch is worked in two journeys and consists of two vertical rows of diagonal straight stitches arranged to form 'V' shapes. The centre of the two rows is then defined by working a row of back stitch *(see page 14)* down it. Back stitch can also be worked to frame each of the rows. Any type of embroidery thread can be used, but pearl or stranded cotton enhances the light and shade effect created by the arrangement of the stitches. Broad stem stitch combines well with canvas fern stitch *(see page 132)* when the two are worked in alternate rows and when two different colours are used.

431 Tweed stitch ☆☆
Tweed stitch is a canvas stitch used on single and double canvas. It makes a tweedy texture on the surface of the fabric, as its name implies, and is very useful for filling a shape or background of any size. It looks most attractive when worked in a soft wool thread, such as tapestry or Persian wool, and different colours can be used to accentuate its tweedy appearance.

Cover the area with large upright cross stitches *(see page 137)*, each worked over six vertical and six horizontal canvas threads. Superimpose an ordinary cross stitch *(see page 14)* over two threads at the centre of each upright cross and work a tiny ordinary cross stitch at the centre of the remaining areas of canvas, alternating the top diagonals. Tweed stitch makes a good covering for chair seats and stools, as it is extremely hard-wearing when worked in a durable thread like tapestry wool.

432 Scallop stitch ☆☆☆
Scallop stitch is a canvas stitch used on single canvas. It makes a large pattern of scallop shapes on the surface and is used for filling large areas and backgrounds. Care should be taken when considering using this

stitch, as the pattern can be rather dominant and may swamp a more delicate canvas stitch if used near it. The scallops are worked over eight vertical and twelve horizontal canvas threads and consist of sixteen slanting straight stitches, radiating from the base of a long, vertical straight stitch worked in the centre. The scallops are worked in horizontal rows across the area to be covered, and the second and subsequent rows interlock with each preceding row. A soft wool thread, such as tapestry or Persian wool, looks very good with this stitch and gives excellent canvas coverage if it is compatible with the gauge of the canvas.

433 Eastern stitch ☆☆☆
also known as Eastern buttonhole stitch

Eastern stitch is a looped canvas stitch used on single canvas. It has a complex lacy appearance and looks most effective when worked with a lustrous thread, such as stranded cotton or silk. It is generally used for filling shapes but can also be used for backgrounds, although it is rather a slow stitch to work. Each stitch covers a square of four canvas threads, and the stitches are worked in horizontal rows from left to right. A foundation of two straight stitches is worked first along the top and left-hand side of the square. The thread is then brought to the surface at the opposite corner, and a looped stitch made over the foundation stitches. The thread enters the canvas through the same hole from which it emerged before making the foundation for the next stitch.

434 Woven tent stitch ☆☆☆
Woven tent stitch is a modern canvas stitch used on single canvas. It makes a textured surface and can be used for filling shapes or backgrounds of any size. This stitch is a variation of ordinary tent stitch *(see page 121)*, and is based on a square consisting of sixteen tent stitches. The square is worked first, and then two straight stitches are added: one runs along the lower edge of the square and the other is placed along the right-hand side of it. The thread is then interwoven diagonally backwards and forwards between these two stitches to create a closely woven triangle. During the weaving process do not pick up any of the tent stitches. A soft wool thread, such as tapestry or Persian wool, works well with this stitch, providing that the gauge of the canvas is compatible.

435 Sunburst stitch ☆☆☆
Sunburst stitch is a modern canvas stitch used on single canvas. It has a highly textured surface with a large pattern reminiscent of the sun and its rays, and is used for filling large shapes and backgrounds. The stitch is worked in vertical rows, which are then threaded on a second journey with a thicker thread. A soft wool thread, such as tapestry or Persian wool, is needed to cover the canvas adequately and can be used double in the needle for the threading. Each stitch covers a large, rectangular block of twelve vertical and six horizontal canvas threads. The blocks are worked first over the entire area to be covered, and each consists of two groups of four straight stitches radiating from the same central hole to the left and right of the rectangle. The second, thicker thread is then laced downwards through the rows at the left-hand side, making a circular movement round the central hole of each block. When the lower edge is reached, the thread is taken through the right-hand side of the blocks back up to the top to begin lacing the next row. The thread passes under the stitches and should not pick up any canvas threads.

436 Curtain stitch ☆☆☆
Curtain stitch is a complex canvas stitch used on single canvas. It makes a very bold pattern in blocks, each block reminiscent of a pair of swagged curtains. Care should be taken in deciding where to use this stitch since the pattern is rather dominant, especially if the stitch is worked in a thick thread on a large-gauge canvas; however, this stitch can look really spectacular. It can be worked in two contrasting threads. Each block fills a square of eight canvas threads, and the blocks are arranged side by side in rows. The blocks are first covered with a series of graduating diagonal straight stitches, the direction of which changes on alternate blocks. This stage should be worked over the whole area first. On the second journey, the 'curtains' are made, using the same or a contrasting thread. These consist of eight vertical straight stitches worked loosely across each block, which are then pulled towards the outside of the block in groups of four and tied down by a short horizontal stitch. It is important to maintain the correct tension of the vertical stitches, as they must be loose enough to be tied back. Any type of embroidery thread can be used, providing that it is compatible with the gauge of the canvas.

166 CANVAS STITCHES

427/1 Vee stitch ☆☆	428/2 Compact filling stitch ☆☆	430 Broad stem stitch ☆☆
427/2 Vee stitch ☆☆	429/1 Spring stitch ☆☆	431 Tweed stitch ☆☆
428/1 Compact filling stitch ☆☆	429/2 Spring stitch ☆☆	432 Scallop stitch ☆☆☆

COMPOSITE STITCHES

167

433/1 **Eastern stitch** ☆☆☆   434/1 **Woven tent stitch** ☆☆☆   435/1 **Sunburst stitch** ☆☆☆

433/2 **Eastern stitch** ☆☆☆   434/2 **Woven tent stitch** ☆☆☆   435/2 **Sunburst stitch** ☆☆☆

433/3 **Eastern stitch** ☆☆☆   434/3 **Woven tent stitch** ☆☆☆   436 **Curtain stitch** ☆☆☆

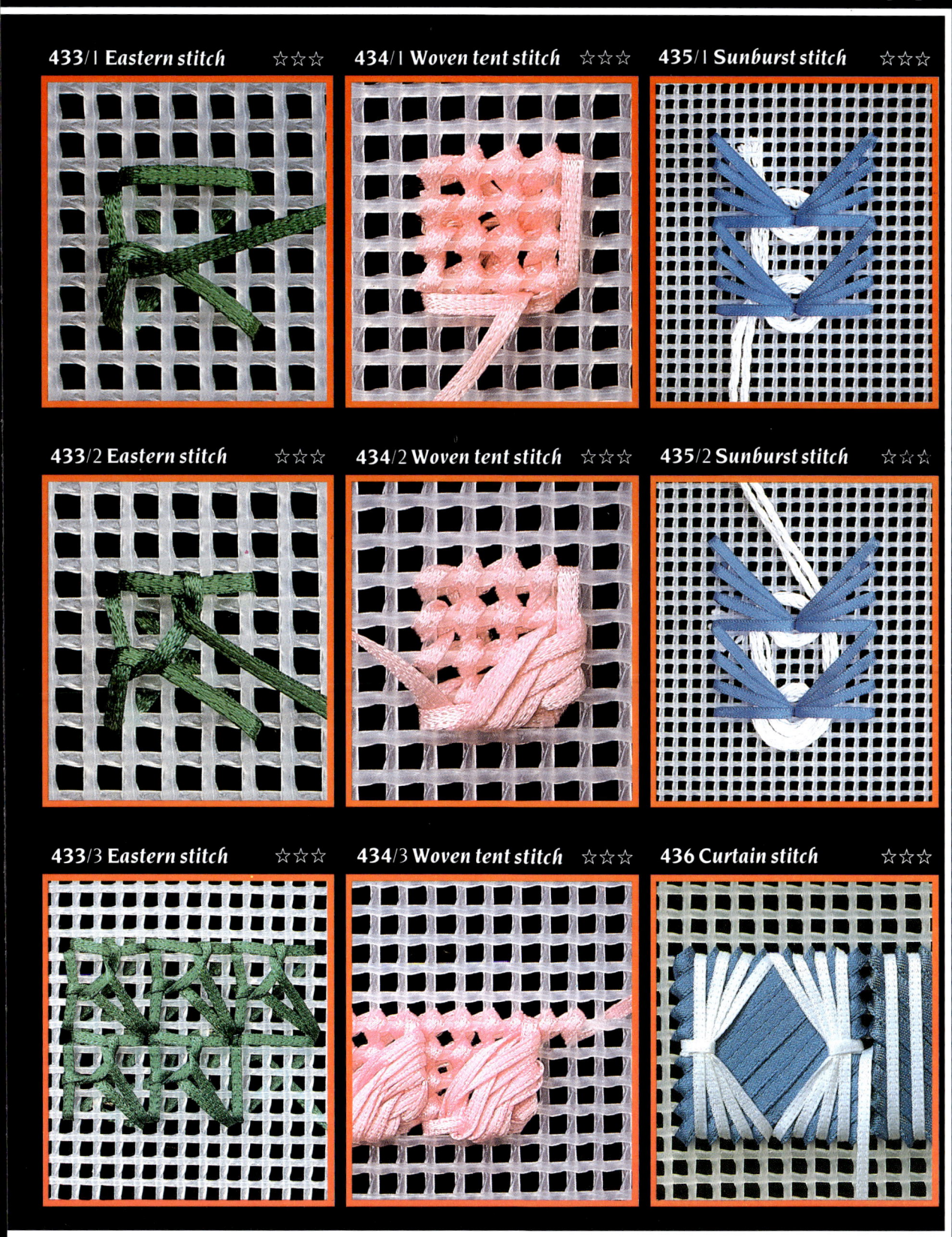

Other canvas stitches

437 Raised spot stitch ☆
Raised spot stitch is a canvas stitch used on single and double canvas, which can be used in rows for an outline or border, or worked solidly to fill a shape where a dense, raised texture is needed. It is extremely simple to work and the finished stitch depends greatly on the type of yarn chosen. Each spot stitch is worked over four horizontal canvas threads and consists of straight stitches worked over each other into the same holes at the top and bottom. The stitches should be packed tightly in order to make a really firm raised spot and as many as fifteen or twenty stitches can be worked over each other before the holes become too full to allow the needle to pass through again.

438 Algerian eye stitch ☆
also known as **star stitch** *and* **star eyelet stitch**

Algerian eye stitch is used in canvas work and in open-work embroidery on a loosely woven even-weave fabric. It consists of eight stitches, all worked into the same central point, and forms a star within a square. When used as a canvas stitch, it should be worked on single canvas with a heavy thread; on an even-weave fabric, the stitches should be pulled quite tightly during the stitching to emphasize the holes that form at the centre of each eyelet. The eyelets can be spaced alternately to give a chessboard effect or worked as an all-over pattern. Alphabets on early samplers were often worked in Algerian eye stitch.

439 Ray stitch ☆
also known as **fan stitch**

Ray stitch is a canvas stitch used on single canvas. It makes a regular pattern of square blocks on the surface and can be worked to give three different effects.

The stitch is normally worked over a square of three canvas threads and is very effective for filling small shapes. The blocks can be made larger by the addition of further stitches and they can be as large as six or eight threads, creating a striking effect for large shapes and backgrounds. When worked over three threads, each square block consists of seven straight stitches radiating from the same hole at the corner of the square and, if the stitches are pulled tightly, a pattern of holes is also made. The blocks are usually arranged so that the direction of the straight stitches is reversed every alternate block. Different effects can be made by working all the stitches in the same direction, or by working diagonal pairs of blocks into the same central hole, which then becomes quite large. Any type of embroidery thread can be used with ray stitch, providing that it is compatible with the gauge of the canvas, but a lustrous thread, such as stranded cotton, enhances the light and shade effect created by the positioning of the stitches.

440 Radiating stitch ☆
Radiating stitch is a canvas stitch used on single canvas. It is quick and easy to work and ideal for covering large areas and backgrounds. The stitch gives a strong, vertically striped surface, and each stripe consists of a row of triangles. Any type of embroidery thread can be used, providing that it is compatible with the gauge of the canvas. Slight gaps may be visible between the vertical rows, giving a rather untidy appearance to the stitch. This can be remedied by working rows of back stitch *(see page 14)* over the gaps, with each back stitch covering two horizontal canvas threads. The rows of triangles are four vertical canvas threads wide and each triangle consists of five straight stitches radiating from the same central hole. The triangles are worked beneath one another and every alternate triangle faces in the opposite direction.

441 Single knotted stitch ☆
Single knotted stitch is a canvas stitch used on single canvas. The stitch imitates the knots of a pile carpet and should be worked closely together to cover the canvas completely. It is useful in cases where an area of raised stitching is needed to complement a flat, smoothly stitched surface. Use very thick thread or, alternatively, thread several strands of a fine thread through the same needle. Interesting colour effects can be achieved by mixing contrasting or toning colours of a fine thread. The stitch is quite simple to work but the loop must be pulled tight after working each stitch. Trim the ends of the threads to the required length after the stitching is completed.

442 Beaded tent stitch ☆☆
Beaded tent stitch provides a method of attaching beads to a piece of canvas work and is mainly used for working small details and highlights. Each bead is secured by a tent stitch *(see page 121)*: bring the thread to the front of the canvas, thread one bead, and go on to work the stitch. The size of the beads should allow them to sit neatly on the surface but, if they are too large to do this, work tent stitch alternately with beaded tent stitch to give more space for the bead. Beaded tent stitch is usually worked in vertical rows.

443 Turkey rug knot ☆☆
also known as **Turkey stitch, Ghiordes knot, quilt knot stitch, tufted knot stitch** *and* **single knotted Smyrna rug stitch**

Turkey rug knot is a pile stitch used on single canvas. It makes a series of closely worked loops, which are cut and trimmed after the stitching is finished to give a pile which resembles the pile of a carpet. This stitch is used to make very raised areas, sometimes needed to complement a flat, smoothly stitched area of canvas work. A soft, thick wool thread should be used, or several finer threads can be threaded through the needle at the same time. By using several differently coloured threads, this stitch can be made to shade an area gradually by changing some of the coloured threads on successive rows. The loops should be worked round a pencil or large knitting needle to keep the size constant. Each loop is secured by a back stitch *(see page 14)*, as shown. Each row is worked above the preceding row: keep the rows as close together as possible.

OTHER CANVAS STITCHES **169**

444 Eye stitch ☆☆
Eye stitch is primarily a canvas stitch used on single canvas but it can also be successfully worked on an even-weave fabric, providing that a fine thread is used. A filling stitch, it makes a regular, geometric pattern of square blocks, which can be worked in two or more colours. Each block covers eight vertical and eight horizontal canvas threads and consists of sixteen straight stitches of graduated lengths, radiating from the same central point. Around the outside of each square, the stitches are drawn through alternate holes, leaving two canvas threads unworked. The blocks can be framed by rows of back stitch *(see page 14)* in the same or a contrasting thread. Any type of embroidery thread can be used, although the thread should not be too thick or the stitches making up the blocks will be difficult to work.

445 Diamond eye stitch ☆☆
Diamond eye stitch is a canvas stitch used primarily on single canvas; it can also be successfully worked on an even-weave fabric, providing that a fine thread is used. A variation of eye stitch *(see above)*, it also makes a regular, geometric pattern of blocks but in this case the blocks are diamond-shaped. The blocks can be worked in two colours and, as with eye stitch, any type of embroidery thread can be used, although the thread should not be too thick or the stitches that make up the blocks will be difficult to work. Each block consists of twenty straight stitches of graduated lengths, radiating from the same central point and arranged to make a diamond. Each diamond shape spans ten vertical and ten horizontal canvas threads. After the diamond shapes have been worked, they can be framed by rows of back stitch *(see page 14)*, in the same way as eye stitch can be framed, or by long straight stitches worked from corner to corner round each diamond.

446 Half eye stitch ☆☆
Half eye stitch is a canvas stitch used on single canvas with a fairly heavy thread, such as soft cotton or the heaviest available weight of pearl cotton. A variation of eye stitch *(see above)*, it makes a heavy, geometric pattern of rectangular blocks arranged with a half drop. Each block consists of half an eye stitch worked over four vertical and eight horizontal canvas threads. The stitches are packed together very closely, and seventeen straight stitches are worked into the same hole; a stiletto may be needed to open up this hole while the stitching is in progress. Each straight stitch should be pulled quite tightly, and this stitch is not suitable for use with a soft wool thread as it may snap or shred. For ease of working, the needle should always emerge from the canvas on the outside edge and re-enter by the central hole.

447 Quick stitch ☆☆
Quick stitch is a canvas stitch used on single canvas. As its name reveals, this stitch covers the canvas very quickly. It creates a diagonally woven pattern and is an adaptation of one fabric technique, laid-work. It should never be used on an article (such as a cushion cover) that is subject to much wear and tear, as the stitches are very long and snag easily, but it works well on a picture as a background. Care should be taken when using quick stitch to choose an embroidery thread which covers the canvas adequately; it is advisable to work a small sample first to test the compatibility of the thread to the canvas. The stitch consists of long threads laid diagonally across the area to be worked and entering the canvas only at the beginning and end of the rows. It is essential that these threads are laid correctly and follow the intersections of the canvas. The laid threads are then crossed at right angles by groups of three diagonal stitches, arranged as shown. Interesting colour changes can be made by graduating the colours used for both the laid threads and the crossing stitches.

448 Surrey stitch ☆☆
Surrey stitch is a pile stitch used on single canvas. It forms a series of closely worked loops, which can be cut after the stitching is finished to give a pile which resembles carpet pile. This stitch is used to make very raised areas, which are sometimes needed to complement a flat, smoothly stitched area of canvas work. Use either a soft, thick wool thread or several finer threads threaded through the needle at once. Work the loops round a pencil or a large knitting needle to keep the size constant. Secure each loop with a short diagonal stitch. Work each row above the preceding row, keeping the rows as close together as possible.

449 Rococo stitch ☆☆☆
also known as **queen stitch**
Rococo stitch is a canvas stitch used on wide-mesh canvas. Dating from the seventeenth century, it became fashionable again during the nineteenth century and examples of it are found on numerous tiny articles of the period, such as pin cushions and purses. It should be worked with a fairly thick thread and it makes a dramatic background stitch. Care should be taken when matching the weight of the thread to the gauge of the canvas to ensure that the canvas is completely covered by the stitching; a small test sample can be worked to check this.

Rococo stitch consists of a group of four vertical stitches worked into the same space with each one crossed by a tiny horizontal stitch. The two outside vertical stitches are anchored to the canvas and curve slightly, giving a globe-shaped appearance to the stitch. The groups are arranged alternately in the spaces of the canvas and make a dense, closely stitched surface punctuated by small holes. They should be worked in diagonal rows, from the top right to the bottom left of the area to be covered.

170 CANVAS STITCHES

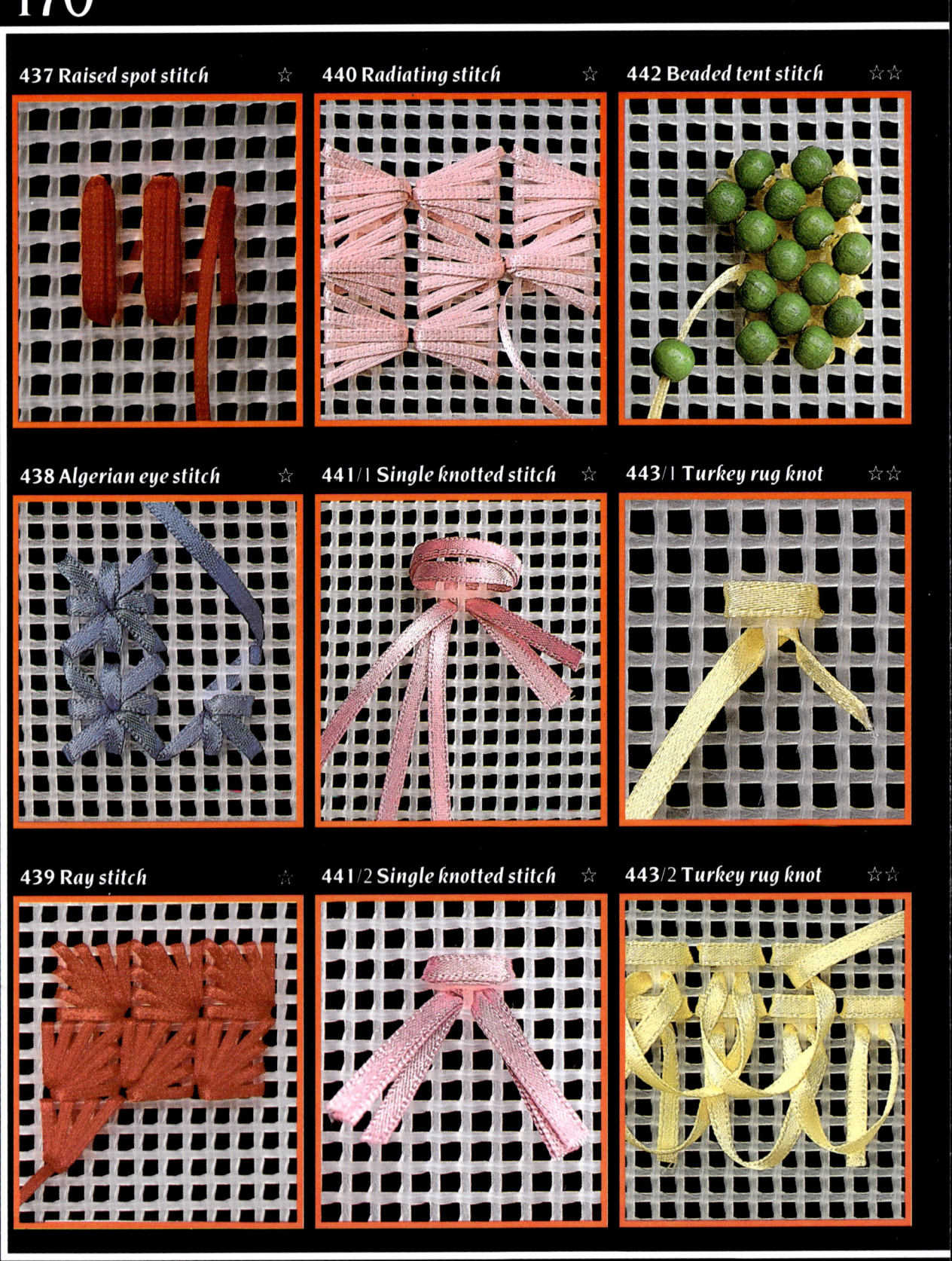

437 Raised spot stitch ☆
440 Radiating stitch ☆
442 Beaded tent stitch ☆☆

438 Algerian eye stitch ☆
441/1 Single knotted stitch ☆
443/1 Turkey rug knot ☆☆

439 Ray stitch ☆
441/2 Single knotted stitch ☆
443/2 Turkey rug knot ☆☆

OTHER CANVAS STITCHES **171**

444 Eye stitch ☆☆

447 Quick stitch ☆☆

448/3 Surrey stitch ☆☆

445 Diamond eye stitch ☆☆

448/1 Surrey stitch ☆☆

449/1 Rococo stitch ☆☆☆

446 Half eye stitch ☆☆

448/2 Surrey stitch ☆☆

449/2 Rococo stitch ☆☆☆

Glossary

Accent stitch An embroidery stitch which is chiefly used to provide a splash of colour or texture to enliven a monotone or flat area of stitching.

Appliqué or **applied work** A technique in which shapes of different fabrics are placed on the ground fabric to form a design. The edges are secured by tiny stitches which are hardly seen, or by a decorative embroidery stitch.

Assisi work A type of counted thread embroidery originating in Assisi, Northern Italy. The patterns or motifs are outlined before the background is filled in using cross stitch or long-armed cross stitch, leaving the motifs unstitched.

Ayrshire embroidery A type of embroidery stitched in a fine white thread on white muslin and characterized by areas of inset lace stitches. Ayrshire embroidery was worked in Scotland from the late-eighteenth to the mid-nineteenth century and was used for baby garments and collars and cuffs.

Berlin woolwork A technique of working designs in coloured wools on canvas, following a chart in which each square represents one stitch. The wools and charts were originally produced in Germany but the work spread to Europe and the United States and was popular during the nineteenth century.

Black-work An embroidery technique used on clothing and household linen during the sixteenth century and revived during the twentieth century. It consists of outline and filling stitches worked in black thread on a white fabric to create geometric designs.

Border stitch A wide embroidery stitch which is always used in a straight line and makes a very attractive border. Multiple rows can be worked to make a more complex decorative border.

Broderie Anglaise A type of cut-work embroidery which evolved from Ayrshire embroidery *circa* 1850, and became very popular as a decoration on children's garments and ladies' underclothes. The formalized designs consist of a series of tiny round and oval holes.

Canvas The ground material for canvas work in which vertical and horizontal threads are woven together to produce precisely spaced holes between the threads. Canvas has a regular grid-like structure and is available in several different sizes of grid.

Canvas work A general term for embroidery on canvas, also known as needlepoint. The entire surface of the canvas is covered with stitching and a wide range of stitches is used.

Closed finish The term used when an embroidery stitch is compressed in order to completely cover the ground fabric.

Composite stitch A combination of two or more simple embroidery stitches to give a more decorative effect than if they were used singly.

Coton à broder A tightly twisted pearlized thread similar to pearl cotton but with a less lustrous finish.

Couching A technique in which a thick thread or group of threads is attached to the ground fabric by means of a finer thread. It is particularly suitable for textured and metallic threads which cannot be stitched directly into the fabric.

Counted thread embroidery An embroidery technique in which the scale and placing of the stitches is determined by counting the warp and weft threads of the ground fabric over which each stitch is worked.

Crane, Walter English illustrator, painter and designer (1845–1915), known primarily for his imaginative illustrations for children's books, who had a great influence on embroidery design at the turn of the century.

Crazy patchwork A technique in which irregularly shaped pieces of fabric are sewn at random onto a ground fabric. The raw edges where the pieces join are secured by decorative stitching.

Crewel embroidery Embroidery stitched with crewel wools on a linen background, using a variety of stitches. The designs are often naturalistic.

Crewel wool A fine two-ply wool for delicate canvas work or free embroidery.

Cut-work A technique in which motifs or patterns are oulined with close buttonhole stitching and the ground fabric is cut away in various sections of the design.

Detached stitch An embroidery stitch which is anchored to the ground fabric at the edges only, with the main part of the stitching remaining free.

Double canvas Canvas in which the weave is formed by the intersection of pairs of vertical and horizontal threads.

Drawn fabric work A type of embroidery in which threads are withdrawn from a loosely woven ground fabric and the spaces left are then filled or edged with different stitches.

Edging stitch An embroidery stitch used to finish a raw edge to prevent the fabric from fraying, or to decorate a plain hemmed edge.

Encroaching stitches A term used to describe the overlap of one row of stitching with the preceding row.

Even-weave fabric A fabric with warp and weft threads of identical thicknesses, which provide the same number of threads over a given area, enabling the threads to be counted to keep the stitching even.

Fabric grain The line of the warp thread in a piece of fabric.

Filling stitch An embroidery stitch which is used to fill a shape on the ground fabric. Filling stitches can be light and delicate with a lacy appearance, or they can completely cover the ground fabric.

Foundation grid The regular arrangement of threads laid across a shape to provide a framework for an embroidery stitch.

Foundation row A row of stitching which provides the basis for a composite stitch. This term is also used to describe the stitched outline which anchors a detached filling stitch to the ground fabric.

Frame A square or rectangular wooden frame used to keep fabric taut during stitching.

Gauge The number of threads that can be stitched in 2.5cm (1in) of canvas. Also the number of threads or woven blocks that can be stitched in 2.5cm (1in) of even-weave fabric.

Grounding stitch A term used in canvas work to describe a stitch that is suitable for covering large areas of background.

Ground fabric Any fabric on which embroidery is worked.

Half drop A term used in canvas work to describe an arrangement of stitches. The top of the second and subsequent stitches aligns with the centre of the preceding stitch.

Holbein, Hans German painter and engraver (1497–1543) who was Court Painter to Henry VIII from 1536 to 1543. He is noted particularly for his portraits.

Hoop A round frame for stretching the ground fabric while embroidery stitches are worked.

Isolated stitch An embroidery stitch which is worked individually and can be used alone or massed together to fill a shape.

Jacobean embroidery A type of free embroidery worked on linen, popular during the seventeenth and eighteenth centuries.

Journey In embroidery a term used to describe working a stitch along a line. Many stitches are completed on one journey but others will require two or three.

Laid filling stitch An embroidery stitch consisting of a foundation grid of spaced laid threads which are then anchored to the ground fabric in a decorative manner.

Laid-work An embroidery technique used to fill a shape solidly. Long threads are laid across the shape, covering the fabric completely. They are then anchored to the fabric by a second thread to create a pattern.

Lark's head knot A knot used in macramé to mount the knotting cords onto a support, such as a length of cord, a dowel, or a ring.

Line stitch Any embroidery stitch which forms a line during the working.

Morris, William English poet, Pre-Raphaelite painter, designer, craftsman and socialist writer (1834–1896). Among his many achievements he created magnificent wallpaper and fabric designs which remain popular today.

Motif stitch An embroidery stitch which is worked individually with each stitch, making a distinctive shape, such as a star or triangle.

Naturalistic embroidery Embroidery in which natural forms such as plants and animals are depicted in a realistic manner.

Needlepoint lace Lace made with a needle rather than a bobbin.

Open finish the term used when an embroidery stitch is spaced out to let the fabric ground show through.

Opus Anglicanum The name given to English embroidery, chiefly ecclesiastical, worked during the Middle Ages.

Pearl cotton A twisted two-ply thread with a lustrous sheen. It cannot be divided into separate strands but it is available in three different weights.

Persian wool A loosely twisted three-ply wool which can be divided into separate strands.

Picot A small loop of twisted thread forming a decorative edging to lace or embroidery.

Plain-weave fabric A fabric in which the warp and weft threads are woven too irregularly to provide a grid for working stitches by the counted thread method.

Powdering A light filling for a shape made by scattering an isolated stitch over an area of ground fabric.

Pulled fabric work An embroidery technique in which stitches are pulled tightly so that the threads of the ground fabric are distorted, creating a pattern of tiny holes in the fabric.

Renaissance embroidery A form of cut-work in which the design is outlined in buttonhole stitch before the ground fabric is cut away. Parts of the design are strengthened by buttonhole bars.

Richelieu embroidery A form of cut-work similar to Renaissance embroidery; the main difference is the addition of picots to the buttonhole bars which join parts of the design.

Royal School of Needlework A school with royal patronage founded in London in 1872. Its stated aims were: 'the two-fold purpose of supplying suitable employment for Gentlewomen and restoring Ornamental Needlework to the high place it once held among the decorative arts.'

Sampler A piece of embroidery originally worked by an adult needlewoman as a directory of stitches, patterns, and motifs and used as technical reference. Later, the name was applied to needlework exercises carried out by children for practice in stitching techniques.

Shadow embroidery A type of embroidery worked on a semi-transparent fabric.

Shisha embroidery A traditional embroidery technique using tiny mirrors; it originated in India.

Single canvas Canvas in which the weave is formed by the intersection of single vertical and horizontal threads.

Smock Traditionally, a linen outer garment worn by working men in the eighteenth, nineteenth, and early twentieth centuries, decorated with smocking and embroidered motifs, which depicted the type of work done by the owner.

Smocking Evenly spaced gathers in a piece of fabric which are held in place by ornamental stitching.

Soft cotton A tightly twisted five-ply thread with a matt finish, always used as a single thread.

Stiletto A sharp pointed instrument used for making holes in fabric.

Stranded cotton A loosely twisted, slightly shiny, six-strand thread. For fine embroidery, the threads can be separated and used in twos or threes.

Stranded silk A pure silk thread similar to stranded cotton but with a more lustrous finish.

Tapestry needle A long, thick needle with a blunt tip and a large eye.

Tapestry wool A twisted four-ply wool with hard-wearing properties, mainly used in canvas work.

Tramming The preparation of double thread canvas, before the decorative stitching is begun, to make the stitched surface hard-wearing. Horizontal straight stitches are worked between the double canvas threads, using colours that match the design. Tramming fills out the stitch that is worked over it and also helps to cover the canvas ground.

Warp The threads in a woven fabric that run lengthways on the weaving loom.

Waxed thread A thread which has been strengthened by rubbing it against a block of beeswax.

Weft The threads running across the width of a woven fabric that are interwoven with the warp threads.

Whipping A term used in embroidery to describe the method of passing a second thread over and under a simple line stitch to give a raised effect.

Whitework A term referring to all types of embroidery which are traditionally worked in white thread on white fabric. They include cut-work, drawn thread work and pulled fabric work.

Index

Page numbers in bold refer to the illustrations

Algerian eye stitch, 168, **170**
 double, 68
Algerian filling stitch, 120, **122**
 with bar, 120
Algerian stitch, plaited, 144, **146**
alternating cross stitch, 132
antique couching, 81
antique hem stitch, 112, **114**
antique stitch, 77
Antwerp edging stitch, 109, **111**
 fringed, 29
 laced, 29, **31**
Armenian cross stitch, 65
Armenian edging stitch, 108, **110**
arrow stitch, 161, **163**
arrowhead cross stitch, 140
arrowhead stitch, 73, **75**
Astrakhan stitch, 148
Aubusson stitch, 128

back stitch, 14, **15**
 crossed, 60
 double, 60, **62**
 isolated, 68
 oblong cross stitch with, 132, **134**
 threaded, 16, **18**
 trellis, 73, **75**
 whipped, 16, **18**
backstitched spider's web, 100
balcony stitch, 152, **154**
balloon satin stitch, 128, **130**
bar stitch, corded, 116, **118**
barb stitch, 16, **18**
bargello stitch, 120
barred beetle stitch, 153, **155**
barred witch stitch, 45
barrier stitch, 76
basket filling stitch, 72, **74**
basket satin stitch, 72
basket stitch no. 1, 28, **30**
basket stitch no. 2, 80, **82**
Basque knot, 36, **38**
Basque stitch, 16, **18**
battlement couching, 85, **87**
battlement stitch, 49, **51**
bead couching, 116
bead edging stitch, 29
beaded, 9
beaded tent stitch, 168, **170**
beetle stitch, 153, **155**
 barred, 153, **155**
Belgian cross stitch, 53, **55**
Berlin plush stitch, 148
Berlin stitch, 14
Bermuda faggoting, 41
berry stitch, 93, **95**
Berwick stitch, 16, **18**
big writing, 17
blanket stitch, **11**, 13
 knotted, 109
blind knot, 96
blind stitch, 20
Bokhara couching, 77, **79**
bonnet stitch, 28, **30**
border stitch
 Portuguese, 65, **67**
 Yugoslav, 76
Bosnia stitch, 76, **78**
Bosnian stitch, 76
bouclé stitch, 161, **163**
braid edging stitch, 109, **111**
braid stitch, 36, **38**
 plaited, 41, **43**
branch stitch, 44

brave bred stitch, 33
Breton stitch, 29, **31**
briar stitch, 12
brick and cross filling, 68, **70**
brick stitch, 72
 fancy, 124, **126**
 no. 1, 73, **75**
 no. 2, 120, **122**
Brighton stitch, 160, **162**
broad chain stitch, 25, **27**
broad cross, 133
broad cross stitch, 133, **135**
broad diagonal cross stitch, 132, **134**
broad stem stitch, 164, **166**
bullion knot, 97, **99**
bullion picot, 109, **111**
bullion stitch, 97
bunched couching, 8
Burden stitch, 81, **83**
butterfly chain stitch, 48, **50**
button stitch, 13
buttonhole edging stitch, 108, **110**
buttonhole faggot stitch, 113
buttonhole insertion stitch, 113, **115**
buttonhole picot, 109, **110**
buttonhole stitch, **11**, 13
 closed, 24, **26**
 crossed, 17, **19**
 detached, 89, **91**
 double, 21, **23**
 Eastern, 165
 fancy, 88
 German, 29, **31**
 interlaced, 45, **47**
 knotted, 40, **42**
 knotted filling, 88, **90**
 laced, 48, **50**
 mirrored, 32, **34**
 open, 13
 rich, 88, **90**
 shading, 81, **83**
 slanted, 20
 tailor's, 33, **35**
 up and down, 32
buttonhole wheel, 101, **103**
buttonholed herringbone stitch, 52, **54**
Byzantine stitch, 125, **127**

cable chain stitch, 33
cable stitch, 33, **35**
 double, 28
 knotted, 20, **22**
 zigzag, 28, **31**
canvas fern stitch, 132, **134**
canvas herringbone stitch, 133, **135**
canvas stem stitch, 164
canvas stitch, 121
captive rice stitch, 145, **147**
Cashmere stitch, 124, **126**
 straight, 124, **126**
catch stitch, 8
caterpillar stitch, 97
Catherine wheel, 105, **107**
centipede stitch, 33
Ceylon stitch, 88, **90**
chain stitch, **10**, 11
 broad, 25, **27**
 butterfly, 48, **50**
 cable, 33
 chequered, 37, **39**
 crested, 40, **42**
 detached, 92
 detached twisted, 21, **23**
 double, 49, **51**
 feathered, 29, **31**
 heavy, 25, **27**
 heavy braid, 25
 interlaced, 53, **55**
 knotted, 37, **39**
 open, 17, **19**

pendant, 28
reverse, 25
Roman, 17
rosette, 29, **31**
Russian, 100, **102**
Singhalese, 57, **59**
spine, 25, **27**
square, 17
tail, 92
threaded, 44, **46**
three, 100
twisted, 21, **23**
twisted zigzag, 64
Vandyke, 37
whipped, 20, **22**
zigzag, 37, **39**
chained cross stitch, 140, **142**
chained feather stitch, 29
chained stitch, 152, **154**
chequer stitch, 152, **154**
chequered chain band, 61, **63**
chequered chain stitch, 37, **39**
chessboard filling stitch no. 1, 73, **75**
chessboard filling stitch no. 2, 120, **122**
chessboard stitch, 153, **155**
chevron stem stitch, 85, **87**
chevron stitch, 8, **10**
 half, 21, **23**
 pagoda, 17, **19**
 raised, 45, **47**
Chiara stitch, 9
Chinese cross stitch, 44
Chinese knot, 96, **98**
Chinese stitch, 20, 44, **46**
close stitch, 13
closed buttonhole stitch, 24, **26**
closed feather stitch, 16, **18**
closed fly stitch, 17, **19**
closed herringbone stitch, 60, **62**
closed wave stitch, 69, **71**
cloud filling stitch, 69, **71**
coil stitch, 97
coiled stitch, 164
Colcha stitch, 72, **74**
compact filling stitch, 164, **166**
continental stitch, 121
convent stitch, 8
coral knot, 9
coral knotted herringbone stitch, 60
coral stitch, 9, **10**
 double, 28
 single, 12
 Spanish, 40
 tied, 36
 zigzag, 25, **27**
cord stitch, 116, **118**
corded bar stitch, 116, **118**
cordonnet stitch, 17
couched filling stitch, 80, **82**
couching, 8, **10**
 antique, 81
 battlement, 85, **87**
 bead, 116
 Bokhara, 77, **79**
 bunched, 8
 fancy, 57, **59**
 Jacobean, 80
 Oriental, 81
 puffy, 8
 Roumanian, 81, **83**
 satin stitch, 29, **31**
 self, 76
 trellis, 84, **86**
 underside, 77
crested chain stitch, 40, **42**
Cretan stitch, **11**, 13
 crossed, 41, **43**
 French, 61
 knotted, 17, **19**
 laced, 73
 open, 20, **22**
 open filling stitch, 84, **86**

Scottish, 64, **66**
triple, 61, **63**
crewel stitch, 9
criss-cross herringbone stitch, 53
criss-cross stitch, 149, **150**
Croatian flat stitch, 81
Croatian stitch, 73, **75**
cross and twist stitch, 92, **94**
cross corners cross stitch, 136
cross couched filling stitch, 80
cross stitch, 14, **15**
 alternating, 132
 Armenian, 65
 arrowhead, 140
 Belgian, 53, **55**
 broad, 133, **135**
 broad diagonal, 132, **134**
 chained, 140, **142**
 Chinese, 44
 cross corners, 136
 diagonal, 140, **142**
 double, 133, **135**, 136
 double-sided, 33, **35**
 double straight, 133
 double tied oblong, 132
 Dutch, 137
 Dutch double, 132
 Greek, 144
 half, 133, **135**
 Hungarian, 80
 interlaced, 105
 Italian, 140, **142**, 143
 long, 133
 long-armed, 141, **143**
 long-legged, 141
 marking, 37, **39**
 Montenegrin, 144
 oblong, 133, **135**
 oblong with back stitch, 132, **134**
 Persian, 133
 plaited, 141
 plaited double, 149, **150**, 151
 plus two, 132, **134**
 reversed, 136, **138**
 Russian, 56, **58**, 8
 St George, 68, **70**
 Smyrna, 136
 straight, 137
 two-sided Italian, 140
 two-sided Montenegrin, 144
 upright, 137, **139**
 woven, 141, **143**
 wrapped, 104, **106**
crossed back stitch, 60
crossed buttonhole stitch, 17, **19**
crossed corners cushion stitch, 152, **154**
crossed Cretan stitch, 41, **43**
crossed fly stitch, 68
crossed Gobelin stitch, 136, **138**
crown stitch, 93, **95**
crow's foot, 104, **106**
crow's foot stitch, 157, **159**
cup stitch, 101, **103**
curtain stitch, 165, **167**
cushion stitch, 120, 121, 152, **154**
 crossed corners, 152, **154**
 reversed, 120, **122**
czar stitch, 133

daisy border stitch, twisted, 16
daisy stitch, 92, **94**
 long-tailed, 93, **95**
damask darning, 81, **83**
damask stitch, 24
Danish knot, 97, **99**
Danish knotted stitch, 97
darning, 14, **15**
 damask, 81, **83**

double, 69, **71**
Japanese, 73, **75**
surface, 89, **90**
Deerfield stitch, 76
detached buttonhole stitch, 89, **91**
detached chain filling, 69
detached chain stitch, 92
detached overcast stitch, 28, **30**
detached split stitch, 97
detached twisted chain stitch, 21, **23**
diagonal broad cross, 132
diagonal-cross stitch, 140, **142**
diagonal fishbone stitch, 137, **139**
diagonal stitch, 124, **126**
diagonal woven band, 56, **58**
diamond eye stitch, 169, **171**
diamond filling stitch, 85, **87**
diamond stitch, 61, **63**
 knotted, 40, **42**
diamond straight stitch, 124, **126**
dot stitch, 92, **94**
double Algerian eye stitch, 68, **70**
double back stitch, 60, **62**
double buttonhole stitch, 21, **23**
double cable stitch, 28
double chain stitch, 49, **51**
double coral stitch, 28
double cross, 141, **143**
double cross stitch, 133, **135**, 136
double darning, 69, **71**
double Dutch stitch, 132, **134**
double feather stitch, 28, **30**
double fly stitch, 24, **26**
double hem stitch, 112
double herringbone stitch, 53, **55**
double knot, 97
double knot stitch, 36, **38**
double leviathan stitch, 149, **151**
double Parisian stitch, 121, **123**
double Pekinese stitch, 73
double running stitch, 9
double stitch, 132, **134**
double straight cross stitch, 133
double tied oblong cross stitch, 132
double twill stitch, 125, **127**
double-rowed open-work, 112
double-sided cross stitch, 33, **35**
doubled herringbone stitch, 48, **50**
Dutch cross stitch, 137
Dutch double cross stitch, 132
Dutch stitch, 137, **139**

Eastern buttonhole stitch, 165
Eastern stitch, 165, **167**
economic long cross, 133
edge stitch
 plaited, 108, **110**
 sailor, 45
edging stitch
 Antwerp, 109, **111**
 Armenian, 108, **110**
 bead, 29
 braid, 109, **111**
 buttonhole, 108, **110**
 Eskimo, 49, **51**
 fringed Antwerp, 29
 laced Antwerp, 29, **31**
 looped no. 1, 108, **110**
 looped no. 2, 32, **34**

sword, 96, **98**
embroidery stitch, 72
encroaching Gobelin stitch, 125, **127**
encroaching satin stitch, 68, **70**
English stitch, 152, **154**
ermine stitch, 93, **95**
Eskimo edging stitch, 49, **51**
Eskimo laced edge, 49
expanded ray stitch, 157
eye stitch, 169 **171**
 Algerian, 168, **170**
 diamond, 169, **171**
 double Algerian, 68, **70**
 half, 169, **171**
eyelet hole, 117, **119**
eyelet stitch, 84, **86**

faggot filling stitch, 80, **82**, 72
faggot stitch
 buttonhole, 113
 interlaced, 113
 knotted, 113
 laced, 113
faggoting, 113
 Bermuda, 41
fan stitch, 157, **159**, 168
fan vaulting, 160
fancy brick stitch, 124, **126**
fancy bricking, 124
fancy buttonhole filling, 88, **90**
fancy buttonhole stitch, 88
fancy couching, 57, **59**
fancy herringbone stitch, 44, **46**
fancy stitch, 72, **74**
fantail stitch, 157
feather stitch, **11**, 12
 chained, 29
 closed, 16, **18**
 double, 28, **30**
 long-armed, 13
 single, 20, **22**
 Spanish knotted, 64, **66**
feather stitch raised band, 56, **58**
feather-work, 72
feathered chain stitch, 29, **31**
fence stitch, 76
fern stitch, 28, **30**
figure stitch, 81
filet stitch, 89, **91**
filling stitch
 Algerian, 120, **122**
 basket, 72, **74**
 chessboard no. 1, 73, **75**
 chessboard no. 2, 120, **122**
 cloud, 69, **71**
 compact, 164, **166**
 couched, 80, **82**
 Cretan open, 84, **86**
 cross couched, 80
 detached chain, 69
 diamond, 85, **87**
 faggot, 72, 80, **82**
 fancy buttonhole, 88, **90**
 fly, 68, **70**
 Gobelin, 125, **127**
 herringbone ladder, 73, **75**
 honeycomb, 80, **82**
 Indian, 77
 knotted buttonhole, 88, **90**
 lace, 89, **90**
 link, 69, **71**
 loop buttonhole, 88
 Maltese cross, 85, **87**
 open buttonhole, 89, **91**
 plaid, 77, **79**
 raised honeycomb, 89, **91**
 Roman, 69, **71**
 seed, 68
 sheaf, 72, **74**
 spaced buttonhole, 68, **70**
 squared no. 1, 76, **78**
 squared no. 2, 76, **78**
 squared no. 3, 77, **79**

star, 68, **70**
stem, 69, **71**
tête de boeuf, 72, **74**
trellis, 88, **90**
Venetian, 88-9, **90**
fir stitch, 157, **159**
fishbone stitch
 diagonal, 137, **139**
 horizontal, 136, **138**
 no. 1, 80, **82**
 no. 2, 137, **139**
 open, 76, **78**
 raised, 77
 stepped, 137
flame stitch, 120
flat square, 125
flat stitch, 81, **83**
 Croatian, 81
floral stitch, 153, **155**
Florentine stitch, 120, **122**
flower stitch, 153, **155**
flowing fly stitch, 68
fly stitch, 93, **95**
 closed, 17, **19**
 crossed, 68
 double, 24, **26**
 filling, 68, **70**
 flowing, 68
 plaited, 20, **22**
 reversed, 17, **19**
 whipped, 16, **18**
 whipped attached, 16
foliage stitch, 152, **154**
forbidden knot, 96
forbidden stitch, 20
four-legged knot stitch, 92, **94**
French Cretan stitch, 61
French dot, 96
French knot, 96, **98**
French knot border, 56, **58**
French stitch, 153, **155**
fringed Antwerp edging stitch, 29

gate stitch, 161, **163**
German buttonhole stitch, 29, **31**
German interlacing stitch, 65
German knot stitch, 9
Ghiordes knot, 168
Gobelin stitch, 125, **127**
 crossed, 136, **138**
 encroaching, 125, **127**
 filling stitch, 125, **127**
 interlocking, 125
 oblique, 125
 plaited, 128, **130**
 straight, 128
 upright, 128, **130**
 wide, 128, **130**
God's eye stitch, 96, **98**
Gordian knot stitch, 36
Greek cross stitch, 144
Greek stitch, 144, **146**
Griffin stitch, 84, **86**
grub knot, 97
guilloche stitch, 52, **54**

half chevron stitch, 21, **23**
half cross stitch, 133, **135**
half eye stitch, 169, **171**
half Rhodes stitch, 144-5, **147**
half stitch, 133
heavy braid chain stitch, 25
heavy chain stitch, 25, **27**
hem stitch, 112, **114**
 antique, 112, **114**
 double, 112
 Italian, 112, **114**
 ladder, 112, **114**
 Roumanian, 112
 serpentine, 112, **114**
 sham, 44, **46**
 trellis, 112
 zigzag hem, 44
herringbone ladder filling stitch, 73, **75**
herringbone stitch, 8, **10**

buttonholed, 52, **54**
canvas, 133, **135**
closed, 60, **62**
coral knotted, 60
criss-cross, 53
double, 53, **55**
doubled, 48, **50**
fancy, 44, **46**
Indian, 53
interlaced, 65, **67**
laced, 65, **67**
overlapping, 77, **79**
self-padded, 77
square, 145, **147**
square-laced, 105, **107**
threaded, 45, **47**
tied, 60, **62**
triple, 53
woven, 65
zigzag, 76
Holbein stitch, 9, **10**
hollie stitch, 88, **90**
holy point, 88
holy stitch, 88
honeycomb fillling stitch, 80, **82**
honeycomb stitch, 89
horizontal fishbone stitch, 136, **138**
hound's tooth, 160, **162**
Hungarian cross stitch, 80
Hungarian stitch, 124, **126**
Hungary stitch, 120

Indian filling stitch, 77
Indian herringbone stitch, 53
insertion stitch
 buttonhole, 113, **115**
 interlacing, 113, **115**
 knotted, 113, **115**
 laced, 113, **115**
 one-sided, 52, **54**
 plaited, 113, **115**
 twisted, 113, **115**
 two-sided, 57, **59**
interlaced band, 44, **46**
interlaced band stitch, 73
interlaced buttonhole stitch, 45, **47**
interlaced chain stitch, 53, **55**
interlaced cross stitch, 105, **107**
interlaced faggot stitch, 113
interlaced herringbone stitch, 65, **67**
interlaced running stitch, 25, **27**
interlacing insertion stitch, 113, **115**
interlacing stitch, 65
 German, 65
interlocking Gobelin stitch, 125
invisible stitch, 77
Irish stitch, 72, 120
isolated back stitch, 68
Italian cross stitch, 140, **142, 143**
Italian hem stitch, 112, **114**
Italian knot stitch, 96
Italian stitch, 140

Jacobean couching, 80
Jacquard stitch, 121, **123**
Janina stitch, 77
Japanese darning, 73, **75**
Japanese stitch, 76, **78**

kelim stitch, 121
Kensington outline stitch, 9
kloster stitch, 8
knitting stitch, 121, **123**
knot, blind, 96
 bullion, 97, **99**
 Chinese, 96, **98**
 Danish, 97, **99**
 double, 97
 forbidden, 96
 French, 96, **98**
 Ghiordes, 168

grub, 97
long-tailed French, 96
Pekin, 96
raised, 92
Turk's head, 97, **99**
Turkey rug, 168, **170**
knot stitch, 109
 bullion knot, 97
 double, 36, **38**
 four-legged, 92, **94**
 German, 9
 Italian, 96
 knotted, 92
 long tack, 96
 old English, 36
 quilt, 168
 simple, 92
 tufted, 168
 twisted, 96
knotted blanket stitch, 109
knotted buttonhole filling, 88, **90**
knotted buttonhole stitch, 40, **42**
knotted cable chain stitch, 20
knotted cable stitch, 20, **22**
knotted chain stitch, 37, **39**
knotted Cretan stitch, 17, **19**
knotted diamond stitch, 40, **42**
knotted faggot stitch, 113
knotted insertion stitch, 113, **115**
knotted knot stitch, 92
knotted loop stitch, 33, 36
knotted pearl stitch, 32, **34**
knotted stitch, 133, **135**, 9, 96
 Danish, 97
 single, 168, **170**

lace filling stitch, 89, **90**
lace stitch, 41
laced Antwerp edging stitch, 29, **31**
laced buttonhole stitch, 48, **50**
laced Cretan stitch, 73
laced double running stitch, 49, **51**
laced double stitch, 49
laced faggot stitch, 113
laced herringbone stitch, 65, **67**
laced insertion stitch, 113, **115**
laced treble running stitch, 49
ladder hem stitch, 112, **114**
ladder stitch, 60, **62**, 17, 56, 112
laid Oriental stitch, 81
laid stitch, New England, 76, **78**
laid-work, 84, **86**
large petal stitch, 157, **159**
lattice band, twisted, 52, **54**
lattice stitch, twisted, 84-5, **87**
lazy daisy stitch, 92
lazy squaw stitch, 116, **118**
leaf stitch, 80, **82**, 72, 157
leviathan stitch, 136, **138**
 double, 149, **151**
line stitch, 9
 single knotted 24
 two-sided, 9
linen stitch, 128, **130**
link filling stitch, 69, **71**
link powdering stitch, 69
link stitch, 37
linked stitch, 124, **126**
lock stitch, 48, **50**
lock stitch band, 48, **50**
long and short stitch, 72, **74**
long-armed cross stitch, 141, **143**
long-armed feather stitch, 13
long cross stitch, 133

long-legged cross stitch, 141
long stitch, 120, **122**
long tack knot stitch, 96
long-tailed daisy stitch, 93, **95**
long-tailed French knot, 96
loop buttonhole filling stitch, 88
loop picot, 108, **110**
loop stitch, 33, **35**, 92
 knotted, 33, 36
 open, 93
 tied, 93
looped edging stitch no. 1, 108, **110**
looped edging stitch no. 2, 32, **34**
looped shading stitch, 69
lozenge satin stitch, 129, **131**

magic chain, 37
magic stitch, 37
maidenhair stitch, 45, **47**
Maltese cross, 105, **107**
Maltese cross filling stitch, 85, **87**
marking cross stitch, 37, **39**
marking stitch, 33
Mexican stitch, 69
Milanese stitch, 129, **131**
 straight, 129, **131**
mirrored buttonhole stitch, 32, **34**
Montenegrin cross stitch, 144
Montenegrin stitch, 144, **146**
Moorish stitch, 121, **123**
mosaic stitch, 120, **122**
 reversed, 124, **126**
moss stitch, 92
Mossoul stitch, 8
multiplait, 145
multiple rice stitch, 137, **139**

needlepoint stitch, 121
net passing stitch, 80
New England laid stitch, 76, **78**
Norwich stitch, 148

oblique Gobelin stitch, 125
oblique Slav stitch, 128
oblong cross stitch, 133, **135**
 with back stitch, 132, **134**
octagonal Rhodes stitch, 148-9, **150**
old English knot stitch, 36
old Parisian stitch, 121
one-sided insertion stitch, 52, **54**
open buttonhole filling, 89, **91**
open buttonhole stitch, 13
open chain stitch, 17, **19**
open Cretan stitch, 20, **22**
open fishbone stitch, 76, **78**
open loop stitch, 93
open wave stitch, 73, **75**
opus plumarium, 72
Oriental couching, 81
Oriental stitch, 129, **131**, 77
 laid, 81
outline stitch, **11**, 12
 Kensington, 9
overcast stitch, 28, **30**
 detached, 28, **30**
overlapping herringbone stitch, 77, **79**
overlay stitch, 116

padded satin stitch, 160, **162**
pagoda chevron stitch, 17, **19**
Palestrina stitch, 36
Pangolin stitch, 133

Paris stitch, 25, **27**
Parisian stitch, 121, **123**
 double, 121, **123**
 old, 121
pearl stitch, 21, **23**
 knotted, 32, **34**
Pekin knot, 96
Pekinese stitch, 20, **22**
 double, 73
pendant chain stitch, 28
perlen stitch, 121
Persian cross stitch, 133
Persian stitch, 8, 13
perspective stitch, 161, **163**
pessante, 69
petal stitch, 28, **30**
petit point, 121
picot, 92
 bullion, 109, **111**
 buttonhole, 109, **110**
 loop, 108, **110**
 pinned, 108
 ring, 108, **110**
 Venetian, 109
 woven, 109, **111**
pineapple stitch, 156, **158**
pinned picot, 108
plaid filling stitch, 77, **79**
plait stitch, 144, **146**, **147**
plaited Algerian stitch, 144, **146**
plaited braid stitch, 41, **43**
plaited cross stitch, 141
plaited double cross, 149, **150**, **151**
plaited edge stitch, 108, **110**
plaited fly stitch, 20, **22**
plaited Gobelin stitch, 128, **130**
plaited insertion stitch, 113, **115**
plaited Rhodes stitch, 145, **147**
plaited Slav stitch, 141
plaited stitch, 137, **139**, 8
plumage stitch, 72
plush stitch, 148
 Berlin, 148
point à la minute, 101, **103**
point de chainette, 12
point de marque, 14
point de sable, 14
point Russe stitch, 100, **102**
point Turc, 41
Porto Rico rose, 97
Portuguese border stitch, 65, **67**
Portuguese knotted stem stitch, 41, **43**
Portuguese stitch, 141
post stitch, 97
powdering stitch, link, 69
Pueblo stitch, 24, **26**
puffy couching, 8

queen stitch, 169
quick stitch, 169, **171**
quill stitch, 13
quilt knot stitch, 168
Quodlibet stitch, 156, **158**

radiating stitch, 168, **170**
railway stitch, 136
raised chain band, 53, **55**
raised chevron stitch, 45, **47**
raised fishbone stitch, 77
raised honeycomb filling stitch, 89, **91**
raised knot, 92
raised lace band, 61
raised spot stitch, 61, **63**
raised spot stitch, 168, **170**
raised stem stitch band, 64, **66**
raised stitch, 148
rapid stitch, 156, **158**
ray stitch, 168, **170**
 expanded, 157
Renaissance stitch, 129, **131**

tied, 153
rep stitch, 128, **130**
reverse chain stitch, 25
reversed cross stitch, 136, **138**
reversed cushion stitch, 120, **122**
reversed fly stitch, 17, **19**
reversed mosaic stitch, 124, **126**
reversed tent stitch, 121
Rhodes stitch, 144, **147**
 half, 144-5, **147**
 octagonal, 148-9, **150**
 plaited, 145, **147**
ribbed spider's web, 100, **102**
ribbed wheel, 100
rice grain, 92
rice stitch, 136, **138**
 captive, 145, **147**
 multiple, 137, **139**
 triple, 137, **139**
 upright, 136, **138**
rich buttonhole stitch, 88, **90**
ridge stitch, 136, **138**
ring picot, 108, **110**
rococo stitch, 169, **171**
Roman chain stitch, 17
Roman filling, 157, **158**, **159**
Roman filling stitch, 69, **71**
Roman stitch, 44, **46**
rope stitch, 24-5, **27**
rose stitch, 104, **106**
rosette chain stitch, 29, **31**
rosette of thorns stitch, 20, **22**
Roumanian couching, 81, **83**
Roumanian hem stitch, 112
Roumanian stitch, 77, **79**, 9
rug knot, Turkey, 168, **170**
rug stitch, 148
 single knotted Smyrna, 168
running stitch, **11**, 12
 double, 9
 interlaced, 25, **27**
 laced double, 49, **51**
 laced treble, 49
 stepped and threaded, 49, **51**
 threaded, 49, **51**
 threaded treble, 48, **50**
 whipped, 17, **19**
Russian chain stitch, 100, **102**
Russian cross stitch, 56, **58**, 8
Russian stitch, 8

sailor edge stitch, 45
sailor stitch, 45, **47**
St George cross stitch, 68, **70**
sampler stitch, 14
satin stitch, 24, **26**
 balloon, 128, **130**
 basket, 72
 couching, 29, **31**
 encroaching, 68, **70**
 lozenge, 129, **131**
 padded, 160, **162**
 square, 125, **127**
 surface, 72, **74**
 twisted, 93, **95**
 whipped, 32, **34**
scallop stitch, 164-5, **166**
Scottish Cretan stitch, 64, **66**
Scottish stitch, 156-7, **158**
scroll stitch, 24, **26**, 9
seed filling stitch, 68
seed stitch, 68, **70**, 92
seeding stitch, 68
self couching, 76
self-padded herringbone stitch, 77
serpentine hem stitch, 112, **114**
seven stitch, 156, **158**
shading stitch, 72
 buttonhole, 81, **83**
 looped, 69
 stem, 69, **71**
 tapestry, 72
shadow stitch, 60
sham hem stitch, 44, **46**
sheaf filling stitch, 72, **74**
sheaf stitch, 64, **66**
shell stitch, 160, **163**
ship's ladder stitch, 21, **23**
shisha stitch no. 1, 117, **119**
shisha stitch no. 2, 117, **119**
shisha stitch no. 3, 117, **119**
Siennese stitch, 49, **51**
simple knot stitch, 92
Singhalese chain stitch, 57, **59**
single coral stitch, 12
single feather stitch, 20, **22**
single knotted line stitch, 24
single knotted Smyrna rug stitch, 168
single knotted stitch, 168, **170**
slanted buttonhole stitch, 20
Slav stitch, oblique, 128
 plaited, 141
small writing, 17
Smyrna cross stitch, 136
Smyrna stitch, 36
snail trail, 9
Sorbello stitch, 36, **38**
South Kensington stitch, 9
spaced buttonhole filling, 68, **70**
Spanish coral stitch, 40
Spanish knotted feather stitch, 64, **66**
Spanish stitch, 144
 two-sided plaited, 48, **50**
speckling stitch, 68
spider's web, 100, **102**
 backstitched, 100
 ribbed, 100, **102**
spine chain stitch, 25, **27**
split stitch, 9, **10**
 detached, 97
 Swedish, 97, **99**
spoke stitch, woven, 100
spot stitch, 116, **118**
 raised, 168, **170**
sprat's head, 104, **106**
spring stitch, 164, **166**
square boss, 92, **94**
square chain stitch, 17
square herringbone stitch, 145, **147**
square-laced herringbone stitch, 105, **107**
square satin stitch, 125, **127**
square stitch, 9, 73
squared filling stitch no. 1, 76, **78**
squared filling stitch no. 2, 76, **78**
squared filling stitch no. 3, 77, **79**
stalk stitch, 9
star, 104, **106**
Star of David, 101, **103**
star darn, 101, **103**
star eyelet stitch, 168
star filling stitch, 68, **70**
star stitch, 145, **147**, 168
 triangular, 81, **83**
 two-sided triangular, 81
stem stitch, 9, **10**
 broad, 164, **166**
 canvas, 164
 chevron, 85, **87**
 filling, 69, **71**
 Portuguese knotted, 41, **43**
 raised band, 64, **66**

shading, 69, **71**
 whipped, 21, **23**
step stitch, 56, **58**
stepped and threaded running stitch, 49, **51**
stepped fishbone stitch, 137
stitching, 14
straight Cashmere stitch, 124, **126**
straight cross stitch, 137
straight Gobelin stitch, 128
straight Milanese stitch, 129, **131**
straight stitch, 92, **94**
 diamond, 124, **126**
striped woven band, 53, **55**
stroke stitch, 9, 92
 two-sided, 9
sunburst stitch, 165, **167**
surface darning, 89, **90**
surface satin stitch, 72, **74**
Surrey stitch, 169, **171**
Swedish split stitch, 97, **99**
sword-edging stitch, 96, **98**

tacking stitch, 14
tail chain stitch, 92
tailor's buttonhole stitch, 33, **35**
tambour stitch, 12
tapestry shading stitch, 72
tapestry stitch, 121
tartan stitch, 77
tassel stitch, 148
tent stitch, 121, **123**
 beaded, 168, **170**
 reversed, 121
 woven, 165, **167**
tête de boeuf filling stitch, 72, **74**
thorn stitch, 21, **23**
threaded back stitch, 16, **18**
threaded chain stitch, 44, **46**
threaded herringbone stitch, 45, **47**
threaded running stitch, 49, **51**
threaded treble running stitch, 48, **50**
three chain stitch, 100
three-sided stitch, 41, **43**
tied coral stitch, 36
tied herringbone stitch, 60, **62**
tied loop stitch, 92
tied Renaissance stitch, 153
tied stitch, 156, **158**
tile stitch, 160, **162**
Torocko stitch, 80, **82**
trailing stitch, 29
trellis back stitch, 73, **75**
trellis couching, 84, **86**
trellis filling stitch, 88, **90**
trellis hem stitch, 112
trellis stitch, 69, **71**
triangle stitch, 45, **47**
triangular Turkish stitch, 81, **83**
triple Cretan stitch, 61, **63**
triple herringbone stitch, 53
triple rice stitch, 137, **139**
Tudor rose stitch, 161, **163**
tufted knot stitch, 168
tulip stitch, 101, **103**
Turk's head knot, 97, **99**
Turkey rug knot, 168, **170**
Turkey stitch, 168
Turkish stitch, 41
 triangular, 81, **83**
 two-sided triangular, 81
Turkmen stitch, 49
tweed stitch, 164, **166**
twill stitch, 124, **126**
 double, 125, **127**
twist stitch, 141
twisted chain stitch, 21, **23**
twisted daisy border stitch, 16

twisted insertion stitch, 113, **115**
twisted knot stitch, 96
twisted lattice band, 52, **54**
twisted lattice stitch, 84-5, **87**
twisted satin stitch, 93, **95**
twisted zigzag chain stitch, 64
two-sided insertion stitch, 57, **59**
two-sided Italian cross stitch, 140
two-sided line stitch, 9
two-sided Montenegrin cross stitch, 144
two-sided plaited Spanish stitch, 48, **50**
two-sided stroke stitch, 9
two-sided triangular Turkish stitch, 81

underlined stitch, 133, **135**
underside couching, 77, **79**
up and down buttonhole stitch, 32
upright cross stitch, 137, **139**
upright Gobelin stitch, 128, **130**
upright rice stitch, 136, **138**

Valerian stitch, 84, **86**
Vandyke chain stitch, 37
Vandyke stitch, 57, **59**
vault stitch, 160, **162**
vee stitch, 164, **166**
vell stitch, 100, **102**
velvet stitch, 148, **150**
Venetian filling stitch, 88-9, **90**
Venetian picot, 109
Victorian tufting, 116, **118**

waffle stitch, 148, **150**
wave stitch
 closed, 69, **71**
 open, 73, **75**
web stitch, 129, **131**
wheat ear stitch, 32, **34**
wheat sheaf stitch, 156, **158**
wheel stitch, 101
whipped attached fly stitch, 16
whipped back stitch, 16, **18**
whipped chain stitch, 20, **22**
whipped fly stitch, 16, **18**
whipped running stitch, 17, **19**
whipped satin stitch, 32, **34**
whipped stem stitch, 21, **23**
wide Gobelin stitch, 128, **130**
William and Mary stitch, 136
witch stitch, 8
worm stitch, 97
wound stitch, 96
woven cross stitch, 141, **143**
woven herringbone stitch, 65
woven picot, 109, **111**
woven spoke stitch, 100
woven spot, 100
woven star, 101
woven tent stitch, 165, **167**
woven wheel, 100
wrapped cross stitch, 104, **106**

'Y' stitch, 93
Yugoslav border stitch, 76
zigzag cable stitch, 28, **31**
zigzag chain stitch, 37, **39**
zigzag coral stitch, 25, **27**
zigzag Holbein stitch, 76
zigzag sham hem stitch, 44
zigzag stitch, 52, **54**